Remembrance and Renewal

*500 Years of European Wars and Politics
and Their Impact on Five Hebrew Families*

By George S. Sacerdote, Ph.D.

Honor thy father and mother

Dedicated to the memory of my parents

Giorgio Salvatore Sacerdote
Luciana Elda Clara Levi

And all those who came before them

Contents

Foreword

Imagine yourself in my parents' situation in June, 1940. Giorgio and Luciana had just landed in New York after escaping from France as that country was collapsing in the face of the Nazi blitzkrieg early in World War II. Giorgio was thirty-five years old and Luciana twenty-five. They had with them two small children under the age of four, Alberto and Piero, both ill with whooping cough. Also with them was Giorgio's 60-year-old mother, Elvira, who had been widowed twenty years earlier. They knew no one in New York except for Giorgio's younger brother Paolo, who had arrived there just a few months before them. Giorgio was lame in one arm and one knee as a result of a terrible automobile accident thirteen years previous. Giorgio's and Luciana's Italian doctorates in engineering and chemistry were not recognized by the Americans. They had no jobs, no home, and only limited assets at their disposal. And they would soon find most of those assets frozen by presidential order and their employment prospects further limited; they were classified as enemy aliens when the United States entered the war in 1941.

Fifteen months before, with the passage of the Racial Laws of 1938–39, they had been forced to leave their native Italy. Up to that time they had lived a comfortable *haute bourgeois* life, surrounded by friends and family, with a summer home in the country, skiing in the Alps in the winter, and regular trips to the leading European resorts. Giorgio held a respectable position as technical director with the telephone company. Their families had lived in the same region for over four hundred years. They were highly educated, cultured, well-accomplished and respected in the community. Indeed Giorgio's grandfather had been knighted some fifty years before. Both were the children and grandchildren of lawyers. The family was backed by substantial capital that it had accumulated over the centuries first as bankers and later as manufacturers, wholesale merchants and property investors. And with a stroke of the pen Mussolini's Fascist dictatorship had taken all that away from them. They had to start all over as strangers in a strange land.

Despite all this, they managed to rebuild their lives in the New World. After several years' efforts to find suitable employment, Giorgio capitalized on his very brief experience in the French rubber industry in 1939–40 to begin a business manufacturing and distributing waterproofing products, in partnership with several of his relatives who had also found their way to New York in the early 1940s. After the war, he was able to recover his investments in Italy and partially rebuild his capital position. Luciana was ultimately able to find an academic post, through not until the mid-1950s. And they endowed their sons with personal values and quality educations with which they were able to achieve considerable success in their chosen professions.

What was it that enabled Giorgio and Luciana to make this transition despite the bleak situation in which they found themselves in 1940? What gave them the resilience necessary to start life anew and avoid getting lost in self-pity? Were they unique or did they carry values learned over tens of generations, values that had repeatedly enabled their ancestors to succeed despite centuries of European wars and political upheavals?

The history of such troubles recounted in this book dates back to antiquity and our tale begins with a very brief survey of our family's roots in Biblical and Roman times, and also in Medieval Italy and Spain, leading up to the expulsions from Spain in 1492. Our tale begins in earnest when five families among our ancestors arrived in Piemonte in northwestern Italy in the 1500s. According to reports from Spanish diplomats in the mid 1500s, the Sacerdote family had been connected to the best families in Spain and Portugal before it was forced to emigrate, first to Constantinople and then Italy, first to the Duchy of Milan, and subsequently to Piemonte.[1] Within one generation of having arrived in Italy, they

---

[1] Segre, document 1063.

became bankers, diplomats and advisors at the court of the ruling Dukes of Savoy in Torino. Other branches of the family had similar histories, obtaining ducal banking charters and becoming important figures in finance and commerce almost immediately upon their arrival into the Duchy of Savoy from Spain and elsewhere in Italy.

This pattern of dislocation and renewal continued through the dynastic wars among the petty Italian principalities and their Spanish and French sponsors in the 1500s, the Thirty Years' war and the wars of Louis XIV of the 1600s, the enclosure of the Piemontese Hebrews[2] into ghettos in the 1700s, the upending of the old world order by Napoleon followed by its repressive reimposition in early1800s, the Italian wars of unification of the mid-to-late 1800s, and the Fascist dictatorship imposed on Italy in the aftermath of World War I. After each event, Giorgio's and Luciana's ancestors regrouped, learned the rules of the new social order, and drew upon their reserves of personal initiative, intellect and financial capital to take intelligent risks in order to prosper anew. And so it was for my parents in the years following their landing in New York that hot June day in 1940. It is this history that we retell in this volume, that future generations might remember them and benefit from their experiences.

In this volume there is a second, parallel story, that of the ruling Savoia (Savoy) family. This family traces its roots initially to Umberto I Biancamano, who was Count of Savoy in the year 1000. In the 1400s the Savoia absorbed the county of Piemonte (Piedmont), creating a domain that spanned the Alps on what is now the Italian/French border. In 1416, the counts were granted the title Duke of Savoy. They continued to rule their French and Italian territories, gradually adding to them through marriage and conquest until modern times. In 1720 they were granted the title King of Sardinia, having acquired that island in the aftermath of the War of Spanish Succession (1701–14). In the period from 1848 to 1870 they led the nationalist movement that unified Italy under their reign and became kings of Italy. When the Italian monarchy was overthrown in 1946, in the aftermath of World War II, theirs had been the longest-ruling royal family in Europe. In generations when they led movements for personal liberty and economic and social progress, they and their subjects prospered. But when they favored the more reactionary elements of their society, the result was almost always disastrous for both them and their subjects. In juxtaposing the histories of the Duchy of Savoy and Kingdom of Italy with those of five Hebrew families we present these lessons as well.

The Origin of this project

The idea for this book emerged shortly after my mother Luciana died; my brother Peter and I realized that we were among the last in our family to have experienced its life both in Italy and America. We wanted to record that life for posterity. Shortly thereafter, an elderly aunt of mine, Prof. Dott. Eugenia Lustig from Buenos Aires, gave me a copy of a brief unpublished history of the Montalcini family, my paternal grandmother's family; that history had been assembled by my cousin, Prof. Michele Luzzati, a medieval historian at the prestigious University of Pisa. In it Luzzati traced the family back to Mantova (Mantua) during the Renaissance, to Montalcino and Florence in the 1300s and 1400s, and to Rome before that. In addition, Eugenia passed on to me a copy of a Montalcini family genealogy that my great-uncle Emanuele Montalcini had pieced together that went back to about 1700.

Those accounts piqued my interest in the family's origins. At about the same time I received a genealogy of my mother's family from my cousin Marcella Ottolenghi Seropian. Shortly thereafter I came across a three-volume set of documents concerning the Hebrews of Piemonte (Piedmont) from 1297 to 1797. These volumes were assembled by Prof. Renata Segre and published by the University of Tel Aviv. Through these documents I was able to piece together the movements and commercial and political activities of most of our Piemontese ancestors and place these activities in the context of the greater political and social milieu of the times in which they lived.

---

[2] I have elected to use the term "Hebrews" because it is the closest word in English corresponding to the Italian word *Ebrei*, the name by which the Jewish communities in Italy have called themselves since at least the Middle Ages. *Ebrei* in turn is a latinization of the Hebrew word *Ivrim*, which the Israelites called themselves in biblical times.

In assembling this history I have worked with five different branches of the family:

- The Sacerdote family of Chieri, the ancestors of my paternal grandfather, Alberto Sacerdote, son of Emanuele Sacerdote and Emilia Perla Levi. Emanuele and Alberto were born in Chieri.
- The Montalcini family of San Damiano d'Asti, and the Segre family of Torino (Turin) and Savigliano, the ancestors of my paternal grandmother, Elvira Montalcini, daughter of Salvador Montalcini and Eugenia Segre.
- The Levi and DeBenedetti families of Nizza Monferrato and Alessandria, the parents of my maternal grandfather, Leone Levi. (The Nizza Monferrato Levi in my mother's family and the Torino Levi in my father's family *may or may not* have been linked in the 1500s.)

All five of these families immigrated to Piemonte in the mid-1500s and quickly established themselves as bankers, manufacturers, merchants, and, in several cases, influential members of the ducal (later royal) court. Not only have they been witnesses to many important historical events over the last five centuries, but those events have affected their daily lives and, in a few cases, their actions have changed the direction of those events. In this history of our family I seek to tie those events to these families as a way of tying the actions of popes, emperors, kings, and dukes to the rest of society.

The only branches of the family I have not traced in detail are those of my paternal great- grandmother, Emilia Perla Levi of Torino, and of my maternal grandmother, Guite (Marguerite) Orefice Levi. Emilia's father, Samuele Leone Levi, lived in Torino in the first half of the 1800s and, according to family tradition, married an Englishwoman. Emilia was apparently a woman of refined tastes, as shown by the suite of Louis Philippe furniture that she owned and is now in my home. Her epitaph in the family tomb reads, "Exemplary mother, pious, adorned with every virtue, dedicated her life to raising her family". I have not been able to trace her family beyond those few facts.

Guite's mother, Penelope, the wife of a Parisian Hebrew stockbroker, was a convert to Judaism; thus Guite and her parents do not appear in the sources that were so valuable to this study. They perhaps will be the subject of future study.

One of the phenomena that have made tracing this family history possible is the remarkable degree to which these families tended to remain in one place for long periods of time. Our branch of the Sacerdote family settled in Chieri, a town near Torino, in the 1500s and lived there until my grandfather reached adulthood in the late 1800s. Indeed, the family lived in the same house, at 2/4/6/8 Contrada della Pace, for at least 250 years. Similarly, the Montalcini family lived in San Damiano d'Asti from the 1500s until it was forced to move to the Asti ghetto in the 1720s, and returned to San Damiano after the ghettos were permanently opened in 1848. My grandmother Elvira Montalcini, wife of Alberto Sacerdote, was born in San Damiano. The Segre, Levi, and DeBenedetti families changed home city only two or three times during the 500-year span this book covers.

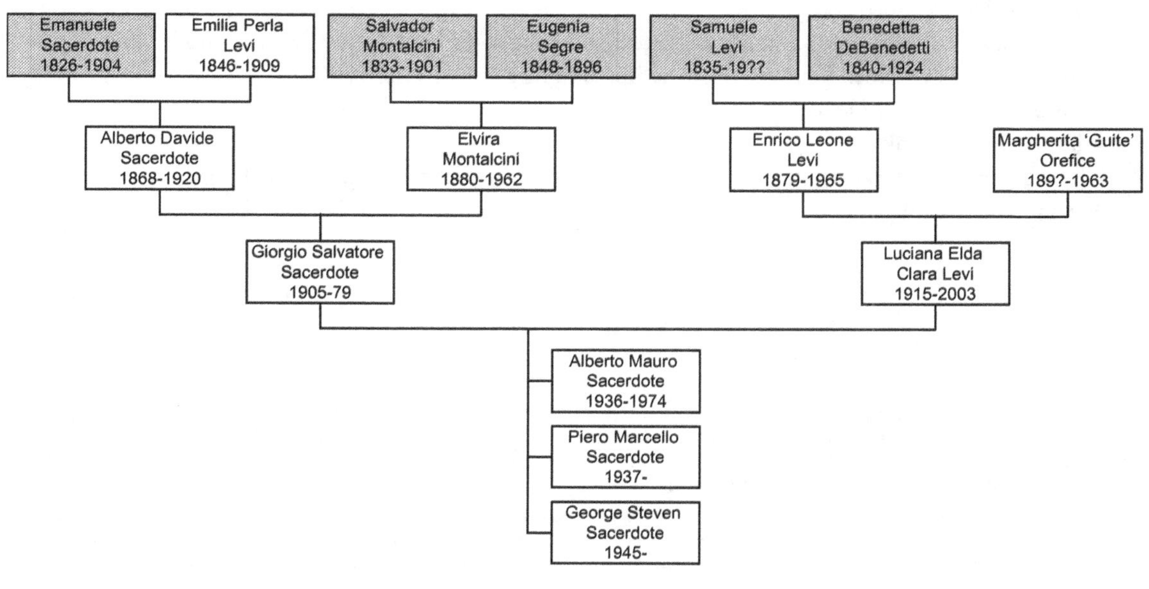

Another very helpful phenomenon is that the Hebrews of Italy and Spain have used surnames for many hundreds of years, unlike most of the Ashkenazim, who adopted surnames only in the 1800s, when they were forced to do so by the Prussian, Russian, and Austrian imperial governments. Surnames had been invented by the ancient Romans, and their use became common among the Hebrews in Italy 2000 years ago. From there the practice spread to the Roman provinces in Spain and southern France. Thus the surnames of our five families were well established in the early 1500s and in all likelihood much earlier; in the case of the Montalcini, they adopted the surname da Montalcino when their branch of the Roman Hebrew family da Sinagoga moved from Rome to the town of Montalcino in the late 1300s. The name da Sinagoga is a direct translation into Latin and Italian of the ancient Hebrew surname Min-ha-Knesset, which was in documented use in Rome at the time of the Caesars. According to Prof. Luzzati, himself a Montalcini descendant, and also my Uncle Paolo and Aunt Eugenia, Montalcini family tradition has it that the da Sinagoga of Rome in the 1300s were descended from the Min-ha-Knesset of ancient Rome.

In general it has been easier to trace the male line than the female line because men were much more likely to be active in finance, commerce, industry, and politics, and thereby create a documentary record.[3] Further, because the Piemontese Hebrews lived in small communities, generally of 200 or fewer individuals, within provincial towns, the normal pattern was for men to seek wives in other towns because they were related to all the eligible women in their own community.[4] In most, but far from all, cases the women moved to their husband's hometown and adopted his surname, making tracing their origins more difficult.

Historical Sources

In completing this research I owe an enormous debt of gratitude to twelve main sources:

- Prof. Cecil Roth of Oxford University; his comprehensive *History of the Jews of Italy* has to be a starting point of any effort of this type.
- Roth's *History of the Marranos.*
- Dott. Sergio Treves of London; his *Gli Ebrei di Chieri* set the example of how to blend family detail with historical context to achieve a complete picture of a community and its times.
- Prof. Renata Segre, whose three-volume collection of documents about the Hebrew communities of Piemonte makes it possible to trace these communities and many individuals in them back to the Middle Ages.
- Prof. Michele Luzzati of the University of Pisa; his unpublished history of the Montalcini family traces its roots in Roman times and its movements through central and northern Italy during the Renaissance and the Baroque.
- Recollections of my Aunt Eugenia Sacerdote de Lustig, of Buenos Aires, and my late uncle Dr. Paolo Sacerdote, of New York.
- Two archives of family documents, pictures, and keepsakes kept by my parents and by my cousin Piera Levi-Montalcini, with some items dating back to the 1700s.
- Annie Sacerdoti's *Guide to Jewish Italy.*
- Gianni Oliva's book *I Savoia.*
- The wonderful archival materials in the Museo del Risorgimento, housed in Torino's Palazzo Carignano.

[3] There were, however, widows with minor children who took over their husbands' businesses. The earliest references I found to this practice were to a Douceta Levi in Torino in the 1400s and to a Hellea Segre in the town of Pinerolo in 1558. In both cases these women were widowed with minor children. Douceta's husband had been a grain broker, and Hellea's a banker. Hellea's litigiousness ensured that she left a particularly rich collection of official records.

[4] In the 1838 census of the ghetto of Chieri, a community of 177 Hebrews and four Protestant servants, fifty-three had been born in other towns, and all but eleven of these fifty-three were women. Among the women, twenty-five had joined their husbands, twelve were servants, two were mothers-in-law, and three were in business for themselves. Of the eleven men, three were students who had come to study with the rabbi.

- James Carroll's *Constantine's Sword*, a comprehensive history of the relationships between the Hebrews and the central hierarchy of the Catholic Church.
- Alexander Stille's *Benevelovence and Betrayal*, an account of the Nazi occupation of Italy from 1943 to 1945. Several of the five families we traced for this book figure prominently in his history.

I owe special thanks to my brother Peter, my Aunt Eugenia, and my dear wife, Carol, for their support and encouragement in preparing this history. This account would not have been possible without their many ideas and suggestions on how best to organize this story.

Finally, I would like to offer my apologies to any professional historians who may read this small volume written by an admitted amateur. While there are, no doubt, errors of fact and analysis that the historical professional will soon discover, I believe that the main line of this brief story is accurate and fairly represents the main actors and actions.

Lexington, Massachusetts
May 2007

Figure 1-1
Moses parting the Red Sea, from a late nineteenth century
Haggadah. In this figure, the Israelites cross on dry land,
pursued by the Egyptians. Note the casket of Jacob being
borne back to Canaan to be buried with his ancestors in
the cave at Hebron. From a Sacerdote family Haggadah.

Figure 1-2
The Egyptians drowning as the waters of the Red Sea close
over them after the Israelites have passed. Note in the upper center Miriam (the sister of Moses) with her tambou-
rine leading the women in singing *Mi Chamocha,* a song of
thanksgiving for their deliverance from the Egyptians. This
song continues to be part of the Jewish liturgy to this day.

Chapter I
In the Beginning: Our Family's Roots in the Biblical, Classical, and Medieval Past

According to the book of Genesis, the Hebrews are descended from one Abram (later called Abraham) who was born in the city-state of Ur of the Chaldees in Mesopotamia.[5] Abram's father was a maker of idols. His son rejected the idol-worshipping polytheistic religion of his parents in favor of worshipping a single unseen and all-powerful god.[6] The Genesis account says that Abram left his parents' house and went to Canaan,[7] where he followed a Bedouin-like life tending his flocks.

Abram had at least two sons. The first, Ishmael, was by his concubine Hagar, and the second, Isaac, was by his wife, Sarah. After the birth of Isaac, Sarah forced Abraham to send Hagar and Ishmael away.[8] Isaac married his cousin Rebecca; they had twin sons, Esau and Jacob. Although Esau was the firstborn, he sold his birthright to Jacob, who inherited the bulk of Isaac's religious and physical estate. Esau and his descendants supposedly settled near the Dead Sea and became the biblical Edomites.

Jacob had two wives, Leah and Rachel, who between them bore twelve sons, the founders of the biblical Twelve Tribes of Israel, as well as twenty-one daughters. These sons were Reuben, Simeon, Levi, Judah, Issachar, Zebulon, Gad, Asher, Joseph, Benjamin, Dan, and Naphtali. The Hebrews with the surname Levi, including Giorgio's wife, Luciana Levi, and the family of Giorgio's grandmother, Emilia Levi, generally claim descent through the male line from Levi, the third son of Jacob.

According to Genesis, Jacob favored his son Joseph, much to the chagrin of his brothers. One day his brothers seized Joseph, tied him up, and left him in the desert to die. However, he was found shortly thereafter by a passing caravan of traders, who took him into Egypt and sold him as a slave.

Joseph claimed the ability to see the future and interpret dreams. This ability came to the attention of Pharaoh, who asked Joseph to interpret a pair of dreams he had had of seven emaciated cattle devouring seven fat ones and of seven meager sheaves of wheat devouring seven full ones. Joseph interpreted the dreams as representing seven years of plenty to be followed by seven years of famine. He recommended that Pharaoh establish a network of granaries to store reserves during the fat years in order to feed the people through the lean ones. Pharaoh put Joseph in charge of building the granaries and securing the reserves of food. The seven fat and seven lean years then occurred, and Joseph was seen as a hero.

According to Genesis, the famine spread to Canaan, and Jacob and the rest of his family went down to Egypt in search of food. There they were reunited with Joseph, who provided them with food and arranged for them to settle in the district of Goshen.[9]

---

[5] The ancient region of Mesopotamia corresponds roughly to the modern country of Iraq. From this region sprang numerous important empires in ancient times, including those of the Assyrians and the Babylonians. After the Arabs conquered the region, in the mid-to-late 600s A.D., they made the city of Baghdad their capital.

[6] A number of Jewish religious practices date back at least to the time of Abraham, including circumcision, observation of the Sabbath, the rejection of human sacrifice (as described in the story of the binding of Isaac), and funeral rites (Abraham, Isaac, Isaac's son Jacob, and their wives were all buried in a cave near Hebron on the West Bank).

[7] Canaan is roughly the region between the Jordan River and the Mediterranean and between the Sinai Peninsula and the mountains of Lebanon—the modern state of Israel plus the Gaza Strip and the West Bank.

[8] Abraham in Hebrew means "father of a people." Actually, Abraham was the father of two peoples—the Arabs claim descent from Ishmael—and the descendants of Isaac and Ishmael are still fighting. Recently there was a bloody skirmish at the Tomb of the Patriarchs, which both Hebrews and Arabs claim houses the body of their national founder, Abraham.

[9] Biblical scholars generally identify Goshen as a region just south of the Nile Delta.

According to the biblical book of Exodus, many years later, a new pharaoh "who knew not Joseph" came to power, and enslaved the descendants of Jacob. They remained slaves for 400 years. The end of slavery came when Moses, a member of the Levite tribe who had been raised in the house of Pharaoh's daughter, led a revolt of the Hebrew slaves during which they escaped from Egypt.[10]

In the following forty years Moses led the Hebrew tribes as they wandered through the Sinai and Arabian deserts. The Book of Exodus says that God directed Moses to establish laws that form the core of the Jewish religion. These laws include the Ten Commandments, but extended into many other domains, including law,[11] commerce,[12] diet,[13] hygiene,[14] charity,[15] and compulsory education.[16] These civil and criminal laws are laid out in detail in Exodus and Deuteronomy.

In the religious domain, Moses set his older brother Aaron as the first in a hereditary line of priests (*Cohanim*). Hebrews with the surname Cohen[17] ["priest" in Hebrew], including the Sacerdotes [Sacerdote is a direct translation of Cohen into Latin, Italian, and Spanish] claim descent in the male line from Aaron. DNA studies on the Y-chromosome in the late 1990s established that about 80 percent of the males making this claim share a common male ancestor who lived about 3500 years ago. The author carries the characteristic twelve genetic markers of the Cohanim.

Aaron and Moses then developed a complex set of sacerdotal rites covering the major holidays that existed at that time, including the celebration of the Sabbath, Passover, the New Year (Rosh Hashanah), the Day of Atonement (Yom Kippur, when Hebrews fast, confess their sins, and make amends), and two lesser feasts, Shavuot (which celebrates the giving of the Ten Commandments) and Succoth (a fall harvest festival). These rites are described in detail in the biblical books of Exodus and Leviticus.

Skipping quickly past the biblical books of Joshua,[18] Judges,[19] and Samuel,[20] we reach the books of Kings. These books recount how David established his kingdom with its capital in Jerusalem. Solomon, the son of David, built a great temple in which to conduct the most important religious rites.[21] This temple was the province of the hereditary priests descended from Aaron, where our presumed male Sacerdote ancestors served.

[10] The Jewish festival of Passover celebrates the exodus from Egypt. Moses created this festival to replace an earlier Abramic feast celebrating the spring planting. Biblical scholars place the exodus from Egypt at shortly after the reign of Pharaoh Akhenaton, who had overthrown the Egyptian religion and replaced it with a monotheistic sun worship. After his death there was a violent reaction in Egypt; the forces representing the old religion retook power and sought to remove all traces of Akhenaton and his religion. Biblical scholars have debated whether or not there are connections between Akhenaton's religious reforms and the Jewish religion as it was formulated by Moses.

[11] "You will give honest judgments, not take bribes, treat the rich and poor equally in judgments, and not bear false witness." The Mosaic laws covered both criminal and civil matters and are remarkably detailed in the areas of criminal law, contracts, torts, and domestic law. Many of the core principles Moses laid down survive into our modern legal system.

[12] "You will deal fairly, using honest weights and measures. You will pay your laborers their wages on the day that they do their work and not keep their wages overnight."

[13] The Jewish dietary laws of not eating pork, shellfish, reptiles, and some other creatures, and also not mixing the meat of mammals with milk. These laws also required the clean and humane slaughter of food animals and the rejection of meat from diseased animals, a practice only recently adopted by the USDA.

[14] All were to wash hands before eating, and women were to bathe after menstruation and childbirth.

[15] "You will give charity, feed the hungry, clothe the naked, care for the poor and sick, and redeem the captive."

[16] "You shall teach your son…." This particular precept is recited in every Jewish service. The requirement of universal (male) education meant that wherever the Hebrews lived, they left an extensive written record (thereby making this book possible). Also, when the Hebrews came to live among other peoples, they tended to be better educated than most of their neighbors, who, until modern times, were mostly illiterate. As a result, Hebrews have figured in the learned professions disproportionately to their numbers in most of their host countries.

[17] Cohen is the Hebrew singular form of Cohanim

[18] Which recounts the reentry of the Hebrews into Canaan after the death of Moses, under the leadership of Joshua.

[19] Judges is a collection of rather disconnected stories recounting the efforts of the Hebrews to establish supremacy in Canaan against their neighbors, especially the Philistines (whose capital was Gaza). This seems to be a precursor of modern troubles. Judges recounts that Samson slew a thousand Philistines with the jawbone of an ass. The level of discourse does not seem to have improved much since then.

[20] The books of Samuel recount the establishment of the Davidian Kingdom.

[21] Solomon was reputed to have had innumerable wives and concubines, including the fabled Queen of Sheba. The Ethiopians, including their last hereditary emperor, claim descent from this union. Late in the nineteenth century the Falasha tribe in Ethiopia was discovered by Europeans. The Falasha practice Jewish rites similar to those of Solomon's time. Most other Ethiopians are Coptic Christians, having been converted by Egyptian missionaries in the first few centuries A.D. The rites of the Ethiopian Christians, however, include celebrating the Sabbath on Saturday rather than Sunday, avoiding pork and other foods proscribed by the Mosaic laws, and circumcising males on the eighth day after birth, as prescribed by Abraham.

After the reign of Solomon, around 900 B.C., the country split into two antagonistic realms known as Israel (or Samaria, after its capital) and Judea (with its capital in Jerusalem), governed by two of Solomon's sons. Samaria had a stormy history and proved to be a very unstable monarchy. It ceased to exist as an independent country in 721 B.C., when it was conquered by King Sargon of Assyria. The Assyrians scattered the population, and little was heard of Samaria thereafter.[22] In their place, the Assyrians brought colonists to Samaria from numerous other parts of their empire. These colonists adopted some of the religious practices of the former inhabitants and became known as Samaritans. There still exist small communities of Samaritans in the Middle East.

Shortly after the Assyrian conquest of Samaria, Assyria itself was conquered by King Sennacherib of Babylonia, in 721 B.C. The southern kingdom, Judea, endured for another 135 years before it was conquered by King Nebuchadnezzar of Babylonia, in 586 B.C. The conquering Babylonians destroyed the city of Jerusalem and Solomon's temple. They elected to partially depopulate the region by exiling the priests and nobles, leaving behind only the lowest classes of society. However, unlike the Assyrians, the Hebrew exiles were deported as a single group to the city of Babylon, thus creating the first diaspora of the Hebrews.[23] This diaspora also led to the founding of innumerable communities of Hebrews throughout the Middle East from Mesopotamia to North Africa as they sought to escape the Babylonian conquest.[24]

The first diaspora forced the Hebrews to develop new institutions to enable them to survive as a minority people in an alien society and new rites to replace those that had been conducted in the temple in Jerusalem.[25] The core institution was the synagogue,[26] which conducted religious services thrice daily. These services centered on readings from the Torah (the first five books of the Bible). Any adult male member of the community could lead the services since all males were required to be literate. Many, but not all, synagogues had a spiritual leader called a rabbi (Hebrew for "teacher"), who was selected from among the Levites. In addition to the synagogue, these communities had a system of law courts to settle both civil and criminal issues in accordance with the Mosaic laws.[27] The communities also established a taxation system to support these institutions and give alms to the poor. Finally, each community had officials trained to perform ritual circumcisions and to conduct the humane slaughter of animals for food. This community structure still existed in the dozens of Hebrew communities scattered throughout the towns and small cities of Piemonte 2000 years later.

In 539 B.C., during the reign of one of Nebuchadnezzar's successors, Belshazzar, Babylonia was conquered by King Cyrus of Persia. The Hebrew community of Babylon petitioned Cyrus for, and was granted, permission to return to its homeland.[28] The Hebrews subsequently returned to Judea in four waves during the reigns of Cyrus and of Darius the Great, bringing with them the temple treasures that

---

[22] There have been innumerable dubious claims throughout history of people "finding" the ten lost tribes of Samaria. Perhaps the most credible is that they were deported to northern Mesopotamia, where they blended with the Kurdish population; this claim is buttressed by the high incidence of the Cohen Modal Haplotype, the DNA signature of the *Cohanim*, in the Y-chromosomes of male Kurds.

[23] A much smaller part of the population fled to Egypt with the prophet Jeremiah. Part of this group went as far as Tunisia, where it settled on the island of Djerba (Jerba). The ancient synagogue of Djerba was bombed by Arab extremists in 2002. In addition, a remnant of the Judean population hid out in the hills and deserts of Judea and avoided deportation.

[24] Most of these ancient Hebrew communities survived until the 1950s, when their inhabitants were summarily driven out of the Arab states. This population of Hebrews from Arab states makes up the majority of the population of the modern state of Israel. Its forced removal is conveniently omitted by the Palestinians and their apologists in their complaints of having been driven out of what is now Israel.

[25] The main institution was the precursor of the modern synagogue, in which rites could be observed in the local community, led by any adult male and without need for a national temple run by the hereditary priests. See the biblical books of Ezra and Nehemiah for details.

[26] Greek for "assembly."

[27] This system of law courts was probably derived from the courts set up by Moses during the Exodus. In Roman times, the Hebrews in Rome were allowed to use their own law courts to judge disputes within the community. Remnants of this system of Hebrew law courts survive to this day. During the British mandate in Palestine, the British administration left domestic law to religious courts so that they would not have to deal with conflicting Moslem, Jewish, and Christian laws on these subjects. Religious courts in Israel still have jurisdiction over family law. Among religious Jews in America, marriages are still governed by contracts drawn up in accordance with these laws, and divorces are not official unless those contracts are dissolved by religious courts.

[28] Some of the Hebrews, however, elected to remain in Mesopotamia, and yet others migrated into Persia (now called Iran). Many years later a Hebrew woman named Esther married King Ahasuerus (better known in the West by his Greek name, Xerxes) of Persia. The story of how Queen Esther foiled a plot by the King's prime minister, Haman, to murder all the Hebrews (including her) is retold in the biblical book of Esther. This victory is celebrated in the Jewish feast of Purim, which features a reading of the book of Esther.

had been taken to Babylon by Nebuchadnezzar. They rebuilt Jerusalem, including the temple, in the years 520–480 B.C. After the conquest of Persia by Alexander the Great and the subsequent division of Alexander's empire among his four top generals, the region of Judea became a province of the Syrian Empire.

In 168–65 B.C., the Hebrews successfully revolted against their Syrian overlords under the leadership of the priestly Hasmonean family, who reestablished Judea as an independent state. For the next century this small state led a precarious existence among the much more powerful kingdoms, including Egypt and Syria, which had been carved out of the empire of Alexander the Great. During this period, Hebrew merchants began to trade quite extensively around the Mediterranean and established communities in Asia Minor (modern-day Turkey), many of the Greek isles, and even Sicily. These communities were modeled on those of the Babylonian Captivity. This was the first recorded presence of Hebrews in what has become Italy.

As the power of Rome grew in the second century B.C., the situation in the Hebrew kingdom became ever more precarious. A deputation of Hebrews went to Rome as early as 161 B.C. to seek its help in defending the kingdom against the twin menaces of Egypt and Syria. Additional delegations went to Rome in 150, 142, and 139 B.C. to renew the relationship between Judea and Rome. At first the Romans paid little attention, but ultimately they chose to exploit this opportunity to establish themselves in the Middle East. The Hebrew kings of the Hasmonean and subsequent Herodean[29] dynasties continued to reign for some time thereafter, but increasingly the Romans ruled, especially after Pompey's military campaigns in Syria and Palestine in the 60s B.C.

During this period, a number of small Hebrew communities sprang up in Rome and surrounding towns. Recent excavations at the Roman port of Ostia turned up a synagogue dating to the last century B.C. By the beginning of the reign of Augustus Caesar (34 B.C.–A.D. 14), there were as many as 30,000 Hebrews and two synagogues in Rome.[30] Julius and Augustus Caesar adopted mostly benevolent policies toward the Hebrews, such as exempting them from military service[31] and from legal proceedings on the Sabbath.

Among the Hebrew families known to have been resident in ancient Rome were the Min-ha-Knesset, Min-ha-Zekenim, Min-ha-Taphuhim, Min-ha-Adomim, and Min-ha-Anavim.[32] These names were in documented usage in the Roman Hebrew community in the Middle Ages in their Italianized forms: da Sinagoga, de Rossi, de Pomi, de Vecchi, and delli Mansi or Piatelli.[33] The modern descendants of these medieval families have at various times claimed that the continuity of their names indicates their lineal descent from the similarly named Hebrews of Roman times.

In Judea there were two major failed revolts against Roman rule. The first, in A.D. 66–70, resulted in the destruction of the temple in Jerusalem and the mass suicide of the rebels at the fortress of Masada. Nearly 100,000 Hebrews were sent to Rome as slaves, the first large influx of Hebrews into Italy. The Arch of Titus in Rome has elaborate carvings showing the Roman victory procession with its Hebrew captives carrying the temple treasures, including a large seven-branched menorah (candelabrum). Most of those who were taken to Rome as slaves were eventually bought out of slavery by their coreligionists who were already established in Italy, following the Mosaic law requiring the redemption of captives.

---

[29] The first Herodean king was an Edomite usurper imposed by the Romans.

[30] Sacerdoti, p. 11.

[31] The Hebrews' requirement that they not work on the Sabbath and their dietary laws made military service problematic.

[32] These names are taken from Cecil Roth's *History of the Jews of Italy* and an unpublished manuscript by Prof. Luzzati. Presumably they obtained them from the inscriptions in the Roman catacombs and surviving texts of that period, such as the histories of Josephus.

[33] Four of these names are direct translations. Da Sinagoga is a direct translation of Min-ha-Knesset from Hebrew into Latin. "Knesset" means "meeting" or "council" in Hebrew, as does "synagogue" in Greek. Min-ha-Adomim translates as "of the red (haired) ones," which translates as De Rossi. Min-ha-Taphuhim means "of the apple growers," which translates as De Pomi. Min-ha-Zekenim translates as "of the old ones," which in Italian is rendered De Vecchi. The da Sinagoga and the De Rossi will reappear in this story in the next several chapters.

At this time the Roman emperor decreed that the voluntary contributions the Diaspora Hebrews formerly sent to Judea to support the temple be institutionalized as a Roman tax, the *Fiscus Judeus,* to be paid to support Roman state religious institutions. This discriminatory Jews' Tax survived in various forms into the mid-to-late 1800s in various parts of Italy.

The second revolt, around A.D. 135, was much more disastrous. The precipitating event occurred when the Roman emperor announced his intention to build a temple dedicated to Jupiter on the site of the former Temple of Solomon. After putting down the revolt, the Romans banished the entire Hebrew population from Judea, producing the second diaspora. Those not deported from Judea in chains by the Romans fled westward across the Mediterranean as far as Spain, northward to Syria and Turkey, south into Egypt and Arabia, or east to Mesopotamia and Persia.[34]

During the latter years of the Roman Empire, there were many well-established communities of Hebrews throughout the empire, especially in Italy, Spain, southern France, Greece, and North Africa. These communities were active in many occupations, of which the most important was international trade. They were naturally drawn to trade because of their extensive kinship networks that spanned the Mediterranean[35] as a direct consequence of the Roman depopulation of Judea. Other occupations ran the full range from peddlers to poets and scavengers to physicians. In Italy, the Hebrew population was concentrated around Rome and the major cities of southern Italy and Sicily. Based on the writings of Josephus, a Hebrew historian during the first century A.D., the sizes of known Hebrew neighborhoods in the city, the extent of their catacombs, and the census of Claudius, Roth and Sacerdoti estimate that Hebrews constituted between 1 percent and 10 percent of the population of the city of Rome. The inscriptions in the catacombs indicate that there were at least a dozen synagogues in the city proper. In Spain, the Hebrew population was mainly in the towns of the eastern and southern coasts.

In the second decade of the 300s A.D., Emperor Constantine made a fateful decision which had direct consequences for the Hebrews of the empire. He established Christianity as the official state religion, although he himself remained a pagan until he was baptized on his deathbed. This change suddenly made the Hebrews and all other non-Christian religious groups into second-class citizens at best and, more often, outsiders.

Constantine also confirmed Diocletian's earlier division of the Roman Empire into two parts and moved to Byzantium, which he renamed Constantinople,[36] as Emperor of the Eastern Roman Empire. The western part included the modern countries of Italy, France, England, Switzerland, Croatia, Slovenia, Spain, Portugal, Morocco, Algeria, and the western half of Libya. The eastern part included the rest of Libya, Egypt, Israel, Jordan, Syria, Lebanon, Turkey, and the Balkan states of Greece, Bulgaria, Romania, Albania, Serbia, Macedonia, and Bosnia.[37] The Western empire went into a gradual decline leading to its conquest by the barbarian Goths in A.D. 476. The Eastern Roman Empire (later known as the Byzantine Empire), with its capital in Constantinople, prospered for a time, and in the 500s expanded back into parts of Italy along the Adriatic coast. Venice was originally a Byzantine city. Over time the Byzantine Empire declined and shrank, but it continued to control Turkey and the Balkan states until A.D. 1453.

During the 400s and 500s a group of Hebrew scholars met in Baghdad, a major city of the Byzantine Empire and an important seat of Hebrew scholarship, to standardize religious practices. They developed a common model for each of the major Jewish rites and determined the best way to celebrate the holidays. As part of their work they also gathered and systematized an enormous body of accumulated learning, the Talmud. The Talmud included collected interpretations of and teachings about the Torah (Five Books of Moses), as well as a vast literature on how to apply the Mosaic laws under a wide variety of circumstances, and how to adapt them to changing conditions or in cases that could not have been

---

[34] Most of these ancient Hebrew communities survived until the 1950s, when their inhabitants were summarily driven out of the Arab states. More than one million Hebrews left Syria, Iraq, Egypt, Saudi Arabia, Yemen, and elsewhere.

[35] This model is remarkably similar to the growth of trading networks in Southeast Asia dominated by the kinship networks among the overseas Chinese.

[36] This city is the modern Istanbul.

[37] Unsurprisingly, the demarcation between which peoples are Orthodox Christians and which are Catholics follows this Constantinian boundary. The recent wars in Bosnia, Croatia, and Kosovo were fought over issues left from this division of 1700 years ago.

foreseen when these laws were written 2000 years earlier. In the late Middle Ages, the Catholic Church deemed the Talmud to be a heretical work because some of its biblical interpretations were at odds with Church dogma. The Talmud was placed on the *Index Librorum Prohibitorum*,[38] alongside the works of Galileo and Luther. As such, both Catholics and non-Catholics were subject to unannounced Church-led searches of their houses. If copies of prohibited books such as the Talmud were found, the books would be burned and their owners severely punished.[39]

With the collapse of the Western Roman Empire came a series of invasions by various Germanic tribes. The Goths set up a government in Italy along Roman lines, but they were soon driven out by much rougher tribes including the Lombards in the north and the Vandals in the south. Domestic order broke down throughout Western Europe, and central government pretty much evaporated. In such an environment, numerous petty chieftains established themselves as controllers of small bits of territory and defenders of the local inhabitants. Life turned into a Hobbesian state of continuous warfare among these chieftains as each sought to seize the property and power of his neighbors.

With the collapse of central government in most of Western Europe, the only remaining force of authority was the Roman Catholic Church. Beginning with Pope Gregory I (590–604), the Church developed a strongly centralized authority over religious affairs. This authority was extended across Western and Central Europe as the barbarian tribes that ruled different parts of that landmass converted to Christianity during the period from 500 to 1000. The Church's position toward the Hebrews was first clearly enunciated by Pope Gregory. While he railed against the Hebrews' refusal to convert to Christianity (and hence become his subjects!), he argued that the Hebrews should be treated humanely and permitted to exercise their legal rights. In Italy, at least, he took steps to curb the outrages upon the Hebrews initiated or condoned by some of his more flagrantly anti-Semitic bishops.[40] This approach appears to have continued through much of the Dark Ages and the early medieval period. While relations between the two Italian communities may have waxed and waned over time, they seem to have been reasonably cordial. Indeed, many late medieval popes had Hebrew physicians. This situation is in sharp contrast with the situation in western Germany, where the assembling army of the First Crusade murdered whole communities of Hebrews in the Rhineland in the 1090s, including the entire Hebrew population of Mainz, which was slaughtered in the courtyard of the bishop's palace as it sought the Church's protection from the marauding Crusaders.[41]

Beginning with the Fourth Lateran Council in 1215, the Church promulgated rules governing the Hebrews, such as requiring them to live apart from Christians and wear distinctive badges. In general, these rules were little enforced in Italy during the late Middle Ages. Relations between the Italian Catholic and Hebrew communities began to change in 1414 under anti-Pope[42] Benedict XIII, a Spaniard whom Roth describes as having a monomania about forcing the conversion of the Hebrews. His energy was particularly focused on Hebrews in southern France, where he held temporal as well as ecclesiastical authority. Perhaps his malevolence was driven by fears that some of the early Protestant movements that had appeared in southern France, northern Italy[43] and in Central Europe were eroding his authority. In any case he established severe rules regulating the Hebrews under his jurisdiction.

---

[38] *The Index Librorum Prohibitorum* was a Church-developed list of books deemed heretical which Catholics were prohibited from reading. During the 1500s-1700s, the Church also prohibited non-Catholics from reading and owning such books, and would enforce this prohibition where it could with inquisitorial raids.

[39] For examples of such inquisitorial raids, see Segre, documents 1461, 1476, 1494.

[40] Roth, *History of the Jews of Italy*, p. 305.

[41] The Hebrews were subsequently banished from England in 1292 and from France in 1394.

[42] In 1378 the Catholic Church split, with two different factions electing their own popes, one ruling from Rome and the other from Avignon in what is now France. The French popes were generally referred to as anti-popes. The state of affairs continued until 1449, when the papacy was once again unified.

[43] About a century before, an obscure Protestant sect, the Waldensians, formed in the mountain valleys of Piemonte and Savoy, and Jan Hus in Bohemia had formed a sect in the 1300s that sought to operate beyond the authority of the papacy. While the Hussite movement was crushed in the 1400s, the Waldensians survived underground until they were at last allowed to practice their faith openly in 1848. Umberto Eco's novel *The Name of the Rose* is set in a Benedictine abbey (modeled very closely after the abbey Sagra di San Michele outside of Torino) during one of the periods in which the Waldensians were being suppressed. Today the only Protestant church in Torino is the Waldensian church. It is situated on Corso Vittorio Emanuele, between the main railway station and the Po River. Immediately behind the Waldensian church is the modern Torino synagogue.

In 1434 Pope Eugenius IV codified and expanded these rules to include such provisions as

- Hebrews were to live apart from Christians[44] and wear a distinguishing badge.
- The Hebrew community was subject to an annual tax.
- Hebrews guilty of insulting Christians or defaming the Church or its doctrines were subject to severe penalties.
- Hebrews could not employ Christians or have them living under their roof; hence they could not rent property to Christians.
- Hebrews could not attend upon Christians as physicians.[45]
- Hebrews could not build new synagogues.
- Hebrews could not attend Christian universities.
- Hebrews could not engage in handicrafts or lend money at interest.
- Hebrews could not study the Talmud or other Hebrew literature deemed heretical by the Church.
- Hebrews were not to have intimate relations with Christians.

There is a striking similarity between these rules and the Jim Crow laws that were applied to blacks in the American South during the century following the Civil War.

Italy being Italy, adherence to these rules was uneven at best, and largely dictated by expedience and the whim of local rulers. In Piemonte, Ferrara, Florence, Siena, Mantova, and other enlightened states, little heed was paid to them from the beginning. Even in Rome they soon fell into disuse until 1555, when Pope Paul IV issued a bull that codified many of the disabilities that the Church had been attempting to impose on the Hebrews over the previous century. In that year the Roman Hebrew community was forcibly moved into a walled compound, later called the Roman ghetto. Hebrews could leave the ghetto only during daylight; at night its gates were locked. While this locking of the gates at sunset may seem harsh, all walled towns closed their gates at sunset to prevent the entry of robbers, vagrants, and other reprobates under the cover of darkness. This rule extended to the Hebrew ghetto, a neighborhood within a town, a rule that was already applied to the town as a whole.

The rise and fall of Arab Spain, and our ancestors' forced departure from that realm

As domestic order, commerce, and learning were collapsing in Western Europe in the centuries immediately following the fall of the Western Roman Empire, Islam emerged in Arabia in the first half of the 600s. The Arab followers of this militant religion quickly conquered much of the Middle East and North Africa. Soon they had an empire stretching from Morocco in the west to Persia in the east. Their capital was Baghdad. Their conquests carried them north as far as Syria, and drove the Byzantines out of all of the Middle East except for Asia Minor.

The conquering Arabs were led by rather ignorant religious fanatics,[46] and among other acts of destruction, they burned the 900-year-old Library of Alexandria, the world's single greatest repository of knowledge. The Arab general responsible for the burning is alleged to have said that the library was useless because its books either agreed with the Koran, and so were superfluous, or they disagreed, and so should be destroyed as blasphemous. However, as the tribesmen from Arabia came in contact with the cultures of the regions they conquered, they quickly recognized the values of these alien cultural heritages. Within a few generations, Baghdad, Cairo, and other major cities of the Arab Empire became the main centers of the arts and learning of the Western world. Much of the literary, scientific, and medical knowledge of the ancients, which had been kept alive by the Byzantines after the collapse of the Western Roman Empire, was taken over and expanded upon by the Arabs. The Arabs also established a network of universities as a mechanism of propagating and furthering knowledge.

---

[44] Beginning in the 1500s, the Church did not view Protestants as "Christian." Consequently one finds Protestants occasionally living in the Hebrew ghettos and working as servants for Hebrew families, particularly in Piemonte which had a small indigenous Protestant movement.

[45] Even though Eugenius himself had a Hebrew physician!

[46] Mohammed himself was an illiterate camel driver. He had to dictate the Koran to scribes.

In the early 700s the Arabs captured Sicily and parts of southern Italy. They invaded Spain and drove north of the Pyrenees into France. They threatened to take over all of Western Europe until they were defeated by the Frankish chieftain Charles Martel at the Battle of Tours in 729. At this point they were driven back into Spain.

In Spain the Arabs established a multiethnic, multireligious society governed by Moorish kings from Morocco. This kingdom was spared much of the cultural and economic collapse that came to the rest of Western Europe during the Dark Ages. The Moors actively promoted the arts, literature, the sciences, and medicine. They also reintroduced much of the learning from classical times, although most of non-Spanish Europe was not ready for it. The Hebrews in Spain were particularly receptive to this inflow of knowledge, probably because of their high literacy rates and compulsory education system. During this period there was a great flowering of cultural life among these Hebrews. Best known among the Hebrew scholars of this time was Moses Maimonides, who was both a physician and a philosopher. Maimonides wrote a compendium of medical knowledge of the day as well as an important book on ethics. The ethics book advocated charity that helped the poor to become self-sustaining rather than merely giving them daily handouts Maimonides was the first to espouse the theory that the former restored self-respect, while the latter merely cemented the poor into lifelong dependency. After an initial career in Spain, Maimonides moved to Egypt, where he was appointed physician to the king.

Around 1000, the Arab Empire in the Middle East began to crumble. First it was invaded by a nomadic people from Central Asia, the Seljuk Turks, who captured Persia early in the eleventh century and took over Baghdad in 1055. Next it was invaded in the Holy Land by Western Europeans during the Crusades in the 1100s and 1200s. Then the Mongols captured Persia in the early 1200s and sacked Baghdad in 1258, ending the Arab caliphate. After the breakup of the Mongol Empire, a central Asian tribe, the Ottoman Turks asserted control. Gradually, the Turkish Empire grew, absorbing modern-day Iraq, Jordan, Syria, Lebanon, Israel, and Egypt in the 1300s. Finally, the Turks captured Constantinople in 1453, putting en end to the Byzantine Empire and acquiring all of its extensive territory in southeastern Europe.

As the Arab Empire in the east crumbled, squabbles among the Moorish royal family in Spain created an opening for a second invasion from Morocco, with power passing to the more austere Almoravid ruling family. Subsequently, the formerly monolithic Moorish kingdom broke apart into smaller kingdoms. At this time several small Christian kingdoms emerged in northern Spain as well. Over time these northern kingdoms conquered bits of Spain from the Moors, and by the 1300s only the Kingdom of Granada, in southern Spain, remained under Moorish control. During the late 1200s, the King of Aragon, in northeastern Spain, who also ruled the Balearic Isles, gained control of Sardinia and Sicily. These new Christian kings preserved as much as they could of the culture of the country. Their new Christian, Moslem, and Jewish subjects were allowed to carry on much as before. The Hebrews prospered under these kingdoms; established themselves as scholars, physicians, politicians and worked in many trades. For example, a Hebrew named Todros Todros living in Catalonia (part of the Kingdom of Aragon) made the first translation of Aristotle's *Poesy* into Spanish in 1404. [47] Best known among the Hebrews in politics was Yehuda ha-Levi, who was finance minister under Pedro the Cruel of Castile in the 1300s.[48] Another Hebrew who rose to political prominence was Isaac Abarbanel, who as Finance Minister under Ferdinand and Isabella organized the financing of Columbus's voyages to America. In a few cases the Hebrews received heraldic titles; in the late 1500s the Segre, Todros and Nizza families of Chieri [a town near Torino in Piemonte] petitioned the Duke of Savoy to resume use of the coats of arms they had borne in Spain.[49]

[47] Todros is a Spanish corruption of the Greek name Theodore, which together with its Hebrew equivalent, Nathaniel, means "gift of God"). The Todros family will figure into our story after it emigrated to Piemonte in the 1500s.

[48] Ha-Levi was also a religious poet, and some of his compositions are part of the Hebrew liturgy to this day. A small synagogue that Ha-Levi donated to the Hebrew community of Toledo, La Sinagoga del Transito, still stands, although it was converted into a Christian church after the expulsion of the Hebrews in 1492.

[49] The Segre's escutcheon featured a lion in an azure field; The Todros's coat of arms featured a winged dragon in a white field; and Nizza's a red tower in a blue field. See Segre, document 1295. We will discuss the Segre and Todros families in more detail in the section of chapter II on the Sacerdotes in Piemonte.

In the 1390s life for the Hebrews in parts of Spain began to change. In Seville a rabble-rousing friar, Fray Martinez, began to preach hatred of the Hebrews, and there followed a series of riots, assaults, attacks, and murders. The troubles then spread to Catalonia, the region around Barcelona, and elsewhere. A few Hebrews emigrated to southern France,[50] to Italy,[51] and elsewhere, but most remained in Spain. Of those who remained, some saw fit to adopt the Catholic religion of the majority Christians to protect themselves. In most cases, however, the conversion was merely a superficial affair of convenience, and the full Jewish religion was practiced in secret. In other cases, the conversions were only partial, with ancient Jewish practices, such as observance of the Sabbath and the dietary laws, continuing. Finally, in a few cases the conversions were complete and sincere.[52] The New Christians who preserved some or all Jewish practice came to be known as Marranos.[53]

Figure 1-3
1631 Map of Spain. The Segre River in Catalonia in
extreme northeastern Spain runs roughly northeast to
southwest, emptying into the Ebro just south of Lerida.
From the collection of George S. Sacerdote.

[50] The town of Lattès in Languedoc was one such point of emigration. From this town came several families of that name who still live in Piemonte.

[51] The first occurrence of the name Segre in Piemonte occurs in 1446; see Segre, document. 443.

[52] Saint Teresa of Avila came from a Marrano family. When she became a passionate Catholic in the 1530s, her parents feared that she would betray the family to the Inquisition, and so sent her brothers to the Americas, to get them out of reach of the Inquisitors.

[53] A medieval Spanish word meaning "swine."

The issue of heretical practices among the nominally Catholic Marranos resulted in institution of the Inquisition in Spain in 1478,[54] at the request of Queen Isabella of Castile. The Inquisition, under the leadership of the General Inquisitor, Tomas de Torquemada,[55] used the most severe medieval tortures to ferret out secret Jews and enforce Catholic orthodoxy. Sins in the eyes of the Inquisition included not only celebrating traditional Jewish holidays and rituals, but also seemingly innocent practices such as avoiding the eating of pork, having a family dinner on Friday night,[56] owning books written in Hebrew (especially a copy of the Talmud), and not eating leavened bread at Eastertime.[57] Those who did not admit to their sins and change their ways were burned at the stake in public rituals called autos-da-fé.

By the mid-1400s, the small kingdoms of Spain had coalesced into four states: Aragon in the northeast, Navarre in north-central Spain, Castile (covering most of central Spain), and Granada, the remaining Moorish kingdom in the far south. In 1469 Ferdinand, heir to the throne of Aragon, married Isabella, heiress to the throne of Castile, and in 1479 those two kingdoms merged. In the early 1490s Ferdinand and Isabella waged war against Granada, culminating in the latter's defeat in 1492. Ferdinand and Isabella completed their consolidation of Spain with their seizure of Navarre 1512.[58]

In the same year as they defeated the Moors of Granada (1492) and the same month in which they authorized Columbus's first voyage,[59] Ferdinand and Isabella, who were violently anti-Semitic, issued an edict requiring all Hebrews in their kingdom to convert to Catholicism or leave.[60, 61] This edict applied as well to Sicily. Some chose to remain in Spain and Sicily as Marranos. This was preferred by those with substantial property holdings or important political offices.[62] These Marranos then became subject to the Inquisition. The rest chose exile and became the first wave of the Sephardic[63] diaspora. This population went to North Africa, Portugal, Italy, and especially the Turkish dominions in the Balkans and the Middle East.[64] The Turkish sultan openly encouraged immigration of the Spanish Hebrews because they were well-educated and had broad commercial and financial skills.

[54] The Inquisition continued in Spain until about 1834. The last public burning of heretics was in the 1730s, and the Holy Office (as the Inquisition was officially called) was not abolished in Spain until Napoleon overthrew the Spanish monarchy around 1800. After Napoleon's fall in 1815, it was reinstituted in Spain and abolished a second time in 1834. The current pope, Benedict XVI, was head of the Holy Office in the Vatican before his election as pope.

[55] Ironically, Torquemada himself was a Hebrew convert to Catholicism.

[56] A Harvard historian, Prof. Barbara Haber, has recently used the archives of the Inquisition to develop a complete picture of the domestic life of the Spanish Hebrews in the last days before the final expulsion of 1492.

[57] The Jewish festival of Passover includes the replacement of conventional bread with unleavened wafers, in remembrance of the Hebrews' hasty departure from Egypt, when their bread did not have time to rise. Because Passover tends to occur around Eastertide, many Marranos held their Passover rituals at this time.

[58] The King of Navarre went into exile with his relatives in France. His grandson became King Henri IV of France in 1589.

[59] Columbus's origin is obscure, though some claim he was a Marrano (a claim based on substantial circumstantial evidence). Columbus is a common surname among the Sephardim. He claimed to be Italian, from Genova (Genoa), although he was able to speak fluent Castilian Spanish at the royal court, suggesting Spanish origin. His father was thought to be from Catalonia. His journals were all kept in Spanish, not Italian. His primary sponsors at the royal court were two high officials who were definitely Marranos, Luis de Santangel and Isaac Abarbanel. Abarbanel was the royal treasurer. When Columbus's ships were ready to leave on their first voyage of discovery, he delayed their departure by a day, thus avoiding the inauspicious ninth of Av, a fast day in the Hebrew calendar commemorating the destruction of the first and second temples in Jerusalem. Finally, numerous notes in Columbus's journals and his letters to his son contain peculiarly Hebrew references.

[60] The Edict of Expulsion of 1492 specified that the Hebrews had to leave by the ninth day of the Hebrew month of Av, the same calendar date as the destruction of the Temples, and it remains a fast day on the Jewish calendar. It endured into modern times. Its core provisions were not revoked until 1968, and the last remaining disabilities placed upon Hebrews in Spain were not eliminated until the eve of the Barcelona Olympics in 1992, the 500th anniversary of the expulsion.

[61] They wanted to drive out the Moslems as well, but were prevented from doing so under the treaty ending the war with Granada. Their successor, Charles V, extended the expulsion order to Moslems in 1527.

[62] The Abarbanel family was among those who chose to stay.

[63] From the Hebrew word for Spain, *Sepharad*.

[64] As recently as 1940, the descendants of those expelled from Spain comprised 25 percent of the population of the city of Salonika in Greece. Most of the Sephardic population of the Balkan states was murdered by the Germans during World War II.

In 1497, as King Manoel I of Portugal prepared to marry Princess Isabella of Spain, her parents, Ferdinand and Isabella, forced Portugal to ban Hebrews from its dominions. In the same year, Portugal required all its Hebrews to convert to Catholicism but did not offer the alternative of emigration. There followed mass baptisms at the point of the sword. This forced conversion swelled the population of Marranos on the Iberian Peninsula. During the next couple of centuries there was a steady emigration of these Marranos, who feared being discovered by the Inquisition. These emigrants followed their coreligionists around the Mediterranean, but some also went northward to the newly emerging Protestant states in England,[65] Holland, and Germany, and the Protestant regions of France. Some wound up in the Americas.[66] A few remained in Spain and Portugal, as evidenced by the continuing activities of the Inquisition until the 1830s.[67]

[65] The Hebrews had been banned from England in 1298 by King Edward I. The Marranos who settled in London in the 1500s and early 1600s lived outwardly as Catholics. One of these Marranos, Ruy Lopez, became the personal physician to Queen Elizabeth I. In 1656, during a war with Spain, the English arrested a Marrano merchant and seized his ships. He was accused of being a Spanish spy and threatened with hanging. His lawyer decided to pursue the risky strategy of revealing that his client was really a Hebrew, and therefore unlikely to have any sympathies for Spain. He won the case, and shortly thereafter, the English Lord Protector, Oliver Cromwell, relaxed the ban on Hebrews in the realm. The entire community then came out of the closet and built a synagogue. This synagogue was destroyed in the great London fire of 1666. It was rebuilt on Beavis Marks in the City in 1700, with material contributions from Princess (later Queen) Anne. It is a beautiful example of Wren-style architecture, modeled on the S'noga Madre of the Spanish Marranos in Amsterdam. When I attended a Rosh Hashanah service there in 2002, the rabbi and a number of the congregants made a great fuss over me. It turns out that the president of the Sephardite community in London was one Cesare Sacerdote, an antiquarian book dealer who was born in Rome. Cesare Sacerdote is unrelated to me.

[66] The Hebrew communities in the Caribbean mostly date to this period. Also, the first Hebrews in New York were a group of Marranos who had escaped to Holland and had become part of the ill-fated Dutch attempt to colonize Brazil in the early 1600s. After the defeat of the Dutch in Brazil, the Marranos set sail for Europe but were captured by Spanish pirates, who robbed them of all their possessions and then dumped them in the Dutch colony of New York in 1654. Their congregation, Shearith Israel, is currently located on Central Park West. It follows to this day the Spanish rite rather than the Ashkenazic rite from Eastern Europe that is used by most U.S. synagogues. The other early Hebrew communities in the United States, those of Philadelphia, Newport, and Charleston, were also founded by Sephardim.

[67] Among the Marranos who remained in Spain and Portugal was a group that held noble titles by right or marriage. There arose among the Portuguese nobles a bitter division between these families and those with no Hebrew ancestry; the latter referred to themselves as being of *sangre limpio* (pure blood). This division grew so bitter in the 1700s that the Marquis de Pombal, prime minister to King João V, decreed in 1768 that all noble families with *sangre limpio* had to marry their daughters to nobles of Hebrew ancestry within four months.

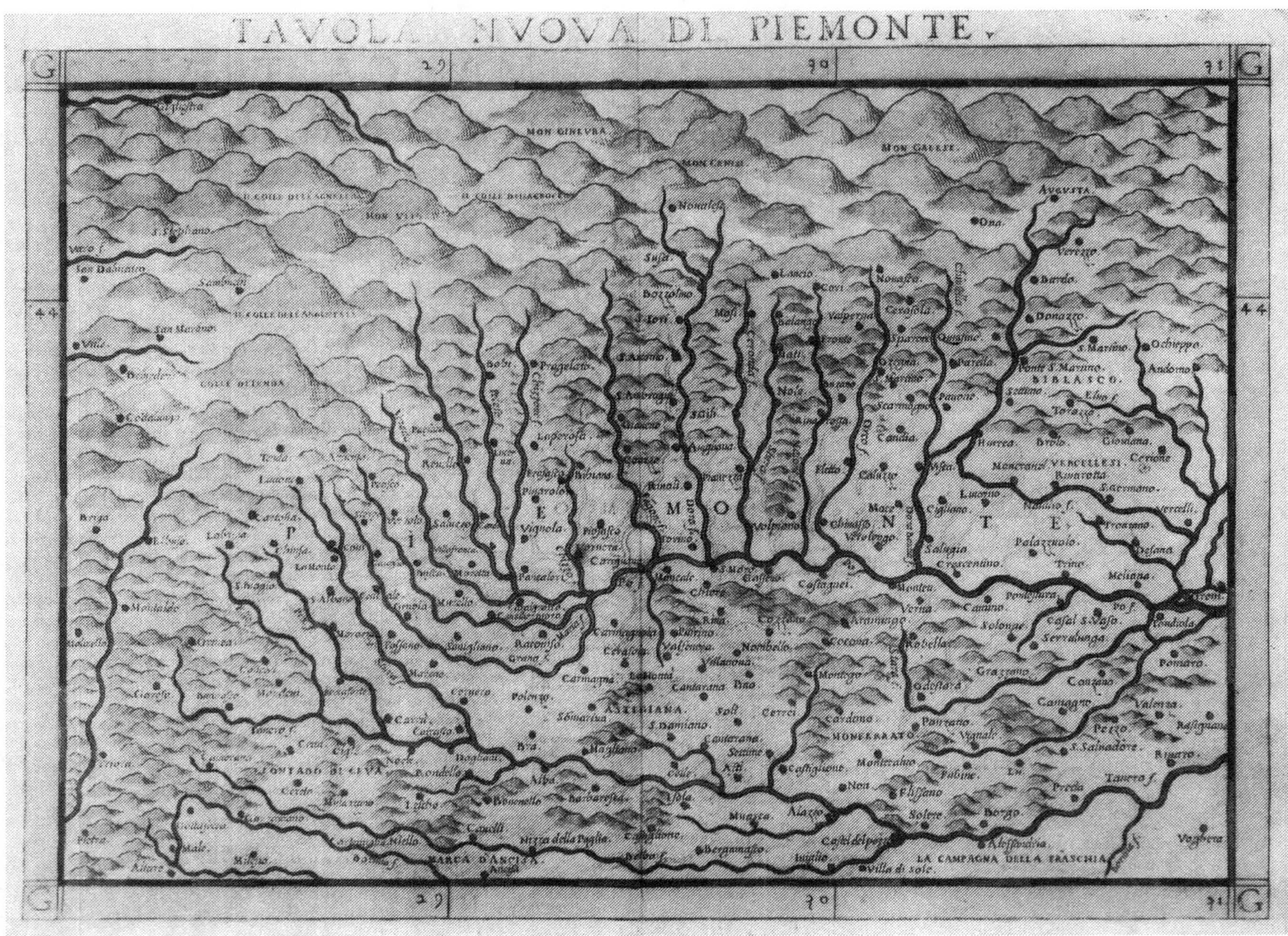

Figure 2-1
Map of Piemonte published in 1574 in the schematic style
pioneered by Herodotus. From the collection of George
Sacerdote.

Chapter II
Piemonte and the Duchy of Savoy in the 1400s and 1500s: The Arrival of Giorgio's and Luciana's Ancestors in Piemonte

We turn next to the development of the Duchy of Savoy in France and Italy, which emerged from the Middle Ages as an independent state straddling the Alps. It was formed through a dynastic marriage in 1419 between the Duke of Savoy, ruler of the French side of the Alps and the Valle d'Aosta, and the Countess of Piemonte, who controlled the eastern slope. West of the mountains it covered most of the territory between Lake Geneva and Nice, including the modern French départements of Haute Savoie, Savoie, and Alpes Maritimes. On the Italian side of the Alps it included the northwestern two-thirds of modern Piemonte and the Valle d'Aosta. It was bounded on the west by France, on the north by the Swiss Alps, on the east by the independent Duchy of Milan, on the southeast by the nominally independent Marquisate of Monferrato,[68] and on the south by the Republic of Genoa east of the Alps and by the Mediterranean in the region around Nice.

The duchy was a relatively poor domain, with much of its land too mountainous to farm. Commerce was limited by the Alps that ran through its middle. Its only important seaport was Nice, on the French side of the mountains, while its most important exports, agricultural products, came mainly from the plains of Piemonte on the Italian side of the Alps. There was little to no indigenous manufacturing industry. Probably on account of its relative poverty, Piemonte was largely untouched by the Renaissance that so enriched Florence, Rome, Venice, and other regions of central and northeastern Italy.

During the 1400s, its nominal political capital was Chambéry, in the Savoy's French domains, although, as in most medieval countries, the capital was of little significance; the duke and his court would move among his castles in the course of his governance, and the effective capital was wherever they happened to be at the moment.[69] The main continuing political issues for the dukes of Savoy during this period had to do with (1) managing and minimizing conflict with the rapidly centralizing power of France[70]; (2) managing and minimizing conflicts with Savoy's nominal overlords, the Holy Roman Emperors[71]; (3) asserting and maintaining political primacy relative to the Church; and (4) wresting political control from the local municipalities, which had gained a great deal of autonomy during the late Middle Ages.[72]

The duchy's geographical position and control of the passes through the Alps made it a prime military and diplomatic target for France. The Valle di Susa, between Torino and the Alps, was France's main invasion route into Italy, and Piemonte frequently found itself in the middle of French wars not of

---

[68] In 1536 the marquisate was formally annexed by the Duchy of Mantova with the blessing of Charles V. Before that, the marquisate was ruled by a branch of the Paleologos family, the former rulers of the Byzantine Empire. It was nominally independent, although since the Middle Ages it had been tightly allied to the Duchy of Mantova, which lay between the Duchy of Milan and the Venetian Republic.

[69] The same held true in France (consider the chateaux of the Loire Valley), Spain, and England

[70] Spain consolidated politically in the 1400s. France consolidated in the 1500s, beginning with the reign of François I (1515-1547). Prior to that time, the central government in France was very weak and real power resided with regional nobles such as the dukes of Burgundy, Aquitaine, Normandy, and the like. The process was not fully completed until the reign of Louis XIV, who broke the power of the last major regional nobles. This consolidation movement did not come to Germany or Italy until the mid-1800s.

[71] As my father loved to point out, the Holy Roman Empire was neither holy, nor Roman, nor an empire. Rather, it was a loose confederation of mainly German-speaking principalities. This confederacy was all that remained of the great Frankish empire of Charlemagne in the Dark Ages. The rulers of the main principalities elected the emperor but generally granted him little authority over their affairs. For example, one document I came across was a letter from Emperor Sigismund in 1434, demanding that the Duke of Savoy turn over the Jews' Tax. A later document said that the Duke of Savoy would look into the matter. A yet later document from Sigismund complained that his first directive had been ignored. The dukes never did turn over the money. During the Middle Ages and into the Renaissance, there were ongoing battles between the Holy Roman Empire and the papacy over political control, especially in Italy, with most of the independent principalities in northern and central Italy taking one side or the other. Florence and Naples tended to side with the popes, while the duchies of Savoy, Milan, and Mantova generally sided with the emperor.

[72] These issues, in one form or another, dominated Savoyard politics for several centuries, and most were not finally resolved until the late 1800s.

its choosing. After two fairly strong dukes, Amedeo VIII (who later became the last anti-pope,[73] Felix V) and Ludovico, the duchy went through a period of decline in the late 1400s. The decline was exacerbated by periodic French incursions into Italy to meddle in territorial squabbles among the Italian principalities and offset the rising influence of Spain on Italian affairs in the first half of the 1500s. In addition, an outbreak of the plague in the 1470s[74] caused a drastic decline in commercial and political activity. By the early 1530s, the duchy was occupied by French troops who ruled it in all but name, including exacting taxes[75] to pay for the occupying troops. During this period most of the moneyed interests in the duchy played it safe; they were content to earn rents on their properties and avoided risky investments.

In the 1400s, the duchy had a small population of Hebrews concentrated in perhaps a dozen towns. Most of this population was on the French side of the Alps, including Nice, Chambéry, Chalon, Orange, and Cremieux. There were also several established Hebrew communities in Piemonte, principally in Savigliano, Torino, and Ciriè. The dominant Hebrew family in the Piemontese towns was the Foa family,[76] which had extensive banking interests and landholdings. A scan of documents from that period reveals fewer than 250 adult male Hebrew names in Piemonte during the 1400s, so the Hebrew population cannot have exceeded 500-1000 in a total population of perhaps 500,000.[77]

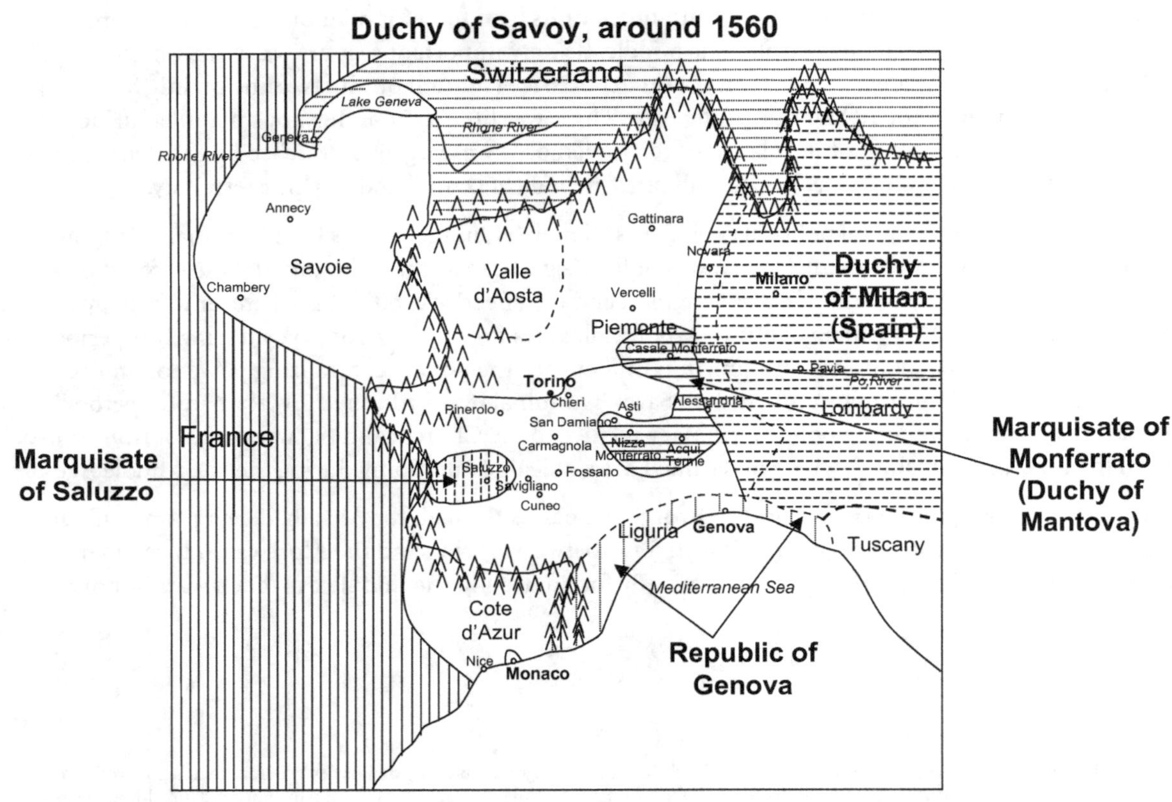

[73] During the years 1378 to 1449, the Catholic Church was split between two competing factions, with each faction electing its own pope, one reigning in Rome and the other in Avignon. Felix was an Avignon pope.

[74] As a measure of the decline of activity in the duchy in the late 1400s, I tallied the number of documents in Segre's book by decade. These documents generally concerned commercial issues, such as contract disputes, licenses for trade and finance, and the like. During the early 1400s, these averaged 103 per decade. During the period from 1470 to 1530, they declined to eleven per decade. During the remainder of the 1500s and the 1600s they rose again to 199 per decade. The obvious conclusion is that commerce had fallen off sharply during the period from 1470 to 1530.

[75] See Segre, pp. xlvi-xlvii.

[76] The Foa are prominent in Italy to this day. Vittorio Foa was an active anti-Fascist during the 1930s and was arrested for subversive activity in 1935. After World War II he was made a senator for life by the newly formed Italian Republic, a post he continues to hold.

[77] Segre, p. xcix.

During the early-to-mid-1500s, things changed for the Duchy of Savoy (indeed, for all of Europe) in very dramatic ways. Charles V, the Hapsburg[78] ruler of Burgundy and Flanders (part of modern Belgium and Holland), inherited the Spanish throne in 1516 as the son of Ferdinand and Isabella's incompetent daughter, Juana la Loca. He was elected Holy Roman Emperor in 1520, making him ruler of half of Europe.

During this time, the Pope allied himself with France, much to the annoyance of Spain. Charles V invaded Italy in the 1520s and in quick succession achieved dominance of major parts of the peninsula. He won Naples in 1521, and took control of the Duchy of Milan in 1522. In 1527 his troops sacked Rome twice.[79] The arrival of the Spaniards caused a mass exodus of Hebrews from the Kingdom of Naples[80] and the Duchy of Milan.[81] Generally these families moved toward Tuscany, Mantova, Ferrara,[82] and Venice. Many settled in the coastal towns of the Adriatic.[83]

The French, in turn, felt greatly threatened by this expansion of Spanish power in Italy, especially in the Duchy of Milan, which was close to France's southeastern border. Their response was to invade Italy. They occupied Piemonte from 1530 on, as a check on Spanish power in Milan. They then backed a rival to the ducal throne in Milan, and succeeded in placing their candidate on the throne for a few years.

Control of Milan passed back and forth between France and Spain until Spain won final control in 1545. The French also began to intervene in Tuscan politics in an effort to bring additional pressure on the Spaniards in Naples and Rome.

Timeline

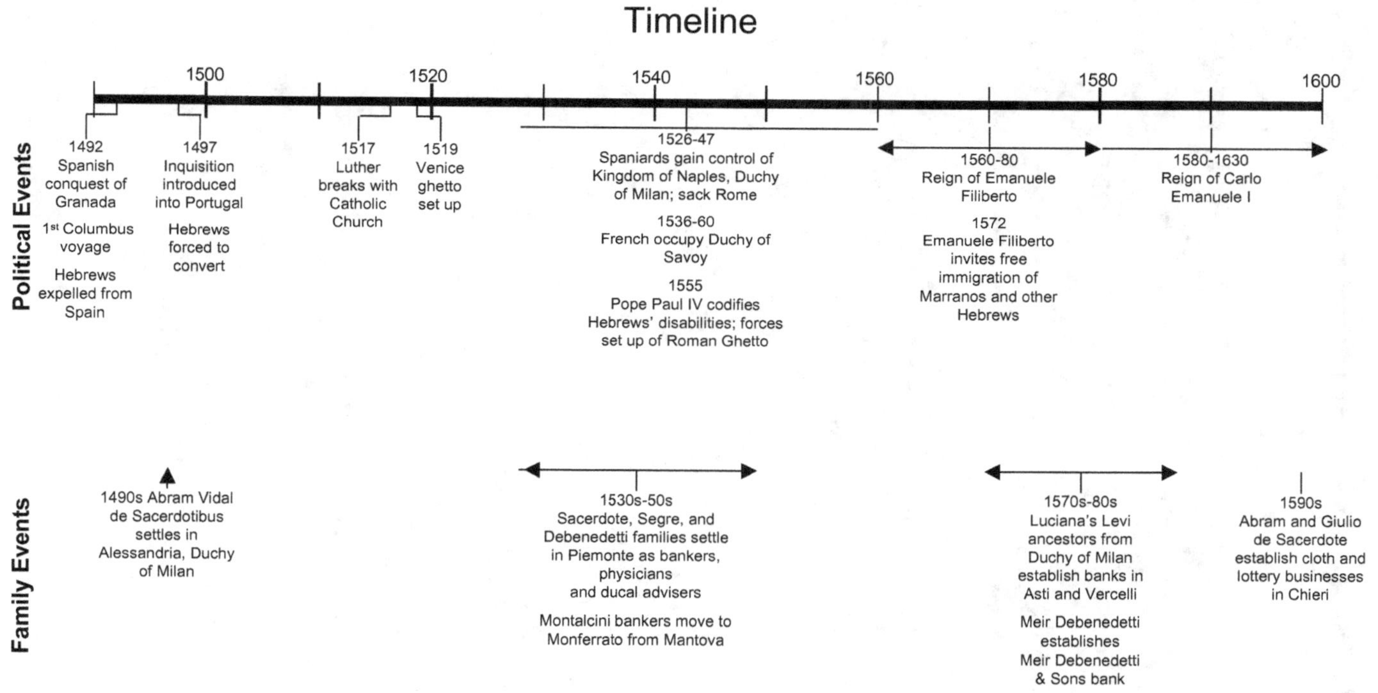

[78] The Hapsburg family were the hereditary emperors of Austria, and had an extensive realm in Central Europe that covered modern Austria, Hungary, the Czech Republic and Slovakia, and parts of Germany and Poland. They later acquired a number of the Turkish possessions in Europe, including Slovenia, Croatia, and Bosnia. They ruled until 1918, when they were deposed in the aftermath of World War I. The tiny principality of Liechtenstein is the only remaining Hapsburg monarchy.

[79] Charles was a devout Catholic and aggressively fought the Reformation with both military means and the use of the Inquisition. Nonetheless, he jealously guarded his powers as emperor vis-à-vis the pope. In fact, he conducted the sack of Rome with Lutheran troops from northern Germany.

[80] Naples had received a great many Hebrew refugees from the expulsion of 1492, especially from Sicily and Spain.

[81] The entire Hebrew population of the Duchy of Milan was expelled except for that of the town of Alessandria, on the border of Piemonte. I do not know why that town was spared, but for the next 160 years it contained the only openly Hebrew community in the Spanish dominions. This community figures prominently in our family history, as we shall see presently. Alessandria was annexed to Piemonte in 1707.

[82] Mantova and Ferrara were two of the more liberal principalities in Italy. They encouraged the arts—Claudio Monteverdi, the first Baroque composer of any note and the composer of the first operas, was the court composer in Mantova.. These cities developed important commerce that was exceeded only by that of Venice, and they openly tolerated their substantial communities of Hebrews.

[83] They often adopted the names of their new native cities as surnames, whence the frequency of the surnames Pesaro, Fano, Ancona, Ravenna, Pitigliano, and the like among Italian Hebrews.

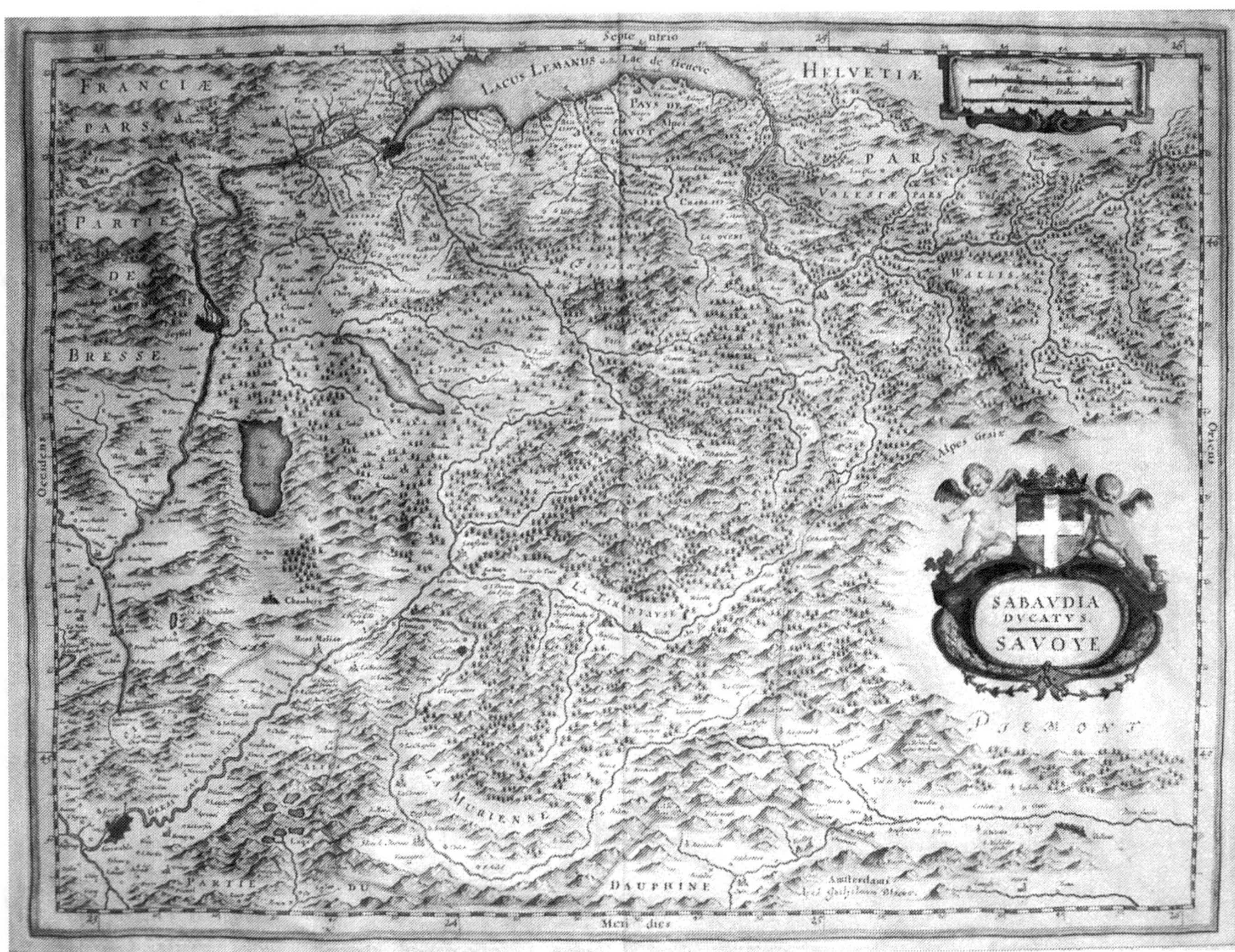

Figure 2-2
Map of Savoie, published mid 1700s. This map was originally in the collection of Baron Arnaldo Levi di Veale, and
was sold to Giorgio in the 1950s.

Figure 2-3
Map of Provence published in the mid 1700s showing the
county of Nice. Nice remained Savoyard territory until the
1850s, when the king traded it to France in exchange for
French support in the conquest of Lombardy. This map
was originally in the collection of Baron Arnaldo Levi di
Veale, and was sold to Giorgio in the 1950s.

At the same time the Reformation swept through Charles's northern domains in Germany and Holland, sparking a series of wars, including the eighty-year war of Dutch independence. Emanuele Filiberto, Duke of Savoy, served Charles, his nominal overlord, as a general in the wars in Flanders. He won several major battles, notably the battle of Saint Quentin in 1557, and eventually ruled parts of Flanders in Charles's name.[84] During this period, Emanuele Filiberto learned the advantages and processes of centralizing state power and developed a strong personal alliance with Charles V.

In 1553, Emanuele Filiberto had inherited the ducal throne of Savoy from his father, the weak Carlo III. After the peace of Le Cateau-Cambrésis in 1559, which ended the war between Spain and France, he returned to Savoy to formally assume the ducal throne. He capitalized on two of his strengths and a major weakness of the French to secure the removal of French troops from his domain:

- His wife was the sister of Henri II of France, so he could appeal to the French king on the basis of personal obligations.
- He had the strong support of Charles V, so he could threaten Henri II with military problems if he did not do as Emanuele Filiberto asked.
- France at the time was wracked with conflict between its Protestant and Catholic citizens, so Henri II had more important things to worry about than the Duchy of Savoy.[85]

Emanuele Filiberto then began a multifaceted program to bring his domains up to date. This program included:

1. Creating a national capital in Torino, centralizing administration there, and thereby taking power away from the cities and towns.
2. Building a civil power capable of challenging papal authority.
3. Playing the French on his western border against the Spaniards, who controlled the Duchy of Milan to his east.
4. Encouraging the arts in his domain by, for example, inviting the great Venetian architect Andrea Palladio to visit Torino for several months in the summer of 1566.
5. Opening commerce, especially with Venice, Ferrara, and other states in eastern Italy, using the Po River, and also with other Mediterranean states through his ports on the Côte d'Azur.
6. Encouraging the growth of mining in the Alps and of manufactures, especially of cotton and silk cloth.
7. Creating a banking system to provide risk capital.
8. Reforming and standardizing the currency.[86]
9. Encouraging the immigration of Hebrews, especially those who had left Spain and settled in the Turkish domains and in the Italian states of Mantova, Ferrara, Venice, and Tuscany; the Milanese city of Alessandria; and the Papal States. He especially sought Hebrew immigrants with financial, manufacturing, and commercial experience.[87]

With this last item begins a detailed examination of Giorgio's and Luciana's family histories. In the early 1530s, there was a sudden influx of new Hebrew families into Piemonte as part of the larger northward movement of Hebrews in the Italian Peninsula. Many new Hebrew names appear at this time in official documents in Segre's collection. This influx of Hebrew immigrants was so great that several Piemontese towns began petitioning the duke to be allowed to exclude them, claiming that they would

---

[84] The Savoys had a long and illustrious history of serving as military leaders for foreign states. Prince Eugene of Savoy led the Austrian troops when they defeated the Turks at the gates of Vienna in 1688. Austria's gift to him for this service was the beautiful Belvedere Palace in Vienna.

[85] These were the lead-up to the French Guerres de la Religion between the Huguenot Protestants and the Catholics. They began in 1562, during the regency of Catherine de Medici's on behalf of her minor son Henri III and were not finally settled until 1598, when the Huguenots defeated the Catholics and the Huguenot leader, Henri de Navarre, was made King Henri IV of France. As a gesture of reconciliation, Henri converted to Catholicism (to satisfy the majority Catholics) and issued the Edict of Nantes, which guaranteed freedom of religion for the minority Huguenots. This edict was revoked by Louis XIV.

[86] See Appendix G.

[87] See pages 28–29 for a summary of this edict.

cause overcrowding. For example, in 1533, the city council of Asti petitioned its ruler, Duchess Beatrice, Countess of Asti and a Portuguese princess, to banish the Hebrews altogether. She issued an expulsion order in 1535, giving the Hebrews two weeks to wind up their affairs. The Hebrews of the town pleaded for a six-month stay of the order. The stay was granted, and the order was subsequently canceled.[88]

Both the Spanish Crown and the papal authorities became alarmed at this rapid immigration of Spanish Hebrews into Piemonte. The Spaniards worried about having an influential population with strong animosities toward Spain settling on the western border of their possession, the Duchy of Milan. The Hebrews might push the Duchy of Savoy even more strongly under the control of Spain's enemy, France. Further, many of the new immigrants into Piemonte were Marranos. As such, they were Spanish subjects who had left Spain without royal permission, and were also heretics in the eyes of the Catholic Church, making them criminals twice over.

The popes were equally upset. They did not like seeing Hebrews settling in Savoy, especially the Marranos, whom they viewed as Catholic heretics. Besides, the popes, who were beholden to Spain after the sack of Rome in 1527, worried about the rising tide of Protestantism in France, Holland, Germany, Switzerland, and Piemonte. They feared that the presence of Hebrews might further encourage freethinkers to rebel against papal authority. Moreover, the popes were increasingly worried about the rising political power of the dukes of Savoy and the manner in which they exercised that power, often in opposition to papal authority.

During the 1500s, especially after 1560, there was intense diplomatic pressure exerted in Torino by both the papal nuncios and the Spanish ambassadors. The record is full of reports of diplomatic initiatives and the activities of secret agents.[89] The diplomatic initiatives sought to have the Dukes of Savoy expel these new Hebrew immigrants, or at least limit their entry. The secret agents sent numerous missives back to their masters in Rome and Spain on the activities of the newly arriving families. The agents also plotted to stem their flow into Piemonte by illegal means, such by arresting immigrants on trumped-up charges as they crossed the Duchy of Milan on the Po River.[90] At the time the Po River was considered an international waterway. As such, harassment of travelers and commerce on it would have been prohibited by international law. In addition, the Hebrew immigrants were typically traveling under safe-conducts guaranteed by the Dukes of Savoy. Arresting them would have caused an international incident. Nonetheless, the Spanish Crown continued to harass Hebrews traveling though the Duchy of Milan. By so doing it could also seize their considerable possessions.

The Sacerdotes Arrive in Chieri[91]

Among the new immigrants during 1530s were families named Todros,[92] de Sacerdotibus,[93] and Segre,[94] who were tightly interlinked by marriage and commercial partnerships. The Todros patriarch, Salvador, had several sons, all of whom became bankers:

---

[88] Segre, documents 794, 797, 798, 799, 804, 806, 807,809, 810.

[89] Segre, documents 1060, 1063, 1064, 1066, 1068.

[90] There are numerous documents in Segre's books referring to protests by the Dukes of Savoy that their citizens were being harassed by the Spanish authorities as they traveled through the Duchy of Milan.

[91] He reader may find the family genealogies in Appendices A–E helpful in going through this and subsequent sections that discuss the five families.

[92] The Todros family is presumably related to the Catalonian scholar Todros Todros of the early 1400s. I mention them because of their extensive intermarriage with the Sacerdote and Segre families in the 1500s.

[93] De Sacerdotibus means "of the priests" in Latin. Sacerdote of course means "priest" in the same language (as does Cohen in Hebrew). The early documents have numerous spellings of their names, but with some effort one can determine which were different spellings of the same person's name by comparing parents' and siblings' given names, birth cities, and other simple facts. Most of the variants reflect different forms of the same noun in Latin or Italian. In Latin, a highly inflected language, each noun had a gender (masculine, feminine, or neuter), a number (singular or plural), and five cases. The cases (nominative, genitive, dative, accusative, and ablative) reflected the noun's role in a sentence, producing up to ten different forms (five cases times two numbers) of the same word.

[94] Some claim that the Segre family took its name from the Segre River in Catalonia, in northeastern Spain. The river runs from the Pyrenees to the Ebro, a large river that empties into the Mediterranean near Barcelona. Others point out that while people's surnames are often taken from the names of cities or regions, the practice of taking one's surname from a river is quite unusual. The earliest reference in Piemonte to the surname Segre that I could find was of an Elia de Segre who was a banker in Savigliano in 1446. Presumably this man and his family left Spain on account of the racial problems that began to surface in the late 1300s. It is unclear from the record how he was related to the Segre families that came to Piemonte ninety years later.

- Moisé and Abram, who settled in Torino and became the personal bankers of the Dukes of Savoy,[95] a role that was continued by their sons. Moisé married into the Foa banking family that had been in that business in Piemonte for many generations. One of Moisé's daughters married Abram Segre of Chieri.

- Benedetto Todros, who settled first in Alessandria, where he was a banker with his brother-in-law Vitale de Sacerdotibus (see below). In 1551 Benedetto and Vitale moved their banking operations to Chieri. In 1560 they jointly purchased an estate outside Alessandria to provide a cemetery for the Hebrews of that town. A cottage on the estate was retained as a residence for the undertaker. As part of the undertaker's contract with them, he was to plant mulberry trees on the grounds. One of the industries that the Hebrews brought to Piemonte in the 1500s was the silk industry. Presumably these mulberry trees were to provide leaves to feed to silkworms and the raw silk was to be used to defray some of the expense of operating the cemetery.[96]

- Todros Todros, who established a bank in Mondovi in partnership with his brother Benedetto.

The de Sacerdotibus families included:

- Abram Vidal de Sacerdotibus, who settled in Alessandria in the 1490s.[97] Alessandria at the time was Milanese territory. Abram Vidal's son Vitale de Sacerdotibus was a banker, diplomat, and merchant in that city in the 1530s.[98] Vitale moved to Piemonte around 1551 with his brother-in-law and business partner, Benedetto Todros, probably as a direct result of the final Spanish takeover of the Duchy of Milan in 1545, which led up to the banning (in 1569) of the Hebrews of Alessandria from banking and money lending. Their admission had to pass muster with Isac de Sacerdotibus of Vercelli, who was likely related to them.[99] While we are not sure where Vitale settled, Todros settled in Chieri, a market town about fifteen miles northeast of Torino on the main route from Torino to the important agricultural center of Asti.[100] Perhaps Vitale made his home there as well.

- One of Vitale's sons was named Simone, and there is strong evidence that others of his sons were the brothers Abram and Consiglio de Sacerdote, who appear in Chieri as industrialists, merchants, and bankers later in the 1500s. Giorgio's family is almost certainly directly descended from Abram or Consiglio.

- Salomone de Sacerdotibus and his sons Giacobbe and Giuseppe[101] [102] were bankers who settled in Asti around 1530. In 1535–38 in the town of Asti there are several mentions of a Salomone de Sacerdotibus and his sons as well-established bankers. They, along with

---

[95] Moisé loaned money to the dukes personally and also to their governments.

[96] Segre, document 1189.

[97] Sacerdoti, p. 18.

[98] Alessandria had the only openly Hebrew community in all of the Spain's global dominions. It is unclear why the Hebrews of this town were permitted to practice their religion. According to one source, it was because Vitale had negotiated a deal with the Spanish authorities in Milan, citing Alessandria's importance as a trading center with Piemonte.

[99] Vitale de Sacerdotibus and Benedetto Todros were almost certainly related to Isac de Sacerdotibus of Vercelli.

[100] Chieri already had a small Hebrew community. The first Hebrew to settle there was Sansone Ebreo, a physician and banker who was invited to settle in the community in 1424. By the early 1500s, there were enough Hebrews in the town to organize a synagogue (that is, at least ten adult males).

[101] When the duchess, a Portuguese princess and also Countess of Asti, ordered the expulsion of all Hebrews on fifteen days' notice, Giacobbe and his brothers along with Helia Segre and his family petitioned for stay of the order, citing the impact on the local populace if they had to call in all their loans on such short notice.

[102] The only other references I can find to Giuseppe and Giacobbe suggest that they may have been of poor character. In 1535 Giuseppe was charged with having intimate relations with a Catholic woman, Bartolomea *la recamatrice* (a *recamatrice* is one who tats lace), speaking against the duchess, and bearing arms. In 1536, Salomone, petitioned the duke to have his son Giacobbe released from jail, where he had languished for the preceding two months. According to the petition, Giacobbe had been accused of having illicit relations with the Catholic landlady of an inn. The accuser was an employee of the landlady, and her accusations came after she had been tortured by the prosecutor on who knows what grounds. He seems, however, to have been rehabilitated in the government's view. In 1539 he was granted permission to continue to live in Asti in exchange for a payment of 50 *scudi d'oro*. Given that these stories occurred at a time when the Countess of Asti, a Portuguese princess, was seeking to expel the Hebrews, an alternative interpretation of them could be that the charges against Giacobbe and Giuseppe were trumped up to harass the family into leaving or to extract money from an obviously wealthy family.

the Segres of Asti, were the petitioners who had the expulsion order delayed and then overturned in 1535.[103]

- Todros (Theodoro) de Sacerdotibus,[104] a doctor, whose permission to enter the duchy was granted in 1531, but whose precise location we do not know. In 1534 the duke granted him a license to practice medicine.

- Isac de Sacerdotibus and his sons Aron, Gesué, Lazzaro, Moisé, and Giuseppe, bankers who settled in Vercelli.[105] They received their first Piemontese bank charter in 1537. When that charter was renewed in 1547, Isac was referred to as having been resident in the town "for many years." He may or may not have been related to Salomone of Asti. In 1551, the duke granted Isac de Sacerdotibus and Giuseppe (Joseph) de Jena[106] the right to determine which new Hebrew immigrants were worthy of admission into the duchy.[107] Aron subsequently left Piemonte and settled in Casale Monferrato, the capital of the then foreign country of Monferrato, sometime in the 1590s. One of Aron's descendants, a broker in grains, lead, and other commodities important for the support of a standing army, became a prominent diplomat in the War of the Spanish Succession in the early 1700s.

As noted earlier, there is strong evidence that the elder de Sacerdotibus were brothers. Vitale was listed as a business partner and brother-in-law of Benedetto Todros. This suggests that his wife was Vitale and Isac's sister. Second, Isac's son Gesué named his first son Vidal Salomone, most likely in honor of his uncles Vitale and Salomone.[108] Third, there is a surviving note from Moisé Todros to his brother Benedetto asking him to make a stop in Asti during a business trip to get some books from "our relatives there"[109] and also to collect a credit from another Hebrew banker named Pugetto. Finally, Vitale's son Abram named one of his sons Aron, probably in honor of his uncle.

In 1572, the Spanish governor of Milan sent a report on Vitale to King Philip II of Spain. That note describes Vitale as "coming from Spain, having been resident for some time in Constantinople, having connections with all the leading families of Spain and Portugal, and being very rich and influential in Piemonte."[110] If one were to try to get more detail on the Spanish origins of the De Sacerdotibus family, I suspect that one would best start in Catalonia, given the close ties between the Todros, Segre, and De Sacerdotibus families. Another source might be the Sacerdote family archive kept in the synagogue in Casale Monferrato.

The Spanish were right to be interested in Vitale and his son Simone. They both had a great deal of access and influence at the ducal court. In 1571 the Duke of Savoy dispatched Vitale to Venice to acquire a large diamond on his behalf. The duke probably sought such a jewel as a symbol of his growing power. There ensued considerable correspondence among Vitale, the duke, and the ducal ambassador to Venice on the relative values of different stones and how to finance the purchase. Ultimately the project was

---

[103] The duchess died before the six months were up, and so her order lapsed. Her successor officially reversed the order.

[104] We know least of Todros de Sacerdotibus. The only tangible reference we have of him is the duke's permission for him to enter the duchy to practice medicine for one year. Perhaps he died young or without heirs, or maybe he was not very active in ways that would leave a trail of official documents.

[105] This de Sacerdotibus family became quite prominent as bankers, with branches in several towns. Several generations later, in the early 1700s, one of them became a diplomat in the employ of the dukes of Savoy to negotiate a peace treaty with Louis XIV of France to end the War of Spanish Succession.

[106] The name de Jena ("from Jena," a city in eastern Germany) was subsequently contracted to Diena. Giorgio had several Diena cousins in Torino, related to him through his mother's family, the Montalcini.

[107] Segre, in the introduction to her book, suggested that this right was given to Jacob de Sacerdotibus, but the document itself refers to Isac.

[108] There is a long tradition among the Sephardim for given names to appear in alternate generations, with children often named for their grandparents or their great-aunts and great-uncles. Thus my father's middle name of Salvatore was the first name of his maternal grandfather. His sister Eugenia is named for her maternal grandmother, Eugenia Segre. My brother Albert is named for his paternal grandfather, Alberto Sacerdote. When we have to deduce lineal descent via indirect means, this generation-skipping naming pattern is often a very useful clue.

[109] The relatives in question are most likely either Salomone de Sacerdotibus's family or the family of Helia Segre discussed below. This note also sheds some light on the Todros' family origins; it is written in rather fractured Italian. Moisé's native language was clearly not Italian, but either Spanish or Catalan. I suspect a linguistic scholar could determine which of those languages is more likely. Segre, document 915.

[110] Segre, document 1063.

abandoned when no suitable jewel could be found at a price the duke was willing to pay. The house of Savoy was never very wealthy as compared with other royal families and therefore tended towards thriftiness rather than royal lavishness.[111]

In 1572 Vitale wrote a secret report to Duke Emanuele Filiberto, in which he advocated improving national commerce by establishing a free port in the coastal town of Villefranche,[112] near Nice. The port would free the duchy from its dependence on the Po River for trade,[113] and would provide an outlet for the duchy's agricultural products and an inlet for cloth and other trade goods from the Turkish dominions. The Spanish and the Venetians were very concerned about this project because it would threaten their predominant positions in the Mediterranean trade. Despite the protests of these nations, the project went ahead, and in 1572 Emanuele Filiberto announced his intention to acquire two ships to operate out of Villefranche. Presumably the De Sacerdotibus and Todros banks helped to finance the project and obtained financial interests in this trade as by-products of Vitale's project.

The second of Vitale's commercial projects was to have the duke lease copper and precious metal mining rights in the Alps to a German consortium in order to develop a metallurgical trade in the duchy. This lease was granted in 1574.[114]

In 1572 Vitale proposed his most important secret project to Duke Emanuele Filiberto. In this scheme, Emanuele Filiberto would encourage the immigration of Hebrews into his domains in order to gain the benefit of their experience in banking, international trade, and manufacturing, especially of cotton and silk textiles. To put this plan in motion, Emanuele Filiberto dispatched Vitale's son Simone on a diplomatic mission to Constantinople.[115] The public purpose of this mission was to obtain the freedom of a Milanese nobleman held captive there. However, Simone was also given coded instructions to recruit Hebrew immigrants from the Turkish dominions, and also from the liberal Italian states to the east: Mantova, Venice, and Ferrara. Spanish agents in Torino learned of Simone's secret instructions and gave orders that he should be captured as he crossed through Milanese territory. However, Simone eluded capture in Milan and completed his mission, though not without serious misadventures. Simone's party was attacked by Uskoks as they passed through what is modern-day Croatia on the way to Turkey. The Uskoks were a tribe of Serbian bandits who began to ravage Croatia after the Turks defeated the Serbs in the Battle of Kosovo. After Simone's party was attacked, there was a flurry of diplomatic activity among the Turks, Venetians, and Piemontese as to whose responsibility it should be to punish the Uskoks for their outrages.[116]

In 1572 Emanuele Filiberto issued an edict promising freedom of worship, full commercial privileges, and ducal protection to Hebrews and Marranos who might enter his lands.[117] These are some highlights of the ducal proclamation:

> At the request of Mr. Vitale di Sacerdoti, a Hebrew, the Duke of Savoy concedes privileges for the entire Hebrew nation, whether originating in Italy, Germany, Spain, Portugal, the Levant, or the Barbary States to live and conduct business in his lands.
>
> They shall have safe conduct and inviolable security for their persons, be allowed to live according to their laws, to keep synagogues, and keep their rituals. The Church is explicitly forbidden to conduct inquisitions into their affairs.
>
> They shall be allowed to conduct all mercantile activities open to Christians.

---

[111] As proof of their modest fortune, we note that the historical record is full of references to their need to levy special taxes to cover major state events such as ducal weddings, state visits of foreign royalty, and supplying dowries for their daughters.

[112] Segre, document. 1056.

[113] The Po was considered an international waterway. Nonetheless, it flowed through the Marquisate of Monferrato and the duchies of Milan and Ferrara before reaching the sea, thus permitting each of those countries to exact tolls and other harassments upon commerce flowing along the river.

[114] Segre, document 1141.

[115] The secret mission to Constantinople is detailed in Segre, documents 1059, 1060, 1061, 1062, 1063, 1063A, 1064, 1066, 1073, 1074, 1075, 1076, 1079, 1082, 1094, 1100, 1104, 1112, and 1123.

[116] The recent years' wars and atrocities in the former Yugoslavia are only the most recent outbreaks of the general lawlessness that has plagued this region since at least the Middle Ages.

[117] Segre document 1059.

They shall be protected from local taxes except for the *gabelle* [excise taxes, e.g., the salt tax] that the Christians pay and shall be immune from having to lodge soldiers in their homes.

The Hebrews shall be allowed to keep the books they need for the exercise of their faith.

They shall be exempt from legal proceedings on their feast days.

They shall be permitted to slaughter animals for food according to their laws.

They shall be allowed to buy or rent houses to live in and workshops to work in.

They are allowed to engage in secured lending.

They may work as physicians.

They shall not be assaulted physically or verbally, nor shall their children under fifteen years old be converted against their parents' will.

They may employ Christian servants, workers, and nursemaids.

The Spaniards and the pope howled complaints[118] which Emanuele Filiberto ignored as long as he could. Finally the papal nuncio induced him to issue an edict at the end of 1573 banishing the Marranos from his duchy.[119] This second edict appears to have been largely for show, as the Hebrews subject to it could buy an exemption, and only three families are known to have left as a result of it.[120]

It goes without saying that the privileges that Emanuele Filiberto bestowed upon his Hebrew subjects came with a price tag. Every ten years, when it was time for the duke to renew the charter of special rights and privileges for the Hebrew community, known as the *condotta*, he would assess the community a flat amount in lieu of the property-based taxes that he assessed on the cities and towns in his domains.

The Hebrews formed a governing council called L'Università degli Ebrei di Piemonte, whose primary task was to apportion this ducal assessment fairly among its members. This council also collected funds among the Hebrews to cover the needs of the poor, widowed, and orphaned among them. Generally speaking, the council would apportion the ducal and charitable assessments according to means. Its proceedings over the years are full of complex rules on how to value hard assets, different types of banking credits, stocks of goods held for resale, real estate, and other assets. Needless to say, there were endless wrangles over these values as members sought to minimize their own taxes. Local subsidiaries of this council established tribunals to adjudicate disputes within the Hebrew communities of Piemonte. Later, during the ghetto period, the council's local branches were responsible for apportioning the available residential and commercial real estate among the community's members. Voting membership in this council was generally limited to male heads of households who would assume responsibility for paying some portion of the assessments, although there are several examples of women being appointed to the council. Those too poor to pay taxes generally had little or no say in community governance.

By the 1580s, there was a highly visible generation change among the Sacerdotibus and Todros families in Segre's documentary record. One by one the names of the first generation of the Todros and de Sacerdotibus brothers disappeared and their sons' names appeared more and more frequently. Salomone and Todros de Sacerdotibus were never mentioned after the 1530s. Isac died in the 1560s. Vitale died in the late 1580s.

The next Sacerdotes whose names appeared relative to the town of Chieri were the brothers Abram and Consiglio (also known as Giulio) de Sacerdote, who were manufacturers and importers of cotton cloth as well as bankers in the town. In 1591 Abram obtained the ducal charter to operate a national lottery in partnership with Simone Todros, a son of Benedetto, and a third partner. While we have no direct evidence that Abram and Giulio were sons of Vitale, the circumstantial evidence is quite strong. First, Vitale's father was named Abram, and it was common practice among the Piemontese Hebrews to name sons after their grandfathers. Second, we know that Vitale had sons other than Simone.[121] Third, only

---

[118] Segre documents 1074-82.

[119] Segre document 1134.

[120] Segre, p. lvi.

[121] Segre, document 1136.

Vitale of his presumed brothers had business and family interests in Chieri. In addition, obtaining the lottery concession would have required close personal connections at the ducal court, and Vitale and his son Simone certainly had plenty of such connections. Fourth, the documentary record is quite complete as to the sons of Isac and Salomone de Sacerdotibus, and neither Abram nor Consiglio appears among them. Finally, Abram named one of his sons Salomone, probably in honor of his uncle Salomone de Sacerdotibus.

In 1596, Abram, Consiglio, and Giacobbe (Jacob) Todros (Giacobbe was another of Benedetto's sons) created a partnership to manufacture and trade in cotton cloth. The common fabrics in Italy at the time were woolens and linens. There was also an Italian silk industry that dated back to the times of Marco Polo, although little silk was made in Piemonte at the time. Cotton was considered a great luxury because the raw fiber had to be imported from Egypt, in the Turkish dominions. It was in considerable demand among the better classes. Few people in Italy knew how to spin and weave cotton, which suggests that the Sacerdotes brought the technology with them from Constantinople. It was just in those years that the Italian textile industry overtook that of the Middle East as the global source of luxury fabrics. In the ensuing several decades, Abram, and to a lesser degree Consiglio, appeared in the commercial and political documents up through 1629. For example, in 1620 Abram Sacerdote of Chieri was paid by the town for supplying fancy *calzette* (long hose or trousers) to the town officials to wear on the occasion of the visit by Princess Christina of Piemonte, daughter of Henri IV and sister of Louis XIII of France. In 1629 he was assessed taxes of 8s 4d, the highest amount after the Segre family of Chieri who controlled the most important bank in the town. He and his brother were regular participants in the work of the Università, the governing council of the Hebrew community. They were periodically assessed customs on the fabrics they were importing. And their tax assessments were among the larger ones for the town of Chieri.

The Montalcini settle in the Monferrato

The Montalcini[122] family was originally from Rome, where, where according to family lore, it had lived since the time of Julius Caesar under the name da Sinagoga or its Hebrew equivalent, Min-ha-Knesset. In Rome they had been bankers since time immemorial. The first documented references to them date to the 1300s, when two branches of the da Sinagoga family moved to Tuscany. At the time that the papacy split in two and one of the two popes ruled from Avignon in France, Rome fell into a significant economic decline, resulting in the exodus of many of its Hebrews, particularly those with capital to invest. The economically more vigorous towns in Tuscany and Umbria, such as Siena, Florence, and Perugia drew many of these migrants. Others went to the port towns on the Adriatic to profit from the growing trade with the Middle East, and adopted the localities' names as their surnames, such as Fano, Pesaro, Ancona, and the like.

The first branch of the da Sinagoga family to leave went to Pisa, where they assumed the name da Pisa[123] and established an important banking franchise with branches throughout northern Tuscany. They also were closely allied with the Medici banking family. The second branch moved to Montalcino, in southern Tuscany near Siena, in the mid-1300s and it adopted the name da Montalcino.[124] By 1381, the family bank had a branch in Perugia,[125] under the direction of a Daniele da Montalcino, son of Vitale.[126] It established branch banks in Cortona and Piombino, under the direction of Dattilo da Montalcino, son of Manovello,[127] by the second decade of the 1400s.

---

[122] This section on the early history of the Montalcini is based heavily on the research of Prof. Michele Luzzati of the University of Pisa. He is a nephew of Giorgio on the Montalcini side of the family and a specialist in family histories of the late Middle Ages.

[123] Literally "from Pisa."

[124] Literally "from Montalcino."

[125] The principal city of Umbria.

[126] According to Luzzati, Vitale died after 1375 and before 1401.

[127] Manovello is a medieval spelling of Emanuele, a name which appears in Spanish as Manuel.

In the 1430s, a Vitale da Montalcino, son of another Dattilo da Montalcino, son of Abram, established branch banks in Fano (1430),[128] Colle Valdelsa (1432),[129] Florence (1436), Siena (1441), and Prato (1441).[130] While he maintained a residence in Montalcino all along, he had by 1459 a house in Florence. The Florence synagogue was part of this house. By the late 1400s, the Montalcino bank in Florence was so busy that Salomone da Montalcino[131] wrote, "This city [Florence] is so full of business and commercial activity that truly from morning to evening there is a crowd of clients who clamor for money. It is incredible to one who has not seen this with his own eyes as I have done today the number of people who are applying for loans at our bank."[132]

In 1461, Vitale was accused of financial irregularities and subjected to a fine of 22,000 golden florins. We do not know what the specific charges were in this case. However, a common scheme for the authorities to extract money from the Hebrew bankers was to set very low maximum interest rates. When the bankers subsequently disregarded the maximums and were caught charging market interest rates, they were fined and threatened with loss of their banking licenses. Vitale then left Florence and moved the headquarters of the family bank to Prato, where he was still living in 1468, although the family must have maintained a branch in Florence, given the comments in the preceding paragraph.

Vitale's brother, known variously as Beniamino or Guglielmo,[133] worked in the family bank, and was also one of the chief rabbis of the Italian Renaissance. He was a Talmudic scholar and philosopher, deeply learned in the Kabbalah.[134] He was well known among both Hebrews and Catholics, and had warm relations with the most important jurist of the time, Mariano Sozzini,[135] and Pietro de Rossi, a professor of philosophy at the University of Siena.

One of Beniamino's sons, Abram da Montalcino, also a banker in the family business, wrote a treatise on mathematics in 1472 that is in the National Library in Florence. This Abram was awarded the degree of Doctor of Medicine. One of the speakers when he took his degree was Pietro Antonio da Vinci, the notary[136] of the Hebrew community of Florence and almost certainly the father of Leonardo da Vinci.[137]

A second son of Beniamino, Davide da Montalcino, moved to Mantova some time after his proposal of marriage to a distant cousin, Clemenza di Vitale da Pisa, was rejected.[138] Initially he remained in Prato and worked as a banker there, in Florence, and in Montepulciano until 1495, when he moved his operations to Mantova. He probably selected Mantova because his sister, Consola, had moved there some years earlier to marry a Hebrew banker. He remained there until at least 1512. In Mantova he married and raised a family.

In the mid-1500s, one of Davide's sons moved to San Damiano di Casale, a smallish town in the Marquisate of Monferrato, to establish a branch of his father's bank.[139] Monferrato, with its capital at Casale, had been tightly allied with the Duchy of Mantova since the Middle Ages, although the two territories were separated by the Duchy of Milan. The Hebrew population moved easily between Mantova and Casale, and also between the countries of Piemonte and Monferrato. At this time the 900-member Hebrew community of Casale was the second largest in the region after Torino. Davide's descendants Simone Montalcino and Salomone Montalcini appear in legal records as bankers in San Damiano Monferrato[140] in 1585–86 and 1603, respectively.

[128] A small port city on the Adriatic coast.

[129] A town south of Florence.

[130] A small city northwest of Florence.

[131] According to Luzzati, this Salomone was a cousin of Vitale, although chronologically it is more likely that he was a son of a cousin.

[132] Quoted in Ariel Toaff's essay "Christian Bankers and Hebrew Moneylenders," *Storia d'Italia* (Einaudi, 1996), vol. 11, p. 287.

[133] Benjamin or William.

[134] A mystical strain of the Jewish religion that has recently become a bit of a fad among certain entertainers, notably Madonna.

[135] Much of the Talmud is interpretations of the Mosaic legal code.

[136] In Italy notaries are trained lawyers who are concerned primarily with contract law. However, they are not permitted to argue cases in court. Thus, they are the rough equivalents of English solicitors.

[137] Leonardo was Pietro's illegitimate son by a peasant woman.

[138] Clemenza ran off with a titled nobleman in 1480.

[139] This may have been around the time that Mantova annexed the marquisate in 1536.

[140] Later known as San Damiano d'Asti, the town was ceded by the Marquisate of Monferrato to the Duchy of Savoy in 1629.

The Arrival of the Segre Families

Three different but probably related Segre families[141, 142] entered Piemonte in the period 1530–50. The first, consisting of Elia[143] Segre and his brothers Simone and Dr. Emanuele Segre, first appeared in the historical record of Asti in 1535, where they are already established as bankers, along with their nephew Giacobbe (Jacob) Foa. Elia joined with Giacobbe and Giuseppe de Sacerdotibus, the sons of Salomone de Sacerdotibus, to petition for a stay of the expulsion order of 1535. After the threat of expulsion from Asti passed a few months later, the Segre brothers set about rapidly expanding their bank. They opened branches in several towns, with each branch under the watchful eyes of one of the Segre brothers or their sons. The locations and approximate founding dates of the branches are as follows:

- Asti, early 1530s. First documented bank charter: 1537; this charter was renewed in 1542 and 1547.

- Pinerolo, 1542; renewed in 1547. This bank operated under Simone's supervision. Interestingly these charters were first granted by the French kings François I and Henri II, even though Hebrews had been prohibited from living in France since the Middle Ages. These French charters were later recognized as valid by the dukes of Piemonte.

- Chieri, 1549, headed by Emanuele and Simone, with an initial fee to the government of 20 scudi. In 1552, Simone was granted an exclusive banking license for the town of Chieri, excluding Richa Della Torre, widow of Dr. Emanuele Della Torre, who had had a banking license in the town. For this exclusive right, Simone agreed to pay 150 scudi to endow the vicar's salary and the cost of wood for the soldiers. In addition he had to agree to lend the town 200 scudi for six months at a monthly interest of 2 grossi. Simone then offered 110 scudi to Richa if she would leave town.[144]

- Cherasco, 1587, headed by Leone, Simone's son.

The second branch of the Segre family was headed by Abram Segre and his wife, Hellea. The first record of these Segres is a court case in the town of Racconigi, where Hellea was settling her late husband's affairs.[145] It appears that the late Abram had had an active banking business based in Pinerolo and branch operations in several nearby towns, including Racconigi and Cuneo. Abram left these to his wife and their several minor children, including sons Aron, Matassia, and Giacobbe. In 1555 documents indicate that Hellea Segre was running Abram's bank with her son Giacobbe. Hellea seems to have been a difficult person. In 1555 she and her son Giacobbe were accused of minting counterfeit gold and silver coins. They were placed under house arrest pending resolution of the case and were ordered to undergo torture. The outcome of the case is unknown. In 1556 she was accused of refusing to do guard duty about the town of Pinerolo. In 1568 she filed judicial proceedings against her sons Matassia and Aron, complaining that they had opened a bank in competition with her, and that Aron had taken her dowry. Their bank was still in operation in 1572.[146]

The patriarch of the third branch of the Segre family to appear in Piemonte was Dr. Bellavigna[147] Segre, who transferred his bank from Lodi in the Duchy of Milan to Piemonte around 1548.[148] Our

---

[141] The first reference to a Segre in Piemonte was to a certain Elia Segre, who was a banker in Savigliano in the 1440s. He may have left Piemonte during the troubled times in the second half of the 1400s. Given the frequency of the name Elia in the three Segre families that settled in Piemonte in the early-to-mid-1500s, one suspects that Elia may have been their common ancestor.

[142] Helia Segre and his brothers, Dr. Emanuele and Simone, also resident in Asti, appear to have been banking jointly. Bellavigna Segre, who entered Piemonte from Lodi in the 1550s, appears to be related to Helia, and perhaps was his uncle. Both of these branches of the Segre family established banking networks across Piemonte, in Asti, Chieri, Pinerolo, and other towns.

[143] He is variously referred to as Helia and Elia. This name corresponds to the English Elias or Elijah and the Hebrew names Eliezer or Eliahu.

[144] Curiously, in 1555 Richa de la Torre and Simone jointly sued the town for nonrepayment of a loan made in 1553; this suit was successful. This action suggests that Simone's bank acquired the Della Torre bank in the transactions of 1552.

[145] Segre, document 828.

[146] Segre, documents 883, 903, 1020, 1023.

[147] The curious name Bellavigna (literally "beautiful vineyard") has no direct analogues in Hebrew. It may have been a fanciful attempt to transliterate the Hebrew name Binyamin, which is ordinarily rendered in Italian as Beniamino, and in English as Benjamin.

[148] Bellavigna was almost certainly the brother of the late Abram, husband of Hellea. In Segre's document 1645, Abram, son of Bellavigna, is listed as a cousin of Aron, son of Abram and Hellea, and also a cousin of yet another Abram Segre, whose parentage I have not been able to trace. I suspect strongly that Bellavigna and his brother were also uncles or cousins of Elia, Emanuele, and Simone.

great-grandmother Eugenia Segre is almost certainly descended from Bellavigna. His sons were Abram, Giacobbe, and Leone. Abram and Giacobbe settled in Pinerolo, although Abram later moved to Chieri and opened a second Segre bank in that town.[149] He married the daughter of Moisé Todros of Torino. His brother Giacobbe remained in Pinerolo. Abram, son of Bellavigna, had three sons, Abram, Angelo, and Manuel, and at least one daughter, Ricca. Abram was a banker in Chieri and Pinerolo, while Manuel and Angelo seem to have settled in Bene Vagienna. The elder Abram's daughter Ricca married a banker named Ottolenghi in the town of Saluzzo.

Bellavigna's son Leone settled in Torino, but returned briefly to Lodi in 1557 after the death of his wife in 1555.[150] Despite his having a passport issued by the Duke of Savoy, the Spanish authorities in the Duchy of Milan arrested Leone and his traveling companion, Benedetto Todros. This arrest was part of their general campaign of harassment which aimed to stem the tide of Hebrew immigration into Piemonte. By 1560, Leone had returned to Piemonte and joined his brothers in Pinerolo.[151] He had three sons, Giacobbe, Giuseppe, and Deodato, and at least one daughter. These sons settled as bankers in Asti, Savigliano, and Cuneo, while the daughter married the banker Israele Nizza of Chieri.

As mentioned earlier, this branch of the Segre appears to have borne heraldic titles in Spain. In 1580, Abram and his nephew Giuseppe, the son of Leone, son of Bellavigna, petitioned the duke for the right to resume use of their family's coat of arms. Benedetto Todros supported their petition and testified that the ancestral Segre coat of arms consisted of a lion holding a folded white banner on a light blue field.[152]

This branch of the Segre family also expanded its banking operations rapidly, and the three brothers were heavily engaged in lending to individuals, merchant operations, and municipalities throughout Piemonte during the second half of the 1500s:

- In 1553, Leone was banking in Torino.[153] In 1557, after his wife died, he returned briefly to Lodi before setting in Pinerolo in 1560.
- In 1556, Abram and Jacob, sons of Bellavigna, received a banking charter for Pinerolo.[154]
- In 1574, Leone opened a branch in Bene Vagienna.[155]
- In 1578, Abram, and Leone's second son, Giacobbe, opened a bank in Chieri.[156]
- In 1584, Leone opened a branch in Cavalleromaggiore, and his older son, Giuseppe, opened a branch in Villanova d'Asti.[157]
- In 1595, Abram, son of Abram, expanded operations into Casale Monferrato.[158]
- In 1599, Abram, son of Abram, was financing trade between Cuneo and Saluzzo.[159]

The banking operations of the three Segre families reflected many of the larger political and social issues that buffeted Piemonte in the mid-to-late 1500s. For example, they had to negotiate their way past the problems of the French occupation. In 1542 Elia and his brothers received a French banking license for the town of Pinerolo, which the French authorities renewed in 1547. In 1556-57 Leone and his brothers received a banking license for the same town from the French government of Henri II. These licenses were recognized as valid by the Duchy of Savoy in 1560,[160] after the departure of the French. In 1552, Simone Segre agreed to lend the town of Chieri 200 scudi for six months, and the town

---

[149] The Elia/Emanuel/Simone and Bellavigna Segre families seem to have been quite competitive with each other. By 1600, each family had competing banks in Chieri, Pinerolo, Cuneo, and other towns.

[150] Segre, document 881.

[151] Segre, document 937.

[152] Segre, document 1295.

[153] Segre, document 880.

[154] Segre, documents 937, 1042, 1047.

[155] Segre, document 1167.

[156] Segre, document 1268.

[157] Segre, document 1361.

[158] Segre, documents 1600, 1616, 1619.

[159] Segre, document 1699.

[160] Part of the issue is that even today, unsecured lending to individuals is a rarity in Italy. The common American practice of distributing credit cards to every Tom, Dick, and Harry is unheard of.

councilors guaranteed the loan personally with jewels and other objects of value.[161] In 1553, Simone lent funds to Chieri to strengthen its walls, presumably to protect it against marauding French troops. In 1555, the town defaulted on its debt; Simone is one of several bankers who successfully sued the town for nonpayment of its debts. Earlier documents suggest that civil unrest and a famine may have been at the root of the problem. In 1557, the French military authorities imposed a tax on the town of Chieri amounting to 5000 scudi,[162] and the Hebrew bankers in the town had to contribute a significant share.

It is commonly thought that the Hebrew banks in Piemonte were not much more than glorified pawnshops. However, the evidence shows that many of them engaged in a broad range of recognizably modern banking services. In addition to municipal lending, the Segres were involved in trade finance,[163] agricultural lending, commodities brokerage, and numerous other types of financial transactions. I came across several clear examples of loans being syndicated across a number of family banks. The one modern lending practice that seems to have been rare was the granting of mortgages. I found only a couple of documents related to mortgages, and the practice was banned by the ducal government in 1576.[164] Even today, mortgage lending is unusual in Italy; mortgaging one's real estate is considered déclassé and a sign of financial distress.

It is unclear whether or not Hebrew banks in Piemonte took deposits, although in several court cases they were accused of fronting loans for Christians. The latter were prohibited from lending at interest by the Church.[165] Such fronting could be construed as deposit-taking of a primitive sort. Finally, the seemingly high rates of interest charged by these banks were only simple interest, as compound interest was explicitly prohibited under the ducal charters.

The Segre banks operated on a significant scale and were able to charge enormous rates of interest. For example, in 1535, when Elia and his brothers were threatened with expulsion from Asti on two weeks' notice, they appealed this order on the grounds that calling in all their credits on such short notice would cause great hardship in the community. This argument suggests that their credits underpinned material commercial interests in the town and county of Asti. In 1574–76 Abram and his brother Leone lent money to the town of Bene Vagienna for various municipal improvements. These loans were secured by the town's expected receipts from the tax on salt. In 1590, this town owed Abram 3200 florins plus 528 florins of interest at 18 percent. In addition the town owed other bankers an estimated 6400 florins in principal and interest on a six-month loan. In 1587, Simone's son Leone won a judgment against the town of Chieri for nonpayment of its debts incurred in 1553 to his late father. The judge set the rate of interest at 24 percent per annum to 1585 and 18 percent thereafter.

The Segre family epitomized the complicated web of marriages among the Hebrew bankers in Piemonte. Abram, son of Bellavigna, married the daughter of Moisé Todros, the duke's personal banker. In 1595, Ricca Segre Ottolenghi, the sister of Abram and Leone Segre, was involved in a case concerning how to divide the assets from a bank in Saluzzo jointly owned by her late husband and his late partner, Isach di Cavaglione. Giuseppe Segre, Leone's son, was named guardian for three of Cavalgione's four daughters, probably because Giuseppe's oldest son, a second Leone, was married to one of those daughters. Shortly thereafter, Giuseppe married the widow Cavaglione, and Giuseppe's second son married another of the daughters. A third daughter was married to Cervio Sacerdote of Vercelli, one of the sons of the Vercelli Sacerdote banking family. To settle the affairs of the two deceased bankers, Giuseppe bought the bank from the heirs, his aunt Ricca Segre Ottolenghi and the Cavaglione daughters. The daughters' share of this settlement was 2000 scudi each. This implies that the Saluzzo bank was capitalized at some 16,000 scudi. In addition, the daughters retained ownership of a family bank in Provence.[166]

---

[161] The convention at the time was that municipal loans were secured either by pledging the receipts of a specific tax or else through personal guarantees of the town leaders.

[162] Each scudo was composed of 3 lire, and the scudo was worth about 10 florins.

[163] Segre, document 913.

[164] Segre, p. lix.

[165] Curiously, the great Florentine banking fortunes, such as those of the Medici, were built on lending to the Church. This appears to be a case of the Church saying to the public, "Do as we say, not as we do."

[166] Segre, document 1619. Giuseppe was then resident in Asti.

Deodato Segre,[167] one of the sons of Leone, son of Bellavigna, was the first in the family to break with its long tradition in banking. In the 1610s he was reported in the town of Cuneo as a jeweler and goldsmith, although he also continued to maintain an interest in the family banks. His sons appear to have followed him in his two professions.

The Arrival of the Levi Families

During the 1400s there are several disconnected documents in Segre's collection concerning Piemontese families bearing the surname Levi. One Ysac Levi and his wife, Gentile, were resident in Savigliano. His lending business first appeared in 1414, and regularly appeared in the documentary record until about 1440, when he and any progeny he may have had disappeared from the documents.

In the 1420s, the names of Peyreto and his wife, Douceta (also known as Joyeta), Levi of Torino appear in the record. He was a banker and grain broker. In 1437 he died, leaving Douceta with minor children. Another Hebrew, Bonafide de Chalon, son of Giuseppe, was named guardian for the family, and Joyeta took over the grain brokerage business, with transactions in her name recorded in the 1440s. Another Levi, Benvegnuto Levi, also of Torino, is listed as winning a settlement for 179 florins in 1445.

Also in Torino in the 1440s there are several documents relating to a Bonafide (also known as Bonafey and Bonafe) Levi, who is variously listed as a son of Moisé or Salomone and was a banker and grain broker near Torino through the 1450s.

In 1456, two more Levis, Abramino Levi and Matassia Levi of Nice, received promises of ducal protection and exemption from the wearing of the badge. In the 1460s, three more Levis, Datolo,[168] Giuseppe, and Jacob, appear briefly in the record as residents in the town of Barge. After that, the record of Levis in the Duchy of Savoy goes cold for a century. This disappearance probably came as a result of the death or departure of most of the Hebrew population in the Duchy of Savoy in the last quarter of the 1400s due to an outbreak of the plague in the 1470s, coupled with the rabble-rousing efforts of Dominican and Franciscan friars to incite the Christian population in many towns to drive out the Hebrews and Protestants, incitements that the dukes of the time were powerless to oppose.

The next appearance of the name surname Levi in the historical record of Piemonte is of one Isachino Levi Finzi, son of Moisé, who was receiving an annual salary of 300 lire in 1562 for services rendered to His Highness.[169] Apparently Isachino was responsible for collecting the ducal taxes, for in 1578 he received a ten-year patent for a recordkeeping system that assured taxpayers their taxes had been duly recorded, and the individual tax collectors that they received credit for the monies they turned over to the ducal treasury.

During the same period, from 1560 to 1600, several Levi families migrated into Piemonte to open banks. Of these individuals, I will focus on two groups. The first settled in Vercelli and a group of small towns in the Alpine foothills north and west of the town, most notably Gatinara.[170] These families and their towns of origin include:

- Pavia[171]
  —Simon de Levitis, a banker in Pavia was lending money in Chivasso, a town between Vercelli and Torino, in 1563.
  —Giuseppe (Joseph) Levi, most likely Simon's son, opened a bank in Vercelli in 1598.
  —Giuseppe's son, Salomone Levi (whose last name was sometimes rendered as Levi Gattinara) was involved with the Hebrew bank in Gattinara. He later rose to prominence as a banker and leader in the Università of Vercelli from the mid-1640s through the

---

[167] Deodato means literally "given by God"; the name is a literal translation into Italian of the Hebrew name Nathaniel, which is generally rendered into English as its Greek equivalent, Theodore. He was also called Todros, a Spanish form of Theodore.

[168] Datolo, meaning "gift," is a translation of the Hebrew name Nathan.

[169] Segre, document 961.

[170] Gattinara today is small town with a population of about 8000; in the 1500s, its population was surely no more than 1000.

[171] Pavia is a university town twenty-five miles due south of Milan. It was besieged in 1525 during the war between France and Spain for the control of Italy. With the Spanish victory in that war, Pavia became part of the Spanish-controlled Duchy of Milan, and subsequently was inhospitable to Hebrews when they were later banished from all of the Duchy of Milan except for city of Alessandria.

1660s.[172] He and his son Isach moved to Casale Monferrato in 1666, probably to avoid an annual tax bill of more than 1000 lire each.[173] A pair of brothers who are direct descendants of this Salomone led to one of two families likely to be the immediate ancestors of Luciana's great-grandfather Israele Levi of Nizza Monferrato.

- Fiorenzuola[174]
  —Very early in the early 1500s, Marco and Angelo Levi, almost certainly brothers, were born in Fiorenzuola, a town in the southern part of the Duchy of Milan, not far from Pavia.
  —Roughly in the 1530s, Marco and Angelo had sons Lazzaro and Aron.
  —Lazzaro opened a bank in Gattinara in 1573[175] which was run by his heirs after 1596. His son Marco (no doubt named for his grandfather) was prominent in banking affairs in Gattinara and Vercelli until his death around 1629.
  —Aron Levi's sons, Donato, Moisé, and Marco Levi, bought a bank in Vercelli from Giacobbe and Consiglio Levi (see below) and settled in Piemonte in 1603. Presumably Marco is named for his great-uncle, Lazzaro's father. These Levi brothers sought to have a German-rite synagogue set up in the town, but that move was vetoed by the local bishop. Clearly these Levis were Ashkenazim, as was Israele Levi, Luciana's direct ancestor, who was born two centuries later.

- Unknown Town of Origin:
  —Giacobbe and Consiglio Levi set up a bank in Arborio in 1597.[176] In 1601, they bought a bank in Vercelli from Gabriele Norzi with the consent of the Hebrew court in Chieri. In 1603, they sold it to Aron Levi's sons (of the Fiorenzuola Levis).[177] During the period 1600-29, Giacobbe and Consiglio operated their own bank in Vercelli and Torino.[178] They were also banking jointly with Donato Levi (also of the Fiorenzuola Levi)[179] and had an interest in the Levi bank in Gattinara.[180]
  —Marco and Abramo Levi, sons of Salomone (born in the 1530s, died in the late 1500s) and grandsons of Moisé (born. early in the 1500s, and died probably in the 1570s), set up banks in 1597-1602 in Gattinara, Favria, Bollengo, and Masserano—these are all towns between Ivrea and Vercelli in the foothills of the Alps.[181] They also became bankers in Vercelli.
  —Isachino Levi, son of Moisé and presumed brother of Salomone, was the duke's "beloved" tax collector in 1562 and received a patent for his method of recording tax payments in 1578.[182] Isachino's son Moisé Levi Finzi was an official witness to a legal settlement in Casale Monferrato in 1595. Isachino's presumed nephew or grandson Isach Levi Gattinara was listed as a banker in Gattinara in 1598.[183]

[172] Segre, documents 2215, 2225, 2310.

[173] Segre, document 2332

[174] Fiorenzuola d'Arda is a small town about forty miles southeast of Milan, about thirty miles from Pavia. In the 1400s and early 1500s it was one of about eighteen towns that made up the tiny independent Marquisate of Cortemaggiore. In the 1500s it was a buffer state between the much more powerful duchies of Milan and Parma. The Duchy of Parma had been carved out of the Duchy of Milan by Pope Paul III to create a fief for his bastard son Pier Luigi Farnese. In the 1520s, during the war between France and Spain, this marquisate was divided between Milan and Parma; it regained its independence around 1557, after a ten-year series of bloody assassinations. It was finally absorbed into the Duchy of Parma in 1584.

[175] Segre, documents 1102, 1294, 1361.

[176] Segre, document 1721.

[177] Segre, document 1753.

[178] Segre, documents 1737, 1794, 1845, 1879, 1908, 1917, 1920, and 2487.

[179] Segre, document 1794.

[180] Segre, documents 2040 and 2106.

[181] Segre, documents 1673, 1739, 1818, 2040, and 2106.

[182] Tax collecting, or as it used to be known, tax farming, was generally seen as a banking-like function. Typically, the collector was a private contractor who would guarantee a certain take to the authorities and get to keep as much as he could extract from the public. In effect, the collector was lending money to the government and recapturing his credits and the associated interest from the taxpayers.

[183] Segre, document 1676.

There is strong circumstantial evidence that all of these Levis were closely related. First, all six of these families had members who worked as bankers in Gattinara, a tiny community that could not have supported more than one bank. Second, three of these family branches named a son Marco, presumably after the first Marco from Fiorenzuola. Third, as one looks through the documents cited in the footnotes, there is a nonstop stream of transactions in which they jointly invested in individual credits and banks in other towns.

A second, much smaller group of Levi, originating from Lodi in the Duchy of Milan,[184] settled in Asti in 1588, and ultimately branched out into several nearby towns, including Casale Monferrato, Alessandria, Acqui Terme, Nizza Monferrato, and other towns in the southeastern part of modern Piemonte. The duke granted a patent in 1588 to Moisé Levi Pavia of Lodi for developing a process for polishing rice (i.e., converting brown rice to white).[185] In the 1580s, an Aron Levi of Lodi, probably the son or brother of Moisé, moved to Asti. His sons, Salomone, Leone, and Ventura Levi, were merchants in the town and appeared in documents beginning in 1589,[186] including the 1596[187] census of Asti. In 1597 Salomone represented the community in the Università. A descendant of Salomone, Giuseppe Salvador Levi, is listed on a 1700s census of Nizza Monferrato as having a home there but living at the time in Acqui Terme.

Luciana Sacerdote's Levi ancestors are almost certainly one of the above two lines. According to Luciana's cousin Giovanna Dompé's genealogy of the Levi family, Israele Levi's ancestors were Ashkenazim who originated in Hungary. When Hebrews were immigrating into Italy in the early 1500s, some Central European Ashkenazim ended up in Lombardy and Venetia because those two countries were the first Italian territories south of the main Alpine passes from Austria, the gateway to Eastern Europe. More specifically, Luciana'a great-grandfather Israele Levi from Nizza Monferrato is almost certainly a direct descendant of either the Salomone Levi from Gattinara who ended up in Acqui and some of whose descendants lived in Nizza Monferrato, or the Salomone Levi from Asti, one of whose descendants, Giuseppe Salvador Levi from Nizza Monferrato, lived for a time in Acqui Terme.

The Debendetti Arrive in Piemonte

In 1547, Benedictis de Benedictis[188] and his two sons, Intendadeo (also known as Tadeo) Debenedictis and Donato Debendetti,[189] immigrated to Piemonte, having left Spain some time before. They settled in the town of Cherasco, where they were granted a banking license. Benedictis was probably born in during the last quarter of the 1400s and his sons in the 1510s or 1520s.

Tadeo was an active banker throughout the period from 1550 to about 1580. The record includes numerous municipal finance transactions for the town of Cherasco. In the mid-1550s he lent the town money to pay off the French troops quartered there when they threatened to riot because they had not been paid by the central government. The French had ordered the duke to meet the troops' payroll and the duke repeatedly promised to do so, but never actually forwarded any funds. The troops threatened to riot and sack the town unless the town saw to it that they were paid. Finally, fearing mayhem, Cherasco borrowed funds from Tadeo to meet the soldiers' demands. In 1559 the town sought to have Tadeo expelled when he pressed for repayment of the loan. In 1560 the troops rioted anyway, and

---

[184] Lodi is southeast of Milan, about twenty miles due east of Pavia, and twenty-five miles northwest of Fiorenzuola.

[185] Segre, document 1432.

[186] Segre, document 1645.

[187] Segre, documents 1467, 2112, 2223, 2289, 2312.

[188] Benedictis, meaning "blessed" in Latin, is a direct translation of *baruch* in Hebrew. It is rendered into Italian as Benedetto, and as Benedict or Bennet in English. Virtually every blessing in the Hebrew liturgy begins with the phrase "Baruch atta Adonai," Blessed art thou, our Lord."

[189] Intendadeo means literally "God listened," and is a direct translation of the biblical name Samuel. The name comes from the biblical story of a barren woman who prayed to God for a son; when that son was born, she named him Samuel because God listened to her prayers. Intendadeo later shortened his name to Tadeo, which is sometimes rendered into English as Thaddeus. Donato is a direct translation into Italian of the biblical name Nathan, meaning gift (of God).

among the houses they looted was Tadeo's. Finally, in 1565, the town and Tadeo patched things up between them, and the town gave him a good conduct letter that he subsequently used to win municipal lending deals with other communities.[190]

About Donato we know much less, other than that he was a banker in Cherasco, in partnership with his brother, and was still actively banking in the 1580s. Sometime before 1550, Donato had a son Meir,[191] who took over the brothers' banking operation from his father in 1580, renaming it Meir Debenedetti & Sons. In 1584, Meir opened branches of his bank in the nearby towns of Fossano and Bra. He lived to about the end of the 1500s.

Meir Debenedetti's sons, Benaia and Donato, were born in the 1560s or 1570s. They continued the family's banking business in partnership with their uncle Tranquillo Lattes, receiving a new charter in 1603 for Cherasco. In 1617 Donato expanded the franchise to include not only the towns of Cherasco, Fossano, and Bra, but also Cuneo and Nizza Monferrato.

---

[190] See Segre, documents 877, 916, 918, 920, 923, 927, 930, 932, 935, 940, 988, 1003, 1006, 1009, 1031, 1038, 1057, 1207, 1223, and 1235.
[191] Meyer in English.

Chapter III
The 1600s: A Century of Warfare, Consolidation, and Cultural Evolution

Emanuele Filiberto died in 1580 and was succeeded by his eighteen-year-old son Carlo Emanuele, who ruled until 1630. Initially Carlo Emanuele continued and expanded many of his father's foreign and domestic policies. For example, in 1582 he renewed his father's *condotta* for the Hebrews almost verbatim.

Carlo Emanuele also worked hard to expand his realm. In 1589-92 he intervened in the French Wars of Religion in an effort to take over the Marquisate of Saluzzo, a small French possession on the eastern side of the Alps. In this adventure he was only partially successful; while he did win control of the Saluzzian territory, he had to give up control of four towns on the French side of the Rhone.

Carlo Emanuele then set his sights on the Marquisate of Monferrato and the Duchy of Mantova. The House of Savoy had had weak claims on the Monferrato dating back to the 1400s. In 1607 he married his daughter Margherita to Francesco Gonzaga, heir to the ducal throne of Mantova, hoping thereby to establish a stronger claim on that throne for his family. In 1612, upon the death of Francesco Gonzaga (after a reign of less than one year), Carlo Emanuele seized the Marquisate of Monferrato, tripping off war with Spain, which supported the Gonzagas. The Spaniards forced Carlo Emanuele to relinquish the Monferrato, but permitted him to retain most of his original domains. Meanwhile, Francesco's brother Ferdinando seized the Mantovan throne and ruled until 1626. Ferdinando was succeeded by yet another brother, Vincenzo II, who died without direct heirs in 1628.

In 1628, a French branch of the Gonzaga family asserted its rights to the Mantovan throne. The Spaniards opposed this claim, not wishing to see French power to the east of their domains in Milan. Carlo Emanuele sided with Spain in this dispute, hoping to secure the Mantovan throne for himself. In the Franco-Spanish war that followed (part of the much larger Thirty Years' War that raged through most of Northern and Central Europe from 1618 to 1648), Carlo Emanuele quickly captured many towns in the Monferrato, including San Damiano, Trino, and Alba, which the French ceded to him in the temporary peace of 1628. Subsequently the French occupied much of Piemonte, and it was left to Carlo Emanuele's successor, Vittorio Amedeo (who reigned from 1630 to 1637), to negotiate the departure of the French in the Treaty of Cherasco in 1631. As part of this treaty, sixty-seven villages and towns in the Monferrato were given to Piemonte, including San Damiano di Casale (renamed San Damiano d'Asti), but the French kept the strategic town of Pinerolo that controlled the Valle di Susa, the main invasion route from France into Italy.

Carlo Emanuele's long reign was marked by a significant development of late Renaissance and early Baroque art, architecture, and music in Piemonte. His personal architect, Vitozzi, reshaped Piazza Castello around the royal palace[192] and laid out the adjacent Via Nuova, today's Via Roma, the main avenue of Torino.[193] To bring the then new Baroque musical style to his court, the duke had Madama Europa de Rossi,[194] the most celebrated female vocalist of the day, sing at the wedding of his daughter to Francesco Gonzaga, and hired her son, Angelo de Rossi, as court composer and music master.

[192] This square existed in Roman times. The Palazzo Madama in the center of Piazza Castello includes elements of the old Roman fortifications of Torino.

[193] In the 1930s, Via Roma was substantially redesigned by the noted architect Gino Levi-Montalcini, a first cousin of both Giorgio and Luciana.

[194] The De Rossi Hebrews descended from the old Roman family of the same name. They were celebrated musicians in Mantova which was an important center of early Baroque music. From 1602 to 1613, the court composer to the Gonzagas was Claudio Monteverdi, the first Baroque composer and the inventor of opera as an art form. In 1613, when Monteverdi left Mantova to become choral director at San Marco in Venice, he was succeeded by Salomone de Rossi, Europa's brother. Salomone was a prolific and very inventive composer in his own right, composing secular music for the Mantovan court and sacred music for the synagogue. Much of his music was lost after the sack of Mantova in 1630, though in the 1800s some of his books fell into the hands of Baron Rothschild, who had them republished. Currently a choral music group in Boston, the Zamir Chorale, has been reviving, performing, and promoting his sacred and secular works.

The duke paid Angelo de Rossi quite well, with his salary set in 1610 as 6 scudi plus 5 ducatoni per month. He received regular raises. De Rossi used his position to obtain banking licenses for Racconigi in 1606 and in Torino in 1613. The Torino license caused considerable alarm among the incumbent bankers, resulting in a lawsuit which the incumbents lost. In 1621 the duke gave De Rossi 300 ducatoni as a dowry for his daughter. In 1611 the Hebrew communities of Fossano and Pinerolo gave him a power of attorney to negotiate a dispute with the central government on their behalf. In 1623 the duke brought De Rossi with him on a state visit to the court of Louis XIII to negotiate a treaty with France. These benefits continued under Vittorio Amedeo and his successor, Carlo Emanuele II. For example, in 1636, the new duke granted de Rossi 100 lire from his own pocket, plus another 80 lire derived from taxes paid by Emanuele Montalcini. De Rossi fell on hard times in his old age, and in 1651 the duke directed Emanuele Montalcini to grant De Rossi an annuity "in view of his long service and current poverty and decrepitude." De Rossi's sons, Giuseppe and Buonaiuto[195] and his grandson Alessandro succeeded him as music masters at the ducal court, serving several generations of dukes.[196]

Carlo Emanuele was succeeded in 1630 by his son Vittorio Amedeo. In 1632, on the occasion of the birth of a new heir to the throne, Francesco Giacinto, the Hebrew community donated 4000 lire to the ducal treasury. In 1637 Vittorio Amedeo died suddenly, leaving a five-year-old heir to the throne. Francesco Giacinto died in 1638 and was succeeded by his younger brother Carlo Emanuele II. There ensued a nasty fight between the dowager duchess, Madama Maria Christina (who was the daughter of King Henri IV of France and sister of Louis XIII; she is sometimes referred to as Madama Reale),

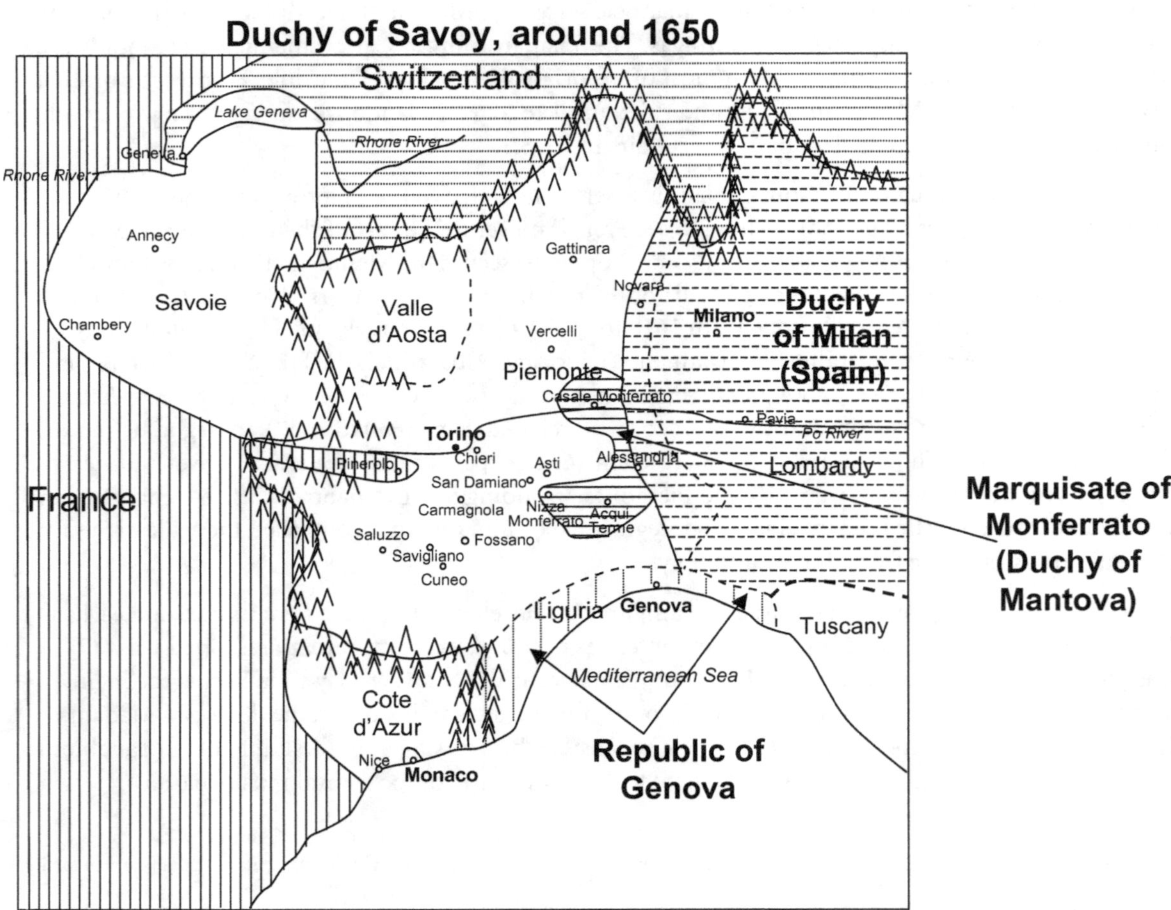

and Vittorio Amedeo's brothers Maurizio and Tomasso[197] over who should hold the regency for the minor duke. The fighting became a civil war that devastated the country, with Madama Maria Christina abandoning Piemonte for Savoie in 1639. King Louis XIII subsequently intervened, occupied Torino in 1640, and reinstalled her as regent. Thus began a long period of increasing French influence in the affairs of Piemonte. This period coincided with the decline in the power of Spain, which had peaked during the reign of Phillip II in the late 1500s. Evidently the fighting had exhausted the duchy economically, as Madama Maria Christina had to give the Hebrews (among others) a tax holiday in 1640. She continued as regent until her son assumed the throne in the 1650s.

Carlo Emanuele II's reign from 1638 to 1675 was a time mostly of peace and prosperity. Except for a weak and failed attempt to capture Genova in 1672, and involving Piemonte in minor ways to support wars of his uncle Louis XIII, Carlo Emanuele II avoided military adventures. During his reign, the duchy's economic policy shifted quite heavily from favoring finance and agriculture to encouraging manufacturing and commerce. For example, in 1648, the duke granted the Sephardic Hebrews in the port of Villefranche an exceptionally long *condotta* of twenty-five years to live, trade, and engage in commerce.[198] In 1649 he established a sugar monopoly under control of families under that *condotta*, in order to have a sugar refining business in the province of Nice. In 1651 the duke granted some of them a monopoly in soap manufacture, to establish that industry in his domains. In 1652 he did the same for the bleaching and manufacture of wax and the production of gunpowder. In 1653 he created a short-term monopoly in the growing and curing of tobacco, also for the same purpose. In 1655 he extended the rights to manufacture soap, provided that manufactures of that commodity be built in several additional towns.

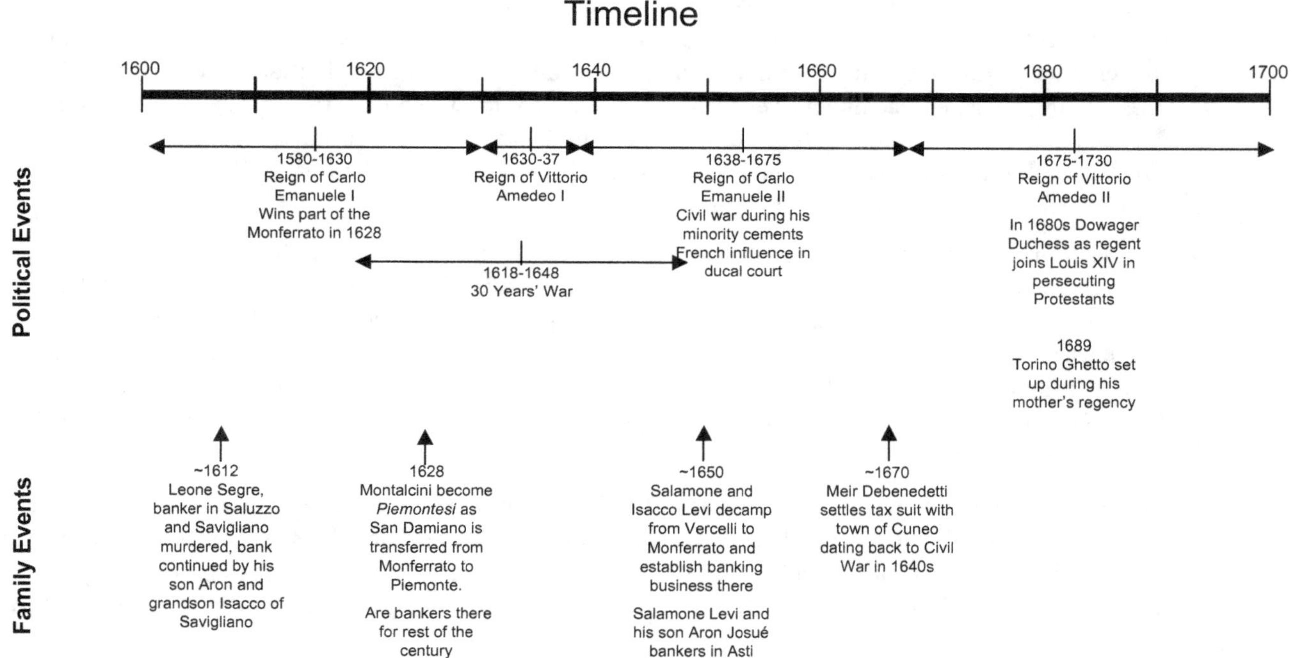

[197] Tomasso's line, the Carignano branch of the Savoia family, went on to produce a number of distinguished public figures, including Prince Eugenio di Savoia, a military hero later in the 1600s. Ultimately, when the main Savoia line died out in 1831, the Carignano branch inherited the house's noble titles.

[198] Segre, document 2221. Its main provisions were: (1) The Hebrews were granted the right to live undisturbed in Villefranche for 25 years, coming and going as they pleased. (2) They were allowed to keep such books as they needed for their religious observances, provided that they were in compliance with the Holy Office. (3) They could not be investigated for any crime they might have committed in other countries (a particularly important provision for those accused by the Inquisition in Spain). (3) They were not to be subject to the Inquisition. (4) They were exempted from all taxes and duties except as were applied to the Hebrews of Torino. (5) Their personal possessions could be imported or exported free of tax. (6) The penalties for intimate relations with Christians could not exceed 100 scudi. (7) Those who slandered these Hebrews would be subject to criminal fines. (8) Dowries and inheritances are to be fully protected by law. (9) Their physicians and surgeons could practice upon both Hebrew and Christian patients, and take university degrees in the Duchy. (10) They were exempted from legal proceedings on Saturdays and their feast days. (11) They were permitted to slaughter meat according to their rules, and butchers could not charge a premium for such meat. (12) They were allowed to bear and use defensive weapons. (13) They were permitted to acquire land for a cemetery. (13) They were permitted to have Christian employees, servants and wet-nurses.

The reign of Carlo Emanuele II was also a period in which arts and education were actively promoted. In 1661, the duke decreed that each town had to establish a public school. In 1666, Carlo Emanuele summoned the Modenese architect Guarino Guarini to Torino, where he remained until 1681. Guarini was already well known, with credits for major churches in Messina and Paris. This architect substantially redesigned the look of central Torino, giving it the Baroque look that survives to this day. More specifically, he designed the grand Piazza San Carlo in the middle of Via Roma. The buildings surrounding the piazza all had (and continue to have) covered walkways, making it possible for people to visit the shops in comfort despite rain, snow, or blazing sun. This system of covered walkways was subsequently extended to many of the main thoroughfares of Torino. Guarini is also credited with the twin churches of San Lorenzo and San Filippo in the Piazza San Carlo; the Capella Sindone in the cathedral, where the Shroud of Torino[199] is kept; and the Palazzo Carignano, the seat of the Carignano branch of the House of Savoy.[200]

Carlo Emanuele II died in 1675 at age forty, and was succeeded by his minor son Vittorio Amedeo II with his mother, the Dowager Duchess Marie Jeanne as regent. She was a granddaughter of Henri IV of France, and thus Carlo Emanuele II's first cousin. Marie Jeanne served as regent until 1680, when her son reached majority.

During her regency, the dowager duchess forced the Hebrews of the capital to move into a segregated ghetto in 1679. This ghetto was located in the former Ospedale della Carità.[201] The Hebrews' rent was to be applied to support the Ospedale at its new location on the periphery of the city. Piemonte was one of the last of the Italian states to impose the ghetto system—the Venetian, Roman, and Florentine ghettos were established in 1516, 1555, and 1571, respectively. The Catholic Church was one of the main driving forces to segregate the Hebrews from the Catholic population. The formation of the ghettoes came at exactly the same time as the Church found itself locked in struggles with the early Protestant movements. Church-led military forces attacked the Waldensians in 1487. Luther posted his theses in 1517; Zwingli began preaching his version of Protestantism in Zurich in 1519; and Calvin introduced his version in Geneva in the 1520s, leading that city to revolt successfully against the House of Savoy. The Church's thinking was that the Hebrews, as people who had resisted it for a millennium and a half, were somehow to blame for the rise of Protestantism.

The Savoyard dukes had considered instituting the ghetto system as early as 1620,[202] but the time never seemed right. This move against the Hebrews of Torino coincided with efforts to suppress the Piemontese Waldensian Protestants and Louis XIV's aggressive moves against the Huguenots, French Waldensians, and other French Protestants.[203] Vittorio Amedeo II remained strongly under his mother's French influence for much of his life. At her recommendation, he married a French princess, a niece of Louis XIV, and during the early part of his long reign (1675–1730) maintained his parents' pro-French, anti-Spanish foreign policy.

In the early 1680s Prince Eugenio di Savoia of the Carignano branch of the Savoia family was refused a commission in the French army.[204] He then slipped out of Paris and offered his services to the Austrian emperor. By all accounts he was a brilliant soldier, and he rose rapidly through the ranks of the Austrian army. In 1688 he led the successful defense of Vienna, which was being attacked by the Turks in an effort

---

[199] The shroud is claimed to be the burial cloth of Jesus. It came into the possession of the House of Savoy in the Middle Ages, and was transferred to Torino from their former capital of Chambéry during the reign of Emanuele Filiberto.

[200] The Carignano branch was a lateral branch of the ducal Savoia family descended from Vittorio Amedeo's brother Tomasso. When the main line died out in 1831, the Carignano branch succeeded to the throne.

[201] The Church-operated charity hostel. This ghetto was located off the modern Piazza Carlo Alberto.

[202] Segre, document 1621.

[203] Louis XIV's mother and wife were both Spanish princesses. One might speculate that their violent hatred of Protestants, which had been Spanish royal policy from the beginning, helped form Louis XIV's determination to suppress the Protestant movements in France. Moreover, during his childhood and his mother's regency, dominated by her prime minister, Cardinal Mazarin, France had been racked by a civil war, the Fronde, in which the Protestant regions of France were mostly arrayed against the boy-king; this experience made him extremely suspicious of the French Protestants as potential resisters against his efforts to consolidate all power in France under his absolute control.

[204] Although he was Vittorio Amedeo II's second cousin, his parents were French aristocrats, and he grew up in the court of Louis XIV.

to expand their European empire beyond their historical holdings in the Balkans.[205] Prince Eugenio then led a military campaign against the Turks in which he conquered Hungary, Serbia, and Bosnia, and added them to the Austrian Empire. This linkage between the House of Savoy and the Austrian Crown turned out to have far-reaching consequences.

Vittorio Amedeo II's pro-French policy continued until the death of the last Hapsburg king of Spain, Charles II.[206] Charles had no direct heir and left the crown to the Duke of Anjou, the grandson and direct heir of Louis XIV.[207] This inheritance threatened to combine France and Spain under one crown and would upset the balance of power in Europe. The War of Spanish Succession (1703– 13) broke out with England and Austria, who were determined to prevent this union on one side, and Spain and France, who were equally determined to pursue it, as their opponents.

At the beginning of the war, the Duchy of Savoy, which was surrounded by France and the Spanish-controlled Duchy of Milan, sided with France. However, when Prince Eugenio's Austrian army crossed the Alps and took control of the Spanish and French possessions in the duchies of Milan and Mantua, the English and the Austrians offered Vittorio Amedeo II a deal he could not refuse. If he would switch sides in the war, the Austrians would give him the Spanish domain of Sicily and the title of King of Sicily, as well as control of Casale and the rest of the Monferrato. He took the bait.[208] The French promptly marched into Piemonte and laid siege to Torino in 1706. The siege was finally broken when a group of Piemontesi, led by Pietro Micca, tunneled out from the city and exploded a massive bomb under the main French camp. At the same time, Prince Eugenio's Austrian army attacked the French from the east, forcing Louis XIV's forces to withdraw across the Alps. Eugenio's Austrian army pursued the French into southern France but was ultimately driven back to the original Franco-Savoyard boundary.

Vittorio Amedeo II eventually made peace with Louis XIV in 1710.[209] His envoy in the negotiations was Raffaele Sacerdote, of the Casale Sacerdotes. Raffaele knew both Louis XIV and Vittorio Amedeo II well, as he had been a leading supplier of commodities to their armies in the years before and during the war. For example, in 1709, the duke asked the Sacerdote brothers to supply 16,000 quintals of lead for the war effort. In the same year, the Sacerdote brothers brokered the sale of 50,000 sacchi of grain to France. Louis's ministers at first refused to deal with Sacerdote because he was a Hebrew. However, after they saw that he was cordially received by both Louis XIV and Vittorio Amedeo II, they swallowed their Gallic pride and conducted their negotiations with him.

In that peace that Sacerdote negotiated, France ceded the Monferrato and the Milanese city of Alessandria to Piemonte. As the war dragged on elsewhere in Europe, France and Spain were ultimately defeated. In the subsequent Treaty of Utrecht, it was agreed that Spain could have a French Bourbon king, but that the crowns of France and Spain could not be united. Further, a Bourbon king would rule in Naples, but not be subject to the Spanish or French Crown. Spanish influence at the papal court was to be replaced by French. The Spanish and French territories in northern Italy were given to Austria,[210] as was Flanders, the Spanish territory in the Netherlands. The English received control of Gibraltar, Malta, and Minorca in the Mediterranean, several Spanish and French islands in the Caribbean, and control of

[205] When the Austrians overran the Turkish camp, they found pots of a dark, aromatic drink. Thus was coffee introduced into Europe, and drinking it became all the rage among the upper classes in the 1700s. Also, to celebrate the victory, the Austrian emperor asked the French bakers in Vienna to create a new pastry; they responded with the croissant because the Turkish flag had a crescent moon on it. Soon it became fashionable to dunk one's croissant into one's coffee. To offer thanks to God for the deliverance of Vienna from the hand of the infidel Turks, the emperor had a new cathedral built, Stefansdom. The cathedral's corbels were all carved in the shape of Turks; for daring to attack Vienna, these infidels were condemned unto eternity to hold up the Christian cathedral's roof!

[206] Charles V, the first Hapsburg king of Spain, had been the fifth Austrian emperor of that name but the first Spanish king Charles. Hence his descendant was Charles II of Spain.

[207] Louis XIV's queen, Marie Thérèse, was Charles's older sister.

[208] The English had earlier offered Vittorio Amedeo II a large bribe (the modern term "foreign aid" had not yet been invented) to join the Anglo-Austrian alliance. He accepted the offer, but the money was never paid. The HMS *Sussex* was dispatched in 1694 to carry roughly $3 billion in gold to Piemonte, but it went down off Gibraltar. The wreck of the *Sussex* was discovered in 2002, and a British diving team is currently excavating it and recovering its treasure.

[209] The larger war continued for several years. Louis tried to conquer Bavaria but was defeated decisively by an Anglo-Austrian army at Blindheim. The victors were led by Prince Eugenio and the English general John Churchill, later created Duke of Marlborough. The English and Austrian governments rewarded these two military heroes in similar fashion. Churchill was given Blenheim Palace in Oxfordshire and Eugenio was given Belvedere Palace in Vienna. Churchill's descendant, Sir Winston Churchill, spent much of his youth at Blenheim.

[210] The Austrian domains in Italy eventually came to include the Grand Duchy of Tuscany as well. When the last Medici duke died in 1737 without heirs, it was agreed that the future grand dukes would be the younger sons of Austrian emperors.

the trade in African slaves in Spain's American colonies. And Vittorio Amedeo II gained Sicily and the coveted title of king. In a subsequent trading of territories, he swapped control of Sicily for Sardinia and was named King of Sardinia.

This wholesale realignment of power in Europe that resulted from the War of the Spanish Succession forced a complete rethinking of Savoyard foreign policy. With the weak Spaniards replaced in Italy by the much more powerful Austrians, the former pro-French policy need to be rethought. The balancing act of the 1500s and early 1600s had to be resuscitated; only now the Savoy kings had to deal on their eastern boundary with the Austrians in place of the Spaniards in Milan, as well as the French to their west. In addition, they had gained an alliance with England, which was now a Mediterranean power with its acquisition of several naval bases on that sea.

In celebration of his victory and new royal title, Vittorio Amedeo set about beautifying Torino to make it a proper royal capital. He invited Filippo Juvarra to Torino as royal architect. One of Juvarra's first projects was to build the magnificent Baroque Basilica of Superga atop a high hill east of the city.[211] Juvarra then undertook to modernize the Palazzo Madama, the ancient palace in the middle of Piazza Castello, by adding a Baroque façade to its western front.[212] Overall, Torino has more than half a dozen major public buildings designed by Juvarra.

As King Vittorio Amedeo II consolidated his new holdings, he had numerous issues with respect to the Hebrew communities in the Monferrato and Alessandria. Each of these had operated under *condotte* with terms quite different from the two *condotte* that had been granted to the Hebrews of Piemonte and Savoie. For example, the Hebrews of Alessandria, under the *condotta* issued by Charles V, were not subject to taxes except for a tax on business receipts; they could employ Christians and carry weapons; and their children were protected from abduction and forced baptism. Conversely, they had been prohibited from lending money since 1569. The Hebrews of Casale were regarded as permanent residents under Mantovan law, and therefore did not have to pay a periodic fee for the right to live in the town.

With respect to the Hebrews, the king's first move was to require these new subjects to swear allegiance to their new sovereign. The Hebrews of Alessandria so swore in 1707. In 1708, the Hebrews of Casale met in their synagogue and authorized Salomone Sacerdote (brother of Raffaele) and Simone Clava to swear loyalty to the king on their behalf.

The war was very expensive, and the king sought new sources of funds to support it. In 1704, he tried to tie the Hebrews' taxes to their incomes, requiring them to declare their incomes; in the ensuing several years, the Università struggled to make this process work. Ultimately, the taxpayers' cleverness at hiding their incomes outran all the schemes developed to enforce this process. In a second effort, when the king had taken over Casale, he immediately borrowed against the projected tax receipts from there to fund the continued prosecution of the war.

The Sacerdotes in Chieri

Let us now turn to how our five families fared during this tumultuous century. In the early 1600s, the Chieri branch of the Sacerdote family expanded from finance to commerce and manufacturing. While they no doubt maintained their investments in the Todros bank in that town, Abram Sacerdote and his brother Consiglio established a business manufacturing and trading in cotton cloth and also obtained the license to operate the national lottery. The Todros bank in Chieri was sold to a branch of the Segre family in 1642.

During the period from roughly 1630 to 1690, the Hebrew community of Chieri seems to have largely settled down to business, and there are but two documents in Segre's collection concerning the town. In 1662, Abram Segre, son of Salomone, son of Leone was required to settle up his back taxes to the Università because he had earlier left the country to live in Casale Monferrato. In 1686 the guild of

---

[211] It is claimed that while the king was surveying the French positions from this hilltop during the siege of Torino, he promised to build a great church on the spot if the capital was delivered from the French besiegers.

[212] Palazzo Madama has elements that date back to Roman times, including a tower that was part of the original Roman wall. Traditionally it was the home of the dowager duchesses of Savoy. It is situated across the street from the royal palace.

cotton merchants[213] complained to the duke that certain individuals were manufacturing socks and other cotton goods without its supervision and then selling them to Hebrews and other members of the public. The duke agreed to levy penalties on those who violated the guild's privileges. While the accused are not named, it is safe to assume that the Sacerdote cotton manufactory in Chieri was among them.

The only other record we have of these families during the mid-1600s is in an undated map of the Hebrew quarter of Chieri that names the heads of households. This document was reprinted in Treves's book and is thought to date to the mid-1600s; it is shown on pages 46–47.

This quarter consisted of two streets, Contrada della Pace and Vicolo Corona Grossa. The diagram tells several stories. First, there are no Todros names on it; the family had probably moved to Torino earlier in the 1600s. Second, there are no Segre names; we know that Abram Segre moved away from Chieri sometime in the 1640s. Since there were Segres in Chieri eighty years later, they must have been living outside the traditional Hebrew quarter. The brothers Salvador and Leone Sacerdote who are listed must have been sons of either Abram or Consilio, who both were already dead and had adult sons when this census was taken in the mid-1600s, and Abram and Consilio were running substantial businesses as late as 1629.

Leone Sacerdote's heirs and his presumed son Moisé Lazzaro Sacerdote were living in the house at 2/4/6/8 Contrada della Pace, a house that Giorgio's great-grandfather owned per the 1838 census of the Chieri ghetto, and that his grandfather had owned in the late 1800s. This house had been in the family for many years. This evidence and the reappearance of the names Leone and Moisé Lazzaro in later generations leading to Giorgio's grandfather suggest that the Moisé Lazzaro of 1650 was his direct ancestor. In the 1670s two Sacerdote brothers, Giacobbe (Jacob) and Samuele, were born in Chieri. Because two of Giacobbe's grandsons bore the names Moisé and Leone, I have inferred that he was the grandson of the Moisé Lazzaro on the map. In 1691 Moisé and Samuele participated in a forced loan of 2776 lire 11 soldi to cover the duke's military expenses.[214] In 1706, when Chieri was occupied by French troops as part of the siege of Torino, the brothers were forced to pay a French war levy of 505 lire, more than one-fourth of the tax on the entire Hebrew community of Chieri.[215] And in 1713, they jointly invested 2800 lire in a block of apartments in the town along with Davide Levi and Israele Nizza.[216]

The Montalcini

Emanuele Montalcini and his brother Giuseppe, whose grandfather had settled in San Damiano di Casale in the 1500s, became a Piemontese citizen in 1628, when San Damiano was captured by Piemonte in the war with France. The transfer was made official in 1631 by the Treaty of Cherasco and the town was renamed San Damiano d'Asti. Thus, the Montalcini did not so much immigrate into Piemonte as they were engulfed by it.

In 1628, the duke confirmed Emanuele's banking charter, which had originally been issued "many years ago" by the Mantovan government, in exchange for an initial fee of 2700 florins followed by ten annual payments of 337.5 florins.[217] In 1629 Emanuele was assessed substantial additional taxes.[218] In 1638, his banking charter was renewed by Madama Reale, the regent for the minor duke.[219]

It would appear that Emanuele was well-known to the ducal family. In 1636, part of Emanuele's taxes was diverted to pay the salary of the ducal music master, Angelo de Rossi.[220] This model was repeated in 1639 and 1643, with the latter payments earmarked to provide a dowry for De Rossi's daughter.[221] In 1649, when De Rossi became old and feeble, Emanuele was asked to grant him an annuity and deduct

---

[213] At that time, Hebrews were not allowed to join the guilds.

[214] Segre, document 2446.

[215] Segre, documents 2600, 2512.

[216] Segre, document 2573.

[217] Segre, document 2090.

[218] Segre, documents 2106 and 2109.

[219] Segre, document 2166.

[220] Segre, document 2146.

[221] Segre, document 2172.

Figure 3-1
The Hebrew quarter of Chieri around 1650. This picture
is taken from Sergio Treves' book which is out of print.
A schematic copy of this picture appears on the opposite
page.

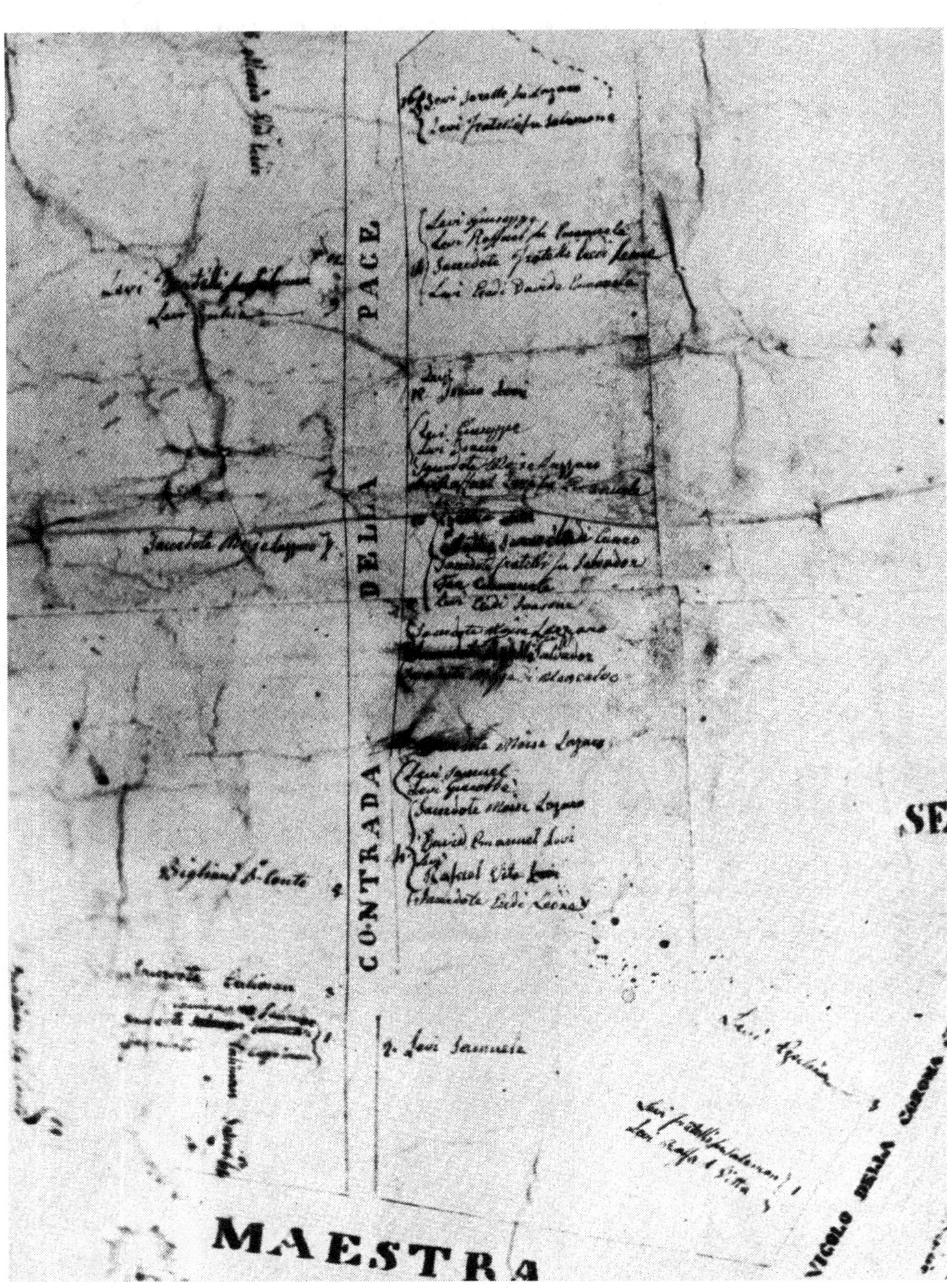

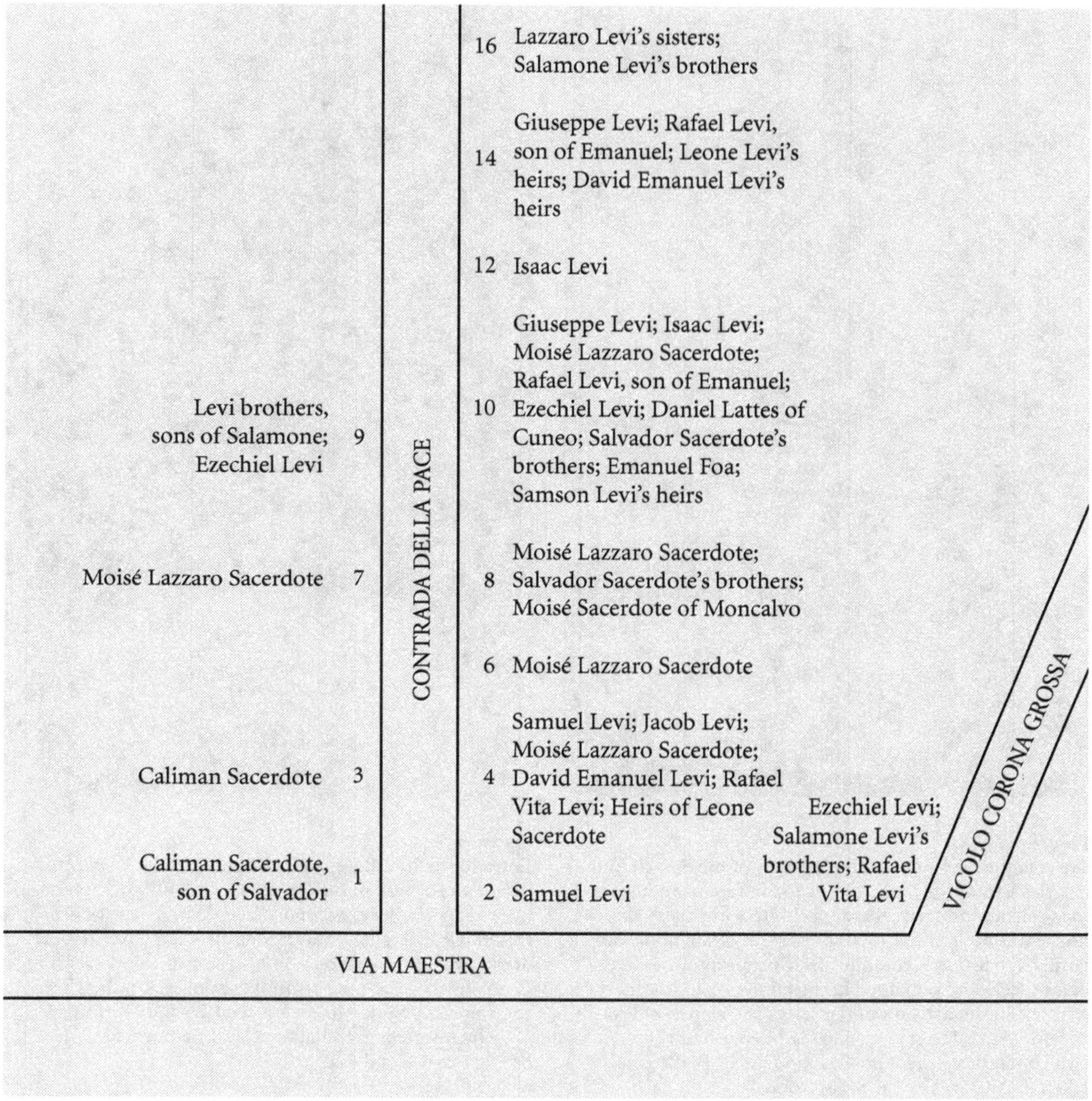

16 Lazzaro Levi's sisters;
Salamone Levi's brothers

Giuseppe Levi; Rafael Levi,
14 son of Emanuel; Leone Levi's
heirs; David Emanuel Levi's
heirs

12 Isaac Levi

Giuseppe Levi; Isaac Levi;
Moisé Lazzaro Sacerdote;
Rafael Levi, son of Emanuel;
10 Ezechiel Levi; Daniel Lattes of
Cuneo; Salvador Sacerdote's
brothers; Emanuel Foa;
Samson Levi's heirs

Moisé Lazzaro Sacerdote;
8 Salvador Sacerdote's brothers;
Moisé Sacerdote of Moncalvo

6 Moisé Lazzaro Sacerdote

Samuel Levi; Jacob Levi;
Moisé Lazzaro Sacerdote;
4 David Emanuel Levi; Rafael
Vita Levi; Heirs of Leone
Sacerdote

2 Samuel Levi

Levi brothers,
sons of Salamone; 9
Ezechiel Levi

Moisé Lazzaro Sacerdote 7

Caliman Sacerdote 3

Caliman Sacerdote,
son of Salvador 1

Ezechiel Levi;
Salamone Levi's
brothers; Rafael
Vita Levi

CONTRADA DELLA PACE

VICOLO CORONA GROSSA

VIA MAESTRA

Figure 3-2
This plaque commemorates the stops of the French king
Charles VIII at the home of the Solara family on his way
to and from military campaigns in Italy in 1400s. This
house was built in the 1300s as the seat of the noble Solara
family. It became Sacerdote family property sometime
before 1650 and remained in the family well into the 20th
century. In the division of the assets of the firm of Fratelli
Sacerdote in 1921, it passed to Cav. Leone Sacerdote, Ada
and Umberto's father and Giorgio's uncle. Photograph
taken in 2005 by George S. Sacerdote.

Figure 3-3
Entrance to Sacerdote family house at 2/4/6/8 *Contrada
della Pace*, Chieri, in the former Ghetto, photograph taken
in 1953 by Umberto Secondo Sacerdote. By the 1950s,
this house had fallen into serious disrepair. Over the main
doorway had once stood a 1400s Flemish wooden carving
of an angel bearing the arms of the Solara family. This
carving was donated to the Museo Civico di Torino in
1875 by my great grandfather, Cav. Emanuele Sacerdote.
See figures 6-4 and 6-5.

Figure 3-4
Details of the alley leading to the entrance, 1950s.
Photograph Umberto Sacerdote.

Figure 3-5
The courtyard stairs leading to the upstairs apartments.
This house was assigned to my great uncle, Cav. Leone
Sacerdote when the assets of the firm Fratelli Sacerdote
were divided after the deaths in 1920 of my grandfather
Alberto and his third brother Balilla. It probably passed
from there to Leone's son Umberto, Giorgio's first cousin.
Photograph Umberto Sacerdote.

Figure 3-6
By the 1980s, the Sacerdote
family house at 2/4/6/8
Contrada della Pace, Chieri, in
the former ghetto, had fallen
into yet worse repair and was
occupied by squatters. Bonnie,
Alisa, Alex and Laurence
Sacerdote are shown in the alley. Photograph taken in 1980s
by Peter M. Sacerdote.

Figure 3-7
In 2004, the Sacerdote family house at 2/4/6/8 Contrada
della Pace, Chieri, in the former
ghetto, was acquired by a
property developer who began
to restore it for use as modern
apartments, offices and shops.
This is the main doorway
shown in figures 3-3 and 3-6.
Photograph taken in 2005 by
George S. Sacerdote

Figure 3-8
This is the restored courtyard.
Photograph taken in 2005 by
George S. Sacerdote

Figure 3-9
Interior details (taken during restoration) of the house
of Sacerdote family house at
2/4/6/8 Contrada *della Pace*,
Chieri in the former ghetto.
Photograph taken in 2005 by
George S. Sacerdote.

Figure 3-10
Sometime in the 18th century, the Sacerdote family decided to cover one of the beautiful coffered ceilings with
'modern' painted plasterwork. When the restorer began
work, part of this plaster had collapsed, exposing the
former wooden ceiling. He retained and restored both ceilings. Photograph taken in 2005 by George S. Sacerdote

Figure 3-11
Details of the restored plaster
ceiling. Photograph taken in
2005 by George S. Sacerdote.

Figure 3-12
Former synagogue in family house at 2/4/6/8 *Contrada della Pace*, Chieri, in the former ghetto. When this picture was taken, the restoration work on the synagogue had not yet begun. The lower floor housed the ghetto school. It was planned to turn these two large rooms into an apartment. Photograph taken in 2005 by George S. Sacerdote.

Figure 3-13
I entered the school, but was afraid to climb the rickety stairs leading up to the old synagogue. Pictured here is the railing at the top of the stairs. Note the as-yet unrestored coffered ceiling. Photograph taken in 2005 by George S. Sacerdote.

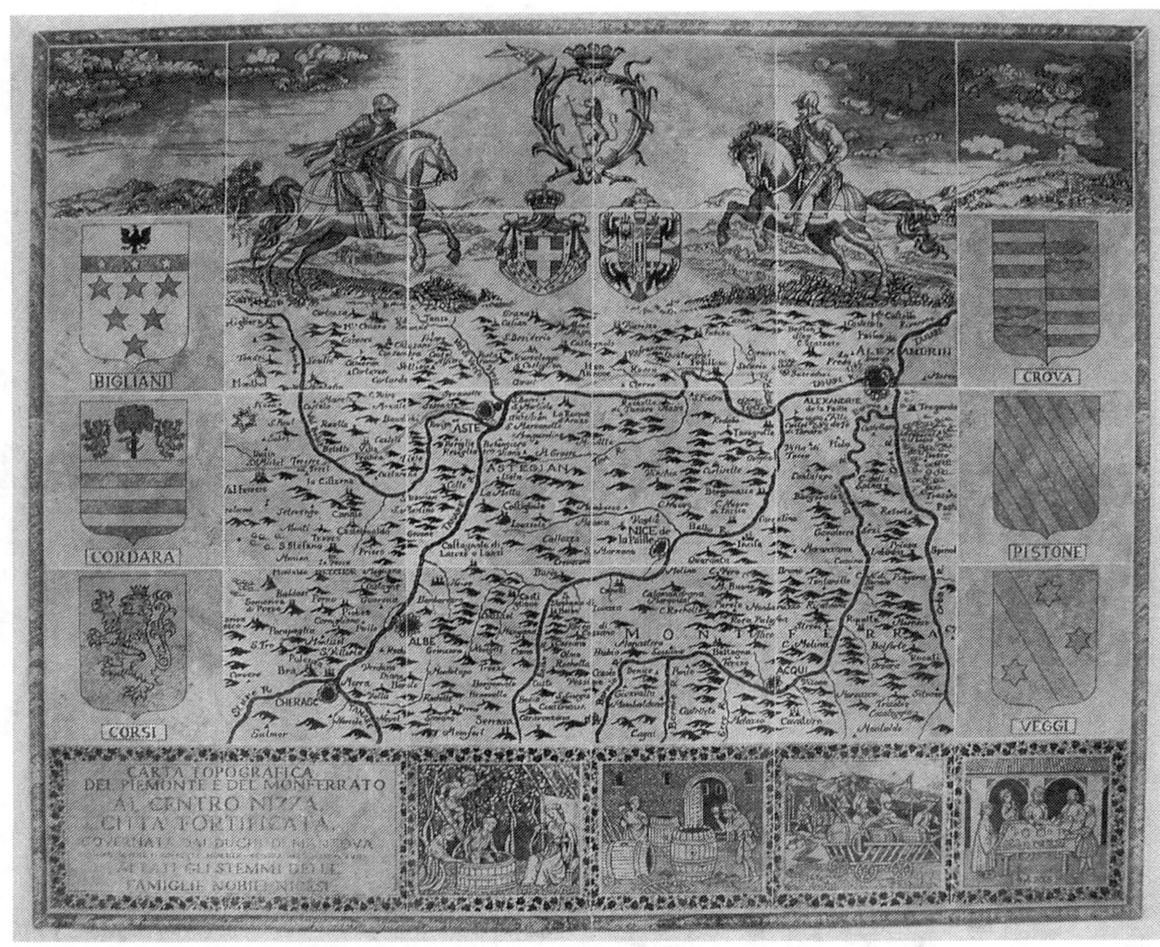

Figure 3-14
Modern copy of old map showing part of the Marquisate
of Monferrato around Nizza Monferrato and Acqui Terme
in early 1600s. This copy is on the exterior wall of the town
hall of Nizza Monferrato.

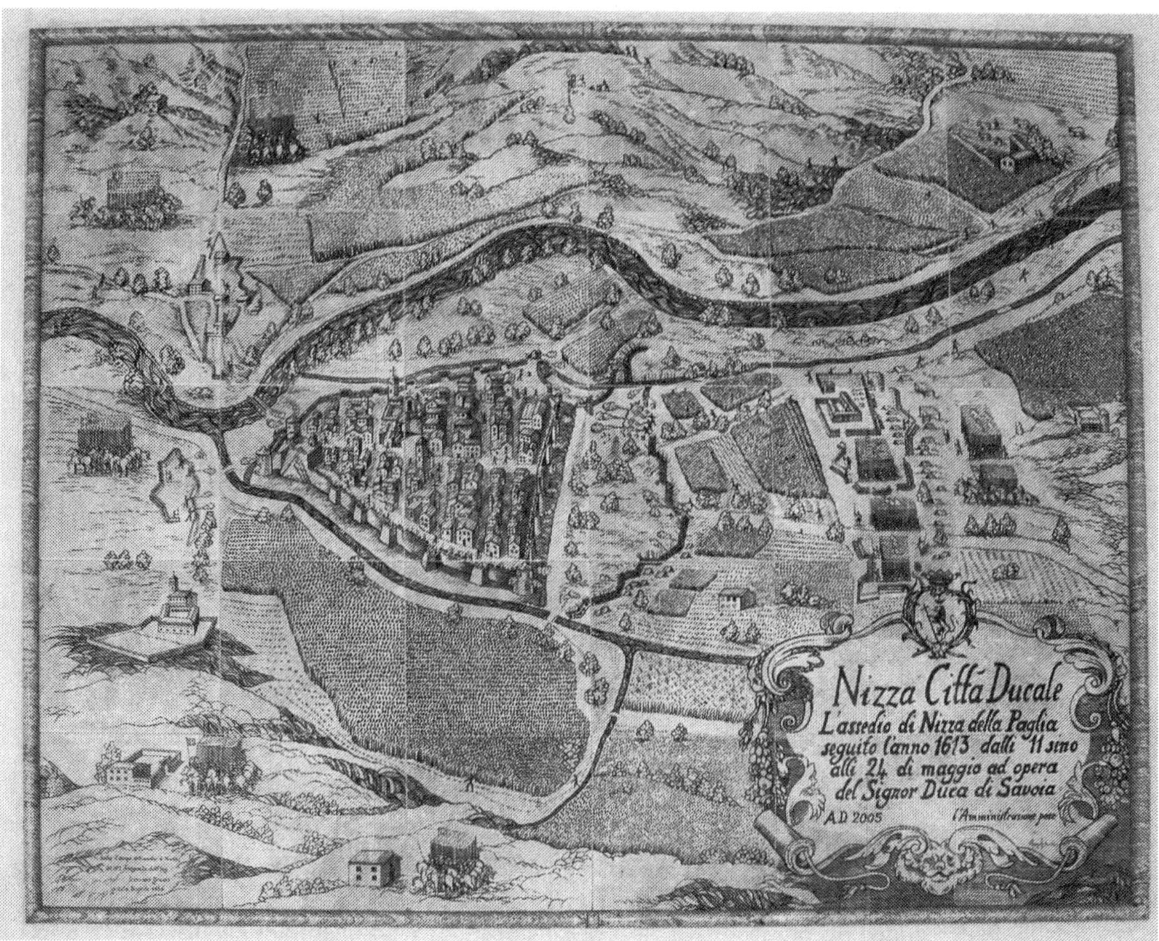

Figure 3-15
Modern copy of old map of Nizza Monferrato in early
1600s. Old Hebrew quarter was just below the fortress on
the left, near the confluence of the two rivers. This copy is
on the exterior wall of the town hall of Nizza Monferrato.

its cost from his taxes.[222] [223] One might speculate that this particular connection among Emanuele, the duke, and De Rossi had its origins in the long linkages between the Montalcini and De Rossi families, first in Rome in the Middle Ages, then in Tuscany in the 1400s, in Mantova in the 1500s, and in Piemonte in the 1600s. Finally, in 1651, Emanuele petitioned the duke for a cut in taxes, and De Rossi agreed to accept a cut in his pension as part of the deal.[224] This petition cites as reasons for needing tax relief financial losses he suffered due to the civil wars and taxes as well as the impact of old age on his capacities. After 1651, Emanuele disappeared from the historical record.[225]

The Segre in the 1600s

The descendants of Abram Segre, son of Bellavigna, continued as bankers for several generations, still operating a bank in Chieri at the end of the 1600s. In 1662, Abram's great-great-grandson, Abram, son of Salomone, shifted his residence to Casale. His brother Todros Segre branched out from banking to establish a silk manufacturing business in Racconigi, which ultimately employed eighty workers in four small factories.

The brothers Leone and Theodoro (also referred to as Deodato), the sons of Giuseppe, son of Leone, son of Bellavigna, continued the family banking business in Pinerolo, Savigliano, and Saluzzo. Deodato's family moved to Pinerolo, and was forced to leave town when that town was ceded to France in 1631—Hebrews had been banned from settling in French territory since 1394. They probably moved to Savigliano, Saluzzo, or Cuneo to live with their cousins. A 1670 census of Pinerolo revealed only one Hebrew family, an elderly widow and her five grandchildren. Leone, Theodoro's older brother, was murdered in 1612, and the family banking business was carried on in Savigliano by his sons. Giorgio's grandmother Eugenia Segre is descended from this line.

The descendants of Deodato, the third son of Leone, son of Bellavigna, who had settled in Cuneo as bankers and goldsmiths, initially prospered and for two generations were leaders of that town's Hebrew community. Unfortunately, they were caught in the French siege of that town during the civil war of the 1640s; Cuneo had sided with the Principisti against Madama Reale and her French allies. After the war, Cuneo imposed a massive tax on all its citizens to pay for its failed defense. The Hebrews argued that that as direct subjects of the duke, they could be taxed only by his government and not by the towns they lived in. There then ensued a several-decades-long lawsuit over the issue which the Hebrews ultimately lost. After it was settled in 1679, the Cuneo Segres were reduced to poverty

Luciana's Levi Ancestors in the 1600s

Luciana's great-grandfather, Israele Levi of Nizza Monferrato, was born in the period 1790–1800. He is almost certainly descended from one of two pairs of Levi brothers whose families had lived at various times in Nizza Monferrato and the nearby spa town of Acqui Terme.[226]

- One of these pairs of brothers, Abram Israele and Samuele Levi, paid taxes in Acqui in 1798 and were the sons of Giuseppe Salvador Levi, who was listed in a 1761 census of the Hebrew community of Nizza Monferrato as having a house there, but being resident at

---

[222] Segre, document 2232.

[223] De Rossi seems to have also gotten a banking charter from the duke. Apparently he was not as clever a banker as he was a musician, as he died "poor and decrepit." He was, however, succeeded in his position as court musician by two more generations of de Rossis.

[224] Segre, document 2242.

[225] The Montalcini financial business survived until the 1980s. In much of the twentieth century it operated as a securities broker-dealer, and many family members invested through it both before and after World War II. In the 1960s-1980s it was led by Giorgio's nephew Sandro Montalcini. It collapsed during the 1980s when Sandro fell victim to a massive swindle. He had supported an investor group that was attempting a hostile takeover of a major Italian company, and loaned money to members of the group that was secured by a portfolio of securities. When the loan came due and the borrowers could not repay it, a substantial portion of the collateral turned out to be worthless and/or multiply pledged. This catastrophe led to the collapse of the Montalcini firm.

[226] The evidence connecting these two families to Israel consists of the following:

    a. Nizza Monferrato had a very small community of Hebrews, numbering in 1761 only ninety-seven souls divided into twenty-one households.

    b. Of these twenty-one households, only six bore the surname Levi.

    c. Of those six, only two had sons of the right ages to potentially be Israele's father, and the given names Israele, Samuele, and Abram that repeated among Israele and his descendants.

the time in Acqui. We will refer to this Levi family as the Vercelli Levi, because their lineage traces back to a banker Giuseppe (Joseph) Levi who had a bank in that city in the late 1500s.

- The other pair of brothers, Abram Israele and Salvador Levi, were in their late teens in 1775 in Nizza Monferrato, and the sons of Salom Levi of Acqui. They appear as children under seven years old in a 1761 census of Acqui. We will refer to these Levi as the Asti Levi, because their ancestry can be traced back to Aron Levi, a banker who moved to Asti in Piemonte in the late 1500s from Lodi, in the Duchy of Milan.

In 1599 Giuseppe Levi of Pavia was granted a ten-year banking license for the city of Vercelli (northeast of Torino and near the border with the Duchy of Milan) for an initial fee of 45 lire, followed by annual installments of 8 lire.[227] His initial license fee was paid by Leone Segre. In the following decade, Giuseppe had two sons, Salomone and Moisé.

By the time of the civil war in Piemonte, Salomone Levi was a prosperous banker in Vercelli and Gattinara. In 1648, he served on a committee appointed by the Hebrew Università of Vercelli to negotiate the renewal of its charter with the town. The key provision of that charter was an exemption from service in the local militia in return for an annual fee of 6 scudi (rated at 9 florins each). Moreover, this fee was waived for the first year (1648) in recognition of the substantial loans that the Hebrews had made to the town during the civil war.[228]

In 1662, Salomone Levi was appointed to a committee of the Università of all of Piemonte to look into the issue of Abram Segre from Chieri. Abram had left town and settled in Casale Monferrato some time before. The Università sought to recover taxes that it had levied on him. The matter was settled when Abram agreed to pay 20 doubloons and hand over a deed for a credit of 350 lire owed by the town of Ferrere,[229] near Asti, on which he had been collecting interest since 1639.[230] His move to Casale was probably prompted by the excessive tax burdens that Piemonte had placed on its Hebrew community to pay for the rebuilding after the civil war of the 1640s. Casale, being foreign territory, had not been affected by the war.

In 1666, Salomone Levi and his son Isach decided to follow in Abram Segre's footsteps and decamped to Casale, prompting a great hue and cry among the members of the Università. In 1670, a committee was appointed to look into the matter, as Salomone and Isach each owed 1100 lire per year.[231]

In 1670, Isach appears in the documentary record as a grain broker of Casale, supplying 1100 sacchi of wheat to the city of Torino at a price of 67½ soldi per sacco.[232] [233] Salomone and Isach next appear in the record in the late 1600s. In 1677, when they were living in the Monferrese town of Acqui Terme, Salomone purchased a bank in Torino from Israele Moisé Levi Fubini; Isach, as Salomone's heir, sold the bank in 1693.[234]

In 1708, Acqui became Piemontese territory, along with the rest of the Monferrato, with the settlement of the War of Spanish Succession.

[227] Segre, document 1697.

[228] Segre, document 2215.

[229] My great-uncle Emanuele Montalcini (Zio Manno, the brother of Elvira Montalcini Sacerdote), who maintained a villa in Ferrere (Castel Rosso). The estate fell into the hands of the Church during World War II. The Church used it as nursing home, and it was largely ruined as a result. Our cousin Piera Levi-Montalcini has been working with the community to have the estate rehabilitated for municipal use.

[230] Segre, document 2310.

[231] Segre, document 2332.

[232] A sacco (literally a sack) was a traditional dry goods measure equivalent to approximately 115 liters or about 3.3 bushels. A soldo was a coin worth 1/20 of a lira, and the lira of the time was worth about .33 ounces of gold or about $200 in modern currency. $200/bushel sounds like a very high price for grains, which today trade for prices more like $3-$5/ bushel, but one has to remember that in the days when transport was by oxcart over very rough roads, when local crop failures caused wild fluctuations in local food prices, and all farming was by hand, food was much more expensive than today. In times of local famines, towns would contract with merchants to supply grain in bulk, and then distribute this grain to the populace, often through the bakers, and often at subsidized prices.

[233] Segre, document 2330.

[234] Segre, document 2487.

The first historical reference to the sons of Aron Levi in the 1600s suggests that they had taken up banking as well as merchant operations. In 1630, Ventura Levi took legal actions to collect unpaid loans from numerous individuals.[235] In 1648, Aron Josué[236] Levi, the minor son of Salomone and Abram Pescarolo's late daughter Richa, was named as the heir of his maternal grandfather Abram; among the assets Aron Josué inherited was a credit from the town of Asti that Pescarolo had been trying to collect since 1632.[237] In 1658, Pescarolo's estate was finally settled, with Salomone (acting on behalf of his son Aron Josué, who was still a minor) buying out the interest in the Asti credit of Pescarolo's late banking partner, Emanuele Artom, for 225 lire.[238] Salomone and Aron Josué finally reached a settlement with the town on this credit in 1663.[239]

This branch of the family then disappeared from the historical record until 1734, when Aron Josué's son Salomone appeared as a sixty-year-old father of a large family in a census of the town of Alessandria.[240] [241]

Luciana's Debenedetti Forebears in the 1600s

In the early 1600s, after considerable expansion of the banking firm of Meir Debenedetti & Sons under the leadership of Meir's son Donato, the Debenedettis' fortunes fell somewhat in the 1620s. In 1623–28 Donato sold his interest in the Nizza Monferrato branch to his Lattes cousins and focused his business energies on the town of Cherasco. By 1629, Donato was the only Debenedetti listed among the Hebrew taxpayers of Piemonte. Donato's first son, Meir, named in honor of Donato's father, was born around 1610. His other two sons, Leone and Salomone, came shortly thereafter.

In their early adulthood, the three Debenedetti brothers, Meir, Leone, and Salomone, settled in the town of Cuneo. During the civil wars of the 1640s, Cuneo sided with the minor duke's uncles and against his mother, Madama Reale. The French forces that entered Piemonte in support of Madama Reale laid siege to Cuneo for two months in 1641, and the town levied a special tax on its citizens to pay for its defense. The Hebrew community insisted that under its ducal charter they were not subject to local taxes, and refused to pay. In 1643, the town obtained a legal judgment against its Hebrews, and the Debenedetti brothers were obliged to pay two installments totaling some 618 lire.[242] The scale of this payment indicates that at least this branch of the family still sustained some level of prosperity in the mid-1600s.

A grandson of one of these three brothers, Tobia, was born around 1660/1670 and died before 1733. He seems to have left little historical record. All we know of him is from a court case in 1733.[243] He must have been a banker in Nizza Monferrato, because the case was brought by his sons, Giacobbe (Jacob) Salvador, born in 1710, and Moisé, born in 1711. The sons sought to recover a 9500 lire credit that their father had extended to the town to help it meet a general levy from the ducal government in 1691–92 to build up the army in the years leading up to the War of Spanish Succession.

[235] Segre, document 2113.

[236] Josué is an Italianization of the Hebrew name Yehoshua, which appears in English as Joshua, in pure Italian as Salvatore, and in Spanish as Salvador.

[237] Segre, documents 2223 and 2126.

[238] Segre, document 2289.

[239] Segre, document 2312.

[240] Segre, document 2841.

[241] Alessandria, a town about 25 km east of Asti, had been ceded to Piemonte as part of the settlement of the War of Spanish Succession. As a town on the border between Piemonte and the Austrian-controlled Duchy of Milan, it was an important and prosperous commercial center.

[242] Segre, documents 2193 and 2195.

[243] Segre, document 2825.

Chapter IV
The 1700s and the Establishment of the Ghettos

After the War of Spanish Succession, Italy in general, and Piemonte in particular, went into a long period of economic and cultural decline. The main locus of political and economic power in Europe shifted northward to France, England, Prussia, and Austria. Spain, which had been in decline since the early 1600s, became a dusty backwater, notwithstanding its vast empire in the Americas and elsewhere. In 1735, the Duchy of Parma fell under Austrian rule. The great Italian cultural centers of Venice and Florence also went into decline, and political control of the Grand Duchy of Tuscany passed to Austria when the last of the ruling Medici family died without an heir in 1737.

In the immediate postwar years, France's Louis XIV died in 1715 and was succeeded by his five-year-old great-grandson, Louis XV. During the regency, France was wracked with a massive inflation whose roots lay in the introduction and profligate printing of paper money in the form of government notes backed by the nonexistent tax receipts from Louisiana, the unsettled French colony on the Mississippi River,[244] as a means of repaying Louis XIV's enormous war debts.

Emperor Leopold I, who had led Austria into the War of Spanish Succession, died in 1705. He was succeeded by his sons: Joseph I ascended to the throne in 1705 and died in 1711; Joseph was succeeded by his younger brother Charles VI. Under Charles VI, Austria focused on expanding its empire eastward into the Balkans, in a series of wars against the Turks. Prince Eugenio of Savoy was Charles's primary military leader in these campaigns.

Piemonte during this period was largely a pawn in the power politics between France to its west and Austria, which controlled the Duchy of Milan, to its east. In 1733, King Augustus II of Poland died. At the time the Polish monarchy was elective, with the nobles having the right to choose the next king. The nobles selected Stanislaus Leszczyński, an ally of France. Fearing a projection of French power onto their borders, the Russians and Austrians backed Augustus's son, Augustus III, and began the War of Polish Succession against France. In 1734, the French bribed the new Piemontese king, Carlo Emanuele III, to enter the war on their side and march his troops into Lombardy. Although he captured nearly all of Lombardy, Carlo Emanuele was forced to return all this territory except for the town of Novara to Austria in 1738 by his erstwhile French allies, as part of the broader settlement of the war. The main European powers—France, England, Prussia, and Austria—had no interest in permitting Carlo Emanuele to establish an enlarged domain as a fifth major power. About all the Piemontese king got for his efforts was recognition as the most important player, albeit still in a minor role, among the Italian princelings in European power politics.

Charles VI of Austria had only one son, who died in infancy, thereby setting up his daughter Maria Theresa as his heir. In 1740, Charles died from eating [presumably poisonous] mushrooms, and was succeeded by this daughter. The Prussians and French, believing that she would be a weak monarch, seized portions of her domains, notably Silesia (in what is now Poland) and Lorraine (in what is now France), setting off the War of Austrian Succession. Spain, hoping to recover its territories in Italy, entered the war on the side of France, and England entered the war on the side of Austria as a means of countering any growth in French power. King Carlo Emanuele III of Piemonte, fearing the return of Spanish rule in Milan, and the territorial designs of the French, entered the war on the side of Austria. The war was settled in 1748 with only minor changes to prewar boundaries.[245]

---

[244] This so-called Mississippi scheme was introduced by a French finance minister of Scottish descent, John Law. Law's machinations are wonderfully described in the classic book *On Extraordinary Popular Delusions and the Madness of Crowds*, by Charles McKay. It is claimed that the near universal distrust of paper money in France dates back to the collapse of the Mississippi scheme.

[245] The main changes were that (1) Prussia got to keep Silesia, and (2) France was given Corsica, formerly a Genoese territory.

On the domestic front, in 1723, King Vittorio Amedeo II set about regularizing the administration of his domains. As they had been acquired through conquest, there were at least four different legal and administrative systems in place: in Piemonte (which had its own legal and administrative traditions), in Savoy and the Valle d'Aosta (where the legal system inherited from Charlemagne's time applied), in the Monferrato (where Mantovan law applied), and in Alessandria (where Milanese law applied). As part of this legal regularization he established laws concerning magistrates and justice, public service, health and welfare, and the like. He also sought to involve the aristocracy, who had been displaced from their feudal political powers as the Italian states consolidated, in leading roles in his administration as government ministers, magistrates, and the like. Further, he expanded his personal powers, weakening the appointive Senate and the Church and establishing an absolutist regime on the model of Louis XIV of France. As part of the realignment of relations with the papacy, he signed the Concordat of 1727, removing the ecclesiastical courts' jurisdiction over civil affairs, eliminating the right of sanctuary in churches from civil authorities, and ending whatever residual powers the Inquisition had in Piemonte.

In 1730, the king, who was in failing health, abdicated in favor of his son Carlo Emanuele III. Initially he sought to sustain his rule through his son, creating a series of crises of power that culminated in an attempt to reassume the throne. The need to act decisively came when Vittorio Amedeo II called upon Austria to intervene in these issues. At this point Carlo Emanuele had his father and stepmother arrested. Vittorio Amedeo II died the same year.

Subsequently, the young king was increasingly concerned with maintaining his absolute powers and became more and more reactionary. He saw the freethinking of the Enlightenment, a powerful force in England, France, Austria, and Germany, as a direct threat to his position and actively suppressed it in Piemonte, driving many intellectuals into exile, including Giuseppe Baretti, Giambattista Bodoni, Giuseppe Luigi Lagrange, and Vittorio Alfey.[246] In government and military affairs he reinforced the status quo by establishing a national bureaucracy and a military academy aimed at the sons of the nobility. In 1742 Carlo Emanuele III signed a treaty with the pope, the most reactionary leader in all of eighteenth-century Italy, reestablishing the Church's political and judicial primacy within his domains.

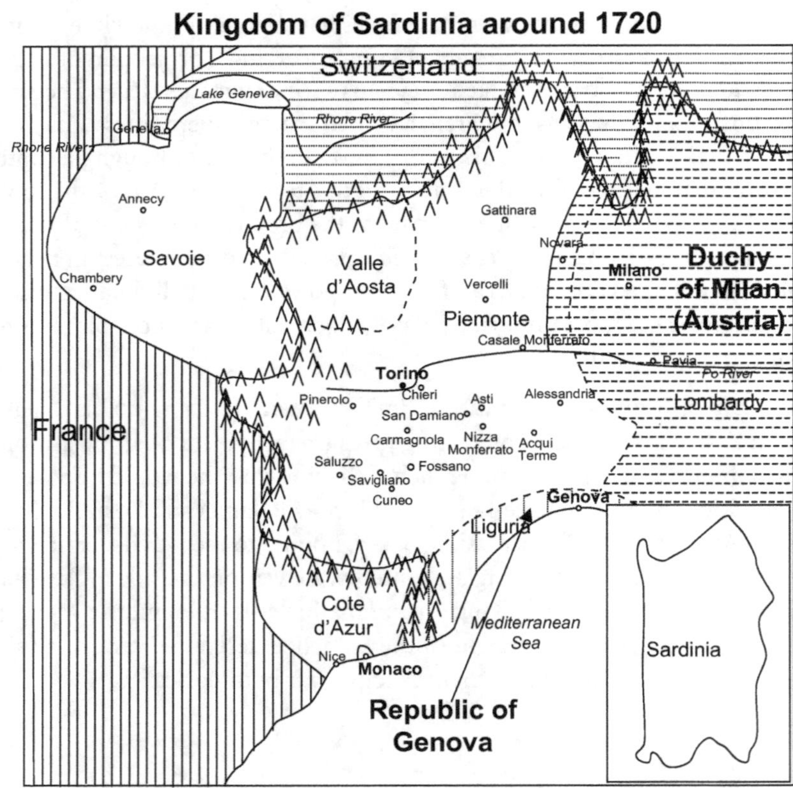

---

[246] Oliva, *I Savoia*, p. 43.

The influence of the Church was so strong during his reign that the king had ten paintings given to him by his cousin Prince Eugenio destroyed upon the command of his father confessor; the priest had determined the paintings to be immoral.

Carlo Emanuele ruled until 1773, when he was succeeded by his even more reactionary son, Vittorio Amedeo III. Vittorio Amedeo's rule was characterized by police repression of free-thinking and his cozying up even more than his father to the Church hierarchy. He imposed a very severe religiosity on the royal court. The governmental administration was jealously guarded by the same small set of noble families that had controlled it since the days of Vittorio Amedeo II.

Spread of the ghetto system across Piemonte

During the 1700s, the relations with the Hebrew community can be summed up in a single word: "ghetto." During the waning years of the reign of Vittorio Amedeo II, things began fairly simply as matters of taxation and legal administration, but deteriorated quickly.

While the rulers of Piemonte now had the grand title King of Sardinia, and a much larger territory to rule than they had had before the Spanish war, both they and that territory had been much impoverished by the war. In 1709, the king sought to raise new taxes from the Hebrews of the newly acquired Monferrato to pay his war debts. The Monferrese Università then developed a complex system apportioning these new taxes among the Hebrews in proportion to their assets. To implement this apportionment system, they enacted a set of rules on how to value various types of assets, such as new goods versus used, household goods versus goods held for resale, locally produced goods versus imports, goods for local consumption versus goods for export, trade versus banking credits, and so on—a system worthy of comparison to the U.S. Internal Revenue Code for its detail and complexity.[247]

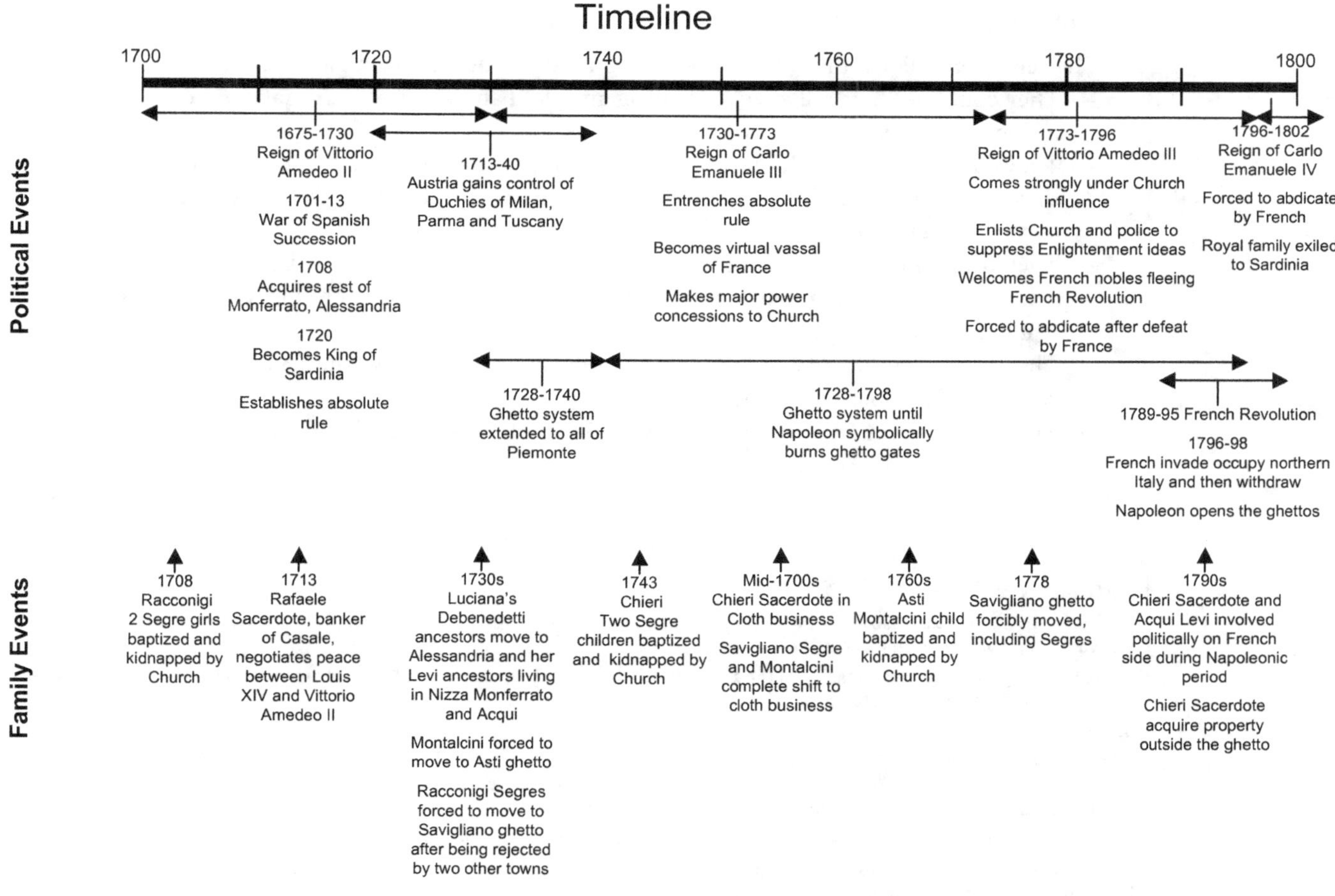

---

[247] Segre, document 2561.

This system was then extended to the other Hebrew communities in Piemonte.[248] The Hebrew communities, in true Italian fashion, became very adept at hiding their assets and income to evade these taxes. The system finally collapsed in 1730,[249] of its own complexity and the community's evasions, at the same time as Vittorio Amedeo II was succeeded by Carlo Emanuele III.

As part of the legal regularization issue discussed above, Vittorio Amedeo II sought to solve the problem that he now had four Hebrew Università—in Piemonte, Savoie, Monferrato, and Alessandria—operating under different and conflicting charters. For example, the Hebrews of Alessandria were not permitted to be bankers under the Spanish charter of 1569. The Hebrews of the Monferrato were not required to purchase a decennial permit to remain, the so-called *condotta*, which was required of the Hebrews of Piemonte. The terms of these permits were little changed since the days of Duke Emanuele Filiberto in the 1500s. Vittorio Amedeo desired to render these rules uniform under a single charter.

In 1723, His Royal Highness engaged in another step to make uniform the rules across his domains by extending the ghetto system to his entire realm, a system which until then he had applied only in Torino.[250] The Torino ghetto had been initiated by his mother, the regent when he was still a minor, in 1679. In his decree of February 20, 1723, he laid out the rules under which the Hebrews were to live in his domains:[251]

- The Hebrews were to live and work in segregated districts, walled off from their Catholic neighbors unless they received permission from the king to reside elsewhere. The gates to these communities were to be closed and locked from sundown to sunup, and all Hebrews had to be inside. The gates were not to be opened at night except in case of fire. Catholics were not allowed to live in these separate districts.

- The Hebrews could not open new synagogues, nor raise their voices to a level audible outside the ghetto during their religious ceremonies.[252]

- The Hebrews had to wear a distinctive yellow badge beginning at age fourteen, except when they were traveling.[253]

- Hebrews were subject to severe restrictions on their trades and occupations:
  — They could not buy, sell, own, or lend against gold and silver objects that had been used in Catholic religious services.
  — They could not buy gold, silver, jewels, clothing, or any other goods except from people they already knew, and they could not buy goods at significantly lower prices than were commonly available in the community.
  — They could not own real estate outside the ghetto without royal permission.
  — They could not lend money to people under fourteen years old or to older persons who still lived with their parents.[254]
  — They had to register all goods pledged as security for loans to Catholics and report it monthly at the local courthouse.[255]
  — They could not sell any goods seized for nonpayment of loans outside of Piemonte.

---

[248] See Segre, document 2368.

[249] The Hebrews, like all other Italians, proved very adept at hiding their assets and incomes from the tax collector, making the entire system unworkable. Segre, document 2783.

[250] I have long suspected that the extension of the ghetto system may have been an unwritten quid pro quo with the papacy in exchange for getting the Church to make the concessions of the Concordat of 1727.

[251] Segre, document 2637.

[252] I never understood this rule until I attended a Sukkoth service in Torino in 2005. The chanting of the prayers and hymn singing were carried out in extraordinarily loud, though not particularly melodious, voices, probably a latter-day reflection of the freedom to pray loudly that came after the emancipation from the ghettos in 1848.

[253] Curiously, when the Nazis re-imposed the wearing of the badge in the 1930s, it too was yellow.

[254] In Italy, then as now, it was customary for children to live with their parents until they married. While some women married in their late teens, it was not uncommon to see adult males still living at home at age forty; such adults would not be permitted to borrow from Hebrew bankers.

[255] This restriction was particularly onerous because of the aversion that most Italians felt, and still feel, toward incurring debt. Most borrowers would not want it known in the community that they were in debt.

— They had to publish the name and address of any borrower and a description of the goods in any case where they had to repossess an item pledged as security for a loan.[256]

— They could sell repossessed goods only at public auction in their locality and had to remit to the original owner any value received beyond the principal and interest owed.

- Hebrews who spoke ill of God, Jesus, or the saints would be subject to corporal punishment.

- The ghetto must remain closed during Holy Week, with all doors and windows facing outside the ghetto also closed. Nor could the inhabitants dance or make sounds that could be heard outside the ghetto during this time.

- Adult Hebrews could not be baptized against their will, nor children against the will of their parents.[257] Neither could they be harmed in word or deed by others.

- Hebrews could not converse with those formerly of their faith who had converted to Catholicism. Further, any Hebrew who converted to Catholicism and who later returned to his ancestral faith would be subject to severe penalties.

- Hebrews who had converted could not be denied their inheritances.

- Catholics were not permitted to live with Hebrews, buy anything from them on Sunday, or work for them in any way that would require them to spend a night under their roofs.

These rules were strengthened in 1729.[258]

The transition to the ghetto communities caused varying levels of dislocation. In communities where most of the Hebrews already lived near each other, the transition was reasonably straightforward.[259] All that was needed was to enclose that community with a wall and gates, at the Hebrews' expense. In other cases, the location of the ghetto turned into a serious local political issue.[260] For example, ecclesiastical authorities would object to the ghetto's being located near churches or on main streets where Catholic religious processions might pass by on holy days.[261] Catholic commercial interests often wanted the ghetto located away from the business district or central market to cut down on competition.[262] Some landlords actively sought to have the ghetto located in buildings they owned, as a way to assure themselves of a steady rental stream. Other landlords sought to avoid being saddled with the ghetto because its rents were fixed for its duration. Of course, Hebrews living in small outlying towns, such as the Segres of Racconigi and the Montalcini of San Damiano d'Asti, or in parts of town far from the ghetto, were forced to move to the ghettos.[263] In a few cases, Hebrews were permitted to keep houses or workshops outside the ghetto.[264] In some communities, the ghettos were set up immediately, while in others it took a decade or more before the Hebrew community was resettled.

Community	Ghetto Established
Torino	1679
Chieri, Ivrea, Fossano, Mondovi, Asti, Carmagnola	1724
Acqui Terme	1731
Nizza Monferrato	1733
Alessandria	1739
Vercelli	1740
Casale Monferrato	1741–42

[256] See the previous note.

[257] These rules were repeatedly violated, as the king was generally powerless to prevent such actions by Church officials.

[258] Segre, document 2774.

[259] Segre, document 2703A.

[260] The location of the ghetto of Casale Monferrato became particularly involved politically. See Segre, document 2812.

[261] Segre, document 2681.

[262] Segre, documents 2663, 2664, 2679.

[263] Segre, documents 2662, 2691, 2696-97, and 2876.

[264] Segre, documents 2719 and 2753.

The establishment of the ghettos gives a brief glimpse into the daily lives of the Piemontese Hebrew communities. For example, in 1731 the town council in Casale Monferrato surveyed the living arrangements of its Hebrew community in order to assess the suitability of various sites as possible ghettos.[265] This survey revealed that the community had 754 individuals in 134 households. They were housed in 554 rooms and had 339 workrooms, shops, and storerooms. In addition, six rooms were reserved for the synagogue, school, ritual bathhouse, and other public uses. Further analysis shows that 207 people in the 44 best-off households occupied living quarters with one or fewer persons per room. Those living with one or two people per room comprised 257 individuals in 45 households, while the remaining 46 households containing 280 people lived with three or more individuals per room, with a handful of families living with eight or nine people per room.

In 1734, the town completed a second, more detailed census of its Hebrew community which gives many details of its socioeconomic makeup.[266] Of the 137 households in which the head of household's occupation is given:

- Twenty-seven had professional occupations that required material fiscal and/or intellectual capital, such as banker, merchant, manufacturer, manager of a substantial enterprise, or "living from rents."
- Fifty-two had middle-class occupations, such as retail storekeeper, innkeeper, or teacher, or were skilled tradesmen such as hatters, weavers, or tailors.
- Fifty were unskilled laborers or live-out servants.
- Eight were poor and living on charity.

About half the population were children under the age of twenty-one. Of these, the three-year age cohorts of 4–6, 7–9, 10–12, 13–15, and 16–18 all had roughly equal populations averaging forty-three children, while the 0–3 cohort comprised seventy-six, which suggests that the majority of children died before reaching age three.

Eighteen households had live-in servants, with four of those households having two servants and two households having three servants. Of those eighteen households with live-in servants, twelve were professional-class households, while the other six were those of prosperous retail shopkeepers. Interestingly, the prosperous shopkeepers employed fifteen of the twenty-six servants.

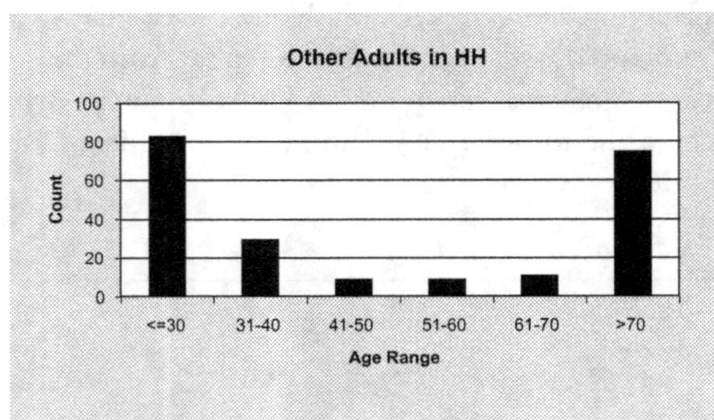

Seventy-three of the households had 148 non-head-of-household adults living in them. The majority of these were elderly parents up to age ninety-one and the householder's adult children under thirty. Others included brothers and sisters of the head of household and, in a few cases, the spouses and children of their adult children. See the adjacent age distribution.

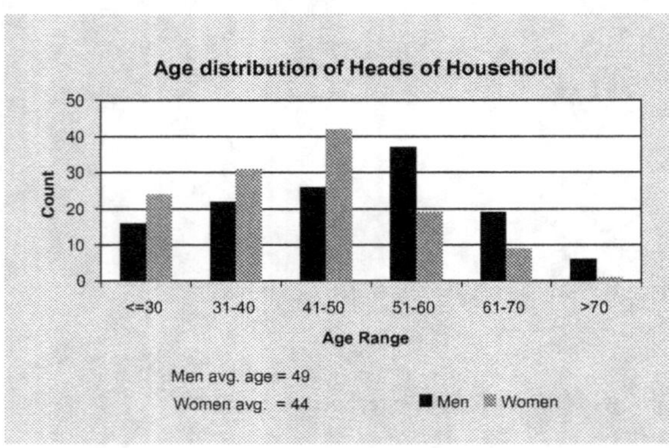

The heads of households ranged in age from nineteen to seventy-five, with the majority in the 40–60 range; see the adjacent distribution. We found sixteen headed by a single man and another sixteen headed by a single woman. Of those headed by a single woman, most appeared to be widows; only one was listed as "abandoned by her husband" (divorce was illegal in Italy until the 1970s) and the husbands of three others were "merchants in the field," merchants who were away on business.

[265] Segre, document 2808.

[266] Segre, document 2843.

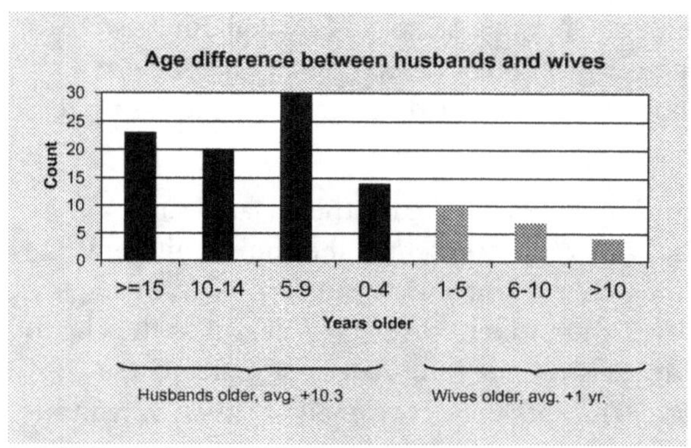

Men generally married women younger than themselves, with an average age difference of 10.3 years. However, in 21 out of 108 households headed by married couples, the wives were older than their husbands.

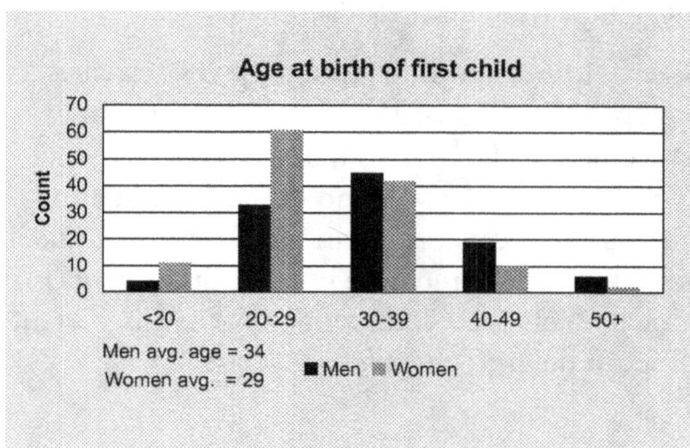

Finally, men generally did not have their first child until they were in their mid-thirties, while women most often had their first child when they were in their twenties. These figures are based on the age of the oldest child living at home, and ignore older emancipated children or firstborn children dying in infancy; the impact of both of these assumptions is to raise the apparent ages of parents at the birth of their first child.

One of the problems of the ghettos is that they were of fixed size, notwithstanding the considerable growth of the population of Piemonte and its Hebrew communities in the eighteenth century. Segre's documents include a few cases in which additional buildings were added to a ghetto after it was established to relieve excessive overcrowding. For example, in 1787, the king agreed to permit the expansion of the Vercelli ghetto to accommodate the needs of the four Sacerdote brothers of that city. In many other cases, petitions to expand the ghettos were denied. For example, in 1797, several Hebrews in the Torino ghetto petitioned to expand the ghetto to accommodate their growing silk manufacturing businesses and the need for new apartments for residents who were getting married and wanted apartments of their own. This petition was opposed by the local chief of police and the state attorney general and was denied.[267]

Three continuing issues in the ghettos were the forced baptisms of children without their parents' consent, the parallel demand that Hebrews be required to attend the baptisms of any of their brethren who abandoned their ancestral faith, and Church requirements that Hebrews attend Church sermons aimed at their conversion. Segre's documents contain numerous other examples of these abuses of the protections guaranteed by royal decree that the king was unable or unwilling to enforce upon the ecclesiastical authorities.

The Sacerdote Family in Chieri during the Ghetto Century

The issues of the ghetto system affected all five of the families we have been following. When we last discussed the brothers Giacobbe and Samuele Sacerdote of Chieri, they were substantial investors, along with Davide Levi, in the brief period between the end of the War of Spanish Succession and the creation of the Chieri ghetto in 1724. The Sacerdote brothers evidently continued the family business of making and trading in cloth: Samuele and his brothers were listed as merchants in a 1728 judgment.[268] In 1740 Samuele was prohibited from improving his lodgings by adding another building to the Chieri ghetto.[269] In the same year, Samuele was elected to the executive committee of the Università degli Ebrei

---

[267] Segre, document 3457.

[268] Segre, document 2761.

[269] Segre, document 2940.

di Piemonte.[270] In 1743 the Sacerdote brothers, Davide Levi, Giuseppe Segre, and several others were fined 75 lire each for renting houses and workshops in areas prohibited to Hebrews.[271] Samuele, who was born in the 1660s, and his younger brother Giacobbe presumably died shortly thereafter, as there is no further documentary reference to them.

The next Sacerdotes to appear in the documentary record of Chieri are the brothers Davide and Emanuele Sacerdote,[272] who were born around 1720. In 1740, they represented the community of Chieri at a national meeting of the Università in Torino.[273] They were evidently merchants: In 1747, during the War of Austrian Succession, they received municipal permission to rent property adjacent to the ghetto in which to store hay they were supplying to Colonel Monseigneur de Montfort's regiment. These French soldiers were stationed in Chieri during the war.[274] In 1755, the city council of Chieri voted to recompense Davide for the furniture that he had either loaned or rented to Monfort in 1747, and that was returned broken.[275] Emanuele lived until about 1790, and Davide until 1810.

Davide Sacerdote had at least one son, Giuseppe Vita Sacerdote, born in 1759, whom Treves describes as an important manufacturer of silk, as his ancestors had been.[276] Giuseppe Vita was so prominent as a silk manufacturer that he was known as Giuseppe or Sacerdote della Seta.[277] Emanuele Sacerdote had at least three sons, Leone Raffaele (b. 1751), Giacobbe, and Moisé. At the very end of the first ghetto period, in 1796, shortly after the 1790 death of their father, they successfully petitioned the town council to permit the addition of another building to the ghetto so that they could have separate apartments for their respective families.[278] Giuseppe and his cousin Leone Raffaele Sacerdote went on to play important political roles during the Napoleonic period, as we shall see in the next chapter.

The Montalcini in the 1700s

With the establishment of the ghettos, the Montalcini, who had lived in San Damiano d'Asti for several generations, were forced to move to Asti, the nearest town with a ghetto. There the family made the transition from banking to commerce. Emanuele Montalcini had been a substantial banker in the early-to-mid-1600s, and this occupation was carried on to lesser degree by his son Elia (active to the 1720s) and nephew Emanuele (active in the early 1700s).

My aunt Eugenia recalled the following story from Montalcini family lore concerning this period. One evening a well-dressed gentleman approached a Montalcini banker, seeking a short-term loan to cover his losses at the gambling tables. When asked what collateral he could offer, the gentleman drew a heavy, finely worked silver box from his sack. The banker examined the box, and decided that it had sufficient value to serve as collateral. Several days later, as Montalcini was walking about the town, he noticed the maids at a great palace hanging out a rug to air on the railing of a balcony. On the rug was a coat of arms matching that on the silver box, from which he concluded that the box must have originated from the palace. Using the box as a calling card, he paid a visit on the countess who was the lady of the house. She immediately recognized the box as belonging to her husband and, upon hearing the story of how the box came into the banker's possession, realized that her secret lover had stolen it from her house. If the story got back to the count, her dalliances would be exposed. She then asked the banker his price to return the box. He replied that all he required was that the principal on the loan be repaid, with a kiss from her for interest. When she paid the interest, he announced that he had just experienced the first kiss between a noblewoman and a Hebrew in two hundred years.

---

[270] Segre, document 2926.

[271] Segre, documents 2975 and 2977.

[272] Davide and Emanuele were presumably the sons of either Samuele or Giacobbe, most likely the latter, since Emanuele had both a son and grandson named Giacobbe.

[273] Segre, document 2926.

[274] Segre, document 3017.

[275] Segre, document 3099.

[276] Treves, p. 168.

[277] Treves, p. 168; *seta* is Italian for silk.

[278] Segre, document 3445.

Sometime in the next two generations, the Montalcini became merchants in addition to bankers. The next recorded link in the family is in 1736, when Moisé Montalcini (1710–61) married Lea (or Dea in some documents) Tedeschi, the daughter of Samuele Tedeschi of Venice.[279] [280] That year of birth would be consistent with his being a grandson or great-grandson of Emanuele. The leader of the next generation, Moisé Montalcini was a merchant importing and trading in woolen cloth. According to the 1761 census[281] of the ghetto of Asti, Lea was already widowed (her husband had died earlier that year) and listed as a merchant and the mother of five children: Samuele, Salvador Vita, Emilio, Abram, and Rosa. She must have taken over the business from her late husband. This family was also touched by a forced baptism of a kidnapped child. Moisé and Lea's youngest son, Abram, born in 1760, was seized from his family at a tender age and was baptized. He eventually became a Catholic priest in Torino under the name Don Giuseppe Lamberti.

In the 1761 census, Moisé and Lea's oldest son, Samuele Montalcini, was listed as a merchant. Later he extended the business into the town of Vercelli, where his wife, Gentile Segre, had been born. Under Samuele's guidance, the business grew to such an extent that by 1782, Samuele was paying by far the largest annual customs tax of the Hebrew cloth merchants in Piemonte, over 144 lire per annum.[282]

The Segre in the 1700s

Even before the ghetto period, a number of the Segre families had begun the shift from a single-minded focus on banking into other lines of endeavor. Todros Segre of Racconigi was a highly successful manufacturer of silk cloth, employing eighty workers in four small factories. The Cuneo Segres had become goldsmiths in the early 1600s, and continued that line of work for several generations. The Savigliano Segres continued the banking tradition the longest, but by the mid-to-late 1700s, they, too, had shifted their attention, entering wholesale trade, especially of woolen cloth.

Several branches of the Segre family suffered from the dislocations and abuses of the ghetto period. The descendants of Todros Segre of Racconigi were forced to leave that community, but it took nearly ten years to determine where they would be forced to move. Each of the proposed communities (Carmagnola, Savigliano, and Saluzzo) rejected the idea that they be absorbed into the local ghetto. Those small ghettos, with roughly 100 inhabitants each, were already crowded, and Todros's children, grandchildren, and their spouses totaled more than a dozen people. Finally, after ten years of wrangling, they ended up in Carmagnola after the town agreed to add a building to the ghetto to accommodate the Racconigi Segres. Much later, in 1778, the Segres of Savigliano, together with all the other Hebrew residents, were forced to move house when the city decided to relocate the ghetto.

The Segres of Savigliano epitomized the crowded conditions of the ghettos. In 1791, a Segre family in Savigliano petitioned to add a building to the ghetto as seven adult brothers and three of their wives were all forced to live together in two damp, insalubrious rooms. They offered to pay the heavily in-debted owner five times the normal rent for such a building and also to lend her 3000 lire to enable her to refinance her existing debts. These figures mean that the family was well off, and that their dreadful living conditions were due solely to lack of adequate space in the ghetto. The new building was added to the ghetto in 1793, after another of the brothers also married. In 1796, three of the Segre brothers purchased the building.[283] This family is almost certainly the family of Elvira's ancestor Israele Segre and his brother Isacco, as their family structure corresponds to the family of Israele Segre family in the Torino census of 1802.

[279] Montalcini family genealogy from Emanuele and Giuliano Montalcini.

[280] In Segre, document 2841, Lea Tedeschi is listed as the seventeen-year-old daughter of the Venice-born Rabbi Samuele Tedeschi of Alessandria.

[281] Segre, document 3151.

[282] Segre, document 3323. The second largest taxpayer paid 89 lire, and the median payment among the thirty-seven importers was under 20 lire.

[283] Segre, documents 3376, 3404, 3406, 3411, 3414, 3442.

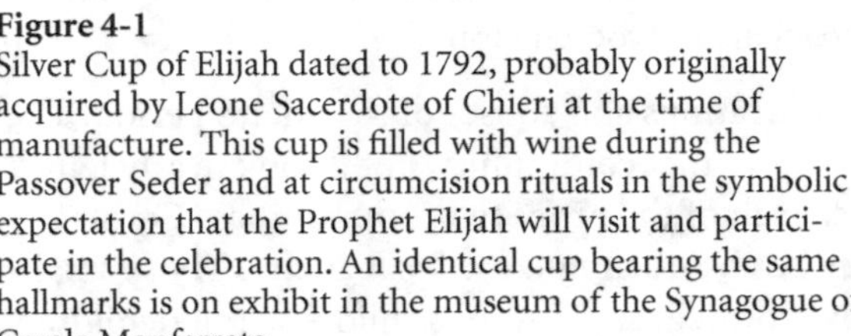

Figure 4-1
Silver Cup of Elijah dated to 1792, probably originally acquired by Leone Sacerdote of Chieri at the time of manufacture. This cup is filled with wine during the Passover Seder and at circumcision rituals in the symbolic expectation that the Prophet Elijah will visit and participate in the celebration. An identical cup bearing the same hallmarks is on exhibit in the museum of the Synagogue of Casale Monferrato.

Figure 4-2
Ornate Baroque *bima* [reader's platform] and *aron ha
kodesh* [holy ark] from former Chieri synagogue. These
came into the possession of the Sacerdote family when the
Chieri synagogue ceased to function and were donated in
the late 1930s to the Torino synagogue. In 1972, when the
Torino synagogue built a chapel in its basement for daily
services, these furnishings were reassembled and are now
in regular use. This is from a postcard from the synagogue
shop.

Figure 4-3
A second view of the Chieri synagogue furnishings in
the Torino synagogue. This is from a postcard from the
synagogue shop.

Figure 4-4
Façade of the former Torino ghetto facing Piazza
Carlo Aberto. Elvira's Segre forbears moved here from
Savigliano at the end of the 1700s. Photograph, 2005 by
George S. Sacerdote.

Figure 4-5
Gates to the former Torino ghetto. These gates were
locked every night at sundown and all residents had to be
inside. Those caught outside were subject to substantial
penalties. Photograph, 2005 by George S. Sacerdote.

The Segres were also afflicted with forced conversions of at least four kidnapped children. Even before the organization of the ghettos outside of Torino, two of Todros Segre's granddaughters, Stella and Rachele, ages eight and seven, were seized in 1708 in Racconigi and cut off from all contact with their parents after a disgruntled maid claimed that she had baptized them. In 1745 two children of the Chieri Segres, Bella and Beniamino, ages seven and six, were seized from their homes by the Church authorities, baptized, and kept from seeing or communicating with their families. In both cases, the families appealed to the king to have their children restored to them, and in both cases, the canonical courts held that the seizures were permissible and the king was unwilling to confront the Church with its open violations of the royal edicts that guaranteed Hebrews that their children would not be baptized without their parents' consent.

Luciana's Levi forebears during the 1700s

The Vercelli Levi who had moved to the Monferrato in the 1660s ultimately ended up in Acqui Terme in the 1690s and Nizza Monferrato by the 1730s. Salomone Levi, son of Giuseppe, found himself the impoverished head of household in Nizza in 1734, unable to pay the salt tax of 5 lire. Since his allocation was the smallest possible, he probably had only recently married and had no children.[284] Indeed, there is no further mention of this wife or any children. Nonetheless, his fortunes seem to have improved, since by 1740, the town was considering requisitioning a house he owned for use as a charity hospice.[285] Presumably this house was outside the ghetto. All through the 1740s he was paying annual taxes in the range of 39-44 lire.[286] Around 1750 he remarried, this time marrying a daughter of the wealthy banker Giuseppe Salvador Ottolenghi from Acqui, and moved to that town. He was listed as paying taxes in Acqui in 1753 and 1755.[287] In 1756 he dealt in silk cocoons and by 1761 he and his second wife had two sons and a daughter.[288] Sometime between 1761 and 1775, Salomone died, leaving minor sons who were living in his former house in Nizza Monferrato. We know that in 1775 their grandfather, Giuseppe Ottolenghi,[289] was their guardian and had to defend their property rights in Nizza against encroachments by the Debenedetti family.[290]

The Asti Levi appear to have fallen on somewhat harder times during the ghetto period. Of the seven children of Salomone listed in the 1734 census,[291] only two sons, Anselmo Grattiadio and Giuseppe, ever married. Anselmo remained in Asti as a dealer in used clothing. He lived there in a household with his three daughters, his brother Beniamino, and three unmarried sisters.[292] Giuseppe moved to Nizza Monferrato, presumably to marry, and brought his unmarried sister Enrica to live with him. The Hebrew community of Nizza Monferrato had become quite poor during the ghetto period. In later life, Giuseppe moved to the nearby town of Acqui.[293] His two sons, Abram Israele and Samuele, while sufficiently well off to pay taxes in that town in 1798, were paying at the lowest levels in that town's Hebrew ghetto.[294]

---

[284] Segre, document 2849.

[285] Segre, document 2934.

[286] Segre, documents 2973, 2991, 3009, and 3046.

[287] Segre, document 3105.

[288] Segre, documents 2108 and 3144.

[289] Giuseppe Ottolenghi went on to have an illustrious career as banker and politician. His political career during the time of Napoleon is detailed on his tombstone in the Acqui cemetery. He lived until 1820. See Figure 5-7.

[290] Segre, document 3277.

[291] Segre, document 2841.

[292] Segre, documents 3082 and 3155.

[293] Segre, document 3147.

[294] Segre, document 3466.

The 1700s for Luciana's Debenedetti ancestors

During the ghetto period, Tobia Debenedetti's sons (from Nizza Monferrato) shifted their principal business activities away from banking. Giacobbe Salvador gained control of the lottery concession of the district around Nizza Monferrato through David Pavia of Alessandria, overall concessionaire of the lottery for Piemonte.[295] Subsequently he moved to Alessandria as personal assistant to Pavia's son Salomone, a wealthy merchant.

Giacobbe Salvador's brother Moisé moved to Alessandria in 1735, and he was married there, becoming a prosperous cloth merchant. In 1754 his household consisted of himself, his wife, their four children (Tobia, Giuseppe Vita, Stella, and Diamante), his wife's seventy-year-old uncle Sanson Amar, and two live-in servants. By 1762 his household had grown to include a fifth child, Susanna. The next year, his son Tobia married Allegra Vitale della Torre, the daughter of a very wealthy merchant, Raffaele Vitale della Torre, and his wife, Benedetta. After they had been married for a year, Tobia and Allegra successfully sued his parents to gain control of her substantial dowry. Sabato Debenedetti, Luciana's great-grandfather, was the grandson of either Tobia or Giuseppe Vita (Giacobbe Salvador's only child was a daughter); moreover, the evidence points toward Tobia, since Sabato's oldest daughter was named Benedetta.

[295] Segre, document 2964.

Figure 5-1

Two pages from a Sacerdote family Haggadah illustrating the ten plagues that God brought upon the Egyptians: 1. Blood, 2. Frogs, 3. Lice, 4. Various Beasts (Note: ערוב was mistranslated into Italian as *Miscuglio d' Insetti* [Various Insects], although the illustration correctly shows people being attacked by lions and other predators), 5. Death of Livestock, 6. Scabies, 7. Hail, 8. Locusts, 9. Darkness, and 10. Slaying of the First-Born.

This particular volume is richly illustrated with woodcuts depicting various biblical stories connected with Abraham, Isaac, Jacob and their families, the tales associated with 400 years of slavery under the Egyptians, the Exodus, and elements of the Passover ritual. This Haggadah was published in Livorno (Leghorn) in the late 1800s. The book bears a signature of Clotilde Sacerdote, Alberto's older sister, dated 1903 and had probably been acquired some time before that.

Livorno had been established as a free port city by the Florentine government in the 1400s and quickly attracted a substantial Hebrew population. It became a center for the printing of Hebrew books. Livorno's Hebrew community was never subjected to the ghetto system, uniquely in Italy.

Chapter V
The Two Emancipations: From Napoleon to 1848

Through the 1700s, Piemonte had become increasingly a backwater both culturally and politically. The French Revolution caused a series of shocks in that small kingdom. Shortly after the fall of the Bastille in Paris in 1789, there was a large influx of French nobles into Torino seeking refuge from the developing catastrophe in France. While these newcomers were just as politically reactionary as Vittorio Amedeo III, they also engaged in the licentious personal behavior that was characteristic of the French royal court, much to the shock of the staid Piemontesi and their stolid king. Piemonte, with its king who preferred going to church to partying, was unprepared for such goings-on. Further, the haughty French aristocrats were openly disdainful of their country-mouse hosts, further upsetting the Piemontesi. While the French were initially welcomed to Torino by the king, they soon wore out their welcome. Nonetheless, that initial welcome had fateful consequences for the royal House of Savoy.

The Revolutionary government in France was equally upset by the goings-on in Piemonte and determined to punish that kingdom for harboring so many people that it viewed as counter-revolutionaries. Piemonte's joining with the other European monarchies to launch an invasion of France to try to reverse the revolution was the final straw. On September 22, 1792, a French army under the leadership of General Montesquiou invaded the Piemontese territories in Savoie, on the western side of the Alps. To counter this invasion, king sent an army under eighty-year-old General De Lazary, a scion of one of the oldest noble families of the kingdom. De Lazary's only battlefield experience had occurred during the reign of Carlo Emanuele III, more than forty years earlier. Faced with the French army, General De Lazary's army promptly melted away without firing a shot, and by the end of the month all of these Piemontese territories were under French Revolutionary control.

Vittorio Amedeo III then spread his troops along the crest of the Alps to keep the French from crossing. In the spring of 1796, the then unknown General Napoleon Bonaparte invaded the Republic of Genoa to Piemonte's south in coastal Liguria. From there he marched northward across the hilly border, thereby evading the Piemontese troops blocking the high Alpine passes. Within a few weeks Napoleon occupied two-thirds of the mainland Piemontese territory and imposed the Armistice of Cherasco on the king. From there he went on to take control of the Austrian territories in Italy (the duchies of Milan, Tuscany and Parma), the Venetian Republic, and the Papal States.

In October of that year, Vittorio Amedeo III died suddenly of apoplexy and was succeeded by his even weaker son, Carlo Emanuele IV. While the Piemontese ambassadors were in Paris negotiating a peace treaty, the new king's army and police were rounding up and sending to the firing squad intellectuals, freethinkers, republicans, and anyone else whose leadership might represent a threat to his throne. The French Directory decided that it had little use for the small reactionary buffer state of Piemonte, and in 1798 took over the rest of mainland Piemonte, sending the king into exile on Sardinia. In the century that Carlo Emanuele IV and his ancestors had held the title of King of Sardinia, he was the first to set foot on that impoverished island. In 1802, Carlo Emanuele IV abdicated and took holy orders. He was succeeded by his brother Vittorio Emanuele I.

Piemonte became Napoleon's base for his efforts to expand his empire eastward and southward. From there he launched his effort to wrest control of Egypt from the Turks and their British allies. When Napoleon was defeated in Egypt by the English in 1799, he fled back across the Alps, leaving a large amount of Egyptian antiquities in Torino. This collection became the base of the collection now housed in Torino's Egyptology Museum, one of the foremost such collections in the world. He reentered Piemonte in 1800 as the first step in taking full control of most of Italy. He drove the Austrians out of the duchies of Milan, Parma, and Tuscany a second time[296] in the same year, defeating them at Marengo, and added those territories to his possessions of Piemonte and Venice. He crowned himself King of Italy in 1805.

Wherever Napoleon conquered, the liberal ideas of the French Revolution followed. The middle classes and peasantry assumed new roles. When his arrival was impending, there would typically be a great deal of unrest in a town as the pro- and anti-French political factions fought it out.

In April 1814, Napoleon was defeated and exiled to the isle of Elba off the Tuscan coast. One month later, Vittorio Emanuele I landed in Genova and made his way back to Torino to re-assume the family throne after twelve years of exile. During 1814–15, the crowned heads of Europe met in Vienna to undo what Napoleon had done. They restored most of the monarchies to more or less their former boundaries, and tried to reestablish some level of military and political balance in Europe. In a few cases, smaller countries such as the Republics of Venice and Genoa were absorbed by their larger neighbors (in these two cases, Austria and Piemonte, respectively).

In continental Europe the period from 1815 to 1848 was marked by very reactionary politics and attempts to stamp out all of the liberal thinking that the French had spread during the twenty years following their revolution. Kings reasserted their absolute governance rights. The nobles reasserted their privileges at the expense of the bourgeois and peasant classes. During this period, many countries developed effective secret police forces which were explicitly chartered to capture and punish liberal thinkers. Periodically there were uprisings against these reactionary initiatives, notably in 1830 in France, Poland, and Hungary, but these were generally put down quite forcefully

In Piemonte, Vittorio Emanuele I immediately set forth decrees abolishing all the changes brought about during the Napoleonic period. Military officers, civil servants, and university professors from the bourgeoisie were replaced by members of the old noble families. All the old rights of the nobility were

Kingdom of Sardinia around 1805

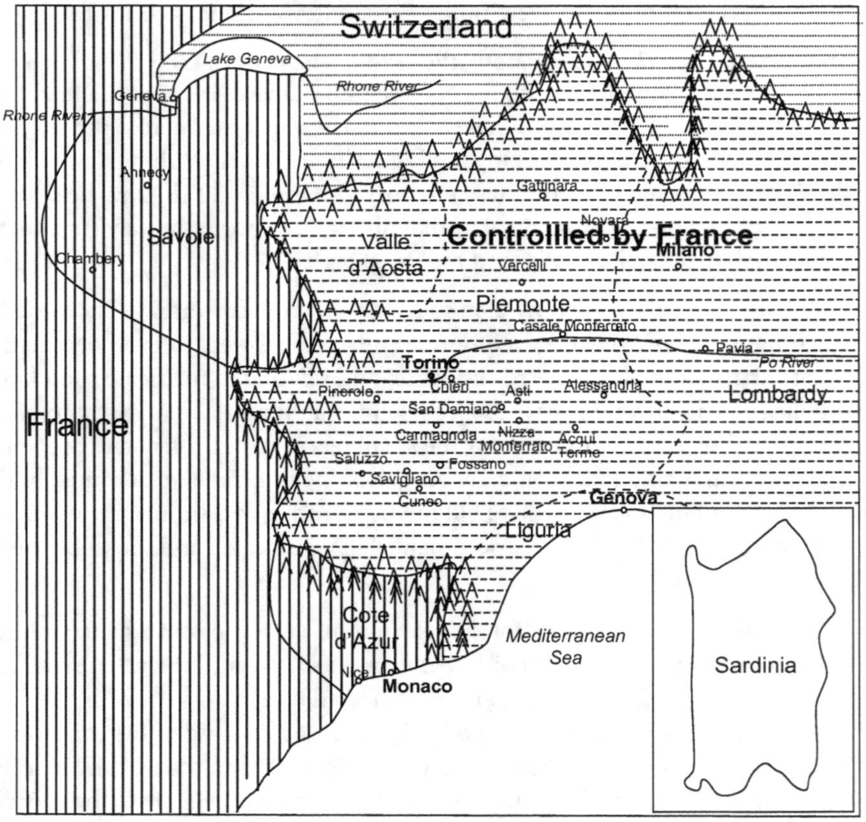

[296] The Austrians had reoccupied them after Napoleon's 1799 retreat across the Alps.

reinstated, and all rights decreed by the French administration were declared null and void. He also reestablished the Church's primacy after twenty years of anticlerical French rule. Faced with a rising crime rate from bands of brigands that formed during the collapse of French rule, the king established the Carabinieri, a type of militarized police, to restore order. They were soon charged with hunting down subversives.

In 1821, four students were arrested and charged as subversives. In reaction, the students from the University of Torino demonstrated in favor of their historical protection from state intervention in academic affairs. The government's response to the demonstration was to order a military crackdown in which thirty-five students were stabbed with bayonets. The resulting public outrage led to a mutiny of several units of the Piemontese army, and Vittorio Emanuele I was forced to abdicate in favor of his brother Carlo Felice.

Carlo Felice was out of the country at the time of his brother's abdication. Given that he was forced out by a military insurrection, Vittorio Emanuele was afraid of leaving the country leaderless. Therefore he named as regent Carlo Alberto of the Carignano branch of the Savoy family.[297] Carlo Alberto, who had been raised in the liberal tradition of the Enlightenment, immediately saw to it that the injured students received medical care, and personally visited them in the hospital. Further, he conceded a democratic constitution, much to the horror of the government officials left over from Vittorio Emanuele's

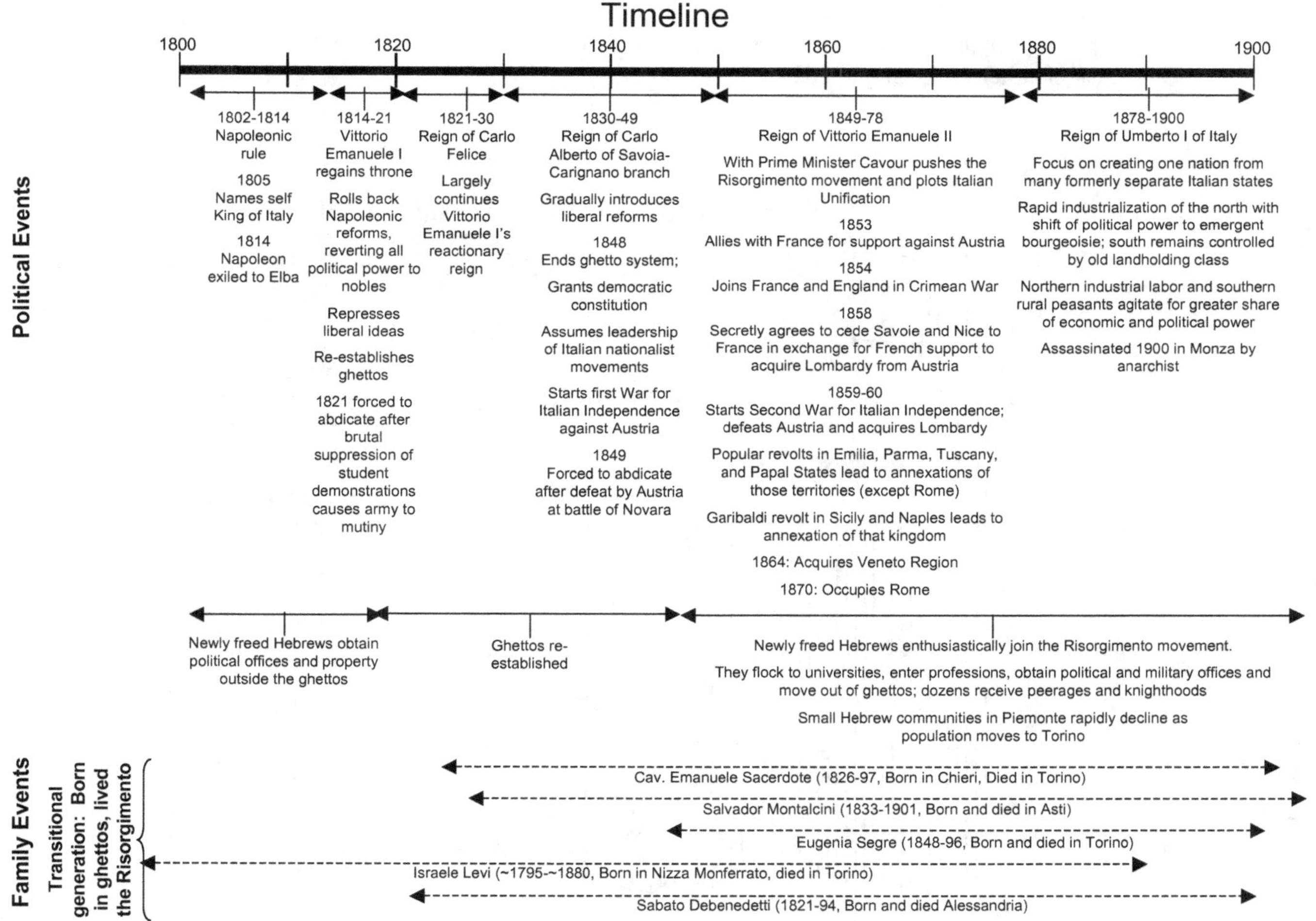

---

[297] The brothers Carlo Emanuele IV, Vittorio Emanuele I, and Carlo Felice were all without surviving sons, and so provided no dynastic continuity. Thus the next in line to the throne was Carlo Alberto of the Carignano branch of the Savoy family, born in 1798. This eventuality had been foreseen by the Congress of Vienna, and Carlo Alberto was named at that time as the legitimate heir to follow Carlo Felice. The Carrignano line descended from Tomasso, brother of Vittorio Amedeo I, who had led the losing side in the civil wars of the 1640s against Vittorio Amedeo's wife for control of the regency of Carlo Emanuele II. Prince Eugenio was also a member of this line; he died without legitimate issue in the mid-1700s.

reign. That constitution was immediately set aside when Carlo Felice arrived and took control of the government. He ruled for ten years, until his death in 1831. His policies were largely continuations of his brothers' reactionary approaches to government.

At age thirty-three, Carlo Alberto became king. During the ten years of Carlo Felice's reign, he had sought to rehabilitate himself in the eyes of the Piemontese establishment by swearing in 1823 never to concede another constitution and by participating in reactionary movements, such as the effort to crush the Spanish revolts of the 1820s. Nonetheless, upon assuming the throne, he brought the first new ideas to the Piemontese monarchy in a full century. His mother had Protestant sympathies, and he himself was a deist. Through his mother he had had a liberal education dominated by Enlightenment ideas, notwithstanding the efforts of Vittorio Emanuele I and his brothers to cleanse him of such "foolish" notions by surrounding him with tutors from the most backward-facing elements of the Church and the military.

Initially, Carlo Alberto sought to placate the Piemontese establishment by maintaining the policies of his predecessors, including sanctioning repressive police-state tactics and granting the Church a great deal of control over the educational system. However, beginning in the mid-1830s, Carlo Alberto began to abolish the ancient privileges of the nobles and the requirements that the peasants supply free services to them. He began to encourage commerce and manufactures with the construction of canals and other public works. During this period the first awakenings of the liberal thinking of the Risorgimento began to be felt in his government, and this movement continued to gather strength in the 1840s. In 1847 Carlo Alberto reformed the penal system to eliminate many of the abuses perpetrated by it and established freedom of the press. Later that year he convened a congress to consider other political reforms.

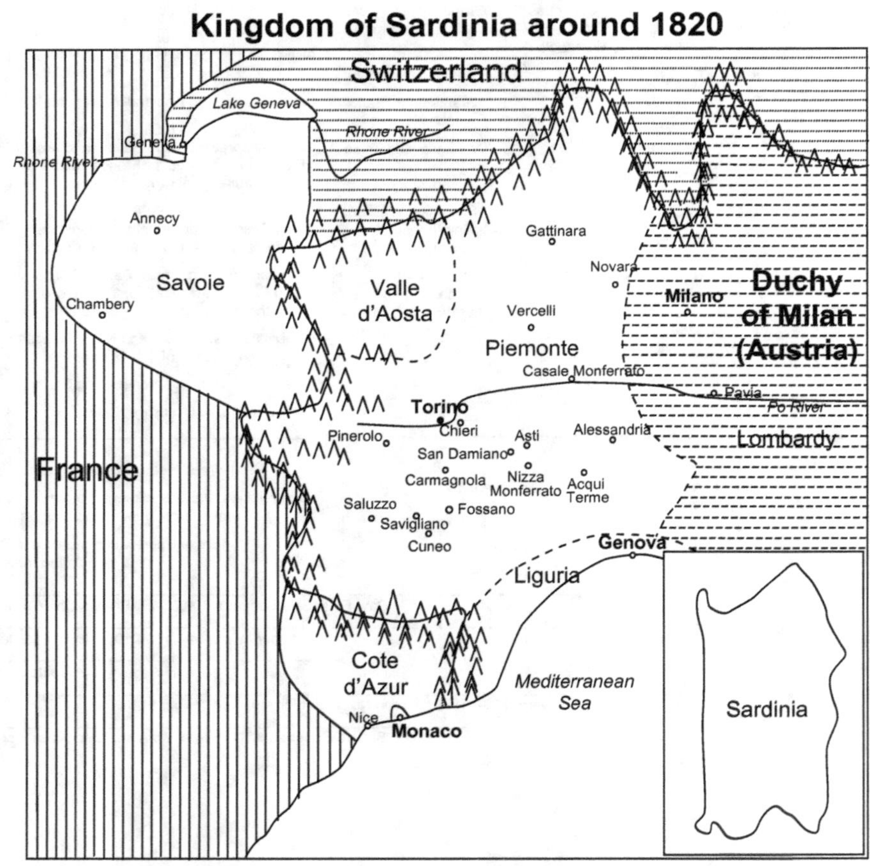

In 1848 there was a widespread set of revolutions across Europe, beginning in France and spreading to many other countries. These revolutions forced out the last king of France in February of that year and forced many other crowned heads to accept constitutions with parliamentary governments, modeled on the English example. Even the pope was forced to accept constitutional government for the Papal States, although, as soon as possible, he suppressed the revolution militarily and abrogated the constitution. Carlo Alberto's political advisers told him that he could either fight these revolutionary forces or join with them and take the lead among the liberal and nationalistic movements in Italy. In March of that year he proclaimed the establishment of a parliamentary government and granted a democratic constitution. Under the new constitution, only foreign and military affairs remained under his direct control.

At the same time Carlo Alberto assumed leadership of the nationalist movements that were beginning to appear in many of the Italian statelets, especially those controlled by Austria. In late March, with insurrections against Austrian rule breaking out in Milan and Venice, he declared war[298] against Austria and marched his army into the Duchy of Milan to aid the local rebellion. Initially the war went very well for him, with several battles won. But after the Austrian Marshal Radetzky brought in reinforcements via the Brenner Pass, Carlo Alberto suffered several defeats during the summer and sought an armistice with the Austrians. The following spring, with local insurrections continuing in Milan and Venice, Carlo Alberto renewed hostilities against Austria. He was decisively defeated at Novara and forced to sue for peace. The Austrians, faced with continuing political unrest in their polyglot empire, wanted no part of controlling Piemonte, which would surely be restive under their control. Besides, Piemonte had a long border with their archenemy, France, and it was much safer to have a weak buffer state between them. Therefore, they agreed to take no Piemontese territory, provided that Carlo Alberto abdicate and that Piemonte pay heavy reparations to Austria. Thus in March 1849 Carlo Alberto abdicated in favor of his son Vittorio Emanuele II and went into exile in Portugal, where he died after a few months.

The Impact on the Hebrews

All of the revolutionary and counterrevolutionary fervor during this period had profound effects upon the Hebrews in Piemonte. During the months leading up to Napoleon's first conquest of Piemonte in 1796, there was considerable unrest in the ghettos, with many of the residents refusing to pay taxes and agitating for ending of the ghetto system.[299] One of Napoleon's first acts upon entering a town with a ghetto was to symbolically burn the ghetto gates and grant the Hebrews and the Waldensian Protestants full citizenship rights. With these rights came the rights to own property and to hire Christian labor, resulting in a rapid expansion of Hebrew-owned manufacturing and property development.

When Napoleon was defeated in 1815, the restored King Vittorio Emanuele I reestablished the ghettos, though typically the gates that Napoleon had burned were not replaced. In principle, the prohibitions on living and owning property outside the ghetto, on being outside the ghetto after dark, and on hiring Christians were reapplied, but in practice these were not enforced as rigorously as before; it was too difficult to close factories and undo property purchases. These restrictions continued through the reigns of Carlo Felice and Carlo Alberto up to 1848. In June of that year, Carlo Alberto abolished the ghetto system throughout Piemonte.[300] Hebrews were now free to work and live wherever they wanted. They could attend universities and public schools. And they could serve in government and the military. Carlo Alberto's declaration of Hebrew emancipation was commemorated in many ways. In the ornate synagogue of Casale Monferrato there are two marble plaques on the wall, one in Italian and the other in Hebrew. In Torino, upon Carlo Alberto's death in 1849, the early Baroque *aron ha kodesh*[301] was painted black in memory of his historic action, and it remains so today in a small chapel in the modern Torino synagogue.

---

[298] The First War for Italian Independence.

[299] Segre, documents 3455-56, 3463.

[300] In so doing, Carlo Alberto was following a precedent set by Austria in the 1830s in granting full citizenship rights to the Hebrew minority.

[301] The Holy Ark, the cabinet in which the scrolls of the Torah are kept between readings.

The Chieri Sacerdotes

Several members of our five families were active participants in the events of the first and second openings of the ghettos. In 1798, a mob of anti-French partisans marched on the ghetto of Chieri, fearing that the Hebrews would side with the French troops who were camped outside the town. Leone Sacerdote, one of the leaders of the community, invited the mob's ringleaders into his wine cellar to sample his wines. As they drank, Leone sent a messenger to the French camp to apprise the commander of the situation. The French responded by sending troops to protect the ghetto and arrest the ringleaders in his cellar.[302]

Under the subsequent French administration, the Chieri industrialist David Levi (unrelated to Giorgio or Luciana) was named *maire adjoint* (vice mayor). He and several of his Sacerdote and Segre partners then bought property outside the ghetto to expand their textile operations. One of those properties was a former convent that had been seized by the French government and that now houses the Chieri textile museum.[303] By 1808 David Levi's textile firm employed more than 100 workers.[304] Likewise, Giuseppe Sacerdote, Leone's cousin, became such an important figure in Chieri's silk industry that be became known as Giuseppe della Seta (Joseph the Silk Man).

After the post-Napoleonic reimposition of the ghetto, the public officials found it difficult to undo the economic expansions of the Chieri Hebrews. Thus David Levi's firm was allowed to remain in family hands. While the royal decrees required Hebrews to divest all real property that they had acquired outside the ghetto, as a practical matter this law was ignored as much as it was enforced. So, for example, the eighteenth-century convent of St. Francis that was jointly acquired by Leone and Giuseppe Sacerdote and Uri Todros (the convent had become French government property when it suppressed the monastic order of St. Francis) remained in family hands to the end of the nineteenth century.[305]

When the universities opened their doors to Hebrews in 1848, Leone Sacerdote's grandson Emanuele (born in 1826 and therefore twenty-two years old in 1848) enrolled in the Faculty of Law at the University of Torino.

The Segre, Levi, and Debenedetti During this Period

During this period, Israele Segre moved from the overcrowded ghetto of Savigliano, where his family had been crowded into two rooms, to Torino, and took his textile business with him.

In 1797, there were refusals to pay increased taxes in the ghettos of Casale, Acqui, Nizza Monferrato, and Moncalvo. When the government tried to force the rabbis to excommunicate the recalcitrants, the populations rose in rebellion and refused to allow the rabbis to enforce such orders. Giuseppe Salvador Ottolenghi of Acqui, uncle and guardian of the brothers Abram Israele and Salvador Leone Levi and a leader of the Universitá of the Monferrato, sought to enforce the rules (probably because he feared that as the richest man in the community, he would be forced to pay the tax for the entire population) and had to leave town briefly for his own safety.[306] Subsequently, when the French took control, he was seized by anti-French forces and imprisoned for six months. After his release he became a city councilor in Acqui.[307]

As soon as the Emancipation Edict was announced, the Levi family began sending its sons to university. Leone, born in 1824 (and therefore twenty-four years old in 1848) was the first; he then pursued an academic career. His younger brother, Samuele, born in 1835, followed in his footsteps and studied law.

---

[302] Treves, p. 155; see also the Sacerdote family genealogy in the appendix.

[303] Treves, p. 181.

[304] Treves, p. 167.

[305] Treves, p. 181.

[306] Segre, document 3455.

[307] From his epitaph in the Acqui cemetery: "Giuseppe Ottolenghi, 1744-1822. Lived in the tumultuous times of the French occupation. In 1800 he suffered greatly on account of the civil disturbances and was kept hostage by the revolutionary army, and later became a council member in the community."

We know less of the activities of the Debenedetti during this period. We know that Sabato Debenedetti was born in Alessandria in 1821, after the reimposition of the ghetto. In 1839, he married Elena Carmi of Casale. Their three daughters and one son were born during the 1840s. Their oldest daughter, Benedetta, Luciana's grandmother, successively married the two sons of Israele Levi: first the professor, and after he died, his younger brother, the lawyer. Their third daughter, Nina, married Cesare Lombroso, who became a well-known physician and professor of criminology, and was active in the then fashionable field of phrenology.

Figure 5-2
A silver *Shaddai* [good luck amulet invoking protection from the Almighty]. In the 1700s through the early 1900s Italian Hebrews often attached such charms to the cradles of new-born children. It probably belonged originally to one of my grandparents. An identical *Shaddai* is in the collection of the Synagogue of Casale Monferrato. Photograph, George S. Sacerdote.

Figure 5-3
Reverse side of the Shaddai. The four Hebrew letters are an acronym referring to a biblical passage.

Figure 5-4
Page from 1838 census of the Chieri ghetto. Cav. Emanuele Sacerdote is entry number 21 as a boy of 12. The five entries above him are his father, Salvador Vita, his mother, Eva Lattes from Cuneo, and his three older brothers, Moisé, Giacobbe, and Salomone. Just below him is the family's live-in servant Perla Segre of Saluzzo. Salvador Vita was listed as the owner of the house. The top two entries were the Rabbi and his wife, his tenants. One should note that under the heading *Patria* [Nationality] is listed the residents' birth cities. This attitude that loyalty to one's locality supersedes national loyalty continues in Italy to this day.

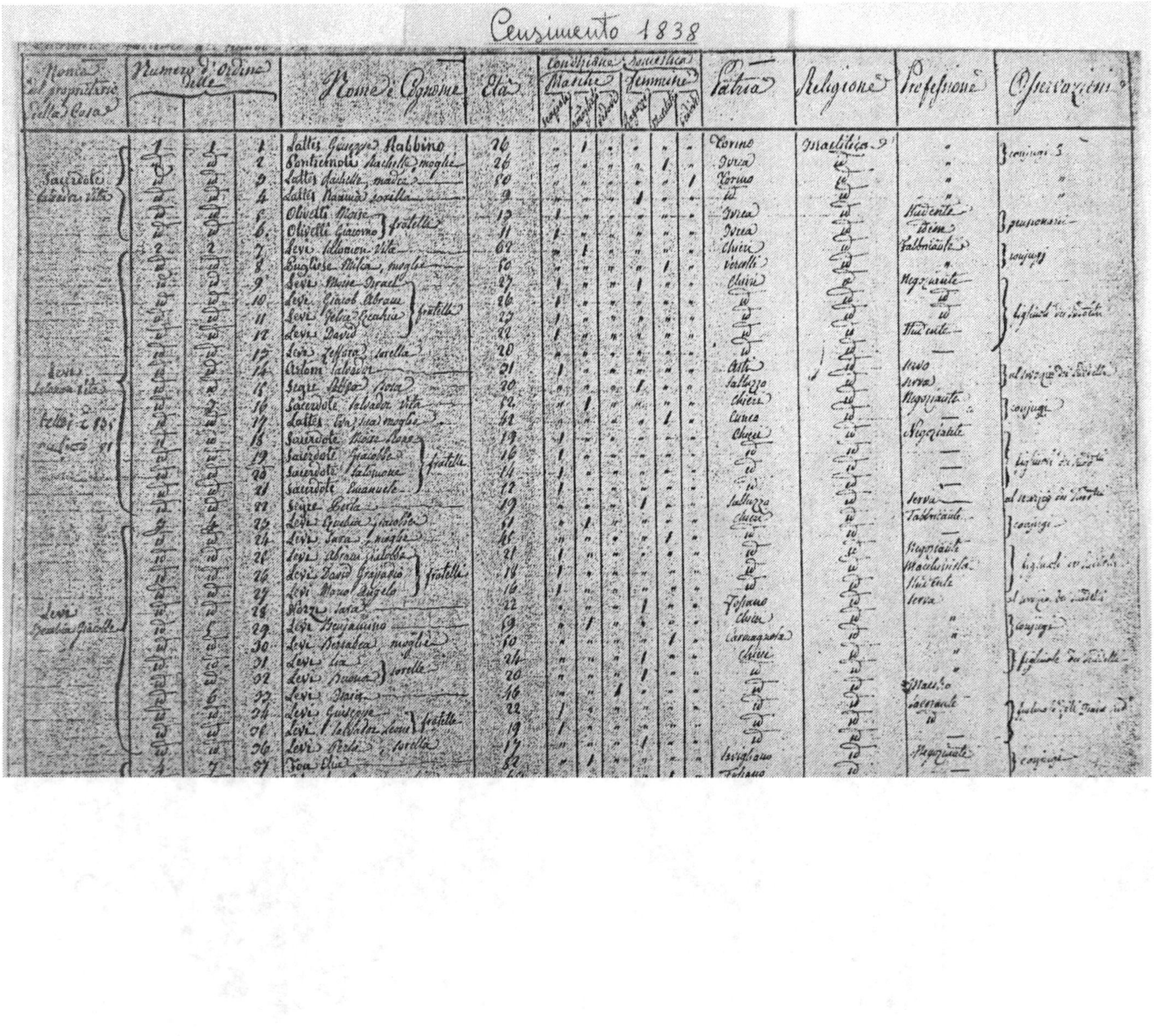

Figure 5-5
Second page from the Chieri census of 1838. Emanuele
Sacerdote's grandfather, Leone Sacerdote is listed as entry
92 at age 87. Listed as entries 93-98 are Leone's 68-year old
wife Ricca Stella, his married son Giacob Israele (age 39),
Giacob's wife Bersabea Levi of Torino (age 31) and their
three daughters Regina, Ricca Stella, and Carlotta (ages 9,
6, and 2)

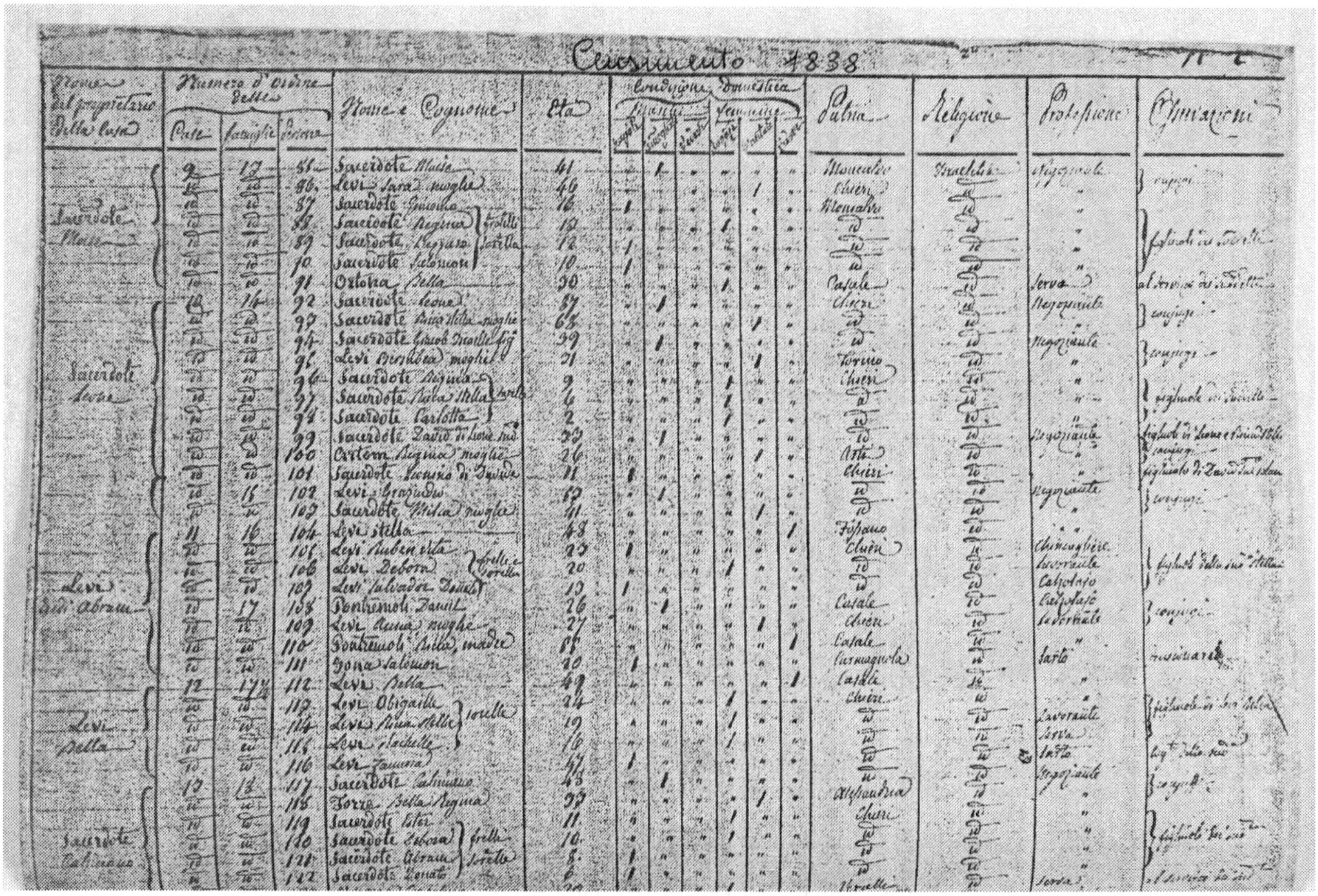

Figure 5-6
Acqui Terme Hebrew Cemetery. This cemetery is largely in
ruins, although there are still occasional burials there when a
descendent from the Acqui community decides to return to his
family roots for eternity. Carol and I visited it in 2005, looking
for graves of Luciana Levi's ancestors and found it locked. We
then went to the town hall in Piazza Abramo Levi, where we
learned that the keeper of the Catholic cemetery was responsible for maintaining the Hebrew cemetery as well. A visit to
the Catholic cemetery on the opposite side of town produced a
key to the Hebrew cemetery, which we then visited. Photograph
2005 by George S. Sacerdote.

Figure 5-7
With 5-8, 2 parts of grave stone of Giuseppe Salvatore
Ottolenghi [1740–1820], uncle and guardian of Luciana's ancestors, the brothers Abram Israel and Salvador Levi [from Nizza
Monferrato], in Acqui Terme. This headstone reads, "He lived in
the turbulent times of the French occupation in 1800. He suffered much during the civil disorders when he was taken hostage
for six months by the revolutionary army. Subsequently he
became a town councilor." Photographs, George S. Sacerdote.

Figure 5-8
The second part of the Giuseppe Salvatore Ottolenghi's headstone.

Figure 5-9
Carol in Piazza Abramo Levi, Acqui Terme, 2005. The city
hall is on this square.

Figure 5-10
Aron ha Kodesh [Holy Ark] from the synagogue in the former Torino ghetto, now housed in the basement chapel of the modern Torino Synagogue. It was painted black after the death of King Carlo Alberto, emancipator of the Piemonte Hebrews. From a postcard from the Torino Synagogue.

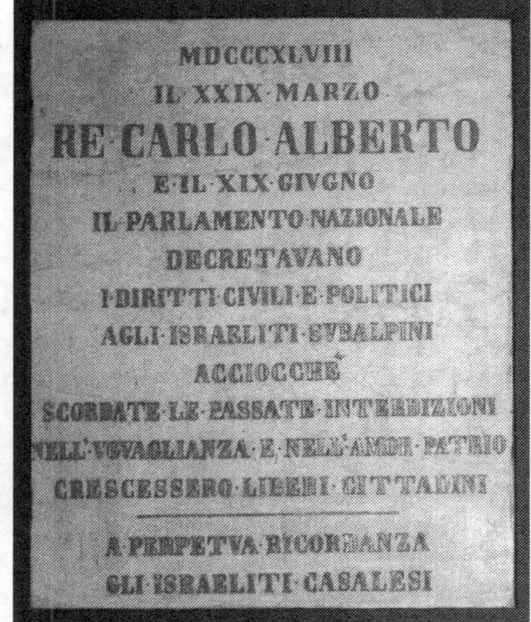

Figure 5-11
Plaque from the Casale Monferrato synagogue commemorating the emancipation proclamation. The synagogue has two such plaques, one in Italian, shown here, and one in Hebrew. It reads: "1848, 29th of March, King Carlo Alberto and on June 19th the national parliament decreed civil and political rights for the sub-Alpine Israelites in order that they should forget the former prohibitions from now on and become free citizens and love their country. For the perpetual remembrance of the Israelites of Casale." From the Catalog of the Synagogue of Casale Monferrato.

Figure 6-1
Cav. Emanuele Sacerdote, portrait taken in the 1890s.
As soon as the ghetto restrictions were lifted in 1848,
Emanuele enrolled in the University of Torino to study
law. He applied his legal training to acquiring distressed
property, often in places where the rapidly growing industrial towns of Piemonte would be expanding.

Fig ure 6-2
Salvador Montalcini, Elvira's father. Salvador was in the
wholesale cloth trade, dealing in silks and woolens, as had
his ancestors back to the early 1700s. Portrait taken in the
1890s. Photograph from the Allais Studio.

Figure 6-3
Eugenia Segre, Elvira's mother. Eugenia's family was also in
the wholesale cloth trade back to the 1700s. Portrait taken
about 1890.

Chapter VI
The Risorgimento and the Establishment of the Italian State: 1849–1900

In 1848, the French overthrew their last king, Louis Philippe, and established the Second Republic. This republic lasted until 1852, when it was overthrown by Louis Napoleon, who styled himself Emperor Napoleon III. Early on, Vittorio Emanuele II allied himself with Napoleon III to have a counterweight to Austria on his eastern border.

In 1853, the Russians began the Crimean War with Turkey with the sinking of the Turkish fleet as part of their efforts to project their power into the Balkans.[308] The British and the French, fearing greater Russian influence in Europe, sided with Turkey. Piemonte, which had little interest in the affairs of the Russians and the Turks, nevertheless joined the war on the side of England and France. The Piemontese participation in the war was actually quite limited, with its troops mostly playing supporting and logistical roles. Nonetheless, by this effort, Vittorio Emanuele II gained two strong supporters to help protect his interests from the Austrians.[309]

As part of the Parliamentary quid pro quo to obtain funding for the Crimean expedition, the king agreed with the liberal parties to declare a land reform in Piemonte. In practical terms, it meant the seizure of much of the Church's lands and their resale to the tenant farmers who worked the land. The pope's reaction was to excommunicate Vittorio Emanuele II and threaten the same for all those who purchased Church lands from the royal government. The only people not threatened by this papal pronouncement were the Hebrews and the Waldensian Protestants, many of whom bought these lands from the government at a discount and then resold it to the public at market rates, earning a substantial profit on the spread.

After the Crimean War, Vittorio Emanuele and his prime minister, Count Cavour, set a course to unify much of Italy under Vittorio Emanuele's rule. In 1858 they concluded a secret treaty with Napoleon III in which Piemonte would cede its territories on the French side of the Alps, Savoie and the county of Nice, in exchange for French military support to dislodge the Austrians from the parts of northern Italy they controlled, including Lombardy, Venetia, Emilia, and Tuscany.

In the spring of 1859, Piemonte staged military maneuvers along its border with Lombardy, provoking an Austrian attack and thus beginning the Second War for Italian Independence. The Austrians were quickly defeated and Piemonte took over Lombardy. Then a series of local insurrections in Emilia, Tuscany, the Papal States, and the Kingdom of Naples caused diplomatic tremors across Europe. Pope Pius IX accused the French of fomenting political problems in his domain. The Prussians, who feared that their ally Austria might be too greatly weakened, massed troops on the French border. Napoleon III then decided to withdraw from the war, forcing Vittorio Emanuele to sign the Treaty of Villafranca ending the war, leaving Piemonte with only the acquisition of Lombardy.

In the succeeding months the publics in several of these insurrectional states voted to join Piemonte via a series of plebiscites in Tuscany, Emilia, and the Duchy of Parma. In the spring of 1860, the revolutionary Giuseppe Garibaldi[310] landed in Sicily with 1000 irregular troops wearing improvised

---

[308] At that time most of the Balkan Peninsula was controlled by Turkey, with the exception of Greece, which had successfully revolted against Turkey in the 1840s, and Croatia, which was part of the Austrian Empire. The Crimean War lasted until 1856.

[309] There is an elaborate monument in Torino commemorating this "glorious" exploit. The monument is in Piazza Crimea, a shady plaza that one crosses just after passing over the Po from central Torino on Corso Vittorio Emanuele, on the way to our former villa in Valsalice.

[310] Garibaldi was one of the most colorful men of the Risorgimento and a lifelong revolutionary. He first saw action in leading a failed revolt of the southernmost province of Brazil. After his defeat, he moved to New York City, where he earned his living making sausages on Staten Island. During the revolutionary period around 1848, he returned to his native Italy and was active in the failed revolutions of that period. He subsequently threw in his lot with King Vittorio Emanuele II and led the campaigns to acquire the Kingdom of Naples for the newly forming Kingdom of Italy.

uniforms with red shirts. Within two months the Red Shirts had defeated the Royal Neapolitan troops and taken control of Sicily. In late August, Garibaldi and his troops crossed the Strait of Messina and entered the mainland portion of the Kingdom of Naples. On September 7, Garibaldi's troops entered Naples.

While Garibaldi was conquering the Kingdom of Naples, the popular insurrection against the papal government grew in intensity. The people of the Papal States were fed up with centuries of papal misrule: Pope Pius IX[311] ran a nasty police state in his temporal domains. In an effort to suppress liberal thinking, his government sought to keep the public ignorant, impoverished, and under tight control. For example, public schools were almost nonexistent in the Papal States even though they had been established in Piemonte more than two hundred years earlier. In 1864 Pius IX published the *Syllabus of Errors*, listing eighty doctrinal deviancies that Catholics must avoid. Among the deviancies he railed against were many principles of modern public policy:

- State-run public schools
- Rational thought not based on Church dogma
- Scientific research that contradicted Church teachings
- Freedom of religion
- Freedom of the press
- Separation of Church and state
- Civil authorities' jurisdiction over Church officials who commit civil crimes
- Political liberalism
- The idea that the Church or the pope could make errors

One of Pius IX's reactions to the political troubles at home was to turn on the Hebrews, much as his predecessors had done in setting up the ghettos in reaction to the Reformation. He ordered the ghetto rules to be enforced with rigor. In 1858, the papal police kidnapped a young boy, Edgardo Mortara, from the ghetto of Bologna and had him forcibly baptized, the last such event in Italy. Despite an international uproar over the incident, including personal appeals from the Austrian, German, and French emperors for Mortara's release, the Church did not allow Edgardo to see his family again for many years.

Count Cavour, Vittorio Emanuele's prime minister, organized a military force to intervene in the Papal States' insurrection on the king's behalf. The papal troops were defeated decisively on September 18, 1860, and the pope's temporal domains were reduced to only the city of Rome.[312] The pope's reaction to the loss of the bulk of his temporal state was to excommunicate Vittorio Emanuele and most of his ministers. This action was no more effective than his earlier excommunication of the king.

Shortly thereafter, the royal Piemontese troops coming from the north met Garibaldi's army marching northward from Naples. In a dramatic moment, Garibaldi met the king, swore loyalty to him, and turned over his conquered territories in the Kingdom of Naples. And thus was born the Kingdom of Italy. It included all of modern Italy except for the region around Venice, Trento, and Trieste (still under Austrian control) and the city of Rome. The act was made official in 1861, when Parliament voted to crown Vittorio Emanuele II as King of Italy.

In 1864, Vittorio Emanuele signed a new treaty with Napoleon III under which he agreed to respect the French guarantee of papal independence in the pope's reduced temporal state consisting only of the city of Rome. In the same year he moved the royal capital from Torino to Florence. In 1866, he signed a treaty with Prussia and France which jointly forced Austria to cede the Veneto region to the newly formed Kingdom of Italy. In 1870, with the collapse of the government of Napoleon III at the end of the disastrous Franco-Prussian War,[313] Vittorio Emanuele was free to capture Rome, which he did on September 20, 1870, thus ending the last vestige of temporal papal government. At same time, Vittorio Emanuele II emancipated the Hebrews of the Rome ghetto, eliminated compulsory attendance at annual conversion sermons, and canceled Rome's Jew's tax, thus eliminating the last such institutions in

---

[311] Pius IX is currently a candidate for sainthood.

[312] Vittorio Emanuele could not enter Rome because it was defended by French troops and he did not want to risk war with his ally, Napoleon III.

[313] Prussia defeated France in a matter of months and occupied Paris shortly thereafter.

Italy.[314] The pope's reaction to the loss of this remnant of his temporal state was to yet again excommunicate Vittorio Emanuele and most of his ministers. This action was no more effective than his earlier royal excommunications. Shortly thereafter, Rome became the capital of a united Italy.

Vittorio Emanuele II died in 1878 and was succeeded by his son Umberto. Although Umberto was the fourth head of the House of Savoy to bear that name, he chose to be designated Umberto I, King of Italy, emphasizing the dynasty's new role. When he assumed the throne, Umberto I not only swore to uphold the constitution granted by his grandfather Carlo Alberto in 1848, but he also placed the throne subordinate to Parliamentary law, thus moving the Crown closer to the British model, where the Crown reigns but does not rule. He did, however, retain direct power over foreign and military affairs independent of Parliament, as had his father. In 1882 he established a triple alliance with Germany and Austria, which was renewed for an additional twenty years in 1887. And in the 1890s he acquired Italy's first African colonies in Eritrea and Italian Somaliland (now part of Somalia) through diplomacy with England. These territories were carved out of areas that had formerly been under the loose control of the Turkish and Ethiopian empires.

If Vittorio Emanuele II had created a unified Italy, Umberto I's main task as king was to create an Italian nation from the disparate principalities that had joined forces under his predecessor's reign.[315] This he accomplished through heavily involving himself in public activities the length and breadth of the country, ranging from supervising flood relief to opening public works and encouraging economic and cultural development.

During this period, the northern half of the country was rapidly industrializing and saw the building of a modern infrastructure of railroads, electrical grids, telephone and telegraph lines, schools, and hospitals. Political power passed to the rapidly growing bourgeoisie. The king and his governments identified their interests closely with this new ruling class. The southern half of the country, corresponding to the old Kingdom of Naples, remained much more backward and controlled by the old landholding class. In response to several outbreaks of unrest among the southern peasantry, the king and his prime minister were forced to establish military rule in the south during 1893–94, perhaps setting precedents for political actions after World War I.

The same model was followed the next year when a crop failure in Lombardy caused the price of bread to rise, leading to street riots by the working class demanding government action. In 1900 Umberto I was assassinated in Monza by Gaetano Bresci. Bresci had been a worker forced into exile to Paterson, New Jersey, as a result of his role in the riots. He had nursed a grudge against the royal family for several years before slipping back into the country with the expressed intent of shooting the king.

As was mentioned above, as soon as the universities were opened to all in 1848, the Hebrews flocked in. The same happened with all walks of public and private life. The newly emancipated Hebrews tended to be ardent supporters of Italian unification. Count Cavour, prime minister under Vittorio Emanuele II, had a Hebrew personal secretary, Isacco Artom from Asti, who was subsequently made a baron. Artom had first come to Cavour's notice in 1852, four years after emancipation, as editor of the pro-unification newspaper *L'Opinione*.

The Hebrews and the Risorgimento

In 1859, Giuseppe Ottolenghi was the first Hebrew admitted to the military academy, and twenty-eight of his coreligionists were admitted in the following year. After distinguished military service during the Wars of Independence of the 1860s, he rose through the ranks, becoming a major general in 1889, and ultimately served as minister of war in the first years of the twentieth century.

With the emancipation, many Hebrews assumed important academic, legal, medical, and commercial positions. Abramo Franchetti, a banker from Livorno, was made a baron in 1858, in honor of his contributions to the development of Piemonte's railroads. Giacobbe Abram Todros of Torino was made a baron in 1860 for his efforts to build the Piemontese silk industry. In 1892, Moisé Zecut Levi di Veali

---

[314] The Roman ghetto had experienced two earlier brief rounds of freedom, under Napoleon I and during the insurrection of 1848.

[315] Even today Italians are much less nationalistic than most nationalities. Their loyalties tend to be local rather than national, a phenomenon known as *campanilismo,* a local loyalty that extends only as far as the nearest church tower.

of Torino was made a baron in honor of his philanthropies—he was in the grain-milling business and supplied free flour to the poor during a famine. By the end of the nineteenth century, eight Italian Hebrews had been ennobled and numerous others had been knighted.

Some years after emancipation, the Hebrew community of Torino decided to erect a grand new synagogue to replace the cramped one in the former ghetto. The new structure was to reflect the community's increasing prosperity and importance. They engaged the well-known architect Antonelli to design the structure and supervise its construction. They broke ground for the building in 1863. As the construction progressed, Antonelli kept on changing his design, making it ever grander. The community could not convince him to settle on a final design and complete the building. After a while they realized that Antonelli had lost sight of their desire for a synagogue and had become obsessed with building the world's tallest building. They became alarmed that his ever-growing ambition would soon outrun their ability to pay for it and halted construction in 1869. One wag at the time is supposed to have asked, "In order to speak to God, does one need a tower that touches Him?" Finally, in 1873, the Hebrew community arranged for the city to buy the partly completed structure and used the city's payment to start work on another building, the Moorish-style modern synagogue on Piazziale Primo Levi that is still in use today. Meanwhile, with municipal funding in hand, Antonelli resumed his mad project and the building soared higher and higher, dominating Torino's skyline. It was mockingly labeled *Il Mole Antonelliana*, Antonelli's Pile. When finally completed, the city engineer feared it would collapse and would not certify it safe for occupancy. It then remained a vacant white elephant for over a century, despite various efforts to reinforce its masonry structure. In the 1950s, when I first noticed the Mole from the garden of our country villa in Valsalice, I asked my father what it was. He shrugged his shoulders and then replied with a touch of embarrassment, "You don't want to know." After the building had stood for a century, it was finally deemed safe. In the millennium year 2000 it was adapted for use as a museum of the Italian film industry.

The Chieri Sacerdotes during the Risorgimento and their move to Torino

During the Risorgimento, the experiences of our five families were similar to those of the rest of the Piemontese Hebrews. In the Sacerdote family, Giorgio's grandfather, Cav. Emanuele Sacerdote, studied law immediately after emancipation, and subsequently used his legal training to build a substantial property portfolio. Many of his transactions involved acquiring property from heavily indebted nineteenth-century landowners and settling their debts for them. At the time there was no equivalent of U.S. title insurance, making such purchases highly risky unless one did his own legal investigations to locate all possible liens on the property and genealogical research into the seller's family to determine that no lateral heirs from earlier generations could make a claim upon it; in Italy, property tends to be very illiquid and trades only once every several generations. The legal steps to complete a purchase often took years, with one case running from 1891 to around 1930; the legal issues in this case dated back to the 1826 will of a man who had left his estate to the Carmelite monastic order in 1831. After Emanuele's death in 1897, his sons made an inventory of his portfolio of property, mortgages, and other investments and estimated its value at 2.6 million lire. [316]

Emanuele was knighted in the 1880s. His granddaughter Marcella Sacerdote (daughter of his eldest son, Balilla) married the second Baron Levi di Veale. Emanuele also made several donations to the Museo Civico di Torino, which was subsequently absorbed by the Museo d'Arte Antica in Palazzo Madama. Emanuele's sons followed him in studying law at the University of Torino. Alberto appears to have been a brilliant student, achieving a perfect grade of 30 out of 30 in every subject, as noted in his grade report for his second year in law school, 1887–8; interestingly, one of the required courses for that year was canon law. After Emanuele's death in 1897, his sons Balilla, Leone, and Alberto continued his property business as partners until the deaths of Balilla and Alberto in 1920. The firm was finally dissolved in the late 1930s when Cav. Leone Sacerdote was near the end of his life.

---

[316] After the deaths of my grandfather Alberto and his brother Balilla in 1920, those properties were devolved to their heirs. Much of this property remained in the family for most of the twentieth century.

Figure 6-4
Sign indicating the former location of a 1400s wooden
statue in front of Sacerdote family house in Chieri in the
former ghetto. The statue was donated by Cav. Emanuele
Sacerdote to the *Museo Civico di Torino* in 1875. The
museum has since merged with the *Museo d'Arte Antica* in
Palazzo Madama. Photograph taken in 1980s by Peter M.
Sacerdote.

Figure 6-5
Wooden statue in storage in the *Museo d'Arte Antica* in
Palazzo Madama, Torino. This statue of an angel bearing
the arms of the Solara family is Flemish, 15th century.
When I sought to find this object in 2005, I learned that
the museum in Palazzo Madama had been closed for
repairs for 25 years. My cousin Piera Levi-Montalcini, a
member of the Torino cultural council, obtained an introduction for me to a curator who let Carol, Mauro Lustig
and me into the museum's collection in a warehouse
outside of Torino to see it. Photograph, 2005 by George S.
Sacerdote.

Figure 6-6
A wooden chest also donated to the *Museo Civico* by Cav.
Emanuele Sacerdote. Note the Judaic symbols including
the *Magen David* (six pointed star) and *Etz Chaim*, the
tree of life that symbolizes the Torah, inlaid into the front
and inside lid of the chest. Photograph, 2005 by George S.
Sacerdote.

Figure 6-7
Louis-Philippe chinoiserie desk. Giorgio inherited this
piece along with a matching chest, washstand and mir-
ror from his grandmother, Emilia Perla Levi Sacerdote.
According to family lore, Emilia's mother was English.
Photograph, 2005 by George S. Sacerdote.

Figure 6-8
Commemorative medal issued by Chieri to Emanuele
Sacerdote in 1875 during an agricultural fair. Emanuele
had already acquired considerable agricultural land near
Chieri and other towns as part of his property business.

Figure 6-9
Commemorative medal reverse side.

Figure 6-10
Alberto Sacerdote, probably as a university student, around 1890. Photograph by the Manfredi Studio, "Photographers of His Majesty the King of Italy and the royal princes."

Figure 6-12
Evalia Sacerdote, sister of Alberto, portrait taken in the 1890s. Photograph by the Montabone Studio, "Photographers of His Majesty the King of Italy."

Figure 6-11
Law school transcript of Alberto Sacerdote for his second year, 1887-8. He studied history of Italian law, philosophy of law, canon law, and constitutional law. His grades were a perfect 30/30 in each subject.

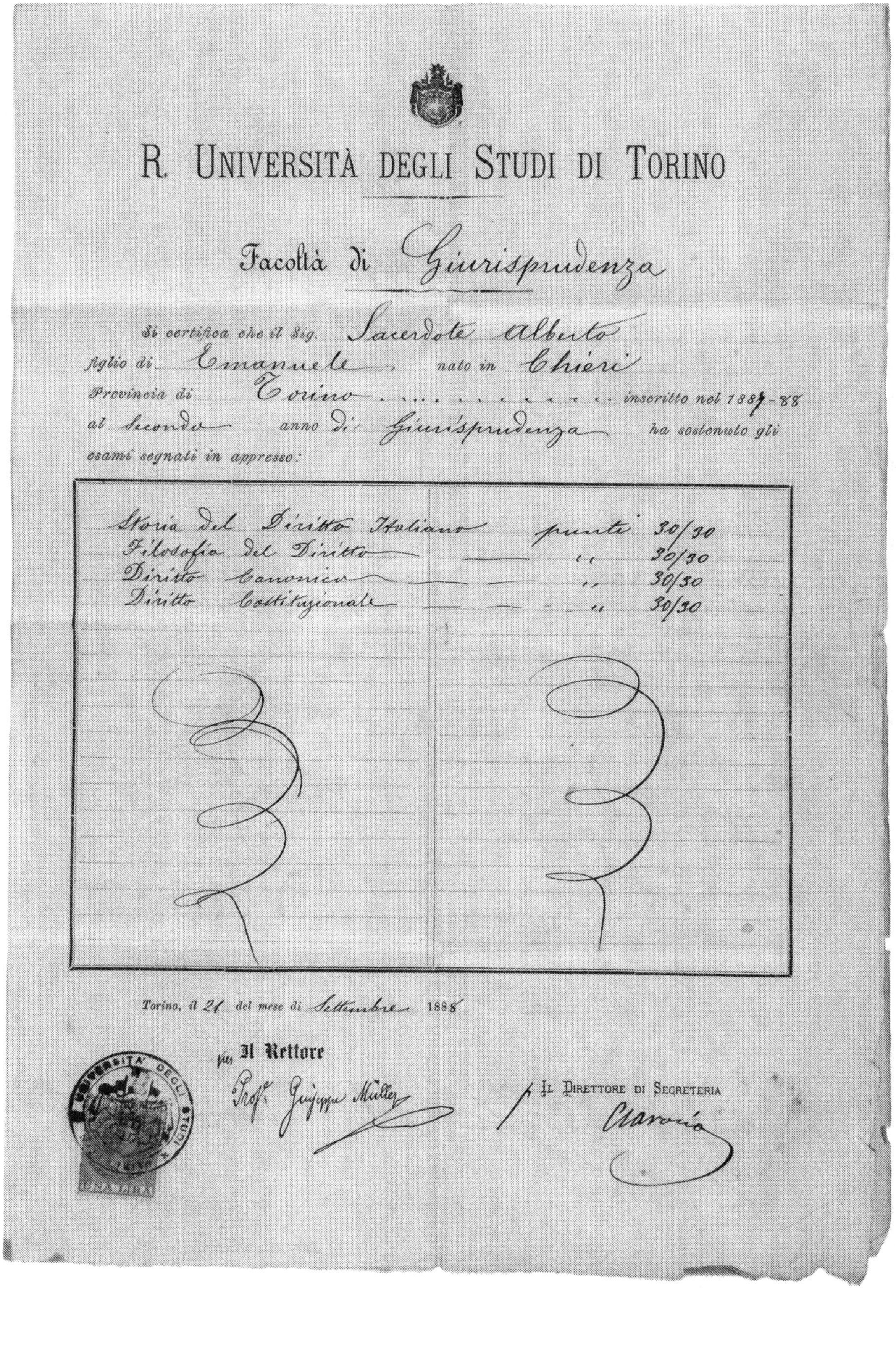

R. UNIVERSITÀ DEGLI STUDI DI TORINO

Facoltà di Giurisprudenza

Si certifica che il Sig. Sacerdote Alberto
figlio di Emanuele nato in Chieri
Provincia di Torino .... inscritto nel 1887-88
al secondo anno di Giurisprudenza ha sostenuto gli
esami segnati in appresso:

Storia del Diritto Italiano	punti	30/30
Filosofia del Diritto	"	30/30
Diritto Canonico	"	30/30
Diritto Costituzionale	"	30/30

Torino, il 21 del mese di Settembre 1888

p. Il Rettore
Prof. Giuseppe Müller

Il Direttore di Segreteria

R. Università degli Studi
Una Lira

Figure 6-13
Wedding contract, Salvador Montalcini and Eugenia Segre,
1867. At the time, marriages were as much business deals
as matters of love. As such, they were solemnized with
formal contracts specifying dowries and the like.

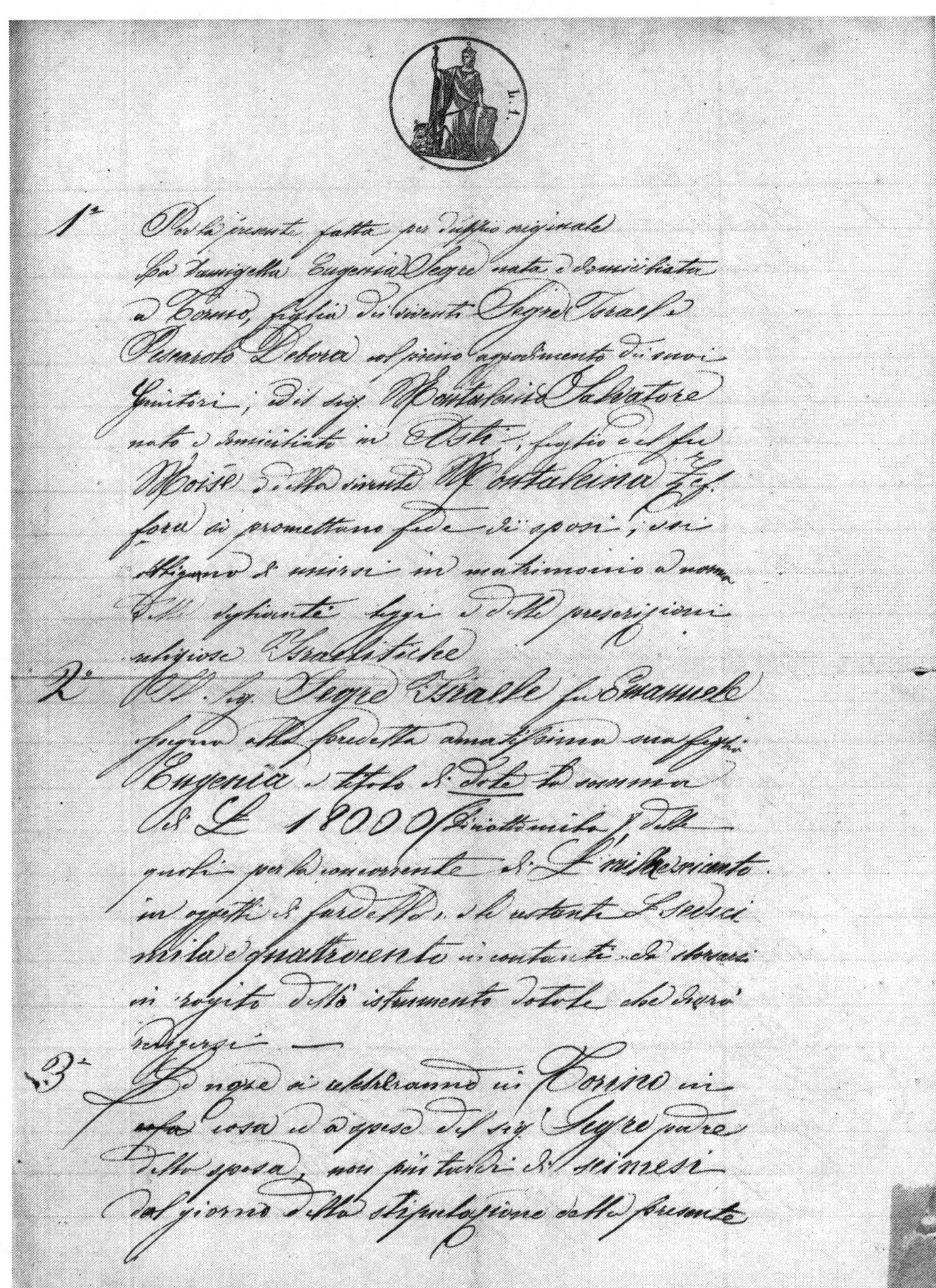

The Hebrew community in Chieri, like many of the smaller Hebrew communities in Piemonte, went into rapid decline after emancipation as the population gravitated toward Torino and other major cities. Emanuele's children were the last generation of the family born there. By the late 1800s, Emanuele's business was based in Torino, in via Roma. The little synagogue in Chieri, which was in a wing of the Sacerdote house in the old ghetto of that town, fell into disuse early in the twentieth century and its beautiful baroque ceremonial objects became Sacerdote family property. They were ultimately donated to the Torino synagogue by the family in the 1930s. In the 1970s, when the Torino synagogue decided to build a chapel in the basement for its daily services, reserving its main sanctuary for major holidays, it built the chapel around the old Chieri *aron ha kodesh* (the cabinet housing the Torah scrolls) and *bimah* (reader's platform).

The Montalcini in the Early Post-Ghetto Years

Among the post-emancipation Montalcini, Giorgio's grandfather, Salvador Montalcini, prospered in the textile industry, as did his wife's family, the Segre. His cousin Camillo Montalcini became secretary of the lower house of Parliament. Unfortunately, Salvador's wife, Eugenia Segre, proved sickly; after bearing five children, she suffered several years of poor health and died in 1896. During her illness and after her death, the maternal role in the family was filled by her childless sister-in-law, Anna Segre[317] née Pesaro. Salvador died relatively young, at the age of sixty-eight, in 1901, leaving an estate worth some 560,000 lire. Of Salvador's three sons, Elvira's brothers, the oldest, Moisé, followed him in the wholesale cloth trade, dealing mainly is silk and fine woolen fabrics; the second, Alessandro, became an ophthalmologist; and the third, Emanuele (Zio Manno), who was trained as a chemist and always referred to as *Il Professore*, spent most of his life as a property investor and was active in politics. For over twenty years, Zio Manno was mayor of Ferrere, a small town near Asti. One of his acts as mayor was to build the first post-primary school in the town in 1925.[318] After the death of Salvador, Zio Manno became the leader of this family.

The Post-Emancipation Generation of the Levi and Debenedetti

Of the first post-emancipation generation of the Levi, Leone became a professor, and his younger brother, Samuele, a lawyer. These brothers were the first and second husbands of Benedetta Debenedetti. Of their and Benedetta's fourteen children, eleven survived into adulthood, entering the legal, engineering, medical, and academic professions or, in the case of the daughters, marrying men in those fields. Two of Leone and Benedetta's daughters were among the first women to enter the university, obtaining doctorates in mathematics and literature. Benedetta's sister Nina Debenedetti married an academic man, Prof. Cesare Lombroso, a medical doctor, criminologist, and phrenologist, who was reputed to control academic appointments at the major Italian universities for two generations.

The Segres during the post-Emancipation Period

Many of the Segres during this period continued the family tradition in commerce, though a number of them achieved professional distinction as well. Most notable in their family was an uncle of Elvira's on the Pescarolo side of her family[319] who became the personal physician to the royal family.

---

[317] Known in the family as Magna Anna, Grandmother Anna.

[318] The school was designed by Giorgio and Luciana's first cousin, Gino Levi-Montalcini, and has since been named after him. The school's lobby contains pictures of the dedication ceremonies, including a large group portrait of much of my family. See Figure 7-29.

[319] Elvira's maternal grandmother was Debora Pescarolo.

Figure 7-1
Alberto Sacerdote, portrait taken about 1904.
Photograph from the Pastal Studio.

Figure 7-2
Portrait of Elvira around the time of her wedding.

Chapter VII
The Twentieth Century: From Monarchy to Republic

The Years before World War I

After the assassination of Umberto I in 1900, the young Vittorio Emanuele III ascended to the throne. The battles between the political left and right that had emerged during the last decade of his father's reign continued in the years leading up to World War I. The rapid industrialization of the northern half of the country, with the development of the steel, rubber, and automotive industries, brought with it labor unions and their agitation for a larger share of the economic pie and political power.

During the first decade of his reign, Vittorio Emanuele III tried to stay above the political fray by appointing Giovanni Giolitti as prime minister leading a center-left coalition government. The Giolitti government sought to placate the unions with the beginnings of the modern welfare state, including the introduction of old-age pensions, a federal dole for the unemployed and poor, and near-universal suffrage. In the realm of foreign policy, Vittorio Emanuele III extended the Triple Alliance Treaty with Germany and Austria in 1902 and again in 1912.

Around 1910, the king sought military glory for his monarchy[320] through the expansion of Italy's African empire. Since the British, French, and Germans had already colonized almost all of Africa, he set his sights on Libya, then controlled by the rapidly waning Turkish Empire. As commander in chief of the military and also having control of foreign policy under the Italian constitution of 1848, Vittorio Emanuele III maneuvered the politicians into backing his African venture and launched an invasion in the fall of 1911 and by 1912 had won control of that desolate territory.[321] My father often repeated the following, probably apocryphal, story about the conquest of Libya. When the Italian troops disembarked to begin their conquest, their general got up on a platform in his white dress uniform, drew his sword, and shouted "*Avanti!* [Charge!]." There being no enemies in sight and no military objective of any sort in the vicinity, the troops looked at each other, a bit puzzled. Then, sensing the absurdity of the general's gesture, they applauded his operatic performance.

During this period before World War I, Alberto Sacerdote married Elvira Montalcini in 1904.[322] Elvira brought a dowry of 70,000 lire into the marriage. Initially they lived on the eastern side of Piazza Carlo Felice at the end of Via Roma, facing the main railway station, Porta Nuova. Sometime after the birth of Giorgio in 1905, the family moved several blocks away to larger quarters at 19 Via Sacchi, opposite the western side of Porta Nuova. There Paolo was born in 1908 and Eugenia in 1910. The family remained in this apartment until 1923. Also living in the same building were Elvira's brothers; Moisé Montalcini used the building's basement as the warehouse for his stocks of silk fabrics.

During this period, Elvira hired two sisters, Teresa (hired in 1905) and Camilla (hired in 1908) Della Valle as cook and maid, respectively. Camilla and Teresa never married and remained in service to the family for nearly seventy years. While Camilla affected a somewhat stern demeanor and was given to complaining, especially if someone left a mess for her to clean up, Teresa was always very warm and kindly, with a twinkle in her eye and good word for everyone.

---

[320] At least since the time of Emanuele Filiberto, the House of Savoy had associated military adventures with national power and glory.

[321] According to articles in the nationalist press of the time, Libya was rich with abundant natural resources. In the 1960s, vast quantities of oil were discovered there, but that oil could not have been found or extracted with the technology of 1912.

[322] They are probably the last ones in our family to have a legal wedding contract (as had their parents and many generations before them). These contracts spelled out dowries and other obligations between the families of the betrothed. They were in addition to the tradition Jewish religious contract known as a *ketubah*.

Alberto, Elvira, and their growing family lived in town in the colder months, but from spring until fall their main center was their country villa, Villa Gurgo, in Valsalice. The Valsalice property was inherited from Emanuele, and it appears in an inventory of his properties prepared in 1907 as his sons settled his estate. Alberto's brother Leone owned the next villa down the hill,[323] and Balilla owned a third nearby villa behind Alberto's and Leone's properties.[324]

Villa Gurgo was set on three terraces on a steeply pitched hill; separate from the main property were two small woodlots further up the hill, from which the farmers cut wood for heating and cooking. The main property had a spectacular view of central Torino and beyond it, the snow-capped peaks of the Alps that mark the border between Italy and France. The topmost terrace was largely devoted to growing grapes and was bordered with hedgerows of hazel bushes. The lowest terrace comprised the bulk of the land area and was devoted to fruit trees (several varieties each of cherries, apricots, peaches, plums, and figs, and also pears, persimmons, medlars,[325] and walnuts), vegetable gardens, berries, more grapes, grain, and pastures for the cows.

The middle terrace contained four buildings: the large main house, the farmer's house and the adjoining stables, the carriage house (which had two small apartments over it), and a small two-story building in the garden that housed a game room with a billiard table upstairs[326] and a small apartment

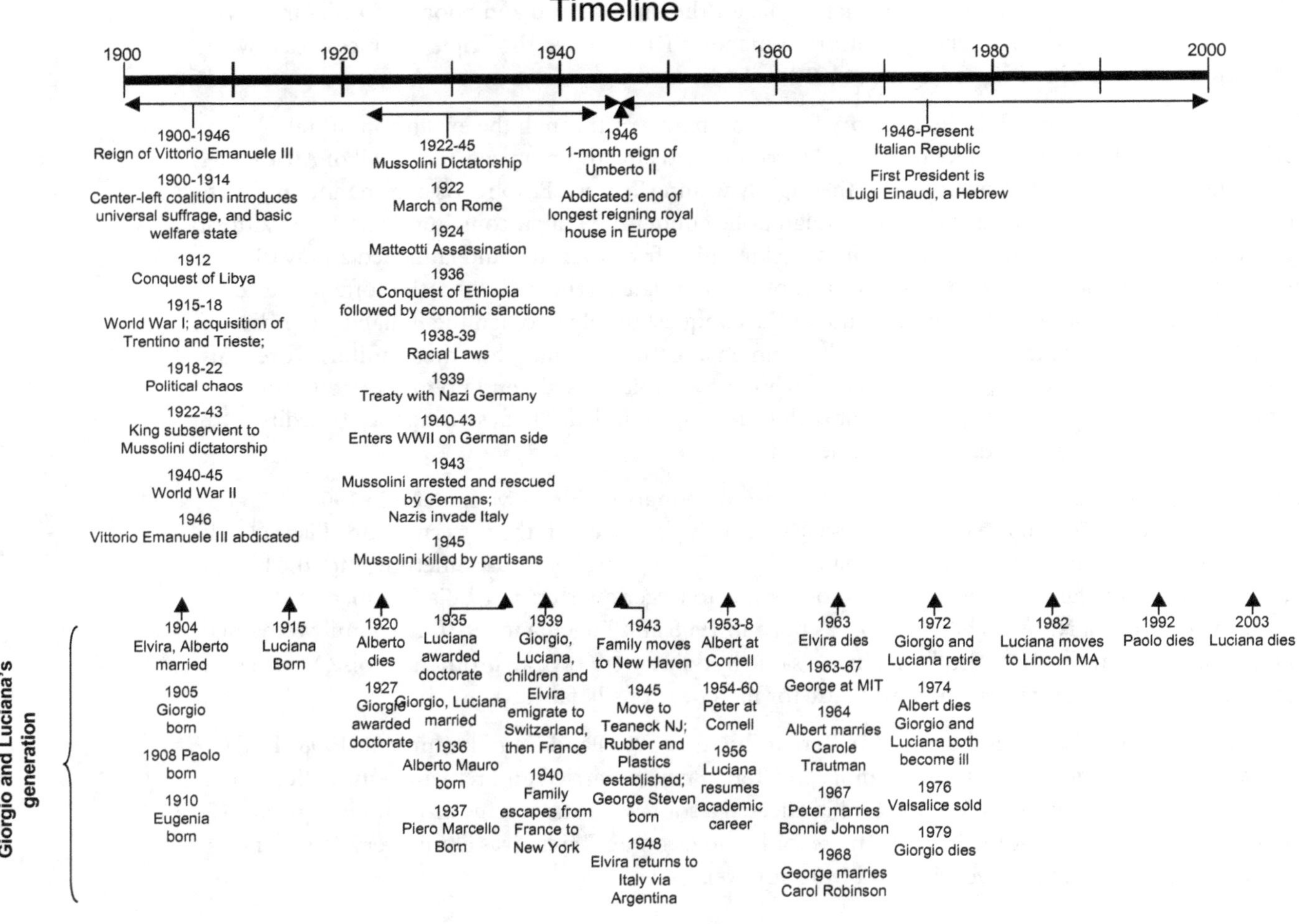

323 Leone's villa was ultimately inherited by his daughter Ada. She lived there with her husband, Angiolo, until his death in 1960, when her second son, Alessandro Treves, took it over; it has since been sold.

324 I have often speculated that these villas were part of the property that was taken from the Church during the land reform of the 1850s, as the property above them on the hillside of Valsalice was a Catholic seminary; with the decline in recent years of Italians interested in entering the priesthood, the former seminary is now a Catholic nursing home.

325 The medlar is a Middle Eastern fruit largely unknown in the United States. It grows on a large tree with shiny leaves, somewhat like a magnolia. The tart fruit resembles an apricot in size and color, and contains four elongated stones.

326 Because of the steepness of the hillside, the upper floor was at the same level as the main house, and the lower floor was at the level of the lowest terrace.

Figure 7-3
Portrait of Elvira around the time of her wedding.

Figure 7-4
Portrait of Marcella Sacerdote, 1906. Marcella was the
daughter of Balilla and Elena Sacerdote. She married the
second Baron Levi di Veale.

Figure 7-5
Elvira Montalcini Sacerdote and her sister-in-law, Elena
Ovazza Sacerdote, wife of Alberto's oldest brother Balilla.
Note the parasol. Portrait taken about 1904.

Figure 7-6
Wedding contract, Alberto Sacerdote and Elvira
Montalcini. This is the last time that weddings in our fam-
ily were formalized with legal contracts specifying dowries.

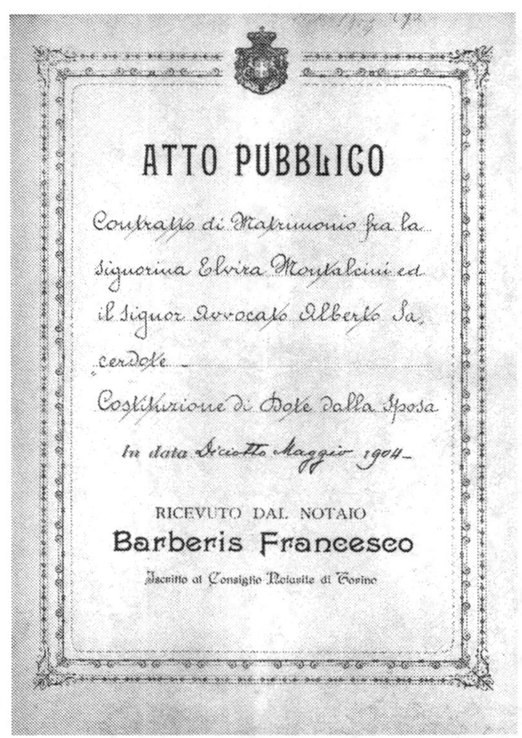

Figure 7-7
Giorgio as an infant, 1905

Figure 7-8
Giorgio at about 1 year, 1906. Photograph from
the A. Colombo studio.

Figure 7-9
Elvira, Alberto and their children, Eugenia and Paolo, Valsalice

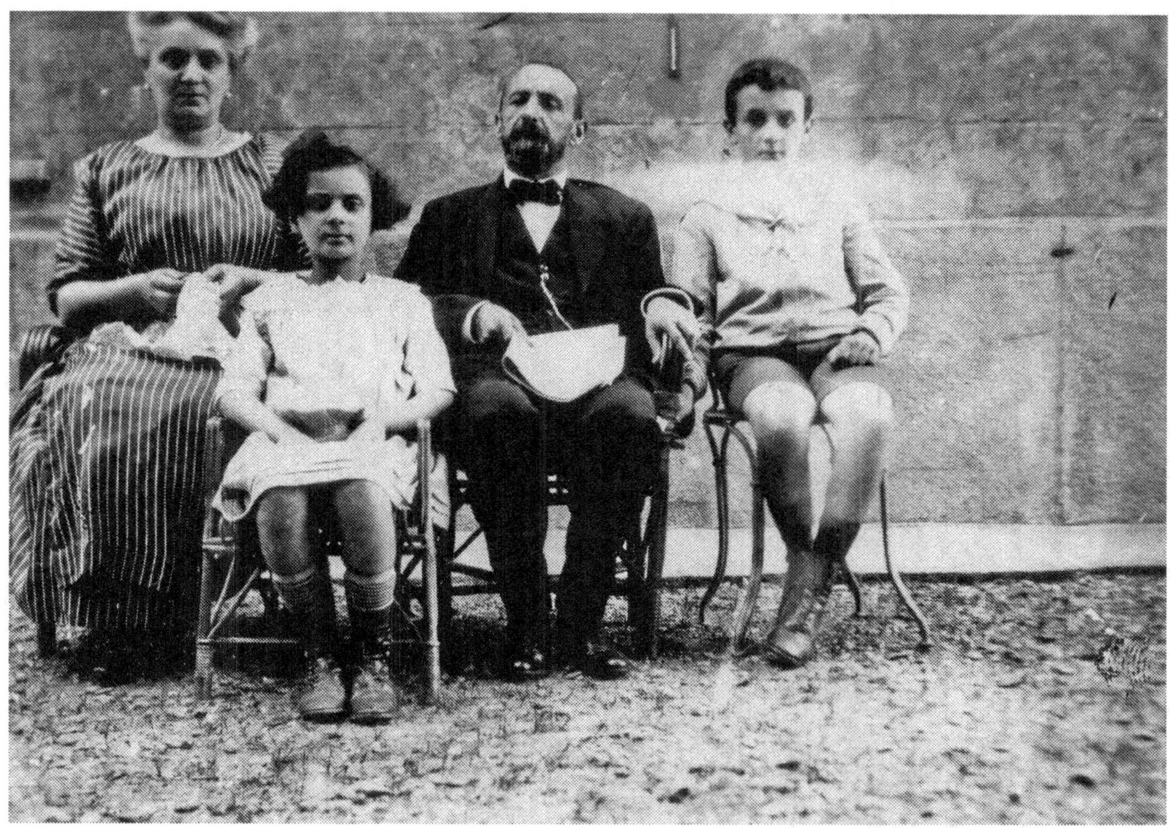

Figure 7-10
Giorgio, Eugenia and Paolo, 1915. At that time and through the 1950s, Italian boys wore short pants all year round, and the sailor suit was the traditional "dress-up" for them. At about this time, Giorgio won a prize at school and was to be presented to the mayor of Torino. When he bent down to tie his just-shined shoes, they left black marks on the seat of his white sailor shorts, creating a crisis which the family maid Camilla had to remedy in short order. When Camilla told me this story fifty years later she smiled, but I have no doubt that at the time she grumbled about the extra work caused by a careless boy.

Figure 7-11
Giorgio as a boy around 1918. This portrait may have been taken on the occasion of his bar mitzvah. Because of his father's fatal illness, the bar mitzvah was probably a very low-key affair. Photograph by the Ambrosetti studio.

Figure 7-12
Watercolor of Castel Rosso, Zio Manno's country villa
in Ferrere, approximately 1913. Original owned by Piera
Levi-Montalcini.

Figure 7-13
Montalcini family portrait 1913, Castel Rosso, Ferrere.
Top row: Moisé Montalcini. Second Row (left to right):
Nina Levi Montalcini, Adamo Levi Montalcini, Elvira
Sacerdote née Montalcini. Third Row (left to right):
Giorgio Sacerdote, Emanuele Montalcini, Gino Levi-
Montalcini, Anna Segre [Magna Anna]. Bottom row (left
to right): Alessandro Montalcini, Alberto Sacerdote, Paolo
Sacerdote, Eugenia Sacerdote, Rita Levi-Montalcini, Paola
Levi-Montalcini, Adelina Levi-Montalcini, Teodoro Segre.

Figure 7-14
Family vacation on the Riviera, 1916. Alberto was un-
dergoing medical treatments for leukemia at the time
and did not join the family. The family archive includes
charming notes to him from Giorgio, Paolo and Eugenia.
Seated in front (left to right): Paolo Sacerdote, Rita Levi-
Montalcini, Nina Levi-Montalcini, Giorgio Sacerdote,
Eugenia Sacerdote. Back row (left to right): Adelina Levi-
Montalcini, Paola Levi-Montalcini, Emanuele Montalcini,
Anna Segre, Adamo Levi-Montalcini, Elvira Sacerdote,
Gino Levi-Montalcini.

Figure 7-15
Alessandro Montalcini, shown in his medical office circa 1920. Alessandro was an ophthalmologist. He reserved one day per week to offer free medical care to the poor.

Figure 7-16
Formal portrait of Alessandro Montalcini. Photograph by
the Lagrange Studio.

Figure 7-17
Formal Portrait of Moisé Montalcini, Elvira's oldest
brother. He continued his father's business in the wholesale cloth trade.

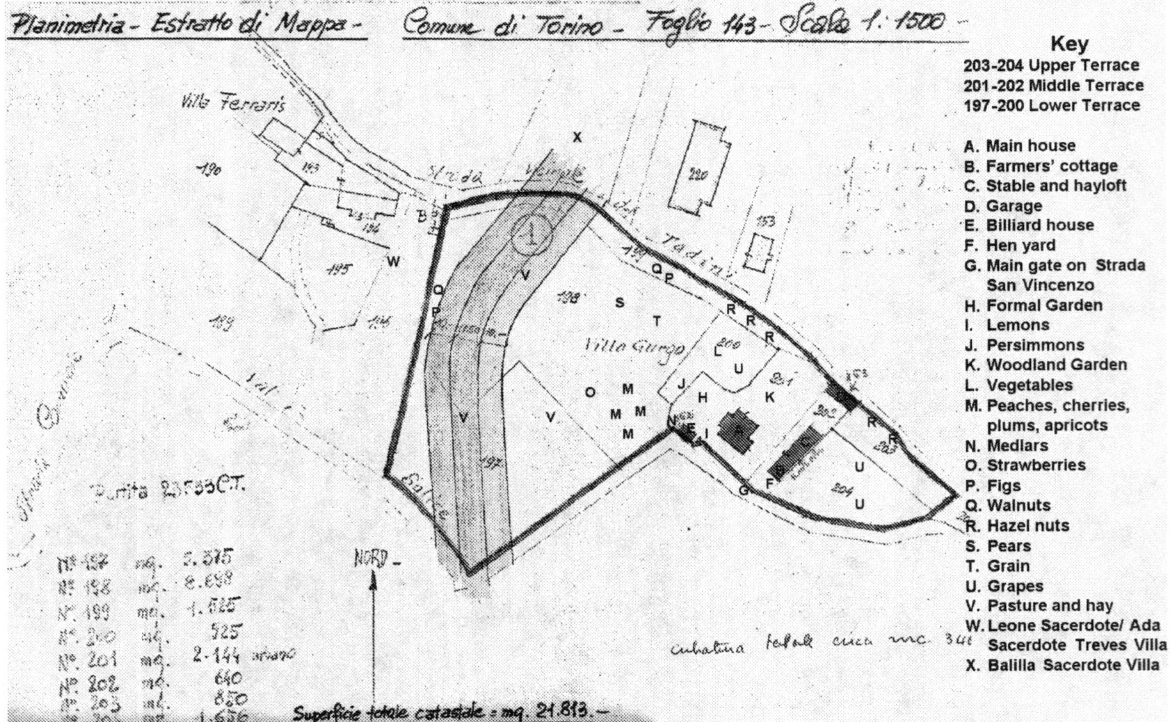

Figure 7-18
Surveyor's plot plan of Villa Gurgo, Valsalice. This villa at
13 Strada San Vincenzo became the focus of family life for
Elvira and Alberto Sacerdote and their children.

Figure 7-19
Valsalice in the 1990s. This view shows the front of the
main house, the billiard house and the current owners, the
Lodi family with Luciana (in the middle). The paved terrace was formerly covered with white pea-sized gravel.

Figure 7-20
The western façade of the main house in Valsalice. The lawn area was formerly part of the formal garden.

Figure 7-21
The western edge of the former formal garden. The new owners had the formal garden replaced by lawn. Alisa, Alex and Laurence Sacerdote are standing in what used to be a bed of roses. The Lodi family also removed the persimmon trees which grew up from the next lower terrace.

Figure 7-22
Valsalice farmer's cottage, stables and carriage house. The building in the foreground used to be the farmer's house with the stables and hayloft at the far end. Vittorio Lodi had the house refurbished for his mother-in-law's use. The stable and hayloft were subsequently converted into a ballroom. In the background is the carriage house with its two small apartments. In Elvira's day, the driveway was unpaved.

Figure 7-23
Alberto, near the end of his life. Alberto died In 1920, at 51, after suffering from chronic leukemia for five years. His drawn face and the way his clothes appear to hang on his body hint at the ravages caused by this disease and its treatment with arsenic compounds.

downstairs. The main house had four large rooms on the ground floor: a kitchen, dining room, living room, and day room; five bedrooms (including four with balconies) and a large bath on the next floor; and several smaller rooms on the top level. Elvira's cook, Teresa, did most of her work on a large wood-fired stove, although there was a small two-burner gas cooktop as well. As most fresh foods came from the farm, the kitchen never had a refrigerator. Instead Teresa kept the few perishables in tubs of cold well-water; fifty years later, when my father insisted that a fridge be installed, Teresa refused to allow it in the kitchen, and so it was kept in the day room. Because the house lacked central heating,[327] the bathroom had a gas-fired water heater covered with a filigreed housing of shiny copper; there was also a small gas jet for heating shaving suds. Since the house had been built long before the invention of flush toilets, its two water closets were in a small nineteenth-century addition.

The main house was separated from the farmer's cottage by a long drive that ran from the entry gate to the carriage house. Alongside this drive were a low wall and two rows of horse chestnut trees. Between the farmer's cottage and the retaining wall for the upper terrace was a hen yard. Attached to the farmer's house was a stable in which he kept two cows and innumerable guinea pigs (destined for the stewpot!), surmounted by a large hayloft.

The billiard room's ceiling was painted dark blue with a moon and stars motif. Its far balcony overlooked the orchard and was close enough to one of the medlar trees that one could pick fruit from it.

On the main level were two gardens. The small formal garden had two tall palm trees and several beds of flowers, mainly roses, and small graveled paths. The tops of the persimmon trees (which were growing up from the lowest terrace) gave it a very pleasant frame. The second, a very cool and shady woodland garden was planted mainly in conifers and was dominated by a huge cedar of Lebanon.[328] Between the formal garden and the billiard house, Elvira kept five large lemon trees. As lemons are not winter hardy, the trees were in huge clay pots on top of wooden wheelbarrows; in the late fall, they were wheeled into the hall of the main house, and then returned to the garden the following spring.

The arrangement between the farmers and the Sacerdote family was a fairly common contract called *mezzadrie.* Under this arrangement, the owners paid to maintain the property, including replacing dead fruit trees. The farmer had rent-free use of his house, the stables, and the agricultural lands in exchange for supplying the main house with milk, eggs, fruits, and vegetables for the table; tending the garden; and returning half the revenue from the market sales of the farm produce. While the supply of foodstuffs to the main house was quite reliable and the farmer made weekly trips to the public market in Torino to sell fruits, vegetables, and surplus garden flowers, somehow there always seemed to be an excuse why the family's share of the market revenue was not forthcoming. One year it was, "The cherries did not fetch a good price." Another year the excuse was, "The tomato crop failed." Yet another time the complaint was "The peaches were small." And so it went year after year.

Farming in Valsalice was all by hand, except that a horse or ox was used to pull the plow and farmer's cart. The only fertilizer used was cow manure and the only pesticide was copper sulfate, which was sprayed on the grapes to prevent mold. Hay and grain were reaped with a scythe. Fruit picking entailed climbing wobbly homemade ladders to reach the upper branches of the trees.

Many of the fondest memories of Giorgio, Paolo, and Eugenia[329] were of their time in Valsalice. They enjoyed running in the fields, sampling the fruits ripe from the tree, gathering wildflowers, collecting chestnuts, and hunting for mushrooms in the woodlots. There were constant visits back and forth with their Sacerdote cousins in nearby villas. Eugenia took it as her special task as a child to teach the farmers and their children how to read and write. Every afternoon, weather permitting, Elvira, who greatly admired English manners and mores, would serve tea with English biscuits in the garden;[330] children

---

[327] It was used only in the summer. When Giorgio and Luciana readied the house for sale in the mid-1970s, they had to live in it in November, which they made tolerable by using fireplaces for heat.

[328] The cedar survived a lightning strike when Giorgio was a boy, after which it was given a lighting rod. When I told the story to the current owner of the villa, Vittorio Lodi, he told me that it had been hit again in the late 1990s.

[329] And mine; I spent many boyhood summers in Valsalice.

[330] The biscuits were made by the English company Huntley and Palmer in Reading. Many years later, when my wife, Carol, and I were living in Oxford, my parents came up from London for a visit. The train passed by the Huntley and Palmer factory, which brought back happy memories of tea in the garden in Valsalice.

had the choice of tea, chocolate, or *amarenata*, a delicious drink made by diluting tart cherry syrup that Teresa preserved each year during cherry season.

In 1910, Elvira's older brother, Zio Manno, acquired a substantial country estate in Ferrere, a small town near Asti, from an impoverished nobleman, Count Gromsi. Zio Manno then sold the agricultural lands to the farm tenants at cost; to help them buy their land, he granted them five-year, interest-free mortgages. As a result of his generosity to Gromsi's former farm tenants, Zio Manno built a lot of goodwill with the Ferrere townsfolk on which he capitalized to start his political career.

He kept the main house and its gardens for himself. This house became a central focus for the extended Montalcini family. Eugenia recalled that the entire family would gather there each fall during the period between Rosh Hashanah and Yom Kippur.

Luciana's life began just before Italy entered World War I. In 1914, Guite Orefice married the Torino lawyer Leone Levi. Guite's mother, Penelope, had converted to the Jewish religion when she married a Parisian Hebrew financier. Because of Guite's French upbringing, she and her husband spoke French most of the time and raised their children biculturally. Their first child, Luciana, was born in 1915, just before Italy entered the war, and their second child, Ruggiero, followed three years later. Because Guite and Leone's marriage fell apart during the 1920s, Luciana spoke only rarely about her parents, especially her father, with whom she had little contact after their separation. They appear to have been quite stern[331], as Luciana used to tell the story that at the dinner table children were permitted only to ask for the salt. One evening, when the family servant had forgotten to serve Luciana, she turned to her father and asked for the salt, to which he replied, "Why do you want the salt? You have nothing in your dish." Nonetheless, one suspects that Luciana grew up in a very intellectually aggressive atmosphere: Among her aunts, uncles, and first cousins, there were at least six practicing lawyers and sixteen people holding doctorates in academic subjects.

World War I and its aftermath

As World War I began in August 1914, Italy adopted a neutral stance, notwithstanding its alliance with the Central Powers, Germany and Austria. However, as the war progressed into 1915, both sides were pressuring Italy to join on their side. By late spring of 1915, Vittorio Emanuele III decided to join England, France, and Russia against Germany, Austria, and Turkey. His near-term objective was to win the last bits of Italian territory still controlled by Austria: the regions around Trento and Trieste, northeast of Milan and Venice, respectively. He also had the ulterior motive of gaining more territory in the Balkans, either from Austria, which controlled Slovenia, Croatia, and Bosnia, or else at the expense of the countries recently freed from Turkish control: Albania, Serbia, Greece, and Montenegro (the native country of his queen, Elena of Montenegro).

Though the king left the management of the military campaigns to his generals, he joined his troops near the front in an effort to imbue them with patriotic fervor. In October 1917, after two years of little to no movement of the front lines, a combined Austrian and German attack broke through the Italian lines in the disastrous battle of Caporetto, north of Venice. The Italians lost over 300,000 troops killed, wounded, or captured, and almost all their artillery.[332] The enemy was able to make a 25 km advance before having to halt their advance due to a lack of supplies, which had to be delivered by horse cart. The king then rallied his troops to repair the breach in their lines and induced the British and French to send several divisions to support his army on the southern front.

During the war, there was great hardship on the home front. Both Eugenia and Paolo wrote of having to live in an unheated house and attend unheated schools because fuel was rationed. Both suffered from chilblains as a result; Elvira tried to soothe them with a steaming infusion of boiled walnut leaves. Paolo

---

[331] I had very limited contact with Guite as a child as she lived in Rome near my Uncle Ruggiero after the war. However, I too remember her as a very stern and imposing woman. Her strict notions about the proper behavior of children tended towards the old maxim that children should be seen but not heard.

[332] The battle of Caporetto touched the Sacerdote household. The husband of one of their servants, Nella, was killed in that debacle. Nella was a married sister of Camilla and Teresa who worked for the family on a live-out basis. Her only compensation for the loss of her husband was to be given a medal.

wrote an essay for a school contest on the suffering of the people who were queuing up to buy rationed foodstuffs. Eugenia in her memoirs described the daily arrival of the Red Cross trains at Porta Nuova [across the street from their apartment] bringing back the dead and wounded from the front.

As part of the war effort, the government whipped up a national anti-German, anti-Austrian hysteria.[333] Giorgio and Paolo did their part to join in the effort: They hanged Eugenia's treasured German doll, Titti, from the ceiling with a noose around its neck. In 1916, when Emperor Franz Josef of Austria died after a sixty-year reign, all the children in Giorgio's school were shepherded into the courtyard to cheer. Giorgio, who even as a boy had strong royalist leanings,[334] quietly shed a tear instead of cheering; in this event he saw the passing of an important era and the loss of a period of order, culture, and grace,[335] to be replaced by a period of disorder and brutality.

When the war was over in 1918, Italy was awarded Trieste and the Trento region, but the country had been exhausted physically and economically. The nation had suffered 680,000 men killed in action and another 450,000 permanently disabled. As the army was demobilized, hundreds of thousands of workers and peasants found themselves without work. These factors, combined with the successful Communist revolution in Russia, led to massive national unrest resulting in running gun battles in the streets between the private militias of the Italian Communists on the left and the extreme right-wing Fascists. Eugenia told of being forced to hide under the pews of a church with her Segre cousin, Nella Basola Maissa during one such gun battle; they had been in the church so that Nella could practice the piano while on vacation at the seashore.[336] In many cases, the workers occupied their factories in sit-down strikes or locked their managers in. Giorgio's uncle Vittorio Tedeschi[337] was imprisoned in his wire factory. Giorgio and Luciana's uncle Adamo Levi,[338] who had just built the first industrial ice plant in the south of Italy, had the factory totally destroyed by rampaging workers.

During this period, Elvira and Alberto Sacerdote were distracted from the political problems by his five-year-long bout with leukemia, and the raising of the children was largely given over to Camilla and Teresa. Alberto's treatments consisted of daily shots of arsenic compounds, the chemotherapy of the day.[339] Alberto died in 1920 when their children, Giorgio, Paolo, and Eugenia, ranged in age from fifteen to ten years old. By all accounts, Alberto and Elvira had been very devoted to each other during their sixteen-year marriage. Paolo describes Alberto as worshiping Elvira, and Elvira as having devoted all her energies to making his life as comfortable as possible, particularly during his long final illness.

When he died, Alberto left an estate with a declared value[340] of 1.5 million lire. This estate was apportioned one third each for Giorgio and Paolo, and one sixth each for Elvira and Eugenia. Although Elvira only received one sixth of the estate outright, she effectively had control of the entire estate because the children were minors and Elvira was their trustee. As a result, she wielded considerable influence over her children's financial affairs, even after they reached majority. Her primary financial advisor was her brother, Zio Manno.

After Alberto's death, Elvira focused on raising her three children and living fairly frugally, though with two live-in servants, Camilla and Teresa. She was always careful not to not to risk exhausting her substantial inheritances from her parents and husband, as these had to last for another forty-plus years; she knew that she would not be able to rebuild her fortune if she squandered it. While the family lived

[333] Similar hysterias were whipped up in other countries. The British royal family, which was of German descent, changed its surname from Hanover (King George I had been ruler of the German principality of Hanover) to Windsor. U.S. streets with German-sounding names were changed to patriotic names such as Liberty Drive and Victory Parkway.

[334] The most extreme royalist in the family was my father's uncle, Leone Sacerdote, who had named his children Emanuele Filiberto, Umberto Secondo, and Ada, after important past and present members of the Italian royal house.

[335] In the aftermath of World War I, several European royal families were swept out of power, including those of Germany, Austria, Russia and Turkey.

[336] Nella subsequently became a concert pianist of some note.

[337] Husband of my grandfather's sister Letizia Sacerdote.

[338] Adamo Levi was a brother of my maternal grandfather, Leone Levi; he was married to Adelina Montalcini, a sister of my paternal grandmother, Elvira Sacerdote, née Montalcini.

[339] One is left to wonder whether he died of cancer or of arsenic poisoning.

[340] At that time in Italy, taxation tended to be more of a negotiated issue than one governed by hard-and-fast rules, and hiding one's assets from the tax collector was considered a matter of honor.

comfortably, nothing was ever wasted. Even the table crumbs were gathered by Camilla to feed the birds. While Elvira spent her money carefully, she always found ways to be generous. Over the years, she would invite many members of the extended family to share the pleasures of Valsalice with her. And she devoted many hours a day to knitting sweaters, gloves, and heavy woolen socks to donate to the poor. She also organized complex family vacations to the mountains or the seashore involving dozens of aunts, uncles, cousins, nieces, and nephews. She was especially close to her brothers and sister. In the mid-1920s they jointly purchased an apartment house at 10-12 Corso Re Umberto in which they all lived, including both Elvira's and Adelina's children. As a result of Elvira's closeness to her sister's family, Giorgio and his cousin Gino Levi-Montalcini, who were only a couple of years apart in age, became the closest of friends, as did Eugenia and Gino's twin sisters, Rita and Paola. In Elvira's later years, she would invite Gino's children to stay with her in Valsalice for a month or more every summer.

The rise of Fascism

Faced with all the postwar unrest, the main Italian politicians dithered, and so did the king. The country rapidly was overtaken by anarchy. Finally, in the fall of 1922, Benito Mussolini mustered his Fascist militia for a march on Rome while his adherents in many regional centers took over police stations and other centers of power. The king, his ministers, and his army were powerless to block this seizure of power, and on October 30 the king asked Mussolini to form a government with himself as prime minister.

While the Fascist government used force to restore social order, its initial rule was not so severe. In 1924, however, the Socialist parliamentarian Giacomo Matteotti was assassinated by Fascist agents shortly after he gave a courageous speech in Parliament denouncing the Fascists. The king was conveniently out of the country at the time, on a state visit to the king of Spain. Initially it appeared that the public had turned against Mussolini, and the king considered having him arrested for murder. Ultimately the king lost his nerve and Mussolini kept his office.

Immediately thereafter, the Fascist regime imposed much harsher laws, banning opposition political parties, introducing press censorship, and rounding up all those suspected of leftist sympathies. Those who were deemed only mild threats to the regime were dosed with castor oil and then released, but others were sentenced to internal exile on remote islands, jailed, tortured, and sometimes executed, depending on how serious a threat they were thought to pose to the regime. Teachers and professors had to teach Fascist doctrine. University students had to wear Fascist uniforms to official university functions such as final examinations. All were compelled to listen to Mussolini's long-winded patriotic speeches, delivered nationally via a system of loudspeakers in city and town squares. Women's education was to be limited to domestic arts so that they might devote their lives to raising children, especially sons for the glorious Fascist army. And membership in the Fascist party became a prerequisite for many types of employment. Finally, in 1929, in an effort to gain more political support from the conservative wing of the Catholic Church, Mussolini signed the Lateran Treaty with the pope, granting him full sovereignty over the modern Vatican City and establishing Roman Catholicism as the official state religion.[341]

Initially there was considerable resistance to the Fascists both among the educated elite and among the mostly Socialist or Communist working class. However, this resistance gradually wore down, and by the end of the 1920s had pretty much disappeared. Life more or less became "normal" under the dictatorship. Elvira settled into her long widowhood, spending winters with her children in the city of Torino and summers at her country villa in Valsalice. Giorgio and Paolo took up skiing and mountaineering; these sports were the height of fashion because they were favored by the crown prince, Umberto II. The House of Savoy, which had originated in the Valle d'Aosta, had long maintained a strong interest in the Alpine life. Vittorio Emanuele II's favorite pastime had been hunting in the mountains, in what was then the royal hunting preserve and is now the Gran Paradiso National Park.

---

[341] One consequence of this treaty was (and continues to be) that the state recognizes only civil or Catholic religious marriages. All non-Catholic couples must have a civil marriage in addition to any religious ceremony they might desire in order to have their marriage recognized by the state.

Elvira's brother, Emanuele Montalcini, remained in office as mayor of Ferrere. The Montalcini did many charitable works in that town. Zio Manno owned the town's only automobile and it was regularly pressed into service as an ambulance to bring the sick and injured to the hospital in Asti. His brother, Alessandro, gave free medical care to the town's poor every Friday. Zio Manno also donated the land on which was built the town's first high school.

Elvira's brother-in-law, Cav. Leone Sacerdote, continued alone in the real estate firm that he and his brothers had inherited from their father, Cav. Emanuele Sacerdote; Leone ultimately became an important city official in Torino as well, and was publicly recognized for his service to the community.

Giorgio and then Paolo attended the selective classical high school in Torino, the Liceo d'Azeglio. The Liceo d'Azeglio's curriculum covered most of what in the United States is covered in the first two or three years at a liberal arts college. Its graduates had seven years of Latin and four of Greek, and were expected to be fluent in French. All students were required to study literature, history, mathematics, and the sciences at what we would consider the collegiate level. In addition they had survey courses in philosophy, art history, music, and economics. When its graduates entered university, they spent four to seven years (depending on the field) doing what in the United States is considered an undergraduate major plus an advanced degree in law or medicine, or a doctorate in an academic subject.

Giorgio and Paolo subsequently entered the university, where Giorgio earned a doctorate in electrical engineering and Paolo a doctorate in economics; Giorgio defended his doctoral thesis on hydroelectric power systems at the University of Milan.[342] While Giorgio and Paolo were at university, Eugenia and her first cousins, the twins Rita and Paola Levi-Montalcini, attended the Liceo Feminile, a cross between a girls' finishing school and a Fascist-style domestic arts school.

After his required peacetime military service, where he commanded a battery of horse-drawn antiaircraft guns,[343] Giorgio went to work as a manager for STIPEL, the regional telephone company for Piemonte and Lombardy. In 1927, as he stood in an open car inspecting the work of a crew that was installing telephone poles in Asti, his car was struck by the lead car in a military motorcade that was driving the king to a public function in the same town. His left elbow and knee were crushed, and he was taken, unconscious, to the hospital in Asti, where the family was well known thanks to the charitable works of Emanuele and Dr. Alessandro Montalcini. Elvira, Paolo, and Eugenia were constantly at his bedside, first in Asti and later at the Institute for Traumatology at the medical school of the University of Bologna, where he went for reconstructive surgery. Despite the best efforts of the surgeon, Giorgio recovered only about 80 percent use of the injured knee and 50 percent use of the elbow. Teresa, Elvira's cook, also sought divine intervention to further Giorgio's recovery by making a pilgrimage to a church where miracles were purported to occur. During his recovery, Giorgio decided to take advantage of his free time and began to attend English classes at the Berlitz School in Torino, a decision that later proved very important.

Having seen firsthand the work of the medical staff attending to Giorgio, Eugenia and Paolo decided upon careers in medicine. For Paolo, it meant completing his studies in economics, and then beginning university all over again in medicine. By a curious coincidence, Rita Levi-Montalcini's former nanny died of cancer the same year; this experience convinced Rita to study medicine as well. For Eugenia and Rita this decision presented a serious problem; their high school studies at the Liceo Feminile did not qualify them to enter university. Consequently they hired as tutors a pair of professors, one in classics and one in physics, and crammed for the university entrance examinations. Their cramming entailed many months of fourteen-hour days of study; they even took their tutors with them on their summer vacation in the Alps. They passed the entrance exams and entered medical school in the fall of 1928, graduating in 1936.

---

[342] He attended the Politecnico, the engineering school in Torino. The laws at the time required that each doctoral candidate submit to a final examination at another university.

[343] Maurizio Lustig, Eugenia's future husband, served as a submarine officer.

Figure 7-24
The Ovazza Bank in Piazza Carlo Alberto. After emancipation, the
Torino Hebrew community grew quite wealthy. One of the wealthiest
families, the Ovazza established an important bank in Piazza Carlo
Alberto, facing the former ghetto. After passage of the racial laws of
1938, Hebrews were no longer allowed to own banks or businesses
with more than one hundred employees. Photograph, 2005 by George
S. Sacerdote.

Figure 7-25
The Ovazza villa. The Ovazzas had a magnificent villa in
Moncalieri that had formerly belonged to the royal fam-
ily. It was just outside of Torino, near a royal palace, the
Castello di Moncalieri, where the crown prince Umberto
II was tutored. They were cousins of Giorgio's through the
marriage of his uncle Balilla Sacerdote to Elena Ovazza.
Balilla's and Elena's second daughter, Nella, also married
an Ovazza. Nella and her immediate family were murdered
by the Nazis.

Figure 7-26
Giorgio's diploma from the Liceo d'Azeglio. Note that
it lists the subjects studied in the last year: Italian, Latin,
Greek, history and geography, philosophy, mathematics, physics and chemistry, natural science (biology), and
physical education. It also lists his final year grades, all
eights and nines on a ten-point scale, where 6 was passing.

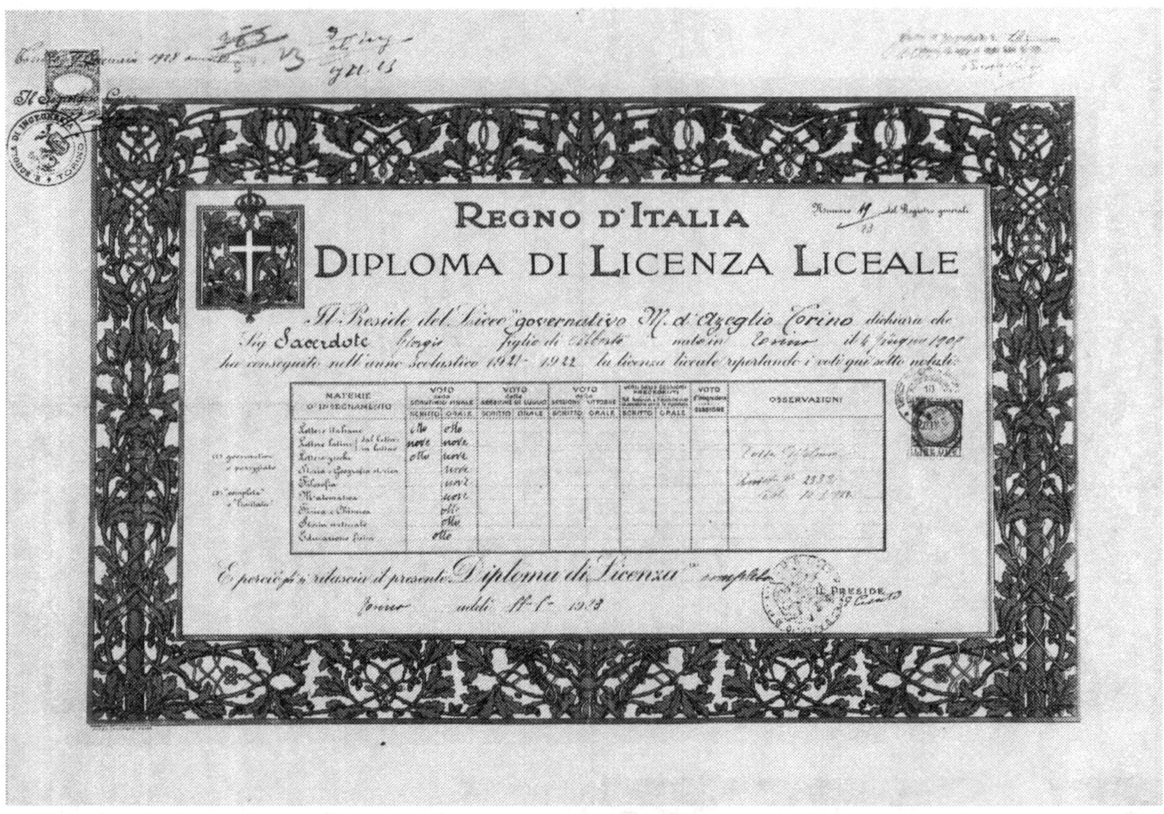

Figure 7-27
Giorgio's university
student ID, 1923

Figure 7-28
Giorgio's doctoral diploma. Note that he scored a 98/100
on his final examinations.

Figure 7-29
The assembled dignitaries at the 1925 dedication of the
school in Ferrere. The land for the school was donated
by Zio Manno [Emanuele Montalcini, Elvira's brother]
when he was mayor of Ferrere. Gino Levi-Montalcini was
the architect; this was his first major commission. When
Carol and I visited the school in 2005 with Eugenia Lustig
and two of her adult children, Livia and Mauro, Carol
discovered this picture behind a sliding bulletin board.
The girl in white in the middle of the picture is Eugenia
at age fifteen. Sprinkled throughout this picture are other
family members.

Figure 7-30
Paolo, 1928 in military uniform. Both Giorgio and Paolo had to serve as officers in the Fascist army. Giorgio commanded a battery of horse-drawn anti aircraft guns during the mid-1920s. The insignia on Paolo's helmet suggest that he was an artillery officer.

Figure 7-31
Zio Manno, Eugenia, another couple, and Elvira in the Swiss Alps, 1930. Not pictured, Giorgio, the photographer.

Figure 7-32
Eugenia, Rita and their tutors, 1930, on vacation in Vico Canavese. Left to right, Prof. Lobetti, Guite Orefice Levi, Elvira Sacerdote, Eugenia, Rita, Professor Bodoni and his daughter, Luciana, and Zio Manno. Because Eugenia, Rita and Paola had gone to a girl's high school rather than an academic school, they were forced to hire tutors to learn the material required to pass the university entrance exams. They kept up a pace of 14-hour days for many months, and even took their tutors with them on vacation. All three women went on to distinguished careers, Rita and Eugenia in medical research, and Paola as an artist. Their example inspired Luciana to insist on an academic education.

Figure 7-33
Luciana as a girl of 13, 1928. This picture may have been taken on the occasion of her bat mitzvah.

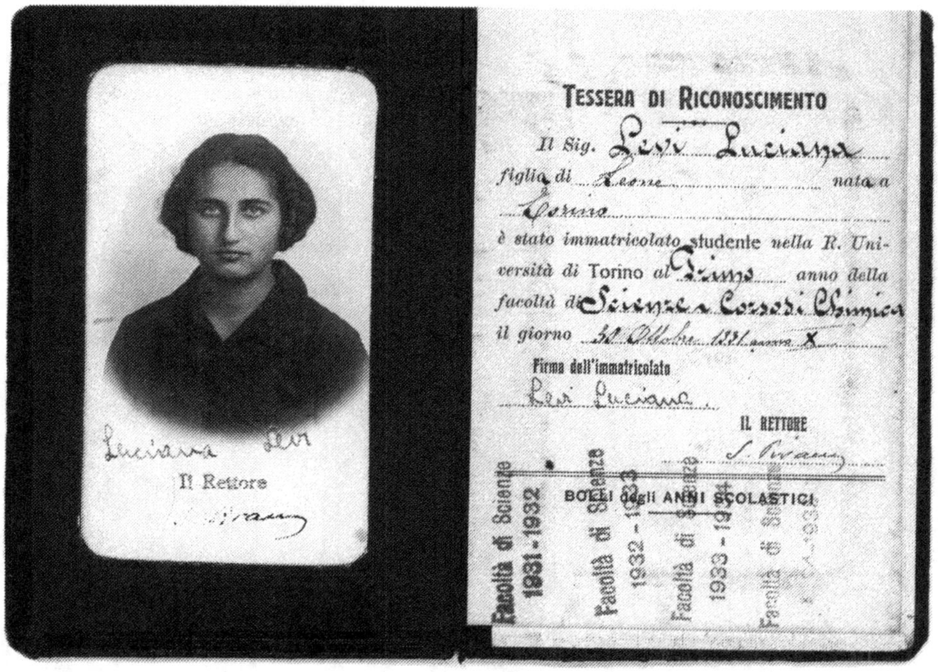
TESSERA DI RICONOSCIMENTO

Il Sig. Levi Luciana
figlia di Leone nata a Torino
è stato immatricolato studente nella R. Università di Torino al Primo anno della facoltà di Scienze e Corso di Chimica
il giorno 30 Ottobre 1931 anno X

Firma dell'immatricolato
Levi Luciana

IL RETTORE

BOLLI degli ANNI SCOLASTICI

Facoltà di Scienze 1931-1932
Facoltà di Scienze 1932-1933
Facoltà di Scienze 1933-1934

Luciana Levi
Il Rettore

Figure 7-34
Luciana's student ID, 1931. Despite being only 16, Luciana was admitted to University in 1931. She then completed her doctorate in four years.

Figure 7-35
Luciana's doctoral diploma. Note that it was sufficiently unusual for women to go to university that her certificate was made out to *Mr.* Luciana Levi, *son* of Leone.

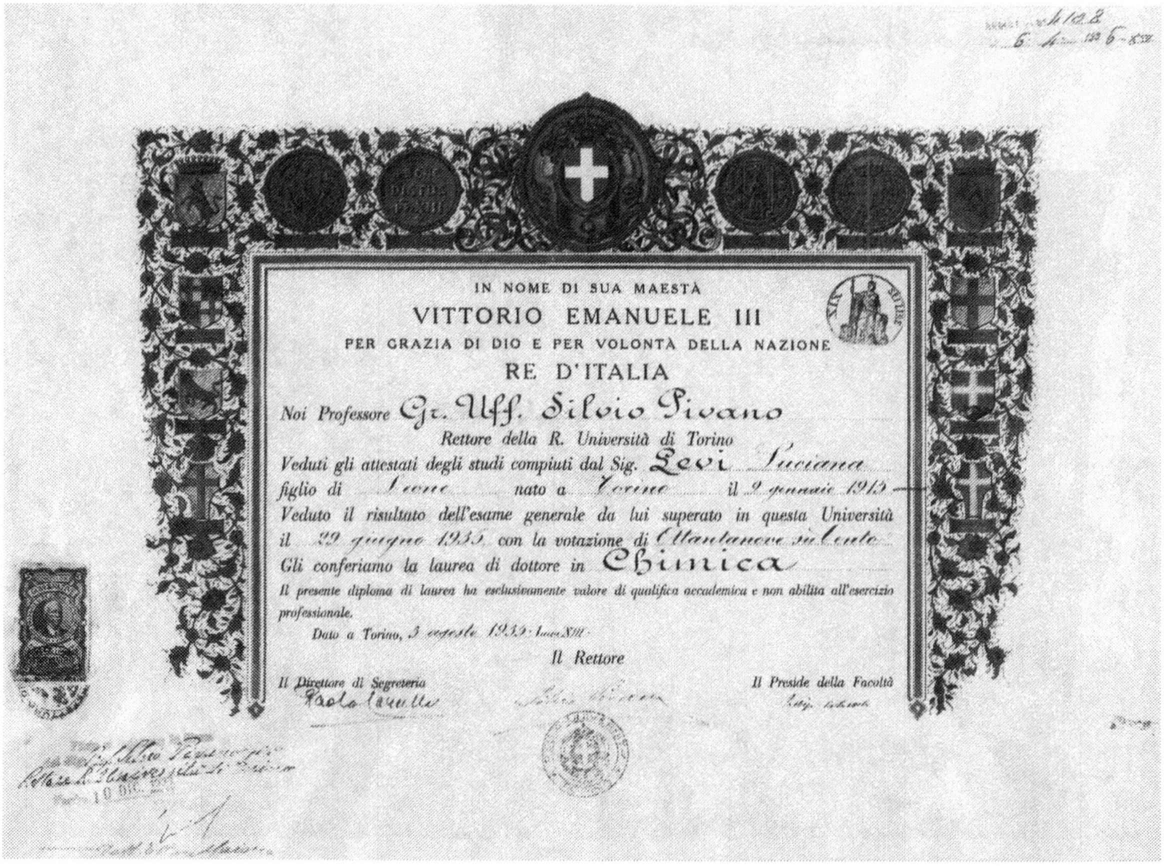
IN NOME DI SUA MAESTÀ
VITTORIO EMANUELE III
PER GRAZIA DI DIO E PER VOLONTÀ DELLA NAZIONE
RE D'ITALIA

Noi Professore Gr. Uff. Silvio Pivano
Rettore della R. Università di Torino
Veduti gli attestati degli studi compiuti dal Sig. Levi Luciana
figlio di Leone *nato a* Torino *il* 9 gennaio 1915
Veduto il risultato dell'esame generale da lui superato in questa Università il 29 giugno 1935 *con la votazione di* Ottantanove su cento
Gli conferiamo la laurea di dottore in Chimica
Il presente diploma di laurea ha esclusivamente valore di qualifica accademica e non abilita all'esercizio professionale.
Dato a Torino, 3 agosto 1935 Anno XIII

Il Rettore

Il Direttore di Segreteria — *Il Preside della Facoltà*

Figure 7-36
Giorgio and Paolo skiing 1935. Note the neckwear and the length of the skis. The crown prince, Umberto II, spent most of his youth in Torino. He was tutored at the Castello di Moncalieri and Palazzo di Stupinigi, two palaces just outside of Torino. He was an avid skier and mountaineer, going often to the Valle d'Aosta, an hour's drive northwest of Torino. Thus, skiing and climbing became very fashionable sports in the city. Paolo was especially taken with climbing, and his mother Elvira was very worried that he would suffer some frightful accident.

Figure 7-37
Giorgio's ID card from when he worked as manager of the
Novara district for the STIPEL telephone company.

Figure 7-38
Giorgio, 1934

Figure 7-39
Luciana, 1935

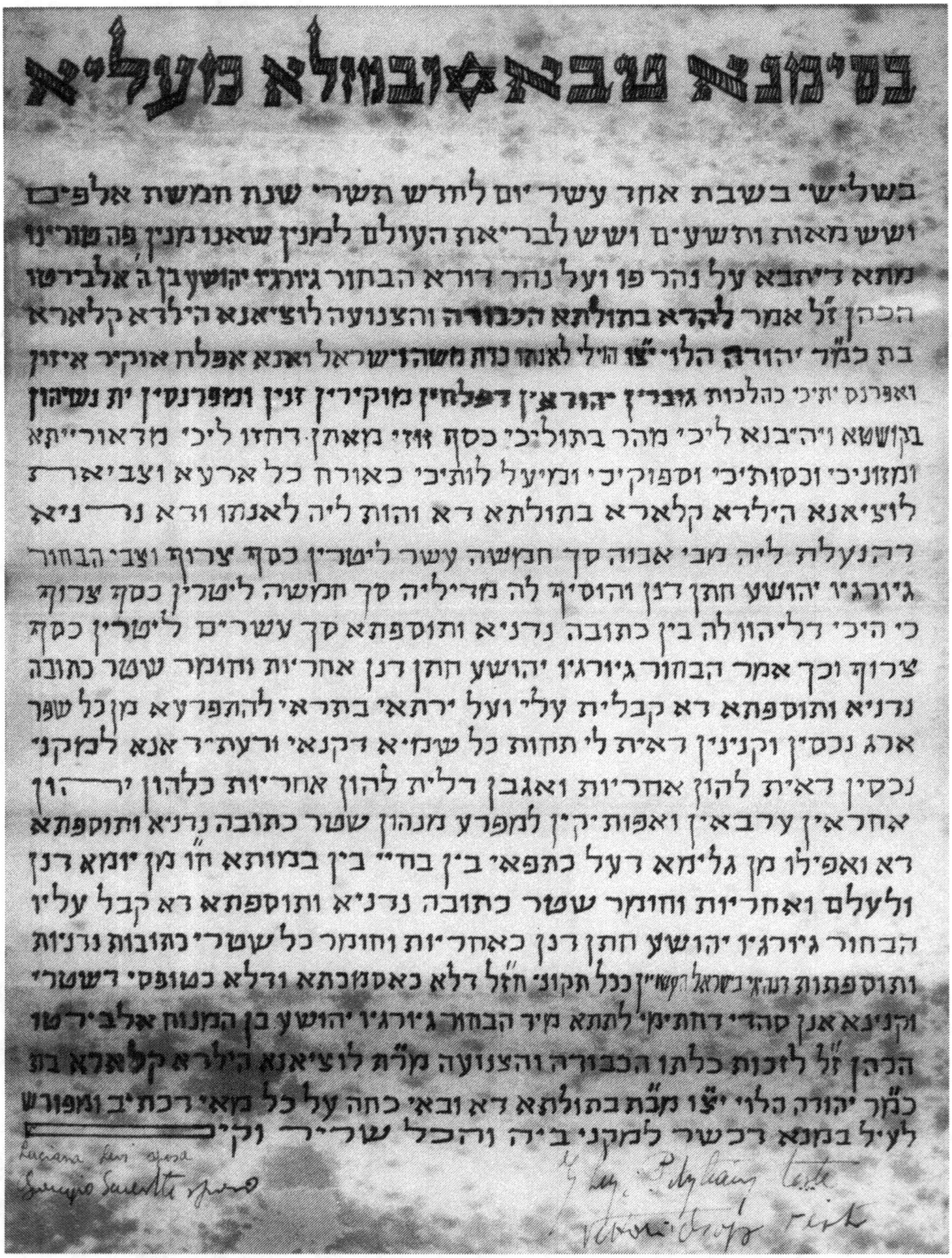

Figure 7-40

Giorgio and Luciana's *Ketubah* [Hebrew wedding contract], hand-written on parchment. As distinct from American Ashkenazic practice, Italian Hebrews did not generally have separate vernacular and Hebrew names, although a few did. If someone had a name that was the same in both languages, so it was. If not, but there was a direct translation then they used the translated name. Otherwise, the Italian name was simply transliterated into Hebrew. In this Ketubah, one can clearly read Giorgio Yehoshua [translation of Salvatore] ben [son of] Alberto haCohen [Cohen being the translation of Sacerdote] in the third and fourth lines up from the bottom. Similarly, Luciana Elda Clara bat [daughter of] Yehuda [Luciana's father Enrico Leone Levi evidently had a distinct Hebrew name, Judah] haLevi [the Levite] appears in the second and third lines up from the bottom. The witnesses were Giuseppe Pitigliani and Vittorio Ovazza. In the family archive, we have a very similar Ketubah from the marriage of Alberto and Elvira, but it was too fragile to photograph.

Figure 7-41
Maurizio Lustig in military uniform, 1938. During the
Ethiopian war, Maurizio was recalled into military service,
where he was an officer in the submarine corps.

Figure 7-42
Luciana and Albert, 1936. This picture was probably taken
in Novara.

Figure 7-43
Luciana and Albert in the formal
garden at Valsalice, May 1937.
In the beds on either side of the
gravel path were rose bushes, and
in the background, growing up
from the terrace on the next level
down, were persimmons.

Figure 7-44
Giorgio and Albert on vacation in the Alps, 1937, a few
months before Peter was born

Figure 7-45
Luciana, Albert and Elvira, in the garden of Valsalice,
spring 1937. Albert was evidently born with a silver spoon
in his mouth. Note also the embroidered Mickey Mouse
bib on baby Albert. Disney's new animated cartoons had
become a big hit in Italy in the mid 1930s, and the Disney
company produced a series of cartoon parodies of the classics of Italian literature and opera.

Figure 7-46
Albert and Peter,
Valsalice, 1938

Figure 7-47
Eugenia and Livia,
Valsalice, 1938

After he recovered from the reconstructive surgery, Giorgio returned to work with the telephone company and was made district manager for a group of towns in the Alpine foothills. He was based in the town of Novara in the extreme northeastern corner of Piemonte. His responsibilities focused on the expansion of telephone service into smaller towns. Giorgio described his formula for opening service in a small town as follows: First he would put the switchboard in the village bar, the place likely to be open the longest hours, and he would train the barkeep's wife or oldest daughter on how to serve as the switchboard operator. Then he would give a few months of free service to two or three leading citizens, generally the mayor, the parish priest, and the principal of the school, in the expectation that others would follow their example and take telephone service as well.

Shortly after Giorgio lost his father to leukemia, Luciana lost hers to a different problem: her parents separated in the mid-1920s[344] and she was sent to a Swiss boarding school at the age of ten while her parents sorted out their difficulties. Having been sent away to school at such a tender age, she realized that it was up to her alone to make her way in the world and she became fiercely independent. After that time she had limited contact with her father. Ultimately she returned to Torino to live with her mother, Guite. Luciana, who was five years younger than Eugenia and six years younger than Rita and Paola (though only three years behind them in school), insisted that she be allowed to attend the classical high school, the Liceo d'Azeglio. It was famous for having a very scholarly and demanding faculty. By all accounts Luciana was a brilliant and precocious student. She skipped several grades and graduated from the Liceo d'Azeglio in 1931, two years earlier than normal, at age sixteen. She then decided to take the very difficult French *baccalauréat* exam as well, as she was fully fluent in French. That summer she went to Grenoble to study for the French exam and passed it with distinction after a few months' study. In 1931 Luciana entered the University of Torino at the age of sixteen to study chemistry, and was awarded her doctorate in 1935, at age twenty. In completing her doctorate in only four years, she finished her studies ahead of Rita and Eugenia, even though they had entered university ahead of her. In those days women were still sufficiently rare as university graduates that her diploma was made out to *Mr.* Luciana Levi, *son* of Leone.

In early 1935, Giorgio proposed to Luciana, and they were married later that year, a few months after she was awarded her doctorate. They had known each other for many years as they had first cousins in common in the Levi-Montalcini. After a honeymoon in Libya, they settled into an apartment in Novara. Nine months later their first son, Alberto Mauro, was born. Shortly after his birth, STIPEL transferred Giorgio back to Torino to become the company's technical director, and the family moved back to its home city. Fifteen months after the birth of Alberto, Giorgio and Luciana had a second son, Piero Marcello.

In the same year Giorgio and Luciana were married, Mussolini decided to rekindle Italy's imperial ambitions and set his sights on the conquest of Ethiopia, one of two remaining independent countries in Africa.[345] In October of that year he launched an invasion of that country from the Italian colony of Eritrea. Within a few months, the Italians triumphed over the under-armed and under-trained Ethiopians. Mussolini granted Vittorio Emanuele III the added title of Emperor of Ethiopia, and the legitimate emperor, Haile Selassie,[346] was sent into exile.

As part of the effort to whip up popular support for the conquest, Mussolini decreed that all married women had to contribute their gold wedding rings to the national treasury; in return they were to be given iron rings. As the wife of an important citizen of Novara, Luciana had to be among the first to contribute; disapproving of the Ethiopian war and having no intention of giving up her wedding ring, she hid her ring, purchased a cheap plated one, and made a great show of donating the latter to the war effort.

Haile Selassie made a dramatic appearance before the League of Nations in Geneva to appeal for help against the invaders. As a result, the invasion was denounced by the League of Nations, and several countries, notably England and France, imposed economic sanctions on Italy. This economic and

---

[344] Until the 1970s, Italy had no divorce law, so that her parents were technically still married thirty-five years later.

[345] The other was Liberia, founded by U.S. abolitionists during the nineteenth century as a home for freed slaves.

[346] Haile Selassie claimed descent from the union of King Solomon and the Queen of Sheba. In Ethiopia at the time there was a tribe, the Falasha, who practiced Hebrew rites from the time of the first Temple. Even the Coptic Christian majority in Ethiopia practices distinctly Jewish rites: They celebrate the Sabbath on Saturday, not Sunday; they shun pork; and all males are circumcised on their eighth day of life. Most of the Falasha were airlifted to Israel during the persecutions under the dictatorship that overthrew Haile Selassie in the 1970s.

diplomatic isolation had the terrible effect of pushing Mussolini closer to Nazi Germany, although at that time the linkage between the two countries was far from strong. Indeed, Mussolini derisively dismissed Hitler as an upstart who had to get himself elected instead of gaining political control through a coup d'état.

In 1936, Italy joined Germany in its backing of the Fascist side during the Spanish Civil War. Mussolini's son, a military pilot, was shot down, and died in that conflict. Nonetheless, when Germany invaded Austria on March 11–12, 1938, Italy nearly went to war against Germany. Several years before, Mussolini had signed a mutual defense treaty with Austria's chancellor, Engelbert Dollfuss,[347] and considered invoking that treaty to prevent the establishment of German power on his northeastern frontier. In May of that year, Hitler paid a state visit to Mussolini and reassured the latter that he had no designs upon Italian territory.[348] Increasingly, German officials were seen shuttling in and out of Rome. Eugenia told the story of when she and her husband, Maurizio, were dining at Alfredo, the famous Roman restaurant, and Marshal Goering, head of the Luftwaffe, entered and ordered out all the patrons so that he could enjoy the restaurant with his officers, unsullied by Italian riffraff. In 1939, Mussolini's son-in-law and foreign minister, Count Ciano, negotiated a full friendship and cooperation treaty between Italy and Germany; thus was born the Berlin-Rome Axis.

The war in Ethiopia and its aftermath rekindled a certain amount of anti-Fascist activity. The Italian exile community in France began to publish anti-Fascist literature which it smuggled into Italy. Inside the country, groups opposed to the regime began to meet clandestinely to plot its overthrow, although most of these plots never got beyond the talking stage. As a result, Mussolini cracked down on the opposition with numerous arrests, imprisonments, and internal exiles. Fascist agents assassinated the Roselli brothers, prominent Italian anti-Fascists, in Paris. Among those arrested in Italy were Luciana's cousin Vittorio Foa,[349] Giorgio's distant cousin Sion Segre, Rita's and Eugenia's thesis adviser, Prof. Giuseppe Levi and his sons, and the left-wing doctor and author Carlo Levi.[350]

The Racial Laws of 1938 and emigration

As Mussolini cozied up to Hitler, the latter began to demand that Italy copy Germany's racial policies. This was a new turn for the Fascist government, as heretofore it had shown no signs of anti-Semitism. The Fascists had as many Hebrew supporters as opponents. Indeed, Mussolini had a Hebrew mistress, Margherita Sarfatti, who ran one of the most prominent artistic salons in Rome. Initially, Hitler demanded that all foreign Hebrews who had taken refuge in Italy, mostly from Germany, be expelled. Beginning in November 1938, and continuing into the next year, Mussolini issued a series of decrees known as the Racial Laws. These new laws were a shock to the nation, especially the Hebrew community, which in many cases had lived in Italy since Roman times. The Hebrews were utterly indistinguishable from their Christian neighbors except in matters of religion.

Some of the highlights of the laws included:

- Marriages between Aryans and Hebrews were prohibited.
- All Hebrews had to register as such, and all official documents pertaining to them had to identify them as such.
- Hebrews could not work in
  —Government offices, civil or military
  —The Fascist party
  —Government-owned or -controlled companies
  —Companies doing business with the government
  —Banks and insurance companies
  —Schools, universities, or hospitals.

---

[347] Dolfuss was assassinated by Nazi agents in 1934.

[348] To show his displeasure at the arrival of Hitler, Pope Pius XI made a special effort to be out of Rome on the day of Hitler's visit.

[349] Foa was a prominent left-wing politician. After the war, he was made a senator for life.

[350] These Levi families were unrelated to each other or to Luciana.

- Hebrews were sharply limited in their rights to own real, personal, or commercial property.
- Hebrews were not allowed to attend schools or universities.
- Hebrews could not be lodged in hotels.

In the following months there were mass firings of Hebrew staff and dismissals of Hebrew students. The Hebrew community of Torino set up a parallel school system for its children, although this was clearly at best a stopgap measure. Various members of the family began to transfer property holdings to Christian nominees who could hold it for them.

As a result of the Racial Laws, Giorgio was summarily dismissed from STIPEL in December, 1938. He was irate at his dismissal; he had had considerable success at STIPEL and had grown the company's business in the Novara district by 15 percent during his brief tenure as district manager. In January 1939 he took the courageous step of writing a letter of protest to Dott. Pio Venturini, the company's director general (CEO). In that letter he complained of the peremptory nature of his dismissal, as if he had been fired for cause. He further complained that he had been given no reason for being let go and that the dismissal letter made no mention of his substantial accomplishments as manager for the preceding ten years. He closed the letter by reminding the Venturini of the serious physical injuries he had sustained in the line of duty. There is no evidence of a reply to his letter.

The rest of the family was sharply divided as to how to respond. Paolo left almost immediately for Paris to continue his medical research since he was banned from professional work in Italy. Others also decided to emigrate while many thought they could remain as second-class citizens, perhaps working in the underground economy. In early 1939, Giorgio's cousin by marriage, Oscar Ghez, arranged to swap his small rubber factory in Italy for a French rubber reclamation plant that was owned by the Pirelli Tire Company. This swap was arranged via Eugenia's husband, Maurizio Lustig, who had befriended the Pirelli brothers in engineering school and who was an executive in their company. Ghez moved to Pont-de-Cheruy (near Lyon) with his wife, Nella Treves; his in-laws, Angiolo and Ada (Sacerdote) Treves and Dario and Egle Treves; and their children. Maurizio arranged to be transferred to Argentina, where Pirelli planned to build a factory to serve the South American market, and in January of 1939, he emigrated to Argentina with his wife Eugenia and their infant daughter Livia. Elvira, Giorgio, and Luciana decided to emigrate to Switzerland with their children. Several of Luciana's cousins[351] left for Peru, Mexico, and the United States. Many others remained, including most of Giorgio's Sacerdote and Montalcini relatives, Luciana's brother Ruggiero, and the vast majority of her Levi and Debenedetti cousins.

Emigration was no simple matter. The family had lived in Piemonte for four hundred years. Leaving meant leaving behind almost all their friends and relatives, their prominent social position in the community, their homes, virtually all their household goods, and their beloved villa in Valsalice. Also, they were prohibited from taking money out of Italy, making it hard to set up a new life for themselves. To deal with the latter problem, Giorgio and Luciana made at least three clandestine trips to Switzerland, France, and Belgium in 1938-39, opening accounts with French, Swiss, and U.S. banks into which they deposited cash, securities, and jewels that they had spirited out of Italy. On one of those trips they skied across the Alps. They were accompanied part of the way by a Fascist *carabiniere* whom they met on the snow. They pretended to be on vacation. After he skied on, they turned toward Switzerland. The Fascist was unaware that Luciana wore a diamond necklace with three diamond pendants under her ski clothes. Many years later, those pendants became the engagement rings worn by her daughters-in-law, Carole Trautman, Bonnie Johnson, and Carol Robinson. One of those rings is now worn by Carole's daughter-in-law Michele Verni.

---

[351] Edmea (Memé), Nadia, and Gisella were double cousins of Luciana's. Their father, Ettore Levi, was an older brother of my maternal grandfather, Leone Levi, and their mother was a sister of my maternal grandmother, Guite Orefice. Memé married Dr. Michelangelo Ottolenghi, who began a pharmaceutical business in Peru and Ecuador. Nadia married a civil engineer, Mario Levi, who became professor at the University of Mexico City. And Gisella married a German sociologist, Prof. Werner Karmann, in New York. Another cousin, Anna Foa, and her husband, Davide Jona, went to New York. Nina Rossi, a Debenedetti cousin, and her husband, Bruno, went to Cambridge, Massachusetts.

I suspect (but do not know) that Luciana's uncle Raoul Orefice,[352] a prominent Paris banker, was instrumental in getting them introductions to these foreign banks. Giorgio and Luciana's cousin Ulrico Montalcini[353] was also more than helpful in using his financial firm to help them obtain bearer securities, jewels, and other easily transportable instruments of value.[354] Later on, after he had left Italy for good, Giorgio helped other family members move assets abroad as well.

As part of the emigration process, Giorgio and Luciana also had to obtain good-conduct certificates from the Italian police as a condition to obtain permission to leave the country. The good conduct certificates were also required for them to obtain entry permits for their destination country. The good-conduct documents were obtained just before Christmas in 1938, and permission to enter Switzerland as temporary residents for six months was granted in March 1939.

In May 1939, Elvira, Giorgio, Luciana, and their two sons, Alberto and Piero, left for Switzerland, going to Lausanne, on the north shore of Lake Geneva. They made one last effort to convince Luciana's brother Ruggiero to join them, but he refused. The clock on their six-month residency had started in March, so they had to decide what to do next by the end of September. Soon after arriving in Switzerland, they decided to join the Ghez/Treves group in France, where Giorgio became the chief engineer for the rubber reclaiming business they had acquired from the Pirellis (he was the only technically trained member of the group). The family rented Villa Humbert, a comfortable house in the town of Cremieux, hired a nanny for the children, and began to settle down. In the meanwhile, Giorgio and his Treves/Ghez cousins purchased some German patents for reclaiming rubber and began to conduct unsuccessful experiments to convert these into a reliable industrial process.

During the summer of 1939, Nazi Germany and the Soviet Union signed a nonaggression treaty and a secret side agreement to divide Poland between them. On September 1, Germany and the Soviet Union invaded Poland, starting World War II. France and England, which were bound by treaty to come to the aid of Poland, declared war on Germany. For the moment, Italy stayed out of the war. After subduing Poland in a few weeks, Germany settled into several uneasy months of inaction, the "Phony War" with England and France.

Giorgio and Luciana were very concerned that Italy could join the war at any moment and they feared that they would be interned by the French as enemy aliens. They had seen the appalling conditions under which the French had interned the refugees from the Spanish Civil War. They had no doubt that France would be even less charitable toward enemy aliens. In retrospect, this was prescient thinking on their part. In 1941–42 the Vichy French[355] government established a network of more than one hundred slave labor camps in the Sahara in its colonies, Morocco, Algeria and Tunisia. Thousands of unfortunate foreign Hebrews and political dissidents were sent to these camps to be worked to death. Giorgio and Luciana were also well aware of the atrocities occurring daily in the Nazi death camps, as documented by the British government in a pamphlet partly reproduced in Appendix I.

Paolo left at once for the United States, gaining entry under the French quota, as the Italian quota had a several-year waiting list. Giorgio began to make the rounds of western hemisphere consulates in Lyon to search for a new haven. When he met with the consul general of the United States, he requested a temporary residency visa. However, when he mentioned his work in the rubber reclaiming industry, the consul general chose to issue immigration papers instead and jumped the family to the head of the waiting list. The United States was anxious to recruit immigrants with critical technical skills, of which experience in the manufacture of rubber was at the top of the list. As a result of the Japanese conquest of Malaya, rubber had become extremely scarce in the United States and was rationed even before the country entered the war in 1941, and experts in reclaiming used rubber were in high demand. The

---

[352] Uncle Raoul was the brother of Luciana's mother, Guite Orefice. Raoul's daughter, Huguette Beres, started a print gallery on the Quai d'Orsay in Paris in the 1950s. During her lifetime, she amassed a world-class collection of Japanese prints. This collection was auctioned off at her death by Sotheby's. Her daughter, Ann-Isabel Beres Montanari, now runs the gallery with her daughter Florence Montanari.

[353] Ulrico was married to their joint cousin Nina Levi-Montalcini. Ulrico and Nina were distant cousins of each other. The Montalcini banking business from the 1600s had come down to Ulrico's side of the family.

[354] Securities in Luciana's portfolio at the time of her death many years later dated to these trips. They included several Swiss stocks, such as Nestlé and UBS.

[355] The Vichy government was the puppet state set up in southern France by the German Nazis.

Angiolo Treves and Oscar Ghez families also received visas for the United States, while Dario Treves and his family could get only a visa for Cuba—you took what you could get in those days.[356]

Luciana began to search for a ship that could take them to America. Each of these searches entailed receiving permission from the French police to travel to a port city to visit the offices of a shipping line. Finally the family obtained tickets for May 1940, on the Champlain, sailing from Bordeaux to New York. In applying for steamship tickets, Giorgio and Luciana were subjected to the very detailed racial classification system associated with the US immigration policy of the time.

On May10, the "Phony War" ended with the German invasion of Holland, Belgium, and France. Those countries' resistance collapsed almost immediately. By May 26 the combined French and British armies were pinned down in the town of Dunkirk, retreating to England. Elvira, Giorgio, Luciana, and the children fled immediately toward Bordeaux, hoping to get out of France before being cut off by the Germans. They got as far as the railway station in Bordeaux, but lacked any sort of transport to take them to the docks; all cars, trucks, and buses had been requisitioned by the French army for the war effort. Finally they found a horse-drawn hearse, minus the horse, which had also been requisitioned. They loaded the children and their baggage into the hearse and pushed it through the streets of Bordeaux to the docks. Once aboard the *Champlain*, they heard a German broadcast promising to sink the ship as it crossed the Atlantic. The Germans made good on their promise on the ship's return voyage from New York.

After an eight-day voyage on the perilous, iceberg-filled northerly route, the family arrived in New York in June 1940, just as Italy entered the war on the German side. The Italians invaded southern France, grabbing the territories that Vittorio Emanuele II had given up to Napoleon III in the 1850s, including the town of Cremieux.

Having landed in Manhattan, the family's next problem was to pass the physical examinations required of all new immigrants. Giorgio and Luciana's sons, Alberto and Piero, had contracted a highly contagious disease, whooping cough, during the ocean voyage and Giorgio was lame in one arm and one leg as a result of his accident many years previous. If they were rejected by the medical examiners, they would be sent back to France or, worse yet, Italy. Luciana sternly told the children to choke down any urge to cough when the doctor was around, and Giorgio managed to convince the examiner that his injuries were no limitation on his ability to do physical work. And so they passed the inspection and were admitted into the United States.

After a few days in a hotel they set about finding more permanent lodging. After a few failed attempts to find suitable housing, they rented an apartment at 76-09 34th Avenue in Jackson Heights, Queens. The next crisis was to prepare the first meal. None of the three adults had ever set foot in a kitchen, let alone cooked anything. Elvira made it clear that at age sixty she was not about to learn cookery. My mother then gave in and boiled some eggs for the family.[357] By the end of their first week in the apartment, the family had become so Americanized that they served corn flakes[358] to Salvador Luria[359] on his first day in the United States. A few weeks before, Paolo had financed Luria's entry into the United States with the required $5000; Luria had been a medical student at the University of Torino with both Eugenia and Paolo.

The next problem was to raise cash for living expenses. Upon leaving France, each adult had been allowed to carry 1000 French francs and 2400 Swiss francs. This was not going to go very far. Luciana found a part-time job as a laboratory technician, paying her about $10–$15 per week. That was not going to go very far either. Giorgio began to visit the U.S. branches of the European banks where he and Luciana had deposited funds before the war. Initially he had some success withdrawing funds, but as the

---

[356] Dario Treves was a painter. We have several landscapes of Cuba that he produced during his sojourn there. After some months in Cuba, the Dario Treves family obtained a visa to enter the US.

[357] Luciana went on to become a master of Piemontese cookery. Some of my fondest memories from my childhood are of the wonderful risottos, polentas, veal dishes, galantines, and desserts that she prepared on a daily basis.

[358] Corn flakes did not exist in France or Italy at the time. Many years later, my grandmother Elvira was still convinced that corn flakes were the quintessential American food. Whenever I would visit her in Valsalice she would try to induce me to eat corn flakes because I was an American child. I suspected that she always offered the same box of corn flakes, because they seemed always to be terribly stale.

[359] When the Racial Laws were passed, Luria moved his research to Belgium. When the Germans invaded that country, he made his way to Portugal. From there he went to New York, arriving about a week after Giorgio and Luciana. He subsequently had a brilliant academic career in the United States, culminating in a Nobel Prize for his research in microbiology.

Figure 7-48

Racial Laws, 1938–9. These laws enforced nearly complete segregation of the Hebrew community from the rest of the Italian population, even though in many cases the Hebrews had lived in Italy longer than their neighbors and differed from them only in their religious tradition. Listed on the cover are laws concerning:

• Prohibition of mixed marriages
• Exclusion of Hebrews from schools
• Limitations of property and business ownership by Hebrews
• Prohibition of Hebrew military service
• Prohibition on Hebrews joining the PNF (Fascist Party)
• Defense of the Italian race
• Exclusion of Hebrews from the professions
• Rights of Aryans with Hebrew-sounding names to change their names

PROVVEDIMENTI PER LA DIFESA

DELLA

RAZZA ITALIANA

Matrimonio - Ebrei stranieri - Discriminazioni.

R. D. L. 17 novembre 1938, n. 1728.
Legge 5 gennaio 1939, n. 274.
Legge 13 luglio 1939, n. 1024.

Difesa della razza nella scuola.

R. D. L. 15 novembre 1938, n. 1779.
Legge 5 gennaio 1939, n. 98.

Limiti proprietà immobiliare - Attività industriale e commerc. - Ente gestione e liquid. immobil.

R. D. L. 9 febbraio 1939, n. 126.
Legge 2 giugno 1939, n. 739.
R. D. 27 marzo 1939, n. 665.

Militari ebrei.

R. D. L. 22 dicembre 1938, n. 2111.

Divieto iscrizione al P. N. F.

R. D. 21 novembre 1938, n. 2154.

Difesa della razza in A. I.

Legge 29 giugno 1939, n. 1004.

Disciplina professioni.

Legge 29 giugno 1939, n. 1054.

Testamenti e cognomi.

Legge 13 luglio 1939, n. 1055.

SECONDA EDIZIONE

Prezzo L. 5.—

MILANO
L. di G. PIROLA
Via Cavallotti, 16
—
1939 (XVII)

N. 977   8-939-d.

Figure 7-49
Giorgio's summary dismissal from the telephone company
as a consequence of the Racial Laws. Adding injury to in-
sult, they would not give him references that might enable
him to find other employment. As this form-letter document shows, they merely certified that he had worked for
them, gave dates of employment and his job titles. Then
even more than now, such a tepid reference from a former
employer would virtually guarantee unemployment.

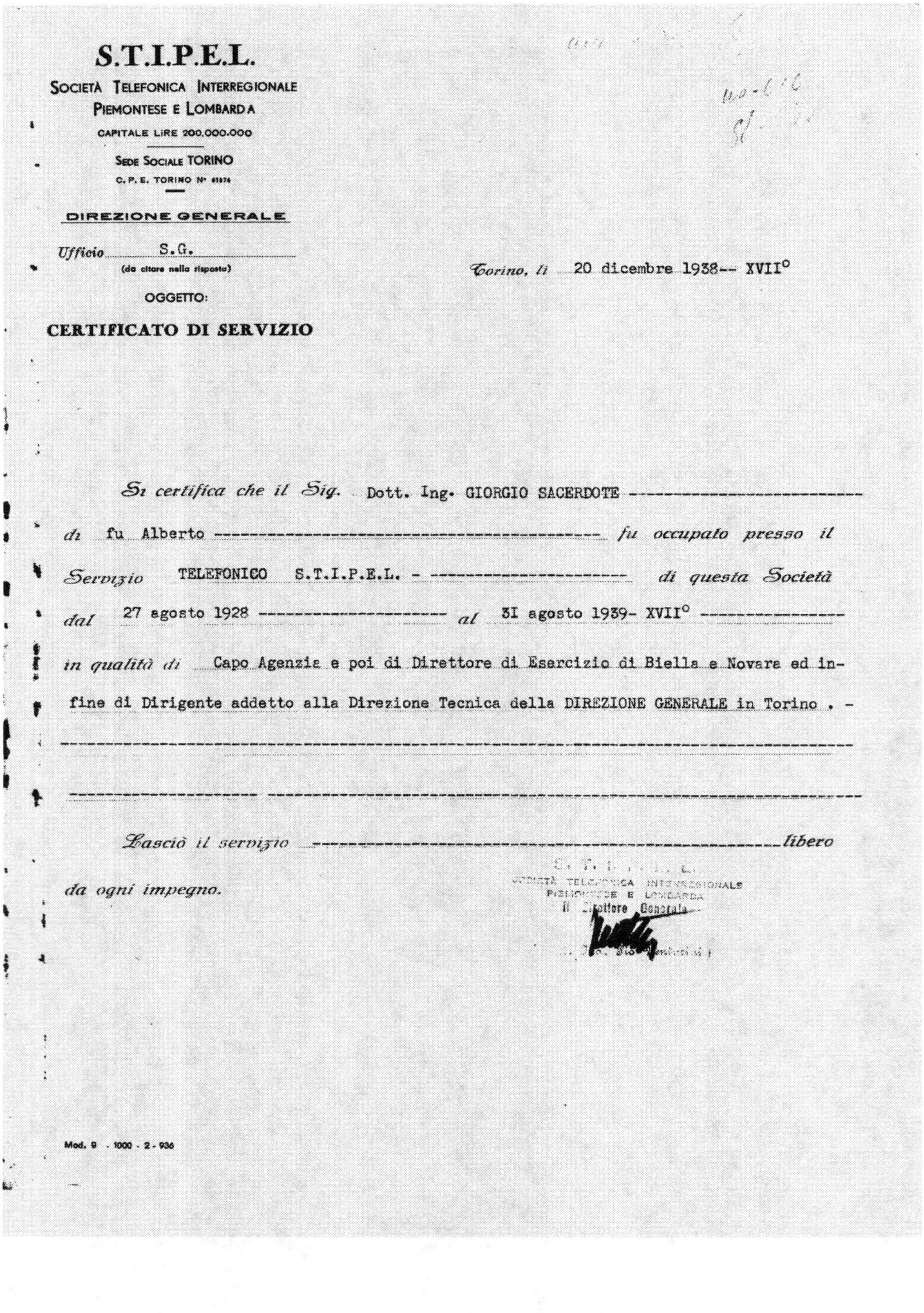

S.T.I.P.E.L.

Società Telefonica Interregionale
Piemontese e Lombarda

CAPITALE LIRE 200.000.000

Sede Sociale TORINO
C. P. E. TORINO N° 61874

DIREZIONE GENERALE

Ufficio   S.G.
(da citare nella risposta)

OGGETTO:

Torino, li 20 dicembre 1938-- XVII°

CERTIFICATO DI SERVIZIO

Si certifica che il Sig. Dott. Ing. GIORGIO SACERDOTE --------------------

di fu Alberto ----------------------------------- fu occupato presso il

Servizio TELEFONICO S.T.I.P.E.L. - ------------------------ di questa Società

dal 27 agosto 1928 --------------------- al 31 agosto 1939- XVII° -------------------

in qualità di Capo Agenzia e poi di Direttore di Esercizio di Biella e Novara ed in-

fine di Dirigente addetto alla Direzione Tecnica della DIREZIONE GENERALE in Torino . -

Lasciò il servizio ---libero

da ogni impegno.

S. T. I. P. E. L.
SOCIETÀ TELEFONICA INTERREGIONALE
PIEMONTESE E LOMBARDA
Il Direttore Generale

Mod. 9 - 1000 - 2 - 936

Figure 7-50
Giorgio's protest at his dismissal. He was incensed that
he had been summarily dismissed as if he had engaged in
misconduct, and courageously wrote a strongly worded
letter of protest. This letter pointed out that he had been a
successful manager for eleven years with increasing levels
of responsibility, and had been seriously injured in the line
of duty. There is no record of a response to his protest.

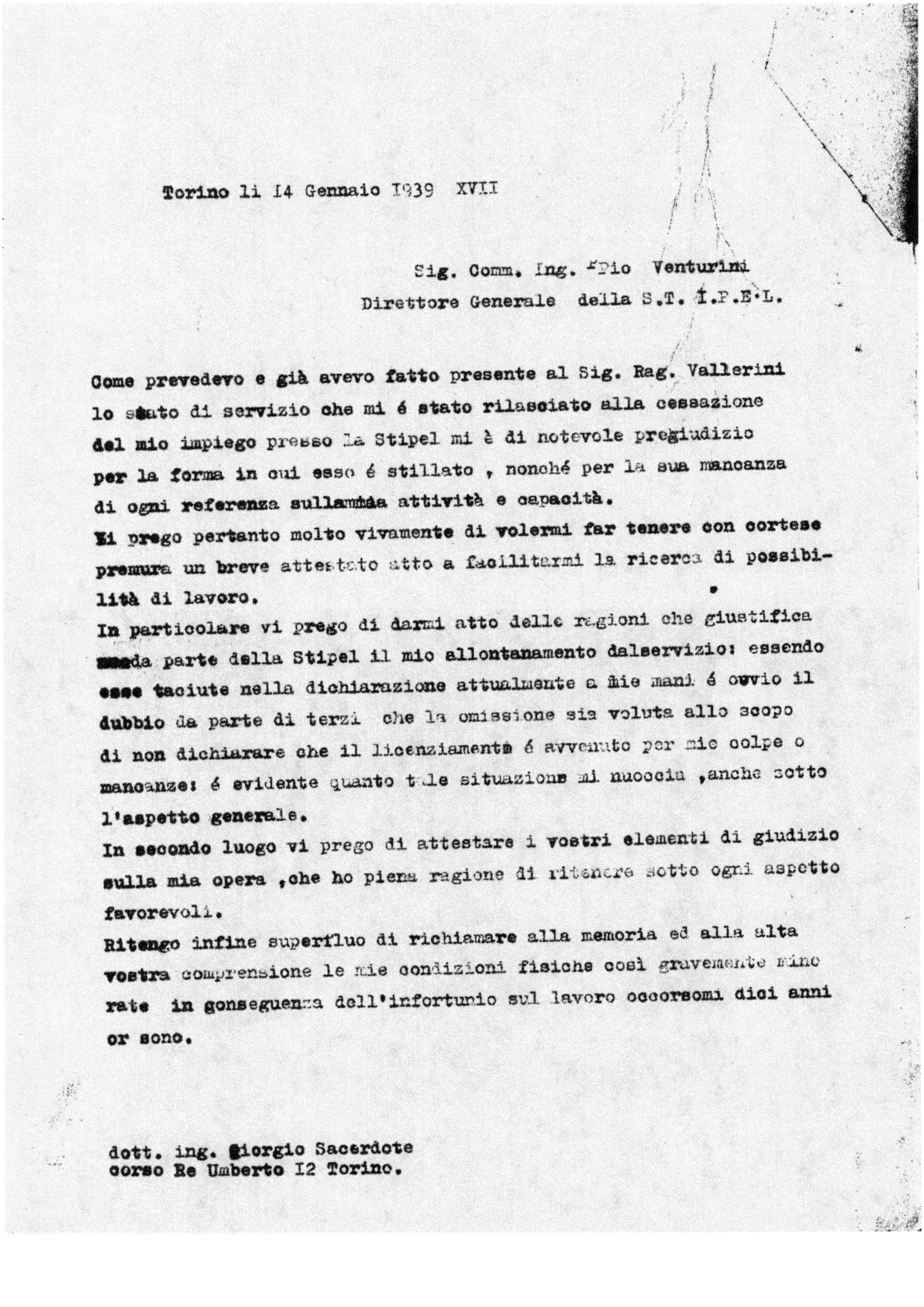

Torino li 14 Gennaio 1939 XVII

Sig. Comm. Ing. Pio Venturini
Direttore Generale della S.T. I.P.E.L.

Come prevedevo e già avevo fatto presente al Sig. Rag. Vallerini
lo stato di servizio che mi é stato rilasciato alla cessazione
del mio impiego presso la Stipel mi è di notevole pregiudizio
per la forma in cui esso é stillato , nonché per la sua mancanza
di ogni referenza sullammia attività e capacità.
Vi prego pertanto molto vivamente di volermi far tenere con cortese
premura un breve attestato atto a facilitarmi la ricerca di possibi-
lità di lavoro.
In particolare vi prego di darmi atto delle ragioni che giustifica
nanda parte della Stipel il mio allontanamento dalservizio: essendo
esse taciute nella dichiarazione attualmente a mie mani é ovvio il
dubbio da parte di terzi che la omissione sia voluta allo scopo
di non dichiarare che il licenziamento é avvenuto per mie colpe o
mancanze: é evidente quanto tale situazione mi nuoccia ,anche sotto
l'aspetto generale.
In secondo luogo vi prego di attestare i vostri elementi di giudizio
sulla mia opera ,che ho piena ragione di ritenere sotto ogni aspetto
favorevoli.
Ritengo infine superfluo di richiamare alla memoria ed alla alta
vostra comprensione le mie condizioni fisiche così gravemente mino
rate in conseguenza dell'infortunio sul lavoro occorsomi dici anni
or sono.

dott. ing. Giorgio Sacerdote
corso Re Umberto 12 Torino.

Figure 7-51
Diamond necklace. Luciana wore this necklace under her clothes during one of Giorgio and Luciana's clandestine trips to spirit assets out of Italy in 1938–39. On this particular trip Giorgio and Luciana skied across the Alps. They were accompanied for part of the trip by a Fascist military officer. After the officer skied off in one direction, they turned towards Switzerland and deposited the securities and jewels that they had hidden in their clothes in a bank. This necklace formerly had three large diamond pendants hanging from the eyelets between the stones 2, 3, 4 and 5. Those pendants were later detached and became the engagement rings that Albert, Peter and George gave to their fiancées, Carole Trautman, Bonnie Johnson, and Carol Robinson. Carole's ring is now worn by Michele Verni Sacerdote, Carole's daughter-in-law.

Figure 7-52
Giorgio, Elvira, Luciana, Piero and Alberto, Lausanne, 1939

Figure 7-53
As foreigners in pre-war France, the family had to have
residency permits issued by the local police. Generally
these permits did not allow travel within the country
beyond a few kilometers from home.

AK 74774

CERTIFICAT DE RESIDENCE

D.A.

Le Premier Adjoint de la Commune de Crémieu,
canton dudit, arrondissement de La Tour-du-Pin,
département de l'Isère, certifie que Madame
SACERDOTE née MONTALCINI Elvira, sans profession,
âgée de 59 ans, de nationalité italienne, titu-
laire de la Carte d'identité N° 38-EK38387, dé-
livrée par la Préfecture de l'Isère, en date du
12 septembre 1939, réside actuellement en notre Commune, depuis le 19 Octobre 1939,
En foi de quoi le présent certificat lui a été
délivré pour servir et valoir ce que de droit.

Crémieu le 8 Mai 1940

Le Premier Adjoint,

Figure 7-54
Giorgio's receipt for a train ticket to a port city to attempt
to buy an ocean passage. Note the handwritten identification *Juif* on the ticket. As foreigners during wartime
Giorgio and Luciana had to get permits to travel even
within France. Those permits were marked *Juif* or *Juive*,
even before the German occupation.

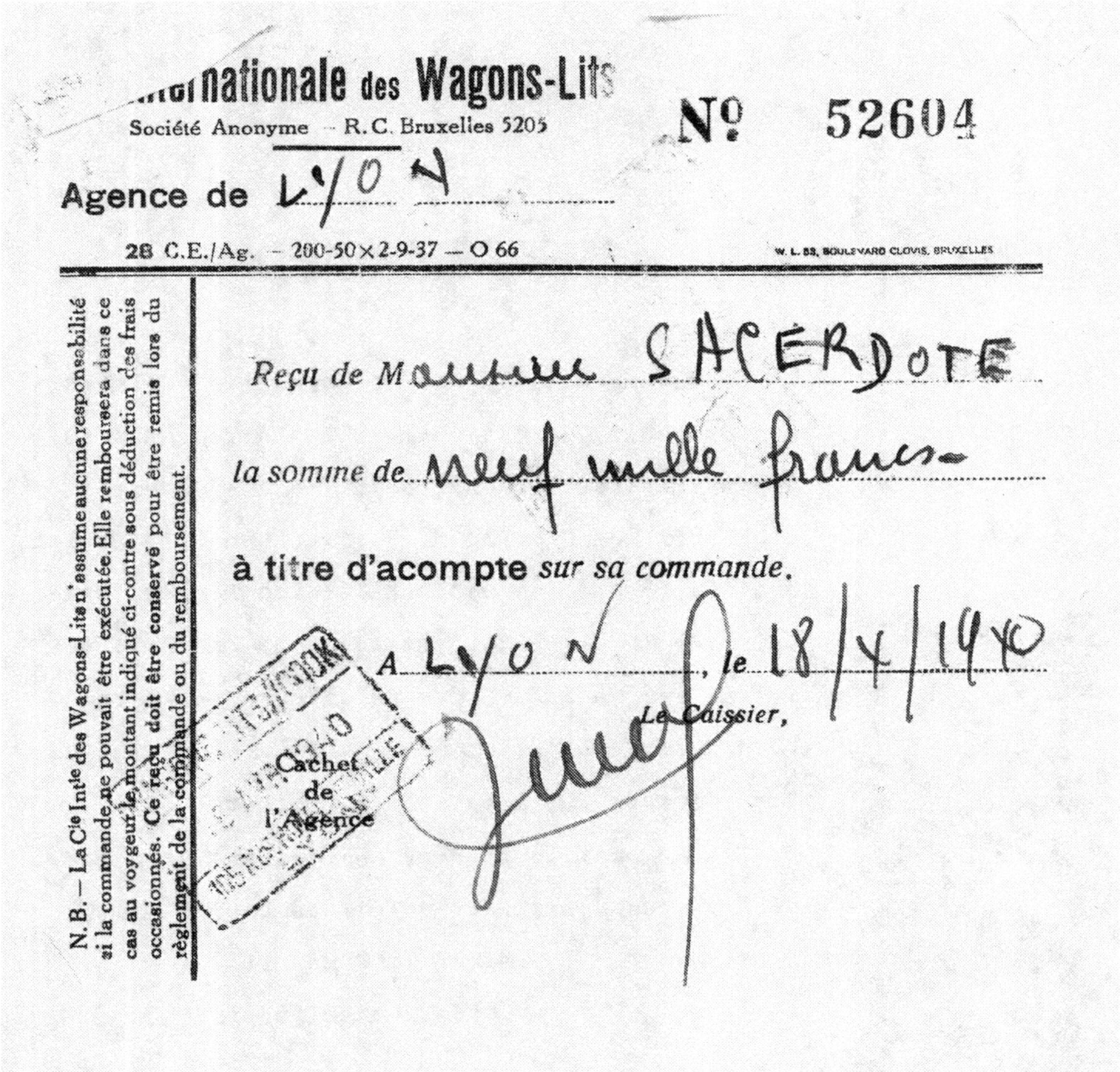

...nationale des **Wagons-Lits**

Société Anonyme – R.C. Bruxelles 5205

N⁰ 52604

Agence de LYON

28 C.E./Ag. – 200-50 × 2-9-37 — O 66

W. L. 88, BOULEVARD CLOVIS, BRUXELLES

N.B. – La Cⁱᵉ Intⁱᵉ des Wagons-Lits n'assume aucune responsabilité si la commande ne pouvait être exécutée. Elle remboursera dans ce cas au voyageur le montant indiqué ci-contre sous déduction des frais occasionnés. Ce reçu doit être conservé pour être remis lors du règlement de la commande ou du remboursement.

Reçu de M.......... SACERDOTE

la somme de neuf mille francs

à titre d'acompte *sur sa commande.*

A LYON, le 18/4/1940

Le Caissier,

Cachet de l'Agence

Figure 7-55

US racial classification form, 1940. In order to apply for a ticket to sail to the US, prospective travelers had to identify themselves racially in conformity with the race-based US immigration policy of the time. It wasn't only the Nazis and Fascists who worried about 'racial purity.' Note that among their fine distinctions, the Americans viewed as distinct 'races' or 'peoples' northern and southern Italians, or Serbs, Croats, Bosnians, Herzegovinians and Montenegrins. This particular listing was on the back of the application for a ticket to sail on the French Line.

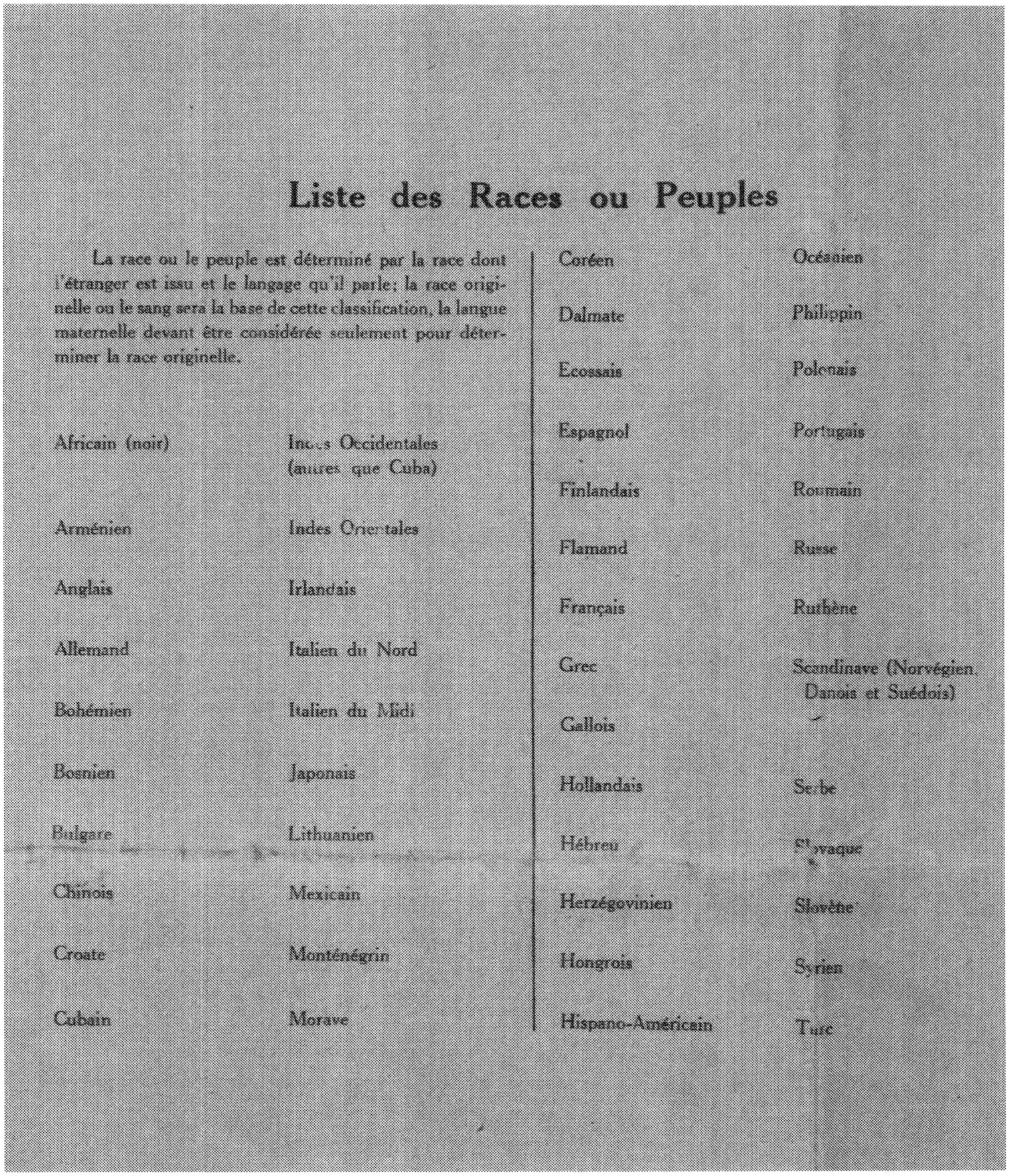

Liste des Races ou Peuples

La race ou le peuple est déterminé par la race dont l'étranger est issu et le langage qu'il parle; la race originelle ou le sang sera la base de cette classification, la langue maternelle devant être considérée seulement pour déterminer la race originelle.

Africain (noir)	Indes Occidentales (autres que Cuba)	Coréen	Océanien
Arménien	Indes Orientales	Dalmate	Philippin
Anglais	Irlandais	Ecossais	Polonais
Allemand	Italien du Nord	Espagnol	Portugais
Bohémien	Italien du Midi	Finlandais	Roumain
Bosnien	Japonais	Flamand	Russe
Bulgare	Lithuanien	Français	Ruthène
Chinois	Mexicain	Grec	Scandinave (Norvégien, Danois et Suédois)
Croate	Monténégrin	Gallois	
Cubain	Morave	Hollandais	Serbe
		Hébreu	Slovaque
		Herzégovinien	Slovène
		Hongrois	Syrien
		Hispano-Américain	Turc

The family's Italian passports severely restricted the list of countries to which they could travel; the US was not on the list of permissible destinations. As Hebrews, it was highly unlikely that they could get the restrictions lifted, particularly in wartime. When the US consul in Lyon heard that Giorgio was experienced in the rubber reclaiming industry, he jumped them to the head of the immigration queue and gave them a permit to use in lieu of a passport. The Japanese had recently conquered the British colony of Malaya, causing a world-wide shortage of natural rubber and the US was aggressively seeking immigrant engineers with expertise in the industry.

AFFIDAVIT IN LIEU OF PASSPORT

REPUBLIC OF FRANCE)
CITY OF LYON) ss.
CONSULATE OF THE UNITED)
   STATES OF AMERICA)

I, Giorgio SACERDOTE, recently residing at Villa Humbert, Cremieu, Isère, France, hereby make oath that I was born at Turin, Italy, on June 4, 1905, that I am an Italian subject, and I further make oath that it is impossible for me to obtain an Italian passport good for travel to the United States of America as an immigrant for myself, my wife, Luciana Elda Clara Levi Sacerdote, born at Turin, Italy on January 9, 1915, and my two minor sons, Alberto Mauro Sacerdote, born July 1, 1936 at Novara, Italy and Piero Marcello Sacerdote, born October 15, 1937 at Turin, Italy.

Description

Height: 5 feet 11 inches
Color of Hair: light brown
Color of Eyes: blue

Subscribed and sworn to before me this sixteenth day of April 1940

John D. Johnson
Consul of the United States of America

Immigration Visa
Non-quota Quota } No. 5725 (Italian Quota)
dated APR 16 1940
Issued to Giorgio Sacerdote (name)
JOHN D. JOHNSON
American Consul at LYON-FRANCE
Immigrant Identification Card
no. 100 5936 issued APR 16 1940

Immigration Visa
Non-quota Quota } No. 5727 (Italian Quota)
dated APR 16 1940
Issued to Alberto Mauro Sacerdote (name)
JOHN D. JOHNSON
American Consul at LYON-FRANCE
Immigrant Identification Card
no. 100 5938 issued APR 16 1940

Immigration Visa
Non-quota Quota } No. 5726 (Italian Quota)
dated APR 16 1940
Issued to Luciana Elda Clara Levi Sacerdote (name)
JOHN D. JOHNSON
American Consul at LYON-FRANCE
Immigrant Identification Card
no. 100 5937 issued APR 16 1940

Figure 7-57
Giorgio, Luciana, Alberto, Piero and Elvira crossed the
Atlantic from Bordeaux to New York on the French liner
Champlain. The Germans announced their intention to
sink the ship as it crossed the Atlantic. On its return voyage
to France, the Champlain stuck a German mine and sank
in 15 minutes.

CHAMPLAIN

Builder: Chantiers & Ateliers de St. Nazaire,
Penhoet, France.
Completed: 1932.
Gross tonnage: 28124.
Dimensions: 645ft × 83ft. Depth 46ft.
Engines: Six Parson steam turbines single-
reduction geared.
Screws: Twin.
Decks: Five.
Normal speed: 20 knots.
Officers and crew: 559.
Passenger accommodation: 548 cabin, 318
tourist and 134 third class.
Maiden voyage: Le Havre—New York on
June 18, 1932.

Engaged in the Le Havre—Southampton—New York
service calling at Plymouth eastbound and cruising
during the off seasonal months. The *Champlain*
had a promenade deck 350ft long and a dining
room two decks high and 65ft long. Struck an
acoustic mine off La Pallice, France, on June 17,
1940, and sank within a quarter of an hour while
she had been working from Bordeaux since the
German invasion. The *Champlain* lived a regret-
fully short time for a liner as did her consorts
Lafayette and *Normandie.*

Figure 7-58
Immigrants had to obtain US sponsors to enter the country. The sponsor's job was to guarantee the immigrant's support. In this document, Paolo sponsored his mother, Elvira even though she also had a letter from a New York bank certifying that she had sufficient assets to support herself. Paolo had come to the United States in November, 1939 and was as yet unemployed in March, 1940, living in the Sloane House YMCA when this document was issued.

Italian Line
624 FIFTH AVENUE, NEW YORK
—

AFFIDAVIT of SUPPORT

PREPAID TICKET No. ____________ CLASS

STATES OF AMERICA
New York
New York ss.:
New York

I, PAOLO SACERDOTE ...., being duly sworn according to law, depose and say:

1: That I am 52 years of age, single, and reside with alone (Name of Relative or Friend) at No. 356 West 34th Street, NYC (Sloane House) (Complete Address)

2: (a) That I am a citizen of the United States, I was Naturalized by the *** and hold Naturalization Court at ** on *** Certificate No. ***** issued by the said Court.

or

(b) That I am an American Citizen by birth. I was born at *** (City and State) on ** and have always maintained my United States Citizenship.

or

(c) That I am an alien and a subject or citizen of Italy. I last arrived in the United States at the port of New York per SS. WASHINGTON as a tourist class passenger and was legally admitted by the U. S. Immigration Authorities on November 1, 1939. I have declared my intention to become an American Citizen and hold Declaration of Intention No. 456028 issued to me by the Southern District Court at New York on March 14th, 1940. I will become an American Citizen as soon as I can possibly do so. I have filed application for verification of my entry (Form 575) with the U. S. Immigration Authorities. Form 575 being filed to-day.

3: That I am employed as, or engaged in the business of unemployed with ....Dollars. ....and derive a net annual income of ....Dollars, at ....Dollars.

4: That I have on deposit in Savings Banks in this Country $5,000.00 and I have other personal property, the reasonable value of which is $6,400. (stocks) ....Dollars.

5: That I own real estate at *** Dollars, with mortgages or other encumbrances thereon amounting to *** Dollars.

6: That it is my intention to have the following relatives at present residing with my brother at Villa Humbert, Cremieu, Isere, France, who are in (Give Name and Complete Foreign Address) good health and in every way admissible under the U. S. Immigration Laws, come to the United States and reside with me until they become self supporting.

NAME	AGE	SEX	MARRIED OR SINGLE	CITIZEN OR SUBJECT OF	RELATIONSHIP TO DEPONENT
Elvira Montalcini ved. Sacerdote.	58	female	widow	Italian	mother

7: That I have filed petition for the issuance of an immigration visa with the Hon. Commissioner of Immigration and Naturalization, Washington, D. C., and the same has been approved. File *** (Give Number on Approval Card)

8: That I am willing and able to receive, maintain and support the above mentioned relatives. I am ready and willing to deposit a bond with the U. S. Immigration Authorities, if that be necessary, to guarantee that they will never become public charges during their stay in this country, and that if any are under 16 years of age that I will send them to school at least until they reach the age of 16 years.

9: That I make this affidavit in good faith to induce the Hon. American Consul in Lyon, France, to issue Immigration Visas to the above named aliens and to induce the U. S. Immigration Authorities to permit them to enter the United States of America.

Signature of Deponent *Paolo Sacerdote* (L.S.)
.... (L.S.)
.... (L.S.)

Subscribed and sworn to before me this 26th day of March 1940.

Teresa Sacciatore
NOTARY PUBLIC

Witness ....
TERESA SACCIATORE
Notary Public, Queens Co. No. 237, Reg. No. 5531
Cert. filed in N. Y. Co. No. 373, Reg. No. 1C245
Commission Expires March 30, 1941

Address ....

Figure 7-59
WW II ration book. Remembering the stories of the food shortages during World War I in Italy and having read the accounts of her former housekeeper from Cremieux in France under the German occupation, Luciana began hoarding as soon as rationing was announced the US. For more than a decade after the war, the family was still eating the canned foods that she had accumulated during the rationing.

Stamps must not be detached except in the presence of the retailer, his employee, or person authorized by him to make delivery.

Certificate of Registrar

This is to Certify that pursuant to the Rationing Orders and Regulations administered by the OFFICE OF PRICE ADMINISTRATION, an agency of the United States Government,

The Stamps contained in this Book are valid only after the lawful holder of this Book has signed the certificate below, and are void if detached contrary to the Regulations. (A father, mother, or guardian may sign the name of a person under 18.) In case of questions, difficulties, or complaints, consult your local Ration Board.

Certificate of Book Holder

I, *the undersigned*, do hereby certify that I have observed all the conditions and regulations governing the issuance of this War Ration Book; that the "Description of Book Holder" contained herein is correct; that an application for issuance of this book has been duly made by me or on my behalf; and that the statements contained in said application are true to the best of my knowledge and belief.

(Signature of, or on behalf of, Book Holder) [Book Holder's Own Name]

Any person signing on behalf of Book Holder must sign his or her own name below and indicate relationship to Book Holder

(Father, Mother, or Guardian)

U. S. GOVERNMENT PRINTING OFFICE : 1942 16—20651-1 OPA Form No. R-302

UNITED STATES OF AMERICA

War Ration Book One

WARNING

1 Punishments ranging as high as *Ten Years' Imprisonment or $10,000 Fine, or Both*, may be imposed under United States Statutes for violations thereof arising out of infractions of Rationing Orders and Regulations.

2 This book must not be transferred. It must be held and used only by or on behalf of the person to whom it has been issued, and anyone presenting it thereby represents to the Office of Price Administration, an agency of the United States Government, that it is being so held and so used. For any misuse of this book it may be taken from the holder by the Office of Price Administration.

3 In the event either of the departure from the United States of the person to whom this book is issued, or his or her death, the book must be surrendered in accordance with the Regulations.

4 Any person finding a lost book must deliver it promptly to the nearest Ration Board.

OFFICE OF PRICE ADMINISTRATION

No. 136897 —355

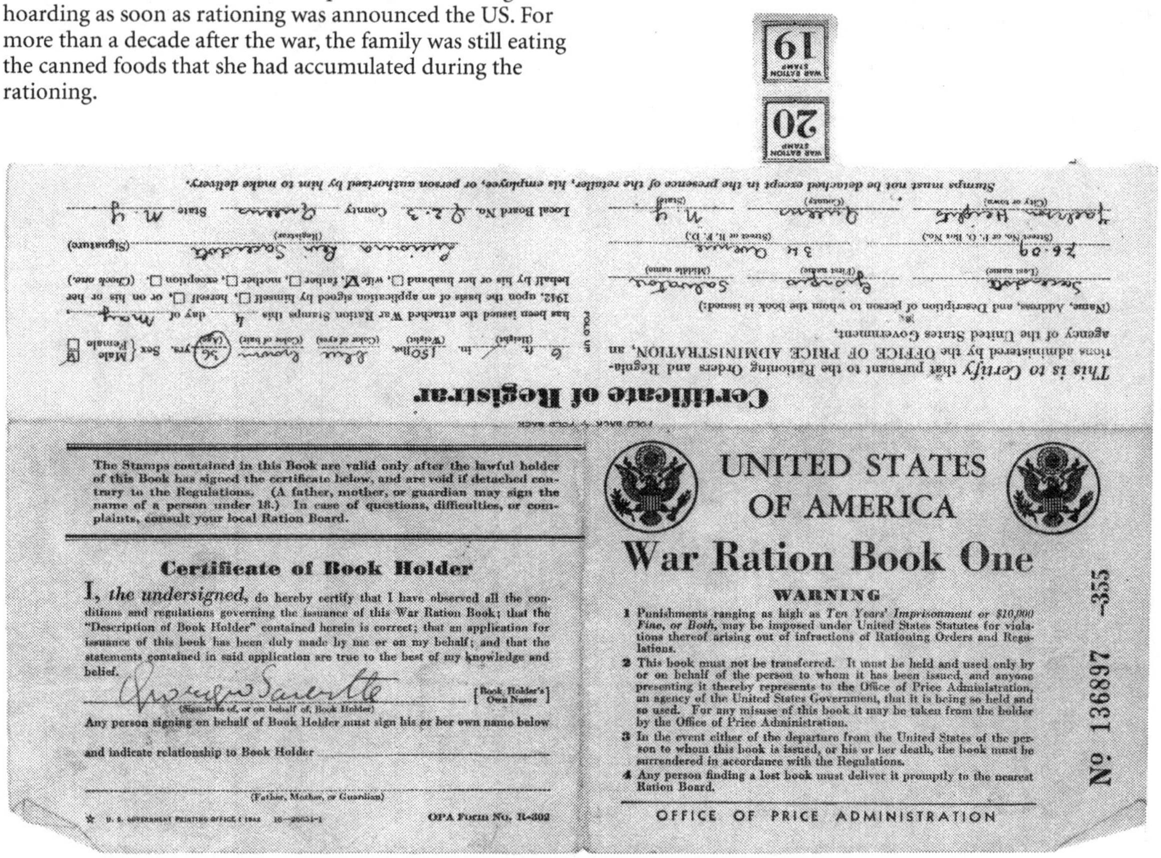

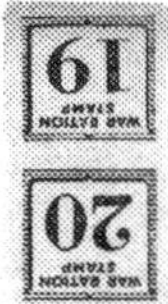

JUNE 14, 1941

"IN ACCORDANCE WITH EXECUTIVE ORDER No. 8785 DATED JUNE 14TH 1941 AND AMENDING EXECUTIVE ORDER No. 8389 DATED APRIL 10TH 1940, WE REGRET THAT WE ARE REQUIRED TO BLOCK YOUR ACCOUNT.

PLEASE NOTE, THEREFORE, THAT NO WITHDRAWALS WILL BE PERMITTED UNLESS PROPERLY AUTHORIZED BY FEDERAL LICENSE."

BROWN BROTHERS HARRIMAN & CO.

Figure 7-60
Bank notification of asset blockage. In 1941, even before entering the war the President Roosevelt issued an executive order freezing the assets of many foreign nationals, including Giorgio, Luciana and Elvira. This note was sent to Giorgio by his bankers Brown Brothers in New York. This asset blockage increased the pressure on Giorgio to find a paying job.

Figure 7-61
Luciana's appointment at Yale, 1943. Yale was one of many universities that joined the war effort by providing accelerated training for future military officers. Luciana found work there in 1943 teaching Italian in a program to train military officers for the future occupational government.

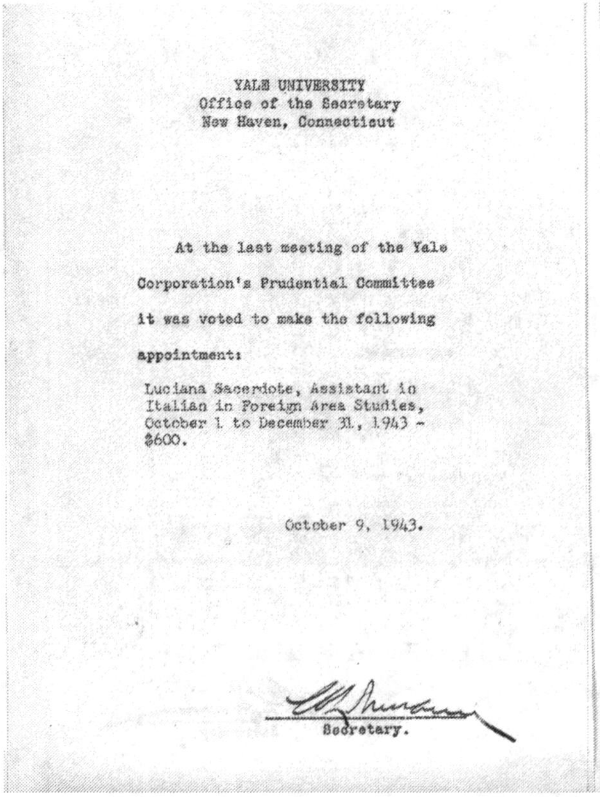

YALE UNIVERSITY
Office of the Secretary
New Haven, Connecticut

At the last meeting of the Yale Corporation's Prudential Committee it was voted to make the following appointment:

Luciana Sacerdote, Assistant in Italian in Foreign Area Studies, October 1 to December 31, 1943 – $600.

October 9, 1943.

Secretary.

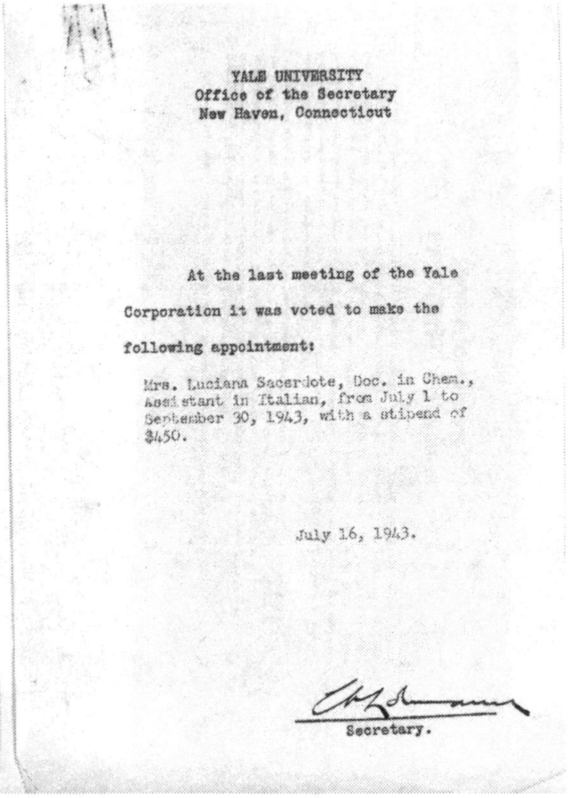

YALE UNIVERSITY
Office of the Secretary
New Haven, Connecticut

At the last meeting of the Yale Corporation it was voted to make the following appointment:

Mrs. Luciana Sacerdote, Doc. in Chem., Assistant in Italian, from July 1 to September 30, 1943, with a stipend of $450.

July 16, 1943.

Secretary.

Figure 7-62
Luciana, Peter and Albert atop the Sleeping Giant in New Haven

Figure 7-63
Pearl Quittel in 1943. Pearl was a technician at the Mount Vernon NY hospital, where Paolo was an attending physician. As an enemy alien, Paolo was ineligible for a commission as a medical officer in the US military and therefore was practicing medicine as a civilian. They were married the following year.

war in Europe worsened, this became more and more difficult. Already in May 1940, their Swiss bankers had informed them that they could no longer send them funds in France. In June 1941, some of their accounts in the United States were blocked by presidential order. Later that year, their Swiss bankers informed them that that it was impossible to transfer any funds, notes, or jewels to the United States because of the unavailability of adequate marine insurance; parenthetically, this letter also informed them that Luciana's uncle Raoul Orefice and his wife had been arrested in Marseilles.[360]

While Giorgio and Luciana had contact with the small circle of Torino émigrés in New York, including Paolo,[361] the Treves family, and part of the Ovazza family,[362] the family was completely cut off from its relatives in Italy. It was too dangerous for Italian Hebrews to make their addresses known. Although Giorgio and Zio Manno had set up a book code for secret correspondence using copies of a certain children's book, in practice they could not correspond. Further, they had lost contact with Eugenia's family in South America, and that contact would remain broken until mid-1942. Luciana maintained a brief correspondence (until the United States entered the war in December 1941) with her housekeeper from Cremieux and learned of the increasing hardships of living in wartime France:

September 1940

Chère Madame

The Germans came to Cremieux, but they did not do anything. We had a ration card for bread but they took it away. We are each allowed a monthly ration of 500 g of sugar and 100 g of rice, 250 g of pasta, 200 g of oil, and 300 g of a mixture of coffee and toasted grain. Maize and chocolate are no longer in the market. Butchers are now closed Sunday to Wednesday. Only milkmen and doctors are permitted to drive cars.

My cousin has been sent to a labor camp. M. X has been arrested by the Germans and the schools are closed.

My father can work only 25 hours a week in the factory for lack of materials.

January 1941

Chère Madame

We can no longer obtain many things. No more coal. No new shoes, no wool for knitting. Meat is very scarce. And we can only get ¼ kg of butter a month. Wood and potatoes are now rationed. And milk is available only for children under 4 years old.

M. X, who had been arrested, has returned safe and sound.

July 1941

Chère Madame

You are so lucky to be in America. Here everything is scarce and we often have to do without. No more meat except from emaciated animals. No more cloth or yarn in the market. We cannot even buy needles to repair our clothes. Papa hardly works anymore because there is no coal for the factory.

November 1941

Chère Madame

Many thanks for your package from America. Here we are lacking almost everything. We are becoming rich because there is nothing to spend our money on. I have bought a sewing machine but cannot buy cloth to make a dress. We have to economize on food and are mostly eating squash and root vegetables.

In the meanwhile, in the expectation that the war would bring serious rationing of foodstuffs, Luciana began to hoard canned goods, sugar, flour and other nonperishables. It was perhaps during this period that she developed the thrifty habits that lasted the rest of her life. Her hoard grew so large that we were still eating tinned meats, fruits, and vegetables from it fifteen years later. During this time she also learned to prepare homemade fruit preserves, probably as a means of storing sugar.

---

[360] I am not sure how Raoul and his family escaped the Nazis. They did, however, survive the war. One of my earliest childhood recollections was having a very formal dinner with them in their Paris apartment in 1948.

[361] Paolo was working at the Mount Vernon, New York, hospital except for a stretch during 1941 when he was at the Lowell, Massachusetts, hospital.

[362] The Ovazzas were a wealthy Torinese banking family. Giorgio's uncle Balilla Sacerdote had married into the family, as did one of his daughters, Nella. Vittorio Ovazza was one of the witnesses to Giorgio and Luciana's Ketubah, their religious marriage agreement.

While in New York, Giorgio joined the anti-Fascist Mazzini Society. One has to wonder how the scion of a strongly pro-royalist family felt about joining a group named after Giuseppe Mazzini, a republican, anti-royalist agitator during the Italian Wars of Independence. Meanwhile, Elvira volunteered to work for a war-relief agency that was making warm clothing with which soldiers could supplement their government-issued uniforms. She welcomed this work, as she could speak with her colleagues in Italian and French and had a break from spoken English, a language she found difficult.

Giorgio continued to look for work as an engineer, but had difficulty getting his European academic credentials and experience recognized. The American Jewish relief agencies were not much use in finding work for professionals; they were used to finding industrial jobs for uneducated Ashkhenazic refugees from Eastern Europe. For example, Davide Jona, the husband of Luciana's cousin Anna Foa, was sent by one of these agencies to work as a laborer in a scrap metal yard, and later, on a poultry farm, notwithstanding his doctorate in architecture. After the war, Jona joined the faculty of the Harvard School of Design and was a colleague of Walter Gropius.

After the US entered the war, Giorgio was classed as an enemy alien, further complicating his search for professional work; this classification made him ineligible for high security jobs such as in the telephone industry. Paolo had a similar experience: As an enemy alien he could not be commissioned into the Army Medical corps, despite its desperate need for doctors. As a result Paolo remained a civilian doctor throughout the war.

At one point Giorgio offered his services to the U.S. government as an expert on the Italian telephone industry, at a consulting fee of $25/day. Eventually the family was down to its last $5000 in ready money. Finally, in 1943, he found work as an engineer with the Armstrong Rubber Company, a tire manufacturer based in New Haven, Connecticut, thanks to his brief experience in the rubber industry in France. The Armstrong plant had been converted to making life rafts for the war effort.

At that time, the major U.S. universities were contributing to the war effort by providing accelerated undergraduate training to young men who were then immediately commissioned as military officers. Luciana found work at Yale University teaching Italian to U.S. military officers about to be shipped to the Italian theater to serve in the occupation government. And so the family moved from New York to Connecticut. Luciana also began her process of American acculturation by volunteering at the Yale New Haven Hospital.[363] She often told another story about her early experiences with American culture: At one point several students in Luciana's first class at Yale took her out to a pizzeria, thinking they were doing her a great favor. My mother had never seen such a dish before in her life—at that time in Italy, pizza was a regional dish served only in the area around Naples.[364]

In New Haven the family rented a two-family house at 659 Whitney Avenue. The tenant in the other half of the house was an FBI agent, whom Giorgio and Luciana referred to as "the real American." Piero and Alberto enrolled in elementary school at the Worthington-Hooker School and began their rapid Americanization, with their grasp of English quickly overtaking the Italian and French spoken at home. The speaking of Italian in public was particularly discouraged, as it was an enemy language.

During this period, Giorgio and Luciana had lost all contact with the families they had left behind in Italy. They groped for connections in an American society that tried to fit them into common stereotypes. They often found themselves lumped together with other Italian immigrants, nearly all of whom were ignorant peasants from the impoverished south of Italy.[365] As educated professional-class people from the economically advanced northern Italy, they had little in common with these working-class southerners. At other times they were lumped with the recent Ashkhenazic Jewish immigrants, most of whom had only recently traded the ignorance and misery of the shtetls of czarist Russia[366] for the tene-

---

[363] Luciana learned fairly quickly how to build networks of friends in the United States. Giorgio, being older, found this much more difficult, and socialized mainly with Italian émigrés.

[364] I wonder if they made her eat it with her fingers, instead of with fork and knife, as any proper Torinese would eat.

[365] Even today, southern Italy is quite poor. Economically it has more in common with the Third World than it does with the economically advanced Italian north.

[366] Russia was the last European country to maintain the feudal institution of serfdom. Legally it was abolished in the 1860s, but many of its rules survived into the twentieth century.

ments and sweatshops of New York City; with these people they had even less in common.[367] Generally they fell back on those with whom they shared an instant bond, other Italian Hebrews. In addition to the small group of Torinesi whom they knew from pre-emigration times, they befriended several others. For example, in New Haven they bonded with the Calabresi family, two of whose sons, Guido and Paolo, later became the deans of the Yale law and medical schools, respectively.

The Italian and German defeats and the postwar years

Some months after the Germans had defeated the French in 1940, they and the Italians occupied the French North African colonies of Morocco, Algeria, and Tunisia, working outward from the Italian colony of Libya. They then attacked British-controlled Egypt, hoping to sever the British lifeline of the Suez Canal. In 1942, the Germans were thrown back from the Suez Canal in the battle of El Alamein. In the ensuing several months a combined British and American force landed in Morocco, putting the Germans and Italians in a pincer between Allied forces on their eastern and western flanks. By the spring of 1943, the Axis forces were driven out of all of North Africa by this combined British and American force. That force then crossed the Mediterranean, occupied Sicily, crossed to the Italian mainland, and fought its way northward up the Italian Peninsula.[368]

In July 1943, with Italy clearly losing the war, the king finally found the courage to order the arrest of Mussolini and placed Marshal Badoglio in charge of the government. Badoglio began secret negotiations with the British concerning a possible armistice even as the fighting continued. When the Germans got wind of what was going on in Rome, they sent special forces troops to spring Mussolini out of jail and launched a full-scale invasion of Italy. They quickly occupied the northern two-thirds of the country and imposed the full brutality of the Nazi regime on the region they controlled. They set Mussolini up as a puppet dictator of a rump state with its capital in the Lombard town of Saló on the shore of the Lago di Garda. Meanwhile, as the Germans invaded Italy, the royal family and its government fled southward to American-controlled Brindisi in the heel of the Italian boot.

In 1943, at the Nazi's command, the Fascists established a camp at Fossoli where Hebrews who were being rounded up by the Nazis and their Fascist henchmen could be interned. Fossoli soon became a way station on the way to the German death camps.

In the north, groups of Italian partisans formed to resist the German invasion, hiding out in the mountainous regions of the Alps and the Apennines, and staging hit-and-run attacks to harass the Germans and their Fascist stooges. The chemist and author Primo Levi joined one of these bands but was soon captured and sent to Fossoli and then Auschwitz.[369] Many heroic Italians, including members of the police, local government, and Catholic clergy,[370] fought successfully in these bands or provided them with safe houses and logistical support.

Luciana's brother Ruggiero joined one of these partisan bands. He soon recognized the extreme danger he was in as both a partisan and a Hebrew, should he fall into the hands of the Germans. His colleagues led him to safety in Switzerland, where he spent the rest of the war in a Swiss refugee camp run by the Red Cross.[371] Through the Red Cross, Ruggiero was able to make contact with Giorgio and Luciana in 1944, and they sent him money for his support through the same channel. This was the first word they had from any of the family who had remained in Italy.

---

[367] The feelings tended to be mutual. Primo Levi described the issue he saw at Auschwitz, where the prisoners were mostly Eastern European Jews from the former Russian domains in Poland, the Baltic states, Belarus, and the Ukraine. They generally would not accept him as a fellow Hebrew because he did not speak Yiddish and was so different from them culturally. The eastern European Jews who control most American Synagogues still do not fully accept those of us from other backgrounds, even though they are the minority of world Jewry.

[368] The main American army in the Italian campaign was the 10th Mountain Division, based in Leadville, Colorado. It had trained in the Rocky Mountains between Leadville and the Vail Valley.

[369] Levi survived a year and a half in Auschwitz and wrote a very moving series of books and short stories based on his experiences.

[370] The local priests, nuns and bishops often went out of their way to help the partisans and protect Hebrews, in stark contrast to the seeming indifference exhibited the central hierarchy of the Church, even in the face of roundups of Hebrews in Rome in neighborhoods bordering the Vatican.

[371] Ruggiero married a woman he met in the camp, by whom he had a daughter, my cousin Gianna, who now lives outside of Naples. After the war, the marriage collapsed, and Ruggiero was left to raise Gianna by himself.

In 1945, when it became clear that Germany was going to be defeated, the left-wing parties which had been operating underground during the Fascist period began to flex their muscles. They staged work slowdowns and strikes throughout northern Italy. Finally they seized Mussolini and his mistress near Lake Como as they sought to escape to Switzerland. The partisans shot Mussolini and his mistress and left their bodies hanging upside down and naked on a major street in Milan.

In the aftermath of the war, in light of his cowardly behavior vis-à-vis Mussolini, the king was pressured to abdicate in favor of his son, Umberto II, to assure the continuity of the monarchy. However, Vittorio Emanuele III temporized, waffled, and dithered. The politicians called for a national referendum on the monarchy. Finally the king abdicated one month before the referendum, leaving precious little time for Umberto II to campaign for a vote to retain the royal family. In June 1946, the public voted to replace the monarchy with a republic, and the royal family was sent into exile. Vittorio Emanuele III went to Egypt, where he soon died, and Umberto II went to Portugal.

In 1945, Giorgio, Oscar Ghez, and the Treves brothers, Angiolo and Dario, decided to try once again to commercialize the rubber patents they had bought in France five years earlier. They formed a company, North Bergen Rubber, in New Jersey, which was initially in the rubber reclaiming business. They also formed a second company, Rubber and Plastics, in New York. Rubber and Plastics was responsible for sales and distribution, while manufacturing was the domain of North Bergen Rubber. As part of this work, Giorgio began to bring home smelly samples of various rubber and plastic products they had concocted to test how they would stand up to hot and cold by heating them on the kitchen stove or storing them overnight in the freezer. These home experiments continued into the 1950s, much to the olfactory annoyance of the rest of the family.

In July, 1945, the family then moved house again, this time to 676 West Englewood Avenue, Teaneck, New Jersey. The previous owners, the Kipp family, had planted a large victory garden in response to the federal government's efforts to encourage householders to grow fruits and vegetables in order to increase the country's war-time food production. For reasons best known only to the Kipps, this garden was mostly planted in Swiss chards. Luciana, who had become very thrifty during the war, refused to let any of these chards go to waste. She served them every day for several months; even now, sixty years later, my brother Peter cannot face that vegetable, no matter how elegantly it is prepared.

Giorgio and Luciana's third son, George, was born a couple of months after they moved to Teaneck, in September, 1945. One month later, Paolo, who had married a hospital technician, Pearl Quittel, the year before, also had a son, Marc. In New Jersey, Luciana began anew to build a social network for herself. She joined the League of Women Voters, an organization of which she was ultimately a member for nearly sixty years. She also began to volunteer in the local hospital.

While Rubber and Plastics struggled in its first years, selling a rather eclectic mix of lubricants, sealants, and other products, it gradually began to focus on selling waterproofing products such as plastic flashing and rubberized sealants to the construction industry under the Nervastral brand. Nervastral's main benefit was that it was far cheaper to buy and install than copper flashing. Initially, the company did its own manufacturing via North Bergen Rubber, but it soon decided to contract out that part of the business, and North Bergen was closed. Rubber and Plastics focused on sales and distribution. The sales process was fairly complex because they had to sell to the architectural and engineering firms that designed major buildings, so that they would specify Nervastral products in their designs. Then they had to sell to the construction companies that actually used the products, to keep them from using cheaper substitutes. On the distribution side, the company sold directly in the U.S. northeast, and then built a network of agents and distributors to cover the rest of North America and Europe. At one point in the 1960s there was a neon sign atop a building in Sintagma Square in Athens with Nervastral's walrus logo on it. As the business grew it had several notable successes, including supplying all of the flashing for the construction of Coop City, a huge housing project in New York's Borough of the Bronx, and also for the Sydney Opera House in Australia.

At about this time, Giorgio, Luciana, and the older boys, Alberto and Piero, became U.S. citizens. In the change Alberto and Piero officially became Albert and Peter. For the adults, the process of becoming citizens entailed passing an examination on U.S. history and government, and then appearing before a judge in Newark, New Jersey, to swear loyalty to the United States. The family and their Torino cousins all had a hard time taking this process seriously. Compared to the country where they had grown up, a country with thousands of years of history, the United States was less than two hundred years old. Their reaction to the story of Washington and the cherry tree was "What a stupid child, to cut down a cherry tree." And when they were asked to swear that they would not attempt to assassinate the president of the United States, they asked, "If we were planning to kill the president, would we refuse to swear?" At the end of the ceremony, when Peter and Albert became citizens,[372] Giorgio asked the judge if there were anything else needed. The judge turned to Giorgio and commanded, "Now take those boys out for an ice cream soda." In the America of that time, as it had been in Italy, a child's reward for achieving an important milestone was to be taken out for ice cream.[373]

In 1946 Giorgio returned to Italy to learn what had become of the family who had remained behind. He heard some remarkable stories of escapes as well as of a few tragedies. When the Germans invaded and roundups of the Hebrews began, most of the family had gone into hiding.

The loyal family servants, Camilla and Teresa, reported that the family villa in Valsalice had been taken over by German officers, who established a command post there to take advantage of its strategic view over the entire city of Torino. Camilla and Teresa were forced to work for the Germans and to sleep in the billiard house. The Germans demanded that their clothes be washed and ironed daily. They also forced the farmers to cut down many of the fruit trees for use as firewood, as the main house had no central heating (it was normally used only in summertime), and they could not be convinced that better firewood was available from the villa's woodlot up the hill or that the fruit trees were the farmer's livelihood. The Germans thought nothing of stealing the farmer's produce for their own use. As they were packing up for their final retreat from Italy, Camilla and Teresa pleaded with them not to destroy the house, a plea which they accepted, notwithstanding their orders to the contrary. When the family returned to Valsalice after the war, they found German military uniforms hanging in the attic as well as piles of old German newspapers. The newspapers found immediate use as toilet paper because all paper products were extremely scarce and had to be purchased on the black market in the early post-war years in Italy. Elvira had always been very thrifty, and her thrift was mirrored by Camilla and Teresa. Many years later, when I broke a shoelace, Camilla found me an old shoelace that the Germans had left behind when they retreated to Germany. Using it gave me a very creepy feeling.

When the Germans invaded Italy in 1943, Zio Manno (Emanuele Montalcini) asked the nuns of the hospital in Asti to take him in. He was well known to them because of his many charitable works for the hospital. They took him in and, whenever a Nazi or Fascist official came in, they would wrap his head in bandages and admonish the visitor, "Don't touch him. He is severely wounded." They kept up the ruse until the end of the war.

When the Germans began to stream over the Alpine passes, Rita, Paola, and Gino Levi-Montalcini fled south together with their mother, Zia Lina (Adelina, the older sister of Elvira), and Gino's wife, Mariuccia, hoping to reach the American lines before the Germans caught them. They got as far as Florence, where they then lived under assumed names and with false identity papers for a year and a half. At one point Rita ran into her former professor, Giuseppe Levi, who slipped up and called her by her real name, potentially betraying them all to their deaths. The family had to quickly change lodgings and adopt a new identity. They lived in fear of being discovered every time they had to buy rationed foodstuffs, because they had to show their identity cards, and their cards were poor fakes. As the Allies closed in on Florence, German snipers took to shooting in the abdomen all who tried to leave the city, causing a very slow and painful death through sepsis. Rita, trained as a doctor, styled herself a nurse and cared for the wounded, though she had no drugs to cure the infections. When the Americans arrived, they brought with them penicillin, which they had learned to manufacture during the war. Those patients who survived until the Americans' arrival were immediately treated with the new drug, and many recovered.

Ulrico and Nina Montalcini (Nina was the sister of Rita, Paola, and Gino) had heard that there was a priest in the Alps leading people across the snows into Switzerland. After several tries, they convinced the Bishop of Asti to introduce them to this priest so they could be led across.[374] When they first tried to

---

[372] The children received citizenship automatically when their parents were naturalized.

[373] At that time, refrigerators had miniscule freezers, barely larger than a couple of ice-cube trays. Consequently, ice cream was a relatively rare treat that could be enjoyed only when eating out.

[374] I suspect that the good offices of Zio Manno played a part in gaining them an audience with the bishop.

reach the border, they were turned back by the police, as Hebrews were prohibited from going to towns within 10 km of the border. On their second attempt, they reached the border, only to see a party of Swiss border patrollers with guns drawn. They hid until the patrol had passed, and then the priest led them to a Red Cross camp in Switzerland.

Giorgio's older cousin, Laura Momigliano (a niece of his father), spent the first part of the war living in her villa in the countryside to escape the Allied bombing of the city. She took in many of her friends to give them shelter. After the German invasion, a party of Fascist officials came to the house looking for the proprietor, whom they knew to be a Hebrew. While her friends were being interrogated in the front room, she slipped out of a rear window, down a ladder, and across the vineyards to a nearby convent, where she was sheltered. Then, fearing that the police might come looking for her in the convent, she slipped back into the city and sought refuge with her dressmaker; that seemed safer, bombing or no bombing. Whenever the dressmaker had a customer, Laura would lock herself in the bathroom until the coast was clear. Her husband, disguised as an altar boy, was hidden by a village priest whom he knew. He spent the German occupation assisting at baptisms and funerals.

Giorgio's cousin, the pianist Nella Maissa, escaped to Portugal with her husband. There they lived a very meager existence. Portugal was a poor country at the time, with a Fascist dictatorship and certainly little money to spend supporting refugee Hebrew pianists.

Other stories finished less happily. Andrea Gonnella, Giorgio's closest friend from engineering school and his former colleague at STIPEL, spent the war commuting into Torino by bicycle from his country villa.[375] While he had to work in town during the day, he needed to be out of the city during the night-time bombing runs. At one point the Allies attempted to blow up a munitions factory not far from his country house, but their bombs missed the mark twice, permitting his family to survive. At other times, as he was bicycling to work, he had to jump into the river to avoid being machine-gunned during Allied strafing runs of the main roads into and out from Torino. Another of their colleagues had joined the partisans in the Valle di Susa, between Torino and the French border. That friend was captured by the Germans; Gonnella was swept up in a police roundup and forced to witness his friend's execution.

Giorgio's cousin Virginia Montalcini was captured by the Nazis in 1944, at age twenty-four. She was deported to the death camps and was killed. According to Primo Levi,[376] of the 653 Torino Hebrews deported by the Germans, only 3 survived. Of the roughly 8000 Italian Hebrews deported to the German death camps, fewer than 500 returned. Another several thousand, mostly the old and sick, were killed in Italy during routine roundups.

After the German invasion, Giorgio's cousin Nella Sacerdote, her husband, Ettore Ovazza, and their children fled to the Alpine village of Gressoney to hide and seek a passage into Switzerland. They stayed in a country inn, depositing a substantial quantity of currency and jewels in the hotel safe. They then made discreet inquiries as to who could safely lead them across the mountains and settled on an experienced Alpine guide. They sent their twenty-year-old son across first, with jewels sewn into his clothes. The guide robbed the young man, and betrayed him to the Nazis. The Nazis tortured him to death and dismembered his body. The guide then betrayed the rest of the family to the police for the bounty that the Nazis had offered for those turning in Hebrews. The rest of the family was also murdered, and their bodies were burned in a school furnace. After the war, the surviving members of the Ovazza family filed war-crimes charges against the perpetrators of these murders. According to the account in Alexander Stille's book, *Benevolence and Betrayal,*[377] the German SS officer in charge, an Austrian national named Gottfried Meir, was tried in absentia and sentenced to prison. However, Austria refused requests that he be extradited to Italy, and he lived out his days as a schoolteacher in his native country.

When Giorgio retuned to Italy in 1946, he also wanted to see what could be salvaged of the family's real estate holdings in and around Torino. As he observed to one of his cousins, he owned several million (prewar) lire worth of real estate, none of which was generating any rent, and which, for all he knew,

---

[375] Gonnella was a gentile and therefore not subject to the Racial Laws.

[376] Primo Levi was a distant cousin of Luciana's through his mother's family. He lived in Corso Re Umberto in Torino, across the street from Elvira, both before and after the war.

[377] Stille's book gives many details of the Ovazza's murders and also of the earlier betrayal of Luciana's cousins, the Foa family, to the Fascists.

had been flattened during the war. When he got there, he was appalled by the level of destruction. Torino, as a major industrial city and transportation hub, had been very heavily bombed. The Engineering Faculty where he had studied twenty years previously was totally destroyed. The synagogue had been hit during a British bombing run and was reduced to a burnt shell. The main railway station was flattened. The Fiat auto works outside of town were obliterated. A large fraction of the housing stock in town was uninhabitable. And the warehouse which had held the family's household furnishings had been destroyed.

As it happened, none of the family's real estate had been seriously damaged. When the Racial Laws had been passed, some of it was placed in the hands of nominees, who turned out to have been honest, and returned it. Other properties had been expropriated during the war and Giorgio had to sue for recovery under the terms of the American-Italian peace treaty that ended the war. Those suits were not finally settled until the late 1950s.

Zio Manno was not so lucky with his real estate arrangements. He had placed his property in Ferrere in the hands of a nominee, to be reclaimed after the war. The nominee then double-crossed him and sold the property to the parish priest. When the local parish could not afford the upkeep on the house, it was taken over by the Asti diocese. During the war, thieves stripped the house of its furnishings and decorative elements. After the war, the diocese turned the house into a home for the aged and it was further damaged. Later, in the 1970s, the diocese built a modern home for the aged in the garden of the house, and left the main house to rot. It currently stands vacant, yet all efforts on the part of the family to buy it back or have it put to productive use have been ignored. For reasons unknown, Zio Manno never sought to recover the property. Perhaps he felt he owed a debt to the Church for the wartime favors it had bestowed on him and his family. Perhaps he was simply embittered by the previously-mentioned double-cross.

Having regained control of the family properties, Giorgio's next task was to repair what damage had been done and fill them with reliable tenants. Because so much of the housing stock had been destroyed or damaged, the municipal government was placing tenants into any available space, so it was important to find tenants to your liking before the government found some for you who might be less reliable. For example, in Valsalice, Giorgio placed two families, relatives of the farmer, in the rooms over the carriage house, and an old widow in the lower level of the billiard house.[378] Further, to repair the damage that the Germans had done to the orchards, he arranged for the planting of several hundred pear trees. He then hired an agent to manage the family's properties on its behalf. In 1947, after an extended absence, he returned to New Jersey.

The next issue for Giorgio and Luciana was whether to remain in America or to return to Torino. Luciana wanted no part of returning after all their recent hardships and her unhappy childhood there. Giorgio was less certain, though the extent of the destruction certainly gave him pause. He had further pause when he witnessed first hand the extent of continuing political and economic instability in the country. The Communists, egged on by their Russian sponsors, were threatening to stage a coup, and inflation had spiraled out of control. The lira, which had stood at six to the dollar before the war, was rapidly converging on 600 to the dollar. Basic commodities like eggs, butter, flour, and paper were scarce and had to be acquired on the black market. Giorgio told the story of being invited out to dinner during this period. His hosts would make a great show of serving up sumptuous meals made up of scarce foodstuffs acquired on the black market. But when he went to the bathroom in these people's houses, he would find newspapers instead of toilet paper. Before the war, Luciana's parents had moved all of their assets into the safest of all investments, Italian government bonds. With the postwar inflation, these bonds became worthless. Guite, and later Leone, required ongoing financial support from Giorgio and Luciana's brother Ruggiero for the rest of their lives.[379]

Even after taking U. S. citizenship Giorgio was undecided for a considerable time on whether or not to return to Italy with the family. In a 1946 letter to Luciana's uncle Raoul Orefice, Giorgio indicated that he had not yet made up his mind. Some months later, Giorgio confided in a letter to one of his cousins

---

[378] This woman's rent was set at the prewar rate of 60 lire/month Because of rent control this rent could not be raised even after the lira
was devalued by 100:1.

[379] This tale shows the validity of the adage "He who follows the 'prudent man' rule is imprudent."

that the final decision for him came as he considered his children. Since the birth of his son Albert in 1936, the family had moved six times and lived in four countries. At last the children were living in a stable country and were at peace. The family would not return.

About 5000 Italian Hebrews had emigrated before the war. Among those we knew who had emigrated to the western hemisphere, about two thirds remained and one third returned. Most of Giorgio's relatives returned to Italy. In 1947, Elvira, who had never liked New York and spoke English with difficulty, left to visit Eugenia in Argentina. They had last seen each other in 1939. She arrived just as Eugenia's third child, Mauro, was born. While she remained in Buenos Aires for many months, she found it no more to her liking than New York. She missed her brother and sister, her friends, and the familiar surroundings of Torino and Valsalice. In 1948 she returned to Torino, where she remained the rest of her life, except for one brief visit to New York in 1949 and a trip to Israel around 1960.

The next to leave were the Vittorio and Cinci Ovazza,[380] their daughters Carla and Franca, and Carla's infant son Alain Elkann. During the war Carla had been briefly married to the French Hebrew financier Jean-Pierre Elkann.[381] In a curious twist of fate, Carla, Alain Elkann and his wife had to resume their exile in New York twenty years later during the political unrest of the late 1960s. At that time, Alain had just married Margherita Agnelli, the daughter of Gianni Agnelli, the richest man in Italy and patriarch of the family that controlled the Fiat automobile fortune. At the same time a group of political radicals, the Red Brigades had begun a campaign of kidnapping, and sometimes murdering, prominent political and business figures. Their most notable murder was of the former prime minister, Aldo Moro. One of those kidnapped was Carla Ovazza, who was held for over a month in an underground cell. Immediately, the Agnellis hustled the rest of the family out of the country. According to a widely circulated rumor, the Agnellis were unwilling to meet the ransom demand for fear of inviting further acts of terrorism against the family; instead Carla was ransomed by the Hebrew community of Torino. Currently John Elkann, the son of Alain and Margherita, is the leader of the Agnelli clan and has control over the family's vast web of industrial, financial and media companies.

Oscar and Nella Ghez were the next to leave New York and return to Europe. Shortly after they returned in the late 1940s, Nella died of cancer. In France, Oscar found that his rubber reclaiming factory was intact and had been heavily overstocked with raw materials by the Germans who had operated it during the war. With rubber still in short supply, he was able to sell the excess stock at a good price. Subsequently he sold the plant to the U.K. firm Dunlop, and invested the proceeds in post-Impressionist art. In the immediate postwar years, such art could be had quite cheaply and he built one of the world's most important collections of such works. Much later this collection formed the base of the Musée du Petit Palais in Geneva.

The Ghez were soon followed back to Europe by Dario and Egle Treves. Dario found he had little interest in business and committed himself full time to his career as a painter.

Angiolo and Ada Treves remained in New York the longest. Angiolo remained an active partner in Rubber and Plastics long after Oscar and Dario had lost interest. He and his wife commuted back and forth between Torino and New York, but during the 1950s their stays in New York grew shorter and shorter, until they, too, had returned to Torino permanently. Angiolo and Ada's sons Edward and Alessandro (whom Ada nicknamed Dino and Dando) went to prep school and college in the United States and served in the American military. Alex was NCAA saber fencing champion in 1949 and 1950 and on the U.S. Olympic team in that sport at the Helsinki games. When their parents were away, Giorgio and Luciana's home was their second home, and they developed very close relationships with the family. After Angiolo's death in 1960, they continued to work as partners with Giorgio through the 1960s, and maintained residences in both Torino and New York into the 1970s. At one point Eddie Treves bought out his brother's interest in Rubber and Plastics. He then began a firm in Italy, Lame Ledal, that embedded metalized plastic fibers into knitting yarns, thus returning to the Sacerdote family roots in the textile industry. During the Red Brigades period in the late 1960s, Eddie Treves's children, Daniel, Susan

---

[380] Vittorio was the brother of the murdered Ettore Ovazza. The third Ovazza brother spent the war years in Uruguay.

[381] Jean-Pierre returned to Paris after the war and resumed his banking career. He later became president of the Communuté des Israelites Français.

and Michael, were sent to school in Switzerland to keep them out of harm's way; they were particularly at risk of being kidnapped because of the role that Eddie's father-in-law, Sion Segre had played in negotiating for the release of Carla Ovazza. Daniel Treves took over leadership of Lame Ledal as a young man just out of college after his father's untimely death in the 1970s.

The only ones of Giorgio's relatives who did not return to Europe were Paolo, Eugenia, and the Segres.

- Paolo married an American, Pearl Quittel. In trying to alleviate the pain of late-stage cancer patients, he conducted a series of experiments in the medical uses of hypnosis. This pioneering work led to a career in psychiatry. Paolo and Pearl's children, Marc and Alan, a teacher and a doctor, continue to live in New York with their families.

- Maurizio and Eugenia's family remained in Argentina. Maurizio continued to work with the Pirelli company's South American operations. Eugenia overcame initial problems in getting her Italian medical degree recognized in Argentina, and eventually achieved academic prominence in cancer research. Their sons Leonardo and Mauro began a successful agribusiness growing and exporting out-of-season fruit to the northern hemisphere. Maurizio and Eugenia's daughter Livia became a professor of medicine, following in her mother's footsteps.

- Ernesto and Anna Segre remained in New York where he developed a successful business as a wine importer. Their sons Eugenio and Gino became physicians in California and Boston.

Among Luciana's cousins who left Italy, fewer returned.

- Her cousin Memé Orefice Ottolenghi and her family moved from Peru to Ecuador in the 1950s, and Memé's husband started a pharmaceutical house there. Their children Roberto, Abramo (Mino), Marcella and Patrizia went to university in the United States and Canada, where the surviving children still live. Mino is an emeritus professor at the Ohio State University Medical School, and Marcella is married to a retired Canadian diplomat.

- Luciana's cousin Gisella, Memé's sister, married a German refugee, Werner Karmann, and they both became professors in New York.

- Nadia and Mario Levi remained in Mexico City, where their daughters continue to live. Mario was a professor at the University of Mexico City. Nadia was another of Memé's sisters.

- Anna Foa and her husband, Davide Jona, who had survived the war doing menial jobs near New York, eventually moved to Cambridge, Massachusetts, where he joined the Harvard faculty.

- Nina and Bruno Rossi went to Los Alamos, New Mexico, where he worked on the Manhattan Project. They later settled in Cambridge, Massachusetts, where he became a professor of physics at MIT.

- Rita Levi-Montalcini came to America after the war to accept a professorship at the Washington University Medical School. After she retired, she returned to Italy.

Giorgio and Luciana's family became reverse commuters. Giorgio had to return to Italy almost every year to look after the family's investments. The rest of the family returned to Torino on an irregular schedule, averaging once every three or four years, beginning in 1948, for nearly thirty years.

During the postwar years, Giorgio and Luciana kept up a lively correspondence with Eugenia and Maurizio; they saw each other relatively infrequently in the United States and Italy because travel to and from South America was difficult and expensive. Eugenia traveled to the United States occasionally on professional business (she had become a professor of medicine at the University of Buenos Aires), and on at least two occasions brought her family to join us for a vacation. On one occasion, in the early 1950s, Eugenia stopped in Atlanta to visit the Centers for Disease Control. The World Health Organization had sent her to the United States to see the early results with the experimental polio vaccines under development, as part of a program she was heading in Argentina to combat an epidemic of that disease.

Figure 7-64
Giorgio's naturalization certificate. Giorgio, Luciana,
Albert and Peter, became US citizens in August, 1946.
Even after becoming a US citizen, Giorgio was undecided
whether to remain in America or return to Italy. When
Albert and Peter turned eighteen years old, the Italian
government sought to draft them into the Italian army and
they had to renounce their Italian citizenship. Only George
retains the right to Italian citizenship since his father was
legally Italian at the time of George's birth.

Figure 7-65
Guite Orefice and her granddaughter Gianna [formally
Jeanette], Rome, October 1945. Gianna was the daughter
of Luciana's brother Ruggiero Levi. Ruggiero was married in a Red Cross refugee camp in Switzerland where he
found a safe haven in 1943. The marriage did not survive
the war. In 1944, Ruggiero was able to make contact with
Giorgio and Luciana in New York through the Red Cross;
this was the first family contact between the US and
Europe in four years. Gianna was raised by her father and
grandmother Guite in Rome and now lives near Naples
with her husband and children.

Figure 7-66
Luciana's naturalization certificate. Unlike, Giorgio,
Luciana did not want to return to Italy after the war. She
had had an unhappy childhood as a result of her parents'
separation and preferred her new home in the United
States.

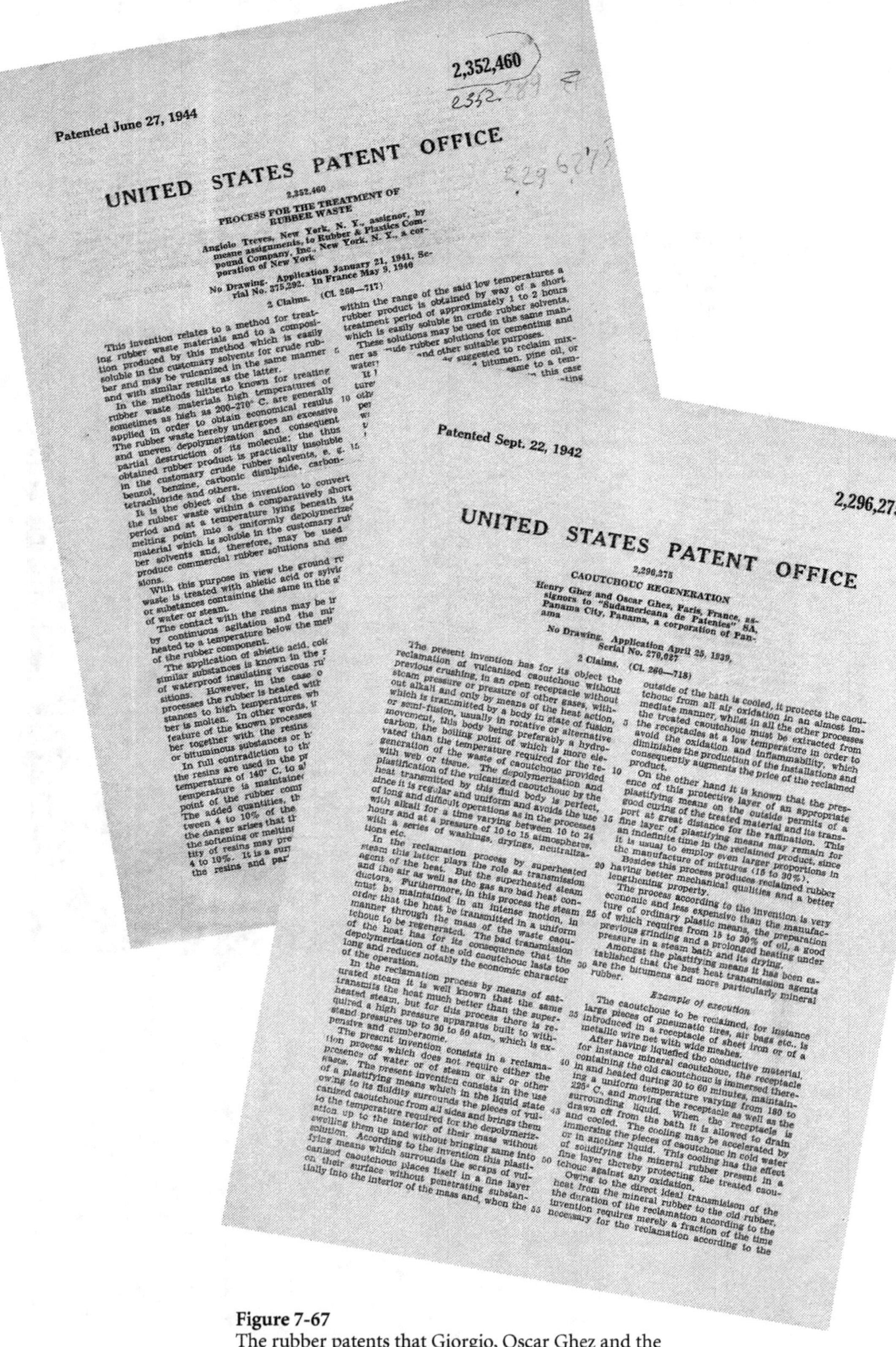

Patented June 27, 1944

2,352,460

UNITED STATES PATENT OFFICE

2,352,460

PROCESS FOR THE TREATMENT OF RUBBER WASTE

Angiolo Treves, New York, N. Y., assignor, by mesne assignments, to Rubber & Plastics Compound Company, Inc., New York, N. Y., a corporation of New York

No Drawing. Application January 21, 1941, Serial No. 375,292. In France May 3, 1940

2 Claims. (Cl. 260—717)

Patented Sept. 22, 1942

2,296,275

UNITED STATES PATENT OFFICE

2,296,275

CAOUTCHOUC REGENERATION

Henry Ghez and Oscar Ghez, Paris, France, assignors to "Sudamericana de Patentes" SA, Panama City, Panama, a corporation of Panama

No Drawing. Application April 25, 1939, Serial No. 270,027

2 Claims. (Cl. 260—718)

Figure 7-67
The rubber patents that Giorgio, Oscar Ghez and the
Treves had purchased while in France were subsequently
also registered in the United States.

Figure 7-68
Giorgio and his third son, George at 676 West Englewood
Avenue, Teaneck, NJ, 1946.

Figure 7-69
Peter at Camp Susquehanna, 1947. In the early post-war
years, Giorgio and Luciana sought to acculturate the family to the American way of life. One step in that process
was sending Peter and Albert to an American camp spe-
cializing in horsemanship.

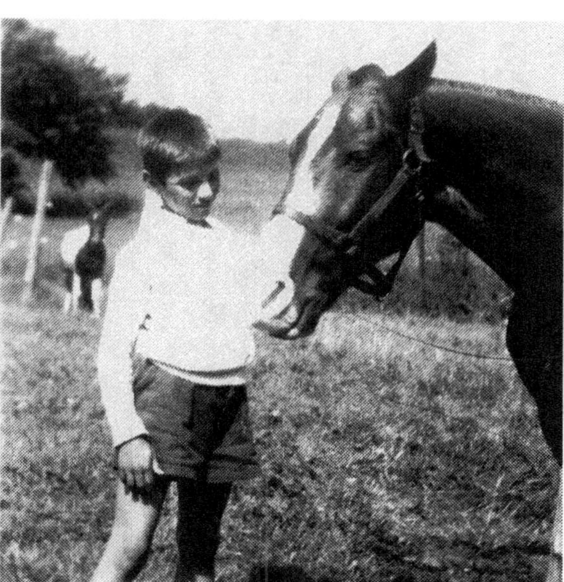

Figure 7-70
Another step in the acculturation process was to take
American style vacations. In 1949, the family went to
Truro on Cape Cod.

Figure 7-71
Albert, Giorgio, Peter, Luciana, and George, Cervinia,
1949. In the late 40s and 1950s, the family alternated
between US-style vacations [Cape Cod, summer camp for
the boys, etc.] and Italian [stays in Valsalice, hiking in the
Alps, visits to the Riviera, etc.].

Figure 7-72
George, Albert, Peter and Marc (son of Paolo), Valsalice,
1949. Note the short pants suits and ties on Peter and
Albert.

Figure 7-73
Paolo, or Paul as he was known by then, with his second son, Alan, 1949.

Figure 7-74
Elvira and Adelina, Paola, Gino, Mariuccia, Emanuele, and Piera Levi-Montalcini, Castel Rosso, 1950s. Elvira never got used to life either in the US or Argentina. She much preferred the familiar surroundings of Torino and Valsalice, spending time with her surviving brother and sister and their close friends to life in those alien environments of the Western Hemisphere. She returned to Italy in 1948.

Castel Rosso had belonged to Elvira and Adelina's brother, Zio Manno—see Figure 7-12. During the war, the property had fallen into the hands of the Diocese of Asti and Zio Manno never recovered it.

Figure 7-75
Albert, Giorgio, Peter, and Eddie Treves, early 1950s. Eddie
(Dino) and his younger brother Alex (Dando) Treves
largely grew up in the US. They both attended prep school
and university in the States, and served in the US military.
During his military service, Alex joined the US Olympic
fencing team in 1952. Ultimately they too returned to
Italy, but were among the last in the family to return.
While they were young men in America and their parents
were in Italy, they often stayed with us in Teaneck as their
second home. After the death of their father in 1960, they
inherited his interest in Rubber and Plastics and became
business partners with Giorgio.

Figure 7-76
In 1955 Eugenia and her family joined us for a trip to Quebec. In this picture are Maurizio, Leonardo, Mauro, Livia and Eugenia Lustig.

Figure 7-77
Rubber and Plastics greeting card, printed on a sheet of Nervastral.

Figure 7-78
Albert was the first Sacerdote to go to university in the
US. Here he is pictured at his graduation from Cornell in
chemical engineering, with George and Peter to his left.
He was also commissioned an ensign in the US Navy upon
his graduation.

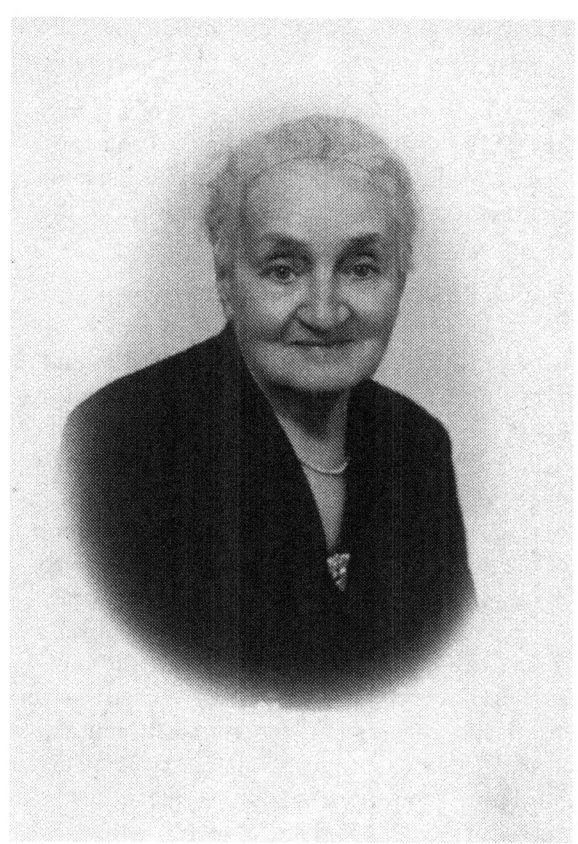

Figure 7-79
Elvira, circa 1960

Dear Mr. and Mrs Sacerdote
I was deeply saddened to hear of Albert's death.
I well remember him as a very bright, attractive and conscientious boy.
I knew he went on to a brilliant career. It is most difficult to understand why such a fine person, with so much to contribute, should be taken at the peak of his life.
My deep sympathy to you and your family
Most Sincerely
Agnes Norton
Tuesday

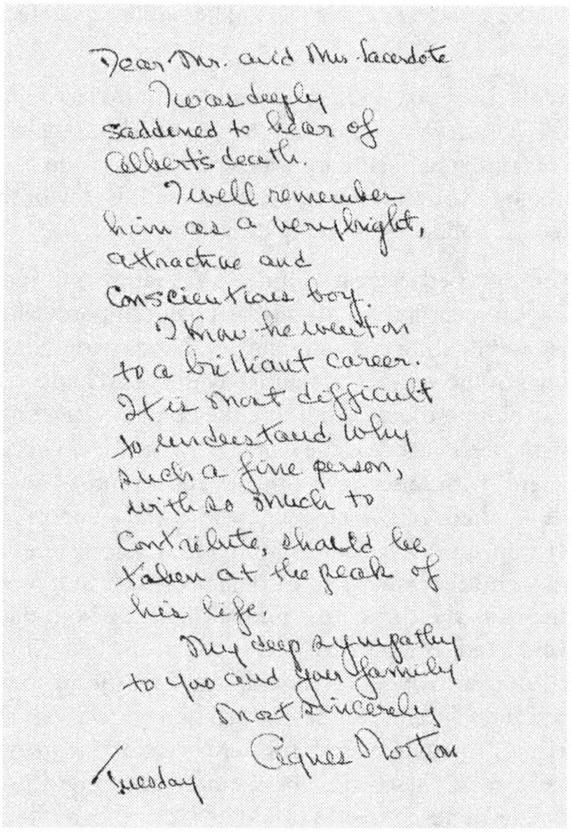

Figure 7-80
Condolence note from Agnes Norton on Albert's death. Albert's sudden death in 1974, at age 37, shocked us all. It took a terrible toll on both Giorgio and Luciana, and of course on Carole, Dean, and Bruce. Luciana preserved hundreds of condolence notes. All who had known Albert were impressed by his brilliance, sincerity and honesty. People never forgot him. Miss Norton had known Albert 20 years earlier as a high-school boy, when he worked part-time in the Teaneck Public Library, of which she was the director. During that time he had been an Eagle Scout, a finalist in the Westinghouse Science Talent search and had been awarded a merit scholarship to Cornell.

While in Atlanta, she boarded a city bus and caused a tremendous furor. Not understanding much English, she could not make out what the fuss was about. It seems that she had unwittingly entered the part of the bus reserved for blacks in the Jim Crow South, upsetting both blacks and whites.

Right after the war, Rita Levi-Montalcini took a professorship at the Washington University School of Medicine, where she taught and did research for many years, ultimately winning a Nobel Prize for her discovery of nerve growth factor. She and Luciana took a long vacation together to the southwestern United States. When she retired from Washington University, she returned to Italy to establish a medical research laboratory in Rome. As a Nobel laureate she became a celebrity in Italy, and would be stopped on the street by people seeking her autograph. She was ultimately given a life appointment to the Italian Senate.

While Giorgio and Luciana had committed to living the United States, their primary circle of friends in this country was composed of people whom they had known in their childhood in Torino: Paolo and his family; Raffaele and Eva Lattes; Ernesto and Anna Segre; the Treves family. Even Giorgio's personal doctor and accountant were Torinesi. It was with these families that they socialized and celebrated the Jewish holidays, especially Passover.

Giorgio tried to create a little of Val Salice in the garden of the Teaneck house. The previous owners, the Kipp family had installed a small fish pond which they stocked with koi. Giorgio added water lilies and floating greens to the pond and surrounded it with a rock garden planted in ferns, azaleas and lilies of the valley. Unfortunately the pond had a serious downside. Each fall we had to spend an entire day netting the fish, draining the pond to clean out the year's accumulated muck, and then refilling it with clean water for the winter. After the war Giorgio replaced the victory garden and its dreaded Swiss chards with raised beds of roses and annuals. Giorgio installed a stone patio at the top of the garden, in the shade of two large dogwoods and an enormous lilac. He and Luciana would entertain afternoon visitors on this patio all summer long. Along one side of the house, Giorgio planted a huge bed of peonies and chrysanthemums. The peonies would produce a sea of red, pink and white blooms in spring time and the chrysanthemums would close out the growing season each fall with their flowers of yellow, white, red, and purple. Next to the peony bed, Giorgio installed a Japanese maple which he would meticulously prune until it became a magnificent specimen. On the other side of the house, adjacent to the screened porch, Giorgio planted honeysuckle which filled the porch with its sweet aroma all summer. His only gardening failures were his efforts to grow fruit trees. At one point he planted several espaliered pear trees. These would blossom well and grew prodigiously, but rarely bore fruit. In another effort he planted a peach tree. It would produce enormous and very aromatic peaches, but never more than three in any one year.

Giorgio and Luciana's children grew up and the older boys left home, Albert in 1953 and Peter in 1955, to attend Cornell University. In 1956 Luciana decided to resume her academic career, which had been interrupted by the arrival of her children and the war. She took a post as professor of chemistry at Fairleigh Dickinson University in Teaneck, New Jersey. There she jumped on the bandwagon of programmed learning, which was the fashion then, and wrote a chemistry textbook using this technique. This book was subsequently translated into half a dozen languages. Luciana subsequently moved to City College in New York.

In 1957, Zio Manno died, followed in 1963 by Elvira. The family kept Elvira's apartment in Corso Re Umberto and the villa in Valsalice for use during family trips to Torino. Elvira left a substantial estate, and there followed a typically Italian, decade-long negotiation with the government on how much estate tax was owed. The negotiations began with the government valuing the estate at three and one-half times what the family thought it was worth.

In 1963, George left home to attend MIT, and Giorgio and Luciana were home alone. Soon thereafter their sons married. Albert married Carole Trautman, a science teacher from Bethlehem, Pennsylvania in 1964; they had two sons, Dean and Bruce. In 1967, Peter married Bonnie Johnson, a graduate of Smith College with a strong interest in art history; they had a daughter, Alisa, and two sons, Alexander and Laurence. In 1968, George married Carol Robinson, a senior at Wellesley College majoring in philosophy; they also had two sons, David and Michael.

With the marriages of their sons and the arrival of their first grandchildren a few years later, a new chapter opened in Giorgio and Luciana's lives. They delighted in their grandchildren. They began to travel more, going to Mexico, western Canada, Central America, the Caribbean, and Spain, among other places. They sold the house in Teaneck, and moved to a more comfortable house at 253 E. Palisade Avenue in the adjacent town of Englewood. Then Giorgio and Eddie Treves sold Rubber and Plastics,[382] and Luciana retired from academic life.

Albert died suddenly in 1974, leaving a widow and two young sons. In the death of Albert, the family lost a brilliant mind. He had graduated from high school at age seventeen, having been an Eagle Scout and a finalist in the Westinghouse Science Talent Search. After graduating from Cornell in chemical engineering, he served as a U.S. naval officer in the Pacific. While he was in the navy, Albert indulged his interest in travel with visits to Hong Kong and Japan. As guest of honor at a dinner in Japan, his diplomatic skills were tested to the utmost; he was offered a rare delicacy: a still-breathing fish from which he was expected to slice off morsels for dinner. He felt obliged to eat it and comment on how delicious it was even though he found the whole idea revolting. After his service in the Navy, Albert won a Fulbright fellowship to attend Canterbury University in Christchurch, New Zealand. As part of his travels to and from New Zealand, Albert organized a round-the-world cruise for himself with stops in Australia, southeast Asia, India, Aden, Egypt and several ports in the Mediterranean. After his Fulbright studies, Albert held a series of engineering positions with W.R. Grace, the Kendall Company, and Colgate-Palmolive. He was a highly intelligent, sensitive, and deeply thoughtful man.

The sudden death of Albert was a terrible blow to his widow Carole and their two small boys, Dean and Bruce. Giorgio and Luciana were also terribly affected and both became seriously depressed. But they thought first and foremost of their fatherless grandchildren and endowed trust funds to ensure their support and education, with Luciana, Peter, and George as trustees.

Soon after Albert's death, Giorgio developed leukemia, as had his father in 1915, and Luciana was operated on for the removal of a large intestinal tumor in 1977. While Luciana recovered well from her surgery, Giorgio's leukemia treatments were no more effective than his father's had been sixty years earlier. As Giorgio's condition worsened and his state of mind declined, Luciana pushed him to wind up his affairs in Italy, divide Elvira's estate, and sell off the remaining bits of property. Valsalice had stood largely unused for several years. As it was the last working farm in its district, the Communist government of the city of Torino wanted to expropriate it for use as a suburban park. Giorgio, Paolo, and Eugenia sold it in 1976 to Vittorio Lodi, an entrepreneur in the auto parts industry.[383] Lodi succeeded in halting the expropriation proceedings and continues to live there to this day.

Giorgio died in 1979, at the age of seventy-four. He had been a gentleman of the old school, highly cultured, enormously well-read, ever polite, scrupulously honest in all his dealings, and with a wry sense of humor. Although he had not learned English—his seventh language after Italian, Piemontese, French, Latin, Greek, and German—until his adult years and always spoke it with a heavy Italian accent, he had an enormous vocabulary in that language, which made him a formidable Scrabble player and a whiz at crossword puzzles. This faculty was no doubt the product of many years of Greek and Latin study at the Liceo d'Azeglio. And he had largely recovered his share of the family fortune from its nadir during the war. Giorgio left a substantial estate at his death, exclusive of the trust funds he had set up for Dean and Bruce and of the generous gifts he had made during the latter part of his life to minimize his exposure to the confiscatory U.S. estate taxes of the time.

Luciana continued to live in Englewood on her own for several years. Several attempted robberies, one of which was successful, finally convinced her to move to a more secure location, and so she moved to 36 Todd Pond Road, Lincoln, Massachusetts, in the early 1980s to be nearer to her Massachusetts grandchildren, Dean, Bruce, David, and Michael. There she fashioned a wholly new life for herself. To meet new people, she threw herself into volunteer activities for the town and joined the local League of Women Voters. She also joined the Harvard Institute for Learning in Retirement, an activity that she enjoyed immensely, both as a student and as a teacher. She broadened her travel, going to China twice, to Australia and New Zealand, to South America, and to Eastern Europe.

---

[382] The firm still exists. It is now headquartered in southern Connecticut.

[383] By a peculiar coincidence, Albert's son Dean was an MBA classmate of Lodi's son Giorgio at Boston University.

Figure 7-81
Exterior of the Sacerdote family tomb, Torino.

Figure 7-82, 83, 84
Three views of the interior of the Sacerdote tomb.
Cav. Emanuele Sacerdote, Alberto and his brothers, their
wives and some of their children are buried here.

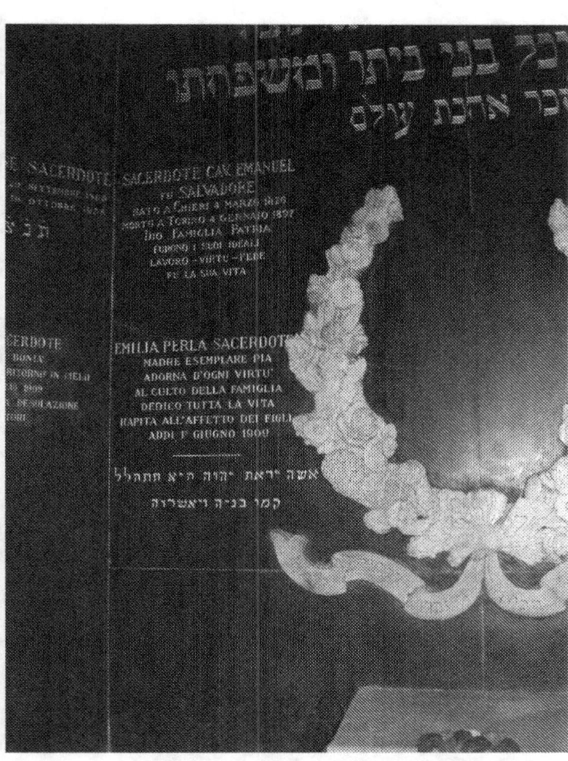

Figure 7-85
Levi family tomb, Torino. This tomb is the final resting place of Luciana's grandparents and many of her dozens of aunts and uncles. The central stone commemorates Leone Levi, Benedetta Debendetti's first husband, and the smaller stones around the sides commemorate her, her second husband, Samuele Levi [Leone's younger brother] and many of their fourteen children. Samuele and Benedetta were Luciana's paternal grandparents.

Figure 7-86
Levi-Montalcini Family tomb, Torino. This monument
was designed by the architect, Gino Levi-Montalcini.
Elvira's sister Adelina and Adamo Levi, brother of
Luciana's father Leone are buried here along with their
descendents.

Figure 7-87
Montalcini-Segre Family tomb Torino. Elvira's brothers,
Moisé, Alessandro and Emanuele, their guardians, Anna
and Teodoro Segre, and Teodoro's sister, Regina Segre
Cassin are buried in this tomb.

Figure 7-88
Treves Family tomb, Torino, containing, among others, the remains of Ada, Angiolo, Dario and Eddie Treves and Nella Treves Ghez.

Figure 7-89
Sacerdote family tomb, Riverside Cemetery, Saddle Brook, NJ, the final resting place for Giorgio and Luciana

As Luciana approached the end of her life, she noticeably began to slow down her activities. She stopped traveling. She cut back on her volunteer work. And she reduced her HILR activities to one class per semester instead of two. Her cancer had recurred, but she refused medical care for it. She could not face another round of major surgery like the one she had been through twenty-five years previously. She died in her sleep in September 2003, at peace with the world, and was buried next to Giorgio in Riverside Cemetery in Saddle Brook, New Jersey.

Giorgio and Luciana played a pivotal role in their family's history. Much as their ancestors had done in the 1500s, they had to reestablish the family in a new country as a result of war and persecution in their former home country. After undergoing considerable hardship, they were able to exploit their intellectual and financial capital to build a new life for themselves and their progeny. They impressed on their children the importance of education,[384] hard work, honest and fair dealing, and their Italian and Hebrew cultural heritage. Their sons all went on to study science and technology at prestigious universities: Albert and Peter at Cornell, having studied chemical and electrical engineering, respectively, and George, a mathematics major at MIT. All three subsequently earned advanced degrees: Albert an MS engineering, Peter an MBA at Harvard, and George a Ph.D. in mathematics. And all three went on to successful careers, rebuilding and expanding the family's fortune; much as we saw with the initial family immigrants to Piemonte in the 1500s, the task fell to the second generation to rebuild the family's estate. That estate will need to be carefully grown in each succeeding generation or it will be destroyed by wars, taxes, inflation, economic depressions and the family's growth over the years, as happened to several of our ancestors in the 1600s and 1700s, and Luciana's parents after World War II

Giorgio and Luciana's values have been passed on to the next generation. Albert's son Dean won admission to the U.S. Naval Academy, served with distinction in the Navy during the Kuwait War, and subsequently earned a MBA at Boston University. While at BU Dean met and later married a fellow student, Lisa Un, with whom he has had two children, Elizabeth and Stephen. Dean has pursued a successful career in the energy industry. Albert's second son, Bruce, was salutatorian of his class at Dartmouth, earned a Ph.D. in economics at Harvard, and returned to Dartmouth as a member of its faculty. He married the former Michele Verni, a teacher, with whom he has two children, Sofia and Sam. Peter's first child, Alisa, graduated from Duke University and later earned an MBA from Northwestern. She and her husband, Curtis Brockelman, jr. have three children, Curtis III, Nina, and Bridget. Peter's second child, Alexander, graduated from Hamilton College, later earned an MBA from Harvard, and has become a highly successful money manager. Alex and his wife, the former Annagret Burtschy have two children, Kate and Peter. Peter's third child, Laurence, attended Duke and graduated from Harvard, and is now studying film in Los Angeles. George's sons continued the family's tradition in science. His older son, David, studied computer science at Cornell and now works in Silicon Valley as does his wife, the former Dorothy Murray, a landscape architect. George's younger son, Michael, studied biochemistry at Harvard and is now a medical student at Washington University. As Peter and I are reaching the ends of our careers, we both look forward to seeing how the values we learned from our parents will play out in the lives of our children, our nieces and nephews, and their growing number of children.

---

[384] Both Peter and I recall the hard questions we were asked on the rare occasions when we brought home a report card that was not straight A's.

Figure 7-90
The Lustig family is descended from three of our five fami-
lies, the Sacerdote, Montalcini and Segre through Eugenia
Sacerdote de Lustig. Back row: Martin Baya, husband of
Daniela Lustig , Leonardo and his son Leonardo, Eugenia
and Sofia (mostly obscured), daughters of Leonardo,
and Sofia's fiancé; second row from the back: Susana
Fernandez, wife of Leonardo, Carola, daughter of Mauro
and Daniela, daughter of Leonardo, Sebastian and Pamela,
son and daughter of Mauro, Livia and her husband Victor
Yohai; front row: Ana and Sonia, wife and daughter of
Mauro, Mauro, Eugenia, Paola, daughter of Livia, and her
husband Horacio Gonzalez. Picture taken January 1, 2007
at Pinar del Mar, Argentina.

Figure 7-91
Paolo and Pearl's older son, Marc and family. Paolo
Sacerdote's descendents have as ancestors the Sacerdote,
Montalcini and Segre families in our narrative. Back row,
Angelo, Kim, Marc, Marysa; front row, Nicolas, Tora and
Marguerite.

Figure 7-92
Paolo and Pearl's younger son Alan and his wife, the former Nancy Greenbaum

Figure 7-93
Alan and Nancy's children, Derek and Allison

Figure 7-94
The modern Levi-Montalcini family is descended from
four of our five families, The Levi and Debenedetti fami-
lies on one side and the Montalcini and Segre families on
the other. Left to Right: Annalisa, Alice, Simona, Leonardo,
Alessandro, Marta Meluzzi nee Levi-Montalcini, Matteo,
Piera, Mariuccia , Emanuele, Paola Laurenzano nee
Geromel, Marco Laurenzano, Erich Terzi, Lorenzo, and
Claudia. Missing: Stefano Meluzzi and his son Davide.
Photograph summer 2006

Figure 7-95
Sacerdote Family Reunion, Nantucket, 2003. The descendents of Giorgio and Luciana and their spouses. Standing: Michael, David and Laurence Sacerdote; middle row: Michelle Verni Sacerdote and Bruce Sacerdote, Carol Robinson Sacerdote and George Sacerdote, Bonnie Johnson Sacerdote and Peter Sacerdote, Alexander Sacerdote; front row: Dean, Lisa Un Sacerdote and Elizabeth Sacerdote, Nina Bockelman, Sofia Sacerdote, Curtis Brockelman III, Alisa Sacerdote Brockelman, Annagret Butschy Sacerdote. Missing, Curtis Brockelman, Jr. Not shown because they came later, Bridget Brockelman, Kate and Peter Sacerdote, children of Alexander and Annagret, Stephen and William Sacerdote, children of Dean and Lisa, Samuel Sacerdote, son of Bruce and Michele, and Dorothy Murray Sacerdote, wife of David.

The Main Sacerdote Families in Piemonte

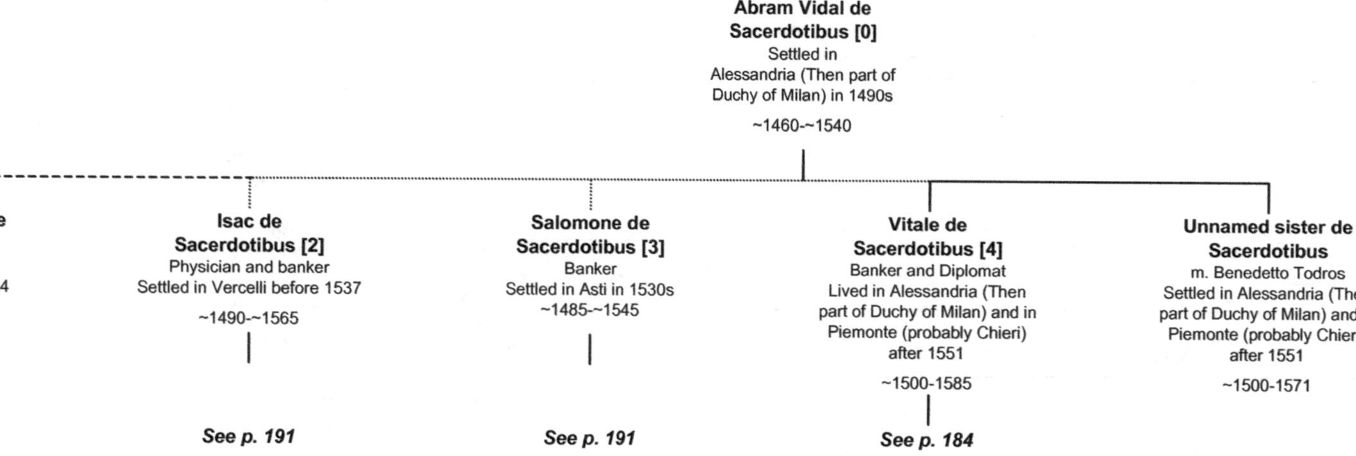

Abram Vidal de Sacerdotibus settled in Alessandria in the 1490s [0].

Vitale de Sacerdotibus and Benedetto Todros were brothers-in-law and business partners [5].

There is considerable circumstantial evidence that Isac and Salomone de Sacerdotibus were close relatives and possibly brothers of Vitale and his sister, wife of Benedetto Todros:

- Both Isac and Salomone had sons named Giuseppe, probably named after a common ancestor.
- Isac's son Aron and Vitale both named sons Abram, probably named after a common ancestor.
- Isac's third son, Josué (a transliteration into Italian of the Hebrew name Yehoshua, Joshua in English, Salvador in Spanish and Salvatore in Italian), named his second son Salomone Vitale, probably after his uncles Salomone and Vitale.
- Correspondence among the Todros family refers to their relatives in Asti, i.e., Salomone's family, related to the Todros through Benedetto's wife [6].
- Benedetto gave a of power of attorney to Isac's son Aron, something he would be unlikely to do with someone outside the family [7].
- Vitale had grandsons named Salomone and Salvador, probably named after Vitale's brother Salomone and nephew Josué.
- Both Isac and Vitale were confidantes of the Duke Emanuele Filiberto and advised him on the issue of Sephardite immigration into the Duke's domains. Isac and his son-in-law were granted the right in 1551 to determine which Hebrews were suitable to settle in Piemonte [8]. Among of the first to pass under this approval scheme were the families of Vitale and his brother In law, Benedetto Todros [9]. 20 years later, Vitale convinced the Duke to aggressively encourage Sephardite immigration [10].

Other than the commonality of names and close dates of immigration, we have no data to link Todros de Sacerdotibus to the others

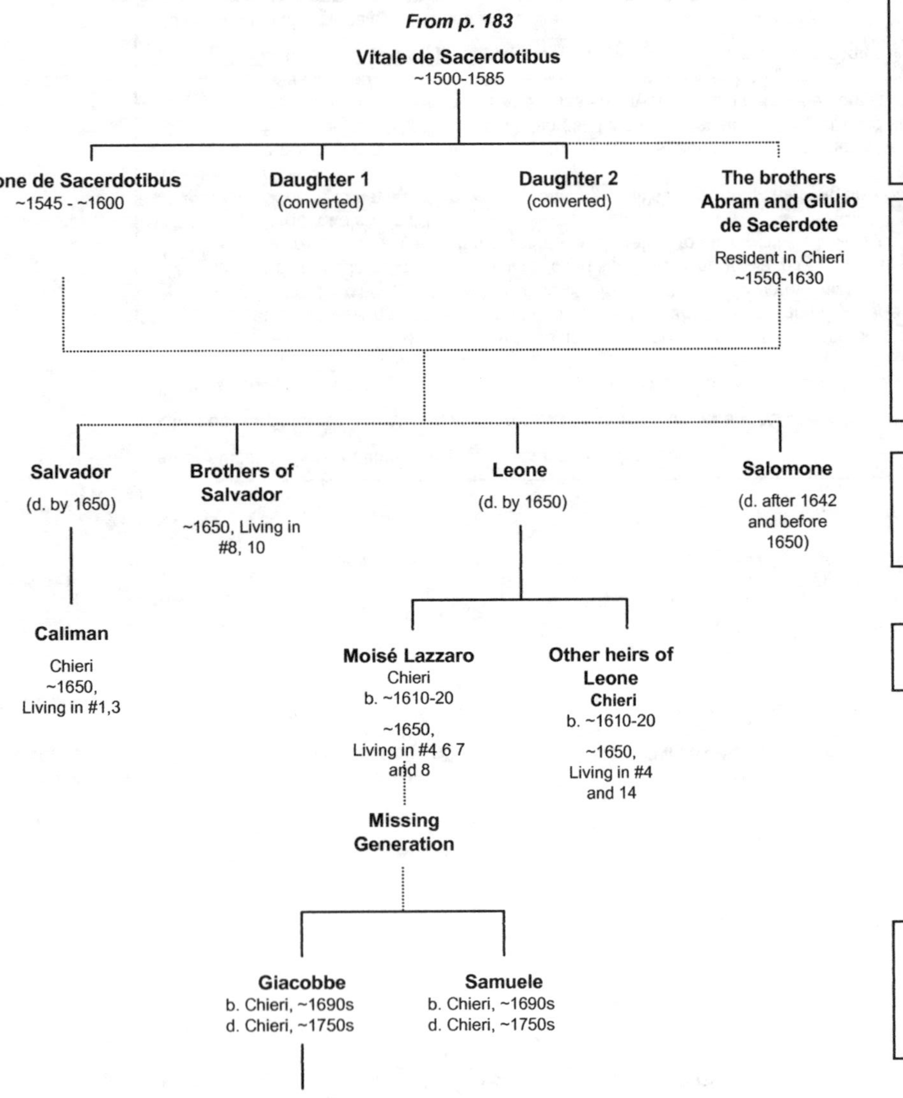

Vitale came from Spain, sojourned in Constantinople and the Duchy of Milan before going to Piemonte around 1551. He was a banker, diplomat and personal advisor to Duke Emanuele Filiberto. The reports to Philip II of Spain describe him as "having excellent connections in Spain and Portugal,… very rich, and influential at the ducal court." Vitale convinced the duke to develop mining in the Alps, open a free port at Villefranche near Nice, establish a merchant fleet on the Mediterranean and encourage free immigration of Sephardim. I presume him to have been in Chieri, since Vitale's sister married his business partner, Benedetto Todros, who had a banking license for Chieri beginning around 1550 [4, 11].

Vitale had several sons, of which we are certain only that Simone, the diplomat, was one of them. Because Abram and Giulio were business partners with one of their Todros cousins and were well-connected at the ducal court, they are presumably his other sons. The Duke sent Simone to Constantinople to recruit Hebrew immigrants as part of implementing the economic policies recommended by Vitale; on the way there he eluded capture by Spanish agents, and was attacked by Serbian bandits. Abram and Giulio started a cotton cloth industry (presumably with Turkish technology) and were the licensees of the state lottery [12].

Presumably brothers or cousins, born to Simone, Abram and/or Giulio, around 1580-1590; Salomone sold the Sacerdote banking interests in Chieri in 1642. (The street addresses are all in Via della Pace, the main street of the Chieri Hebrew community) [13]. Fee Figure 3-1.

Presumably they were about aged 30-40 in 1650, so born around 1610-1620. [13]

Since Giacobbe's (Jacob) heirs were still living in 2, 4, 6 and 8 Via della Pace 200 years later, he and his brother are presumably the grandsons of Moisé Lazzaro. Giacobbe and several others were taken to court and fined in 1743 for having rented property outside the recently set up Chieri ghetto to use for manufacturing, and possibly living, space [14].

Chieri Ghetto

1724-1797
and
1815-1848

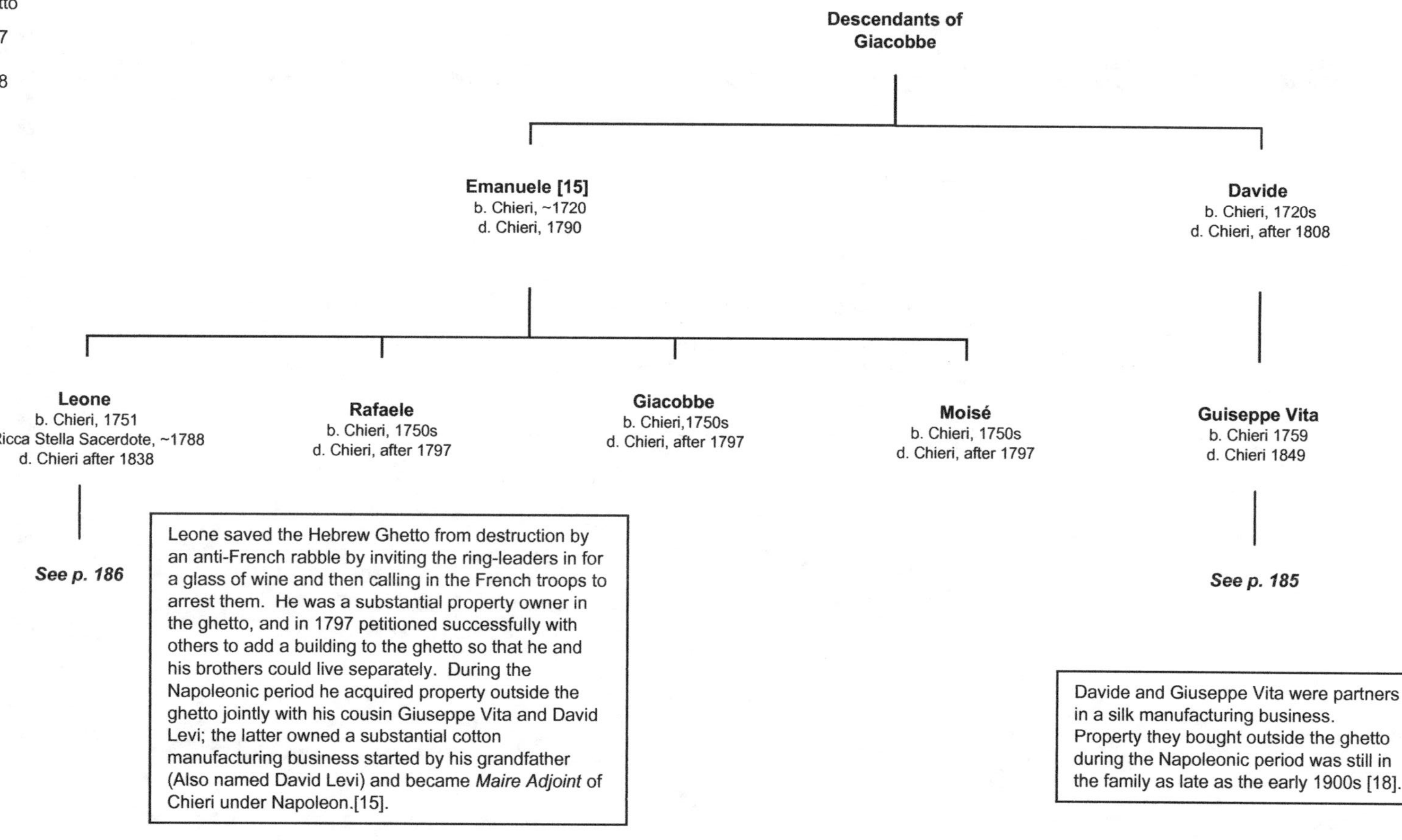

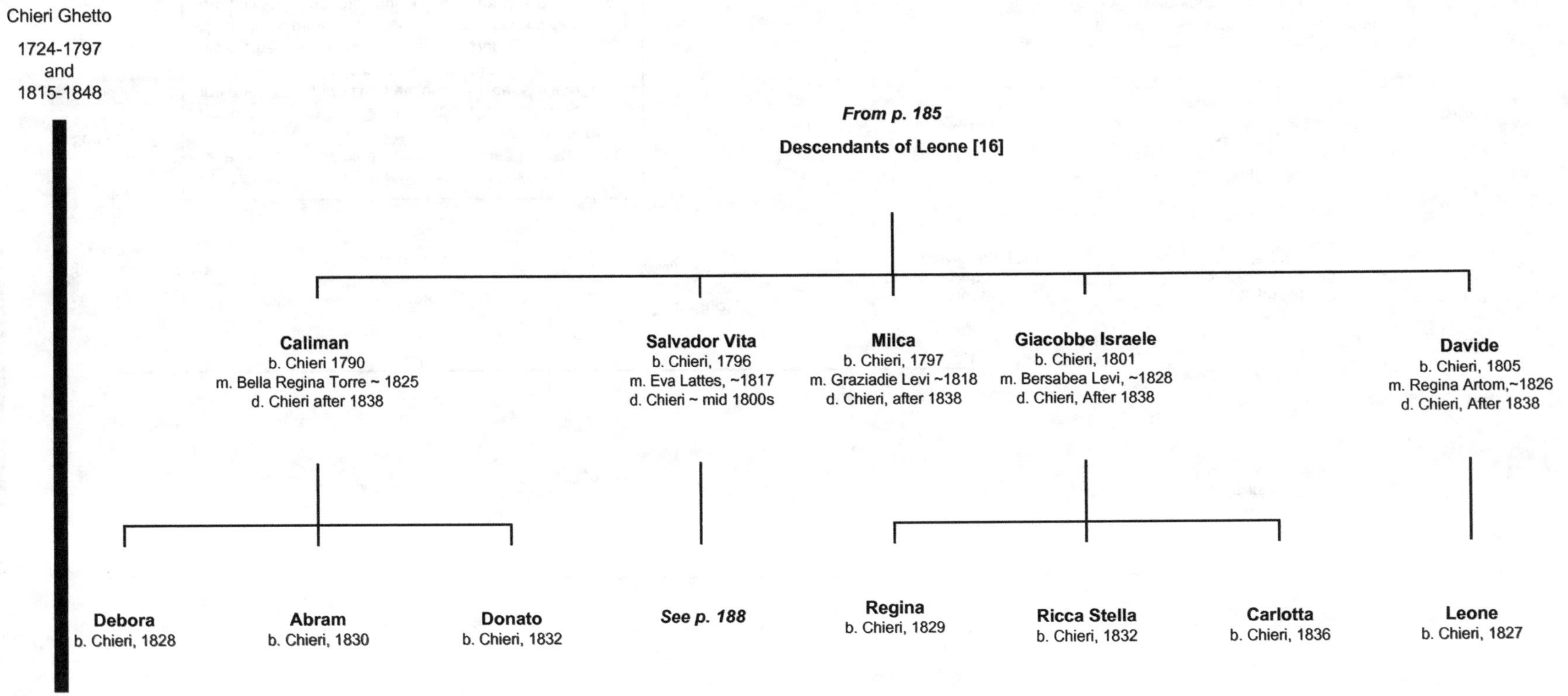

Chieri Ghetto

1724-1797
and
1815-1848

From p. 185

Descendants of Leone [16]

Caliman
b. Chieri 1790
m. Bella Regina Torre ~ 1825
d. Chieri after 1838

Salvador Vita
b. Chieri, 1796
m. Eva Lattes, ~1817
d. Chieri ~ mid 1800s

Milca
b. Chieri, 1797
m. Graziadie Levi ~1818
d. Chieri, after 1838

Giacobbe Israele
b. Chieri, 1801
m. Bersabea Levi, ~1828
d. Chieri, After 1838

Davide
b. Chieri, 1805
m. Regina Artom, ~1826
d. Chieri, After 1838

Debora
b. Chieri, 1828

Abram
b. Chieri, 1830

Donato
b. Chieri, 1832

See p. 188

Regina
b. Chieri, 1829

Ricca Stella
b. Chieri, 1832

Carlotta
b. Chieri, 1836

Leone
b. Chieri, 1827

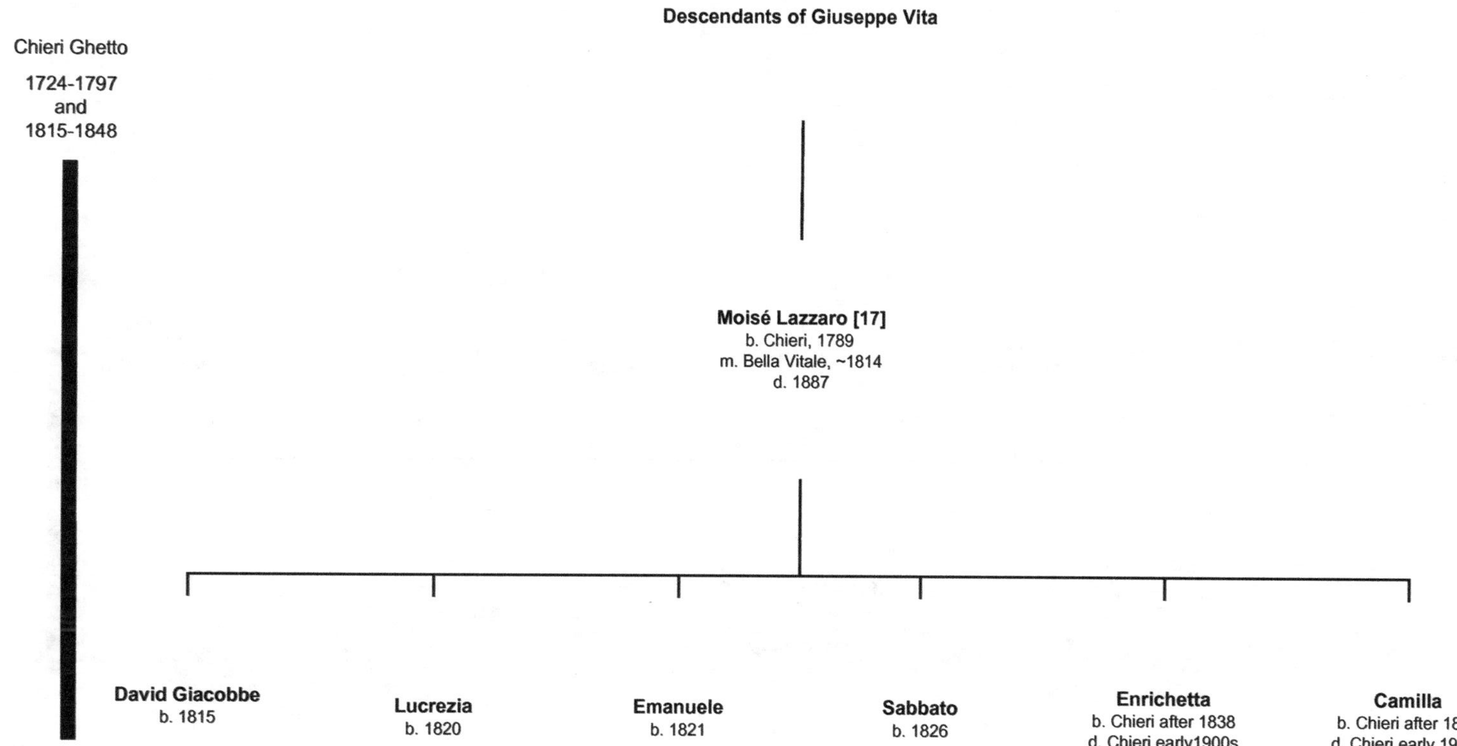

From p. 185
Descendants of Giuseppe Vita

Chieri Ghetto
1724-1797
and
1815-1848

Moisé Lazzaro [17]
b. Chieri, 1789
m. Bella Vitale, ~1814
d. 1887

David Giacobbe
b. 1815

Lucrezia
b. 1820

Emanuele
b. 1821

Sabbato
b. 1826

Enrichetta
b. Chieri after 1838
d. Chieri early1900s

Camilla
b. Chieri after 1838
d. Chieri early 1900s

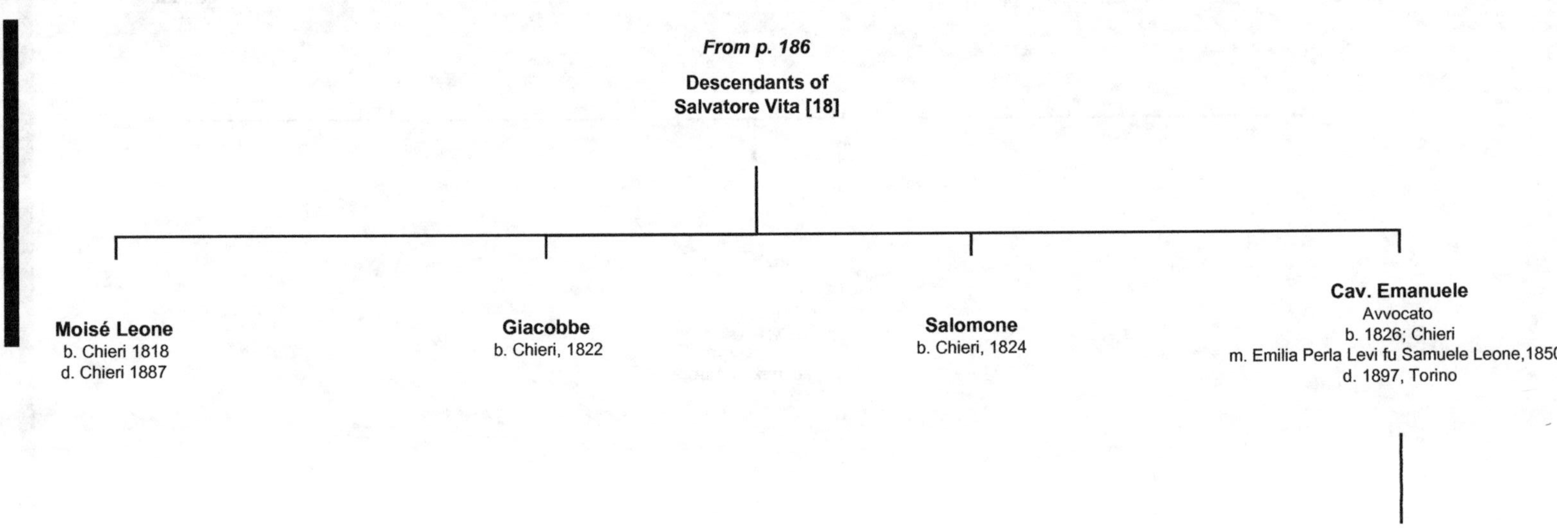

See p. 189

Cav. Emanuele Sacerdote was one of the first in the family to attend university, where be studied law; this was made possible by the emancipation decree of 1848. He became a property investor, buying agricultural properties in the path of urban growth and bidding successfully at foreclosure auctions.

From p. 189

**Descendants of
Cav. Emanuele [19]**

Balilla
Avvocato
b. Chieri 1859
m. Elena Ovazza, ~1894
d. 1920, Torino

Clotilde
b. Chieri 1862
d. Torino 1911

Letizia
b. ? Chieri
m. Vittorio Tedeschi, ?
d. Torino?

See p. 190

Cav. Leone
Grande Ufficiale
b. Chieri, 1866
m. ? , ~1901
d. Torino, 1938

Alberto David
Avvocato
b. 1868 Chieri
m. Elvira Montalcini, 1904
d. Torino. 1920

Evalia
b. ? Chieri
d. Torino?

Marcella
b. 1895, Torino
m. Bar. Arnaldo Levi di Veale,
~1915
d. Torino1988
Children and
grandchildren

Elena (in Israel)
m. Aston Mayer
Maria
Marcella
Maurizio

Alessandra
m. Rodolfo Weisz
Simona
m. Beppe Ferrero
Carlotta

Lidia
m. Ezio Levi
Claudia
Alessandra
Silvia
Arnaldo
m. Luisa
Andrea

Nella
m. Ettore Ovazza
Murdered by Nazis
along with their
children, 1943

Riccardo
b. 1899
d.1905

Vittorio
b. 1890
d. 1891

Umberto Secondo
b. Torino 1903
m. Virginia ?, ~1930
d. Torino 1988

Children

Miriam
m. Stephen Hirsch

Manuela

No surviving
grandchildren

Ada
b. 1905 Torino
m. Angiolo Treves, ~1927
d. Torino, 2003

Children and
Grandchildren

Edward (Dino) 1928-
1982
m. Ghita Segre-Amar
Daniel
Susanna
Michael
Alessandro (Dando)
1929-
Marco
Alessandra

**Emanuele
Filberto**

See p. 190

Cav. Emanuele's real estate business was
continued by his sons and grandsons. The
last of the buildings and agricultural
properties he had bought were sold in the
1970s as my father's health went into
decline

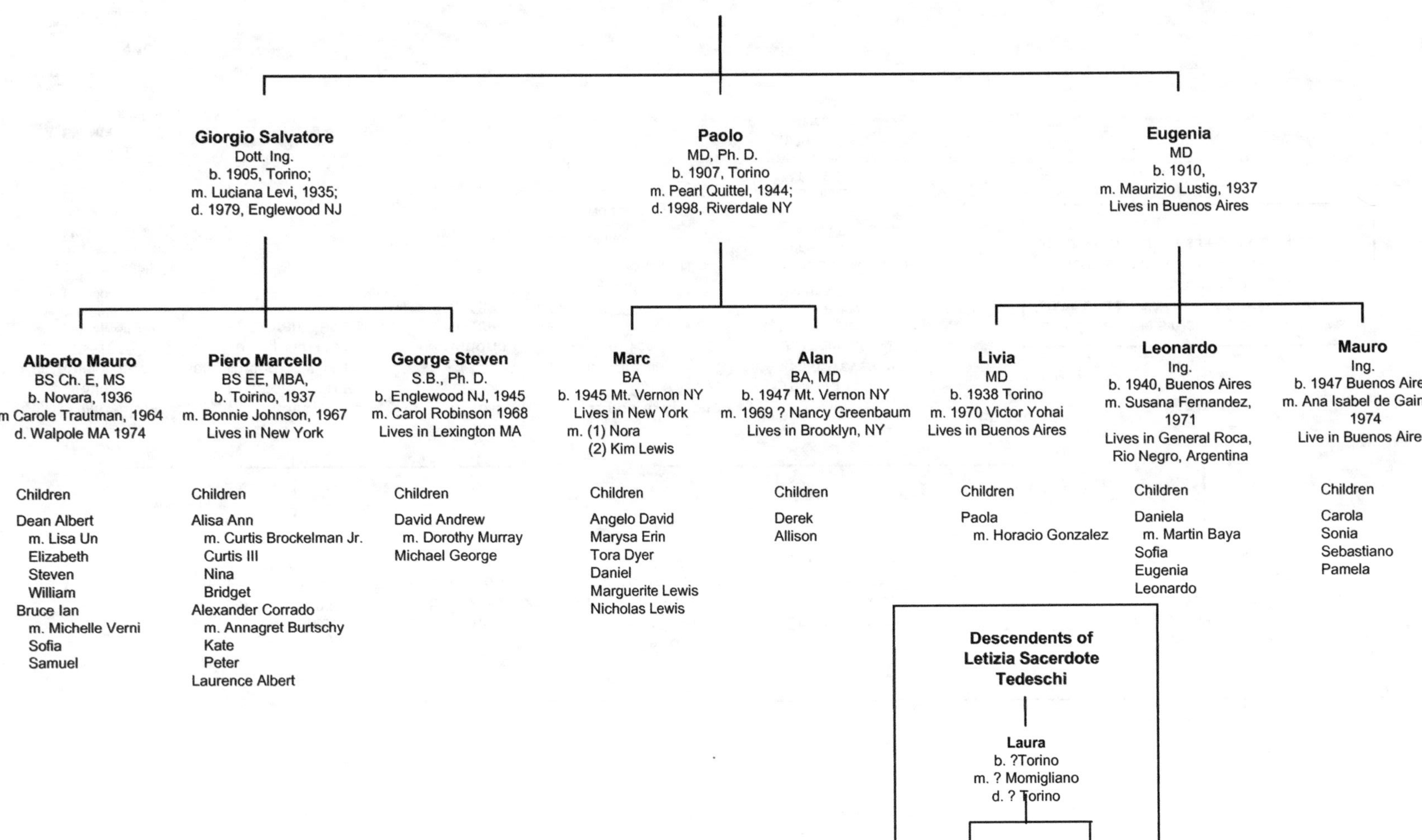
From p. 189
Descendents of
Alberto David

Giorgio Salvatore
Dott. Ing.
b. 1905, Torino;
m. Luciana Levi, 1935;
d. 1979, Englewood NJ

Paolo
MD, Ph. D.
b. 1907, Torino
m. Pearl Quittel, 1944;
d. 1998, Riverdale NY

Eugenia
MD
b. 1910,
m. Maurizio Lustig, 1937
Lives in Buenos Aires

Alberto Mauro
BS Ch. E, MS
b. Novara, 1936
m Carole Trautman, 1964
d. Walpole MA 1974
Children
Dean Albert
m. Lisa Un
Elizabeth
Steven
William
Bruce Ian
m. Michelle Verni
Sofia
Samuel

Piero Marcello
BS EE, MBA,
b. Toirino, 1937
m. Bonnie Johnson, 1967
Lives in New York
Children
Alisa Ann
m. Curtis Brockelman Jr.
Curtis III
Nina
Bridget
Alexander Corrado
m. Annagret Burtschy
Kate
Peter
Laurence Albert

George Steven
S.B., Ph. D.
b. Englewood NJ, 1945
m. Carol Robinson 1968
Lives in Lexington MA
Children
David Andrew
m. Dorothy Murray
Michael George

Marc
BA
b. 1945 Mt. Vernon NY
Lives in New York
m. (1) Nora
(2) Kim Lewis
Children
Angelo David
Marysa Erin
Tora Dyer
Daniel
Marguerite Lewis
Nicholas Lewis

Alan
BA, MD
b. 1947 Mt. Vernon NY
m. 1969 ? Nancy Greenbaum
Lives in Brooklyn, NY
Children
Derek
Allison

Livia
MD
b. 1938 Torino
m. 1970 Victor Yohai
Lives in Buenos Aires
Children
Paola
m. Horacio Gonzalez

Leonardo
Ing.
b. 1940, Buenos Aires
m. Susana Fernandez,
1971
Lives in General Roca,
Rio Negro, Argentina
Children
Daniela
m. Martin Baya
Sofia
Eugenia
Leonardo

Mauro
Ing.
b. 1947 Buenos Aires
m. Ana Isabel de Gainza,
1974
Live in Buenos Aires
Children
Carola
Sonia
Sebastiano
Pamela

Descendents of
Letizia Sacerdote
Tedeschi

Laura
b. ?Torino
m. ? Momigliano
d. ? Torino

Walter
b. ?~1907 Torino
d. ? Torino

Mimmi
b. ?~1910 Torino
d. ? Torino

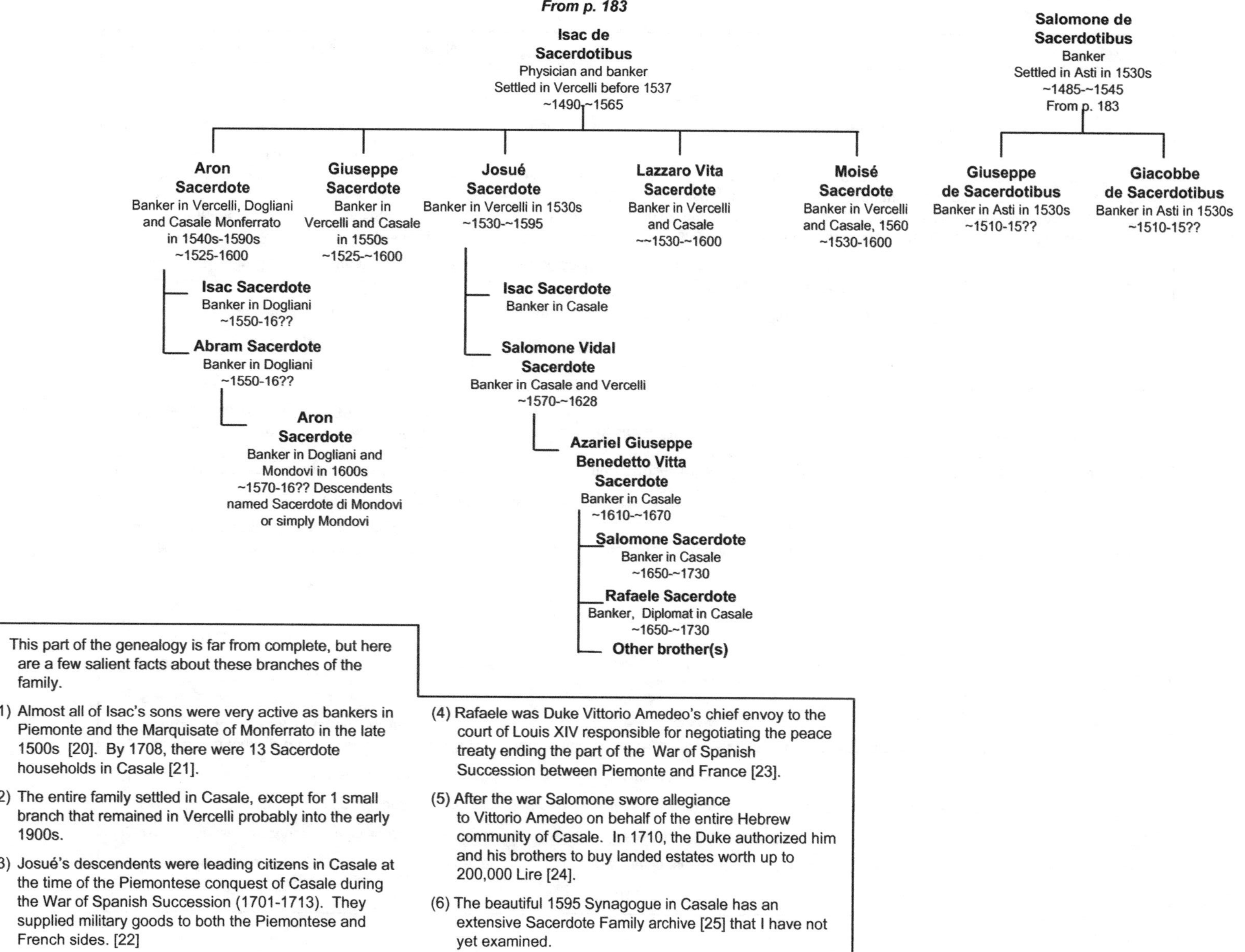

This part of the genealogy is far from complete, but here are a few salient facts about these branches of the family.

(1) Almost all of Isac's sons were very active as bankers in Piemonte and the Marquisate of Monferrato in the late 1500s [20]. By 1708, there were 13 Sacerdote households in Casale [21].

(2) The entire family settled in Casale, except for 1 small branch that remained in Vercelli probably into the early 1900s.

(3) Josué's descendents were leading citizens in Casale at the time of the Piemontese conquest of Casale during the War of Spanish Succession (1701-1713). They supplied military goods to both the Piemontese and French sides. [22]

(4) Rafaele was Duke Vittorio Amedeo's chief envoy to the court of Louis XIV responsible for negotiating the peace treaty ending the part of the War of Spanish Succession between Piemonte and France [23].

(5) After the war Salomone swore allegiance to Vittorio Amedeo on behalf of the entire Hebrew community of Casale. In 1710, the Duke authorized him and his brothers to buy landed estates worth up to 200,000 Lire [24].

(6) The beautiful 1595 Synagogue in Casale has an extensive Sacerdote Family archive [25] that I have not yet examined.

Notes

[0] Abram Vidal de Sacerdotibus was thought to be the first Hebrew to settle in Alessandria in the 1490s, Sacerdoti, p.18.

[1] Todros de Sacerdotibus' immigration appears in Segre, *The Jews in Piedmont,* document 800.

[2] Documents covering Isach de Sacerdotibus include Segre, p. XLVIII and documents 817, 865, 901, 947, 986, 995, 1027, and 1392.

[3] Salomone de Sacerdotibus and his sons are mentioned in Segre, documents 805, 80, 808, and 810.

[4] Vitale's relationship with Emanuele Filiberto is well documented in Segre, pages XLVIII and LV, and documents 1056, 1059, 1062, 1063,1068, 1100, 1104, 1135, 1136, 1141, and 1189.

[5] Segre, page XLVIII.

[6] Segre , document 915.

[7] Segre, document 1119.

[8] Segre, document 865.

[9] Segre, page XLVII.

[10] Segre, document 1059 is the central document, although there are numerous other documents concerning Spanish and Papal diplomatic efforts to prevent the immigration of Hebrews into Piemonte.

[11] Todros' banking license is in Segre, page XLVIII and documents 841, 915, 1119, 1189, 1258, 1295, 1334.

[12] Simon's exploits are documented in Segre, page LV and documents 1054, 1056, 1061, 1063A, 1073, 1079, 1094, 1100, 1104, 1112, and 1123. Abram's and Giulio's activities appear in Segre, documents 1485, 1638, 1645, 1996, and 2106.   The converted daughters of Vitale are mentioned in Segre's article, *Controriforma: Espulsioni, Conversioni, Isolamento,* in *Storia d'Italia, Annali 11, Gli ebrei in Italia,* edited by Corrado Viventi, published by Giulio Einaudi, 1996, Page 760.

[13] The two generations after Simon, Abram and Giulio are documented in the map in Treves, *Gli Ebrei a Chieri,* pages 271-2. Salomone appears in Treves, page 87. That the family still lived at 4,6, and 8 Via della Pace in the late 1800s is documented by an 1875 plaque at #4, and an unpublished letter from Umberto Sacerdote to my father dated 1953.

[14] Giacobbe and Samuele are documented in Segre, documents 2446, 2573, 2600, 276, 2926, 2940, 2975, and 2977.

[15] Emanuele's and Davide's lives and descent from Giacobbe are documented in Segre, documents 2975, 2977, 3099, and 3112.   Leone and his brothers appear in Segre, document 3445. Leone is also well documented in Treves, pages 155, 171, and 181.

[16] Leone's three younger children are listed as living in his household in the 1838 census of the Chieri Ghetto, when he was 87. I have inferred that the brothers Caliman and Salvador (see Treves, pages 173-4) were also his children from three facts: (a) Their birthdates are consistent with the age of Leone's wife, uniquely among all the Sacerdote women in the 1838 census; (b) Salvador's granddaughter Clotilde is buried in the same tomb as Leone's nephew, Moisé Lazzaro and several of his children, suggesting close family connection; and (c) the given names Leone and Emanuele appear among Salvador's descendents.

[17] Moisé Lazzaro and his family are documented in the 1838 Census, the Sacerdote family tomb in Chieri, and Treves, pages 181, 183, and 199.

[18] Salvador Vita's immediate descendents are listed in the Chieri census of 1838.

[19] Cav. Emanuele's immediate descendents are buried in the Sacerdote family tomb in Torino except as follows: Clotilde in Chieri, Letizia probably in a Torino tomb of the Tedeschi family.

Notes

[20] Aron's activities are mentioned in Segre, documents 842, 870, 912, 1037, 1294, 1361, 1494, 1657, 1676. Giuseppe in documents 1651, 1657, and 1676. Gesué's in documents 1003 and 1294. Lazzaro's in 975, 1494, 1651, and 1657. Moisé's in document 975.

[21] The Hebrews of Casale assembled in 1708 to swear allegiance to the Duke of Piemonte; Segre document 2531 enumerates their families.

[22] The activities of Rafaele and his brothers are detailed in Segre, pages LXXX-LXXXI and documents 2533, 2537, 2538, 2561, 2541-2545, 2547, 2549, 2551, 2553, 2554, 2556, 2557, 2559, 2564, 2594, 2604, 2732, 2744, 2808, 2843, 2859, and 2898.

[23] Rafaele's role in the negotiations between Vittorio Amedeo and Louis XIV is detailed in Segre, documents 2538, 2541-45,2547, 2549, 2551, 2553, 2554, 2556, and 2557.

[24] The permission to acquire real estate appears in Segre, document 2604.

[25] DeBenedetti, *La Sinagoga degli Argenti*, published by Pluriverso, 1991.

Appendix B
The Montalcini Family

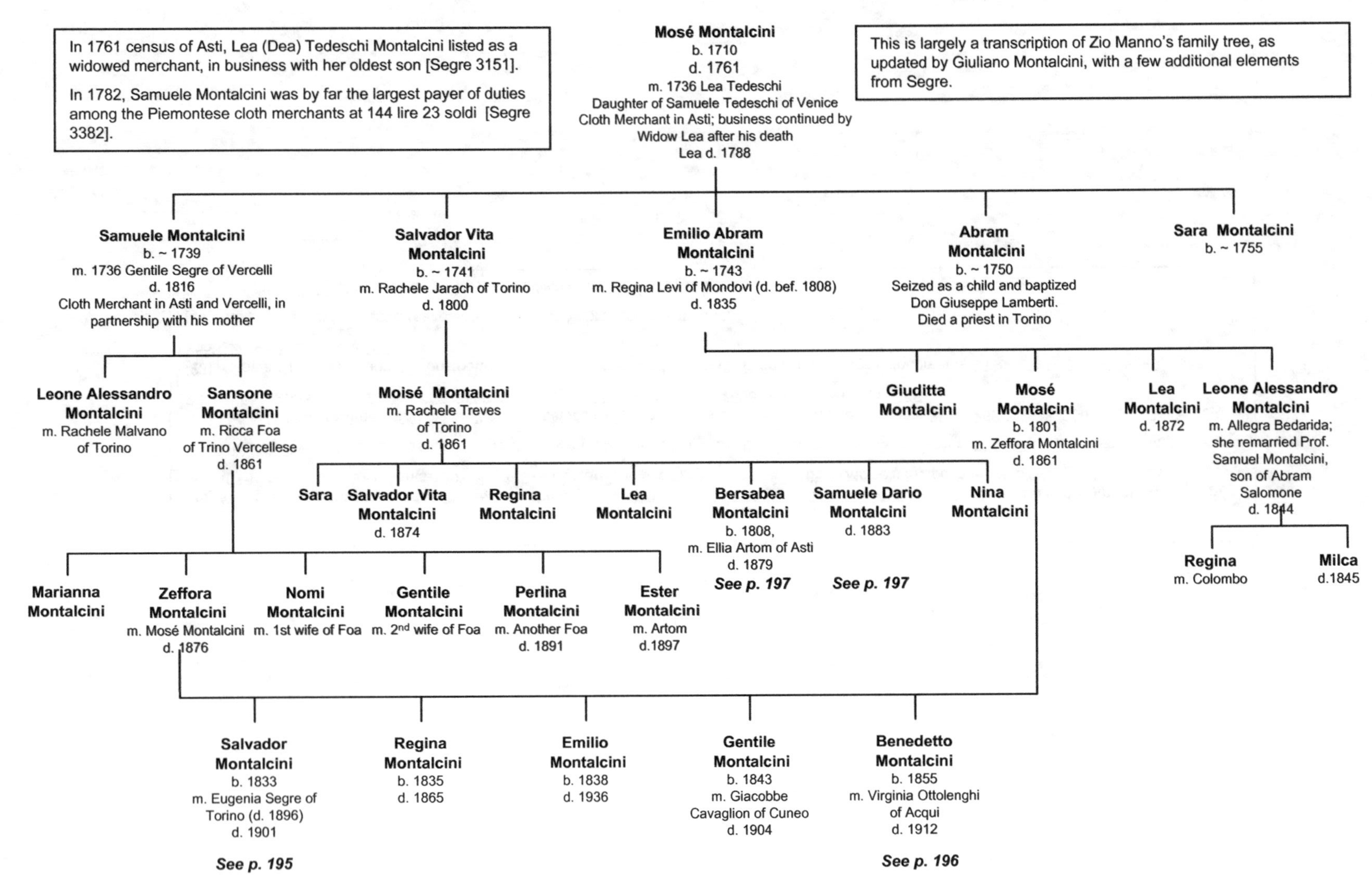

The Montalcini Ancestors of Elvira Montalcini

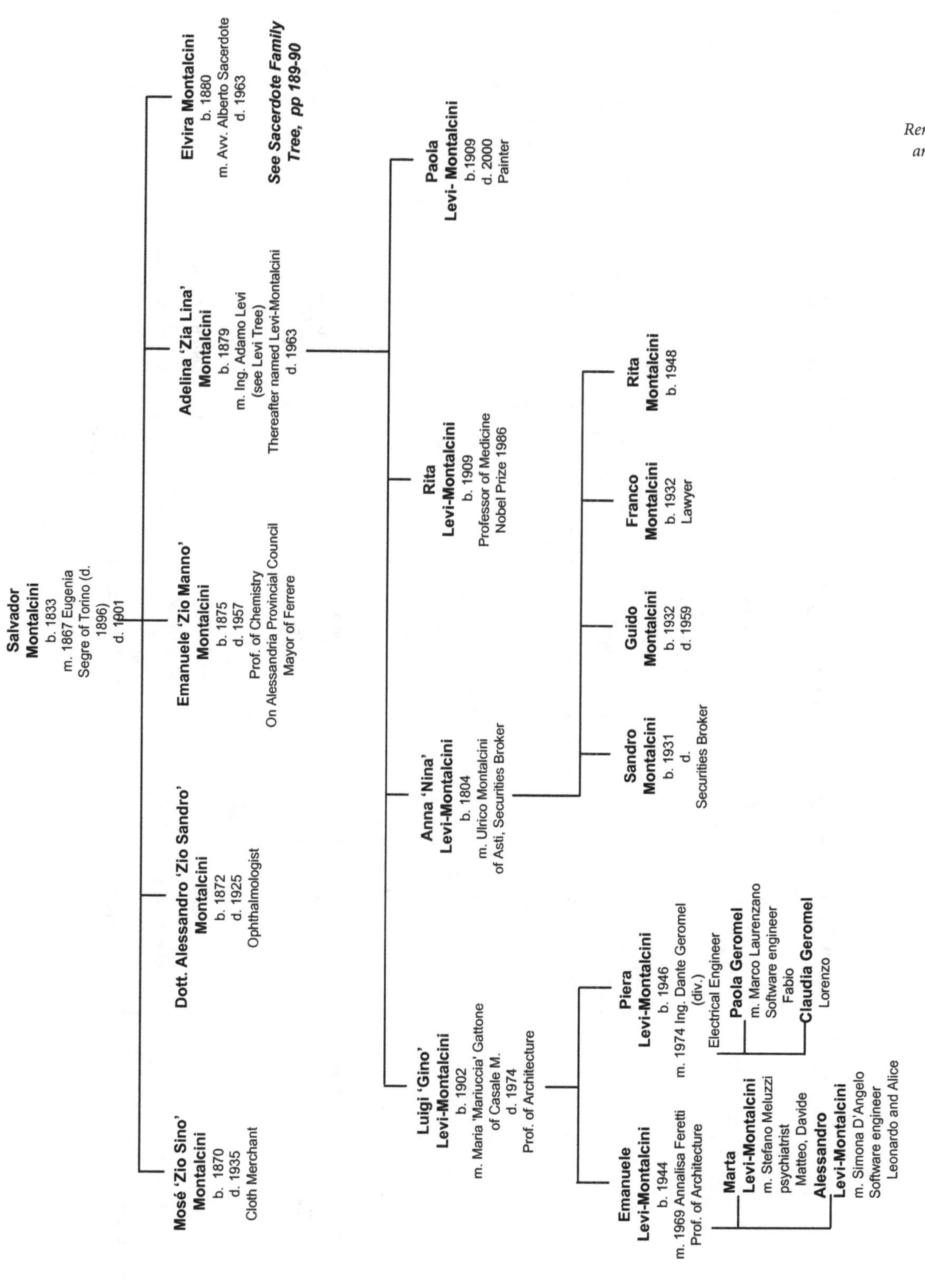

The Montalcini Cousins of Elvira Montalcini

From p. 194

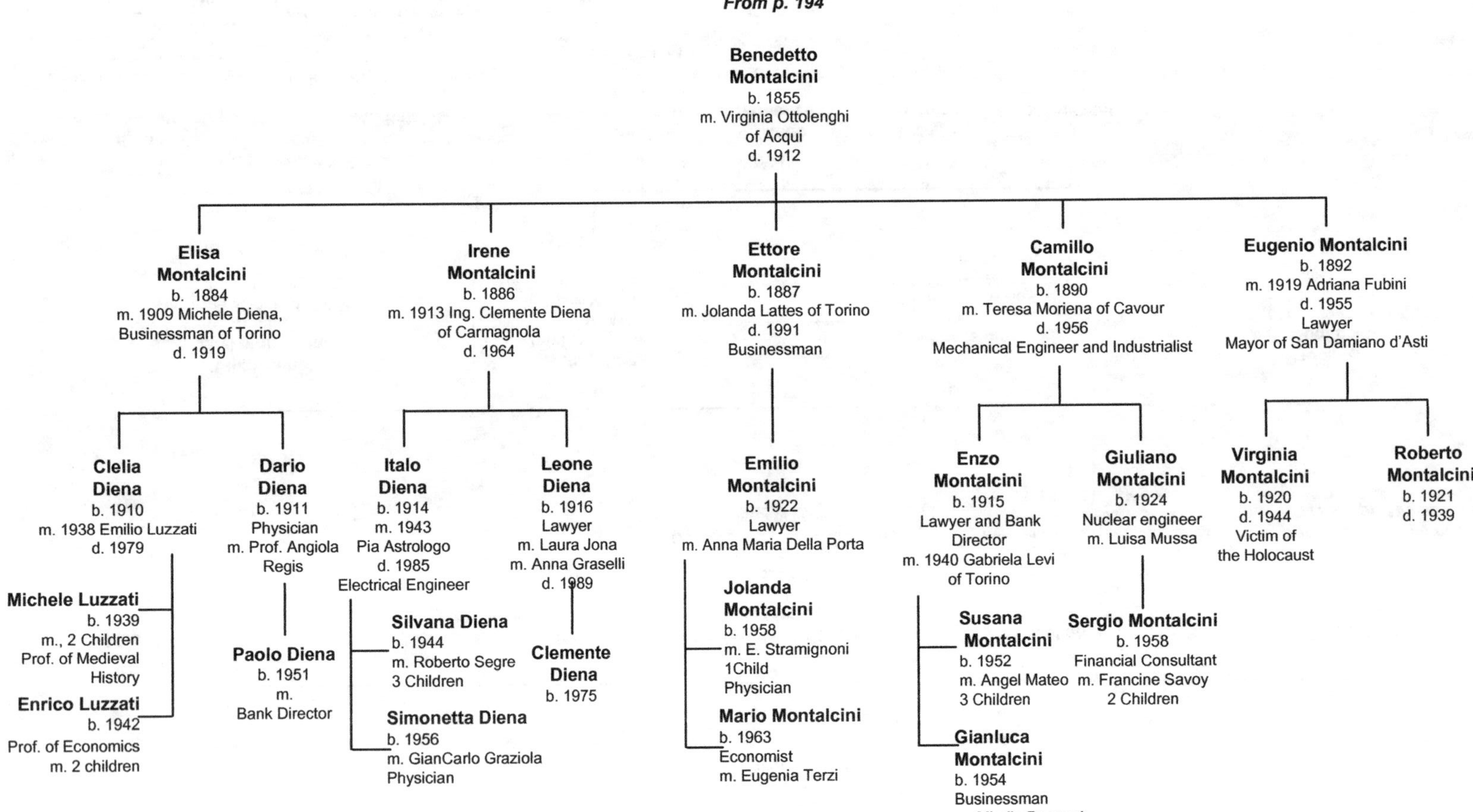

The Montalcini Cousins of Elvira Montalcini

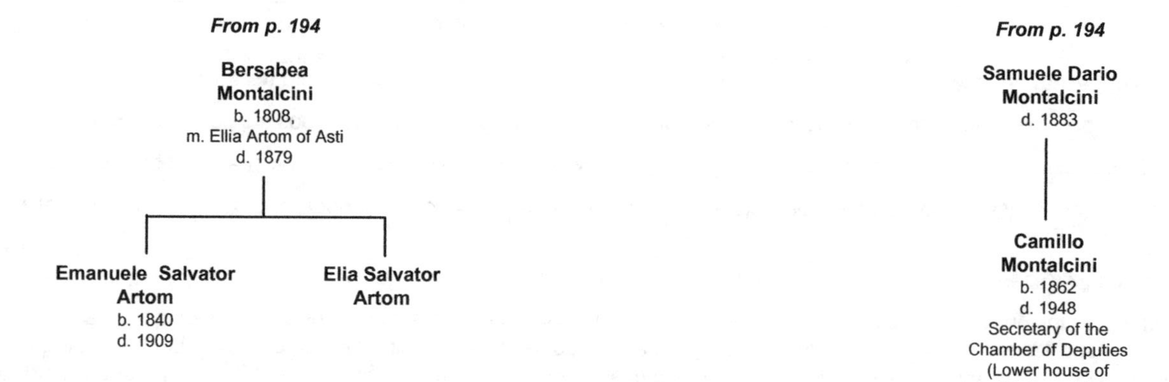

The Segre Ancestors of Elvira Montalcini

The earliest reference to a Segre in Piemonte was to an Elia de Segre, a banker in Savigliano in the mid 1400s. He may or may not have been the father or grandfather of three Segre families that settled in Piemonte in the first half of the 1500s. According to Segre family lore, their family originated from the Spanish region of Catalonia, from a town on the Segre River, though some scholars dispute this origin. At least one branch of the family had a right to use a Spanish coat of arms, as was confirmed by Benedetto Todros' court testimony during the late-1500s.

In any case, those three families, which were almost certainly related to each other, appear to be the forbears of all the Segres in modern Piemonte. They were:

1. The brothers Elia, Doctor Emanuel and Simone Segre who were well-established as bankers in Asti in the 1530s.

2. Abram and Lea (Hellea) Segre and their children, who were bankers in Pinerolo, Racconigi and other towns in the mid-1500s.

3. Bellavigna Segre and his sons. Bellavigna moved to Piemonte in the 1540s from the Milanese town of Lodi.

Working backward from Elvira's mother, Eugenia Segre of Torino, one finds that that her Segre forbears had moved to Torino from Savigliano sometime toward the end of the 1700s, probably during the period when Napoleon had cancelled the ghetto restrictions.   From there one can trace the family back generation by generation to Bellavigna, with only a single generational gap.

The Segre Ancestors of Elvira Montalcini

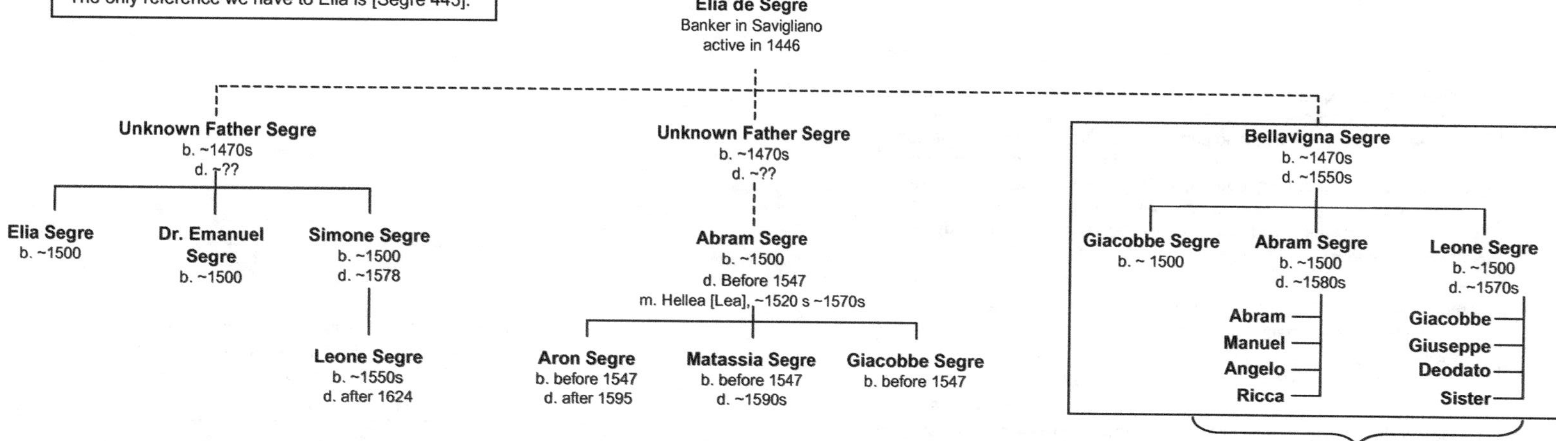

In 1535, The Duchess of Savoy, who was also Countess of Asti sought to have Elia and the other Hebrews in Asti expelled. She was a royal princess of Portugal [Segre 807]. They successfully petitioned for a delay in the expulsion order, which then lapsed with her death in 1538.

Elia, his brothers and nephews received a charter in 1539 from Emanuele Filiberto as heir to the Duchess Beatrice for the county of Asti [Segre xlvi, and documents 809-810]. Under this charter they continued their banking business in that town [Segre 811].

In 1547, the brothers obtained a French banking charter for Pinerolo, which was reconfirmed by Emanuele Filiberto in 1564 [Segre 982].

In 1549, Elia and his brothers obtained a banking charter for Chieri [Segre 845].

Simone took the lead with the Chieri bank from 1549 into the 1570s [Segre, 850, 874, 878, 882, 893, 896, 897, 900, 913, 982].

In 1579, Simone's son Leone sued to recover funds his father had lent to the town of Chieri in earlier years; he won the suit in 1587 [Segre 1286, 1405]. Leone continued the bank in Chieri at least to 1624 [Segre 1645, 1657, 1669, 1670, 1673, 1677, 1697, 2040]. This bank was still owned by Leone's heirs in 1699. [Segre 2487].

The brothers Aron, Matassia, and Giacobbe Segre were the sons of the late Abram Segre and his widow Hellea. The elder Abram was a banker in Pinerolo, Racconigi and other towns. He died in the 1540s, and his widow continued the bank into the 1550s-60s and wound up competing against her older sons [Segre 903, 1020]. Aron and Matassia were bankers from the1560s to 1580s [Segre, 1015, 1020, 1047, 1049, 1051]. In 1589, Matassia is listed as impoverished with a household of 10 [Segre 1398].

One can only speculate the exact relationships among these four Segre families. The following facts however suggest close ties:

- Abram son of Abram of the Bellavigna line is listed as banker in Chieri along with his cousins Aron and Abram.
- The oldest Elia probably had to leave Piemonte in the late 1470s. The three later branches arrived in Piemonte at about the same time, roughly 50-70 years later.
- All three later branches had banks at the same time in Pinerolo.
- The Elia/Emanuel/Simone and Bellavigna branches had banks in Chieri
- The descendents of Leone son of Bellavigna had banks in Savigliano, just like the original Elia
- The given names Elia, Leone, and Emanuele (Manuel), Abram, Giacobbe and Aron repeat through the generations among these families

The Segre Ancestors of Elvira Montalcini

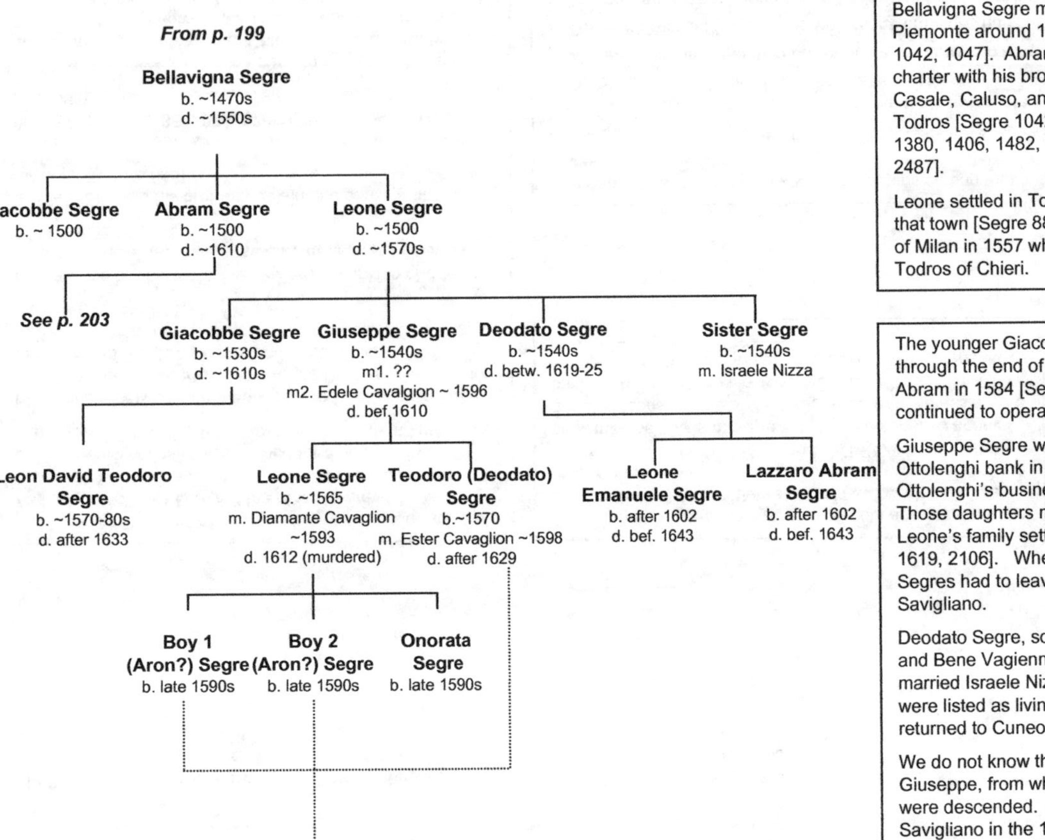

Bellavigna Segre moved his bank from Lodi in the duchy of Milan to Piemonte around 1548. The elder Giacobbe settled in Pinerolo [Segre 1042, 1047]. Abram settled first in Pinerolo, where he had a banking charter with his brother from at least 1556-7 and then opened banks in Casale, Caluso, and Chieri, where he married a daughter of Moisé Todros [Segre 1042, 1047, 1294, 1295, 1333, 1258, 1357, 1359, 1370, 1380, 1406, 1482, 1600, 1616, 1619, 1645, 1648, 1654,1731, 2040, 2487].

Leone settled in Torino in 1548 where he received a bank charter for that town [Segre 881]. He was arrested by the Spaniards in the Duchy of Milan in 1557 when he was traveling back to Lodi with Benedetto Todros of Chieri.

The younger Giacobbe operated banks in Casale and Chieri at least through the end of the 1500s. The Chieri bank was leased to his uncle Abram in 1584 [Segre 1268, 1295, 1357, 1619]. Abram's heirs continued to operate this bank until at least 1699 [Segre 2487].

Giuseppe Segre was a banker in Asti. He assumed control of the Ottolenghi bank in Saluzzo as guardian of two of the four daughters of Ottolenghi's business partner and brother-in-law, Isach de Cavaglione. Those daughters married Giuseppe Segre's sons, Leone and Teodoro; Leone's family settled in Savigliano and Teodoro's in Pinerolo [Segre 1619, 2106]. When Pinerolo came under French control, the Pinerolo Segres had to leave and probably settled in Carmagnola, Saluzzo or Savigliano.

Deodato Segre, son of Leone, was a banker and goldsmith in Cuneo and Bene Vagienne in the 1610s [Segre 1862, 1903, 1926]. His sister married Israele Nizza, Deodato's banking partner. Deodato's children were listed as living in Pinerolo in 1629 [Segre 2106], but subsequently returned to Cuneo.

We do not know the names of the sons of Leone or Teodoro, sons of Giuseppe, from whom we believe most if not all of the Savigliano Segre were descended. However, there was banker Aron Segre active in Savigliano in the 1620-30s. Given the frequent repetition of the names Isacco and Israele among the generations of the Savigliano Segres, one can speculate that Aron's brothers and/or cousins might have been named Isacco after their grandfather Isach de Cavaglion, or Israele, after their great uncle, the prominent banker Israele Nizza. See page 201.

The Segre Ancestors of Elvira Montalcini

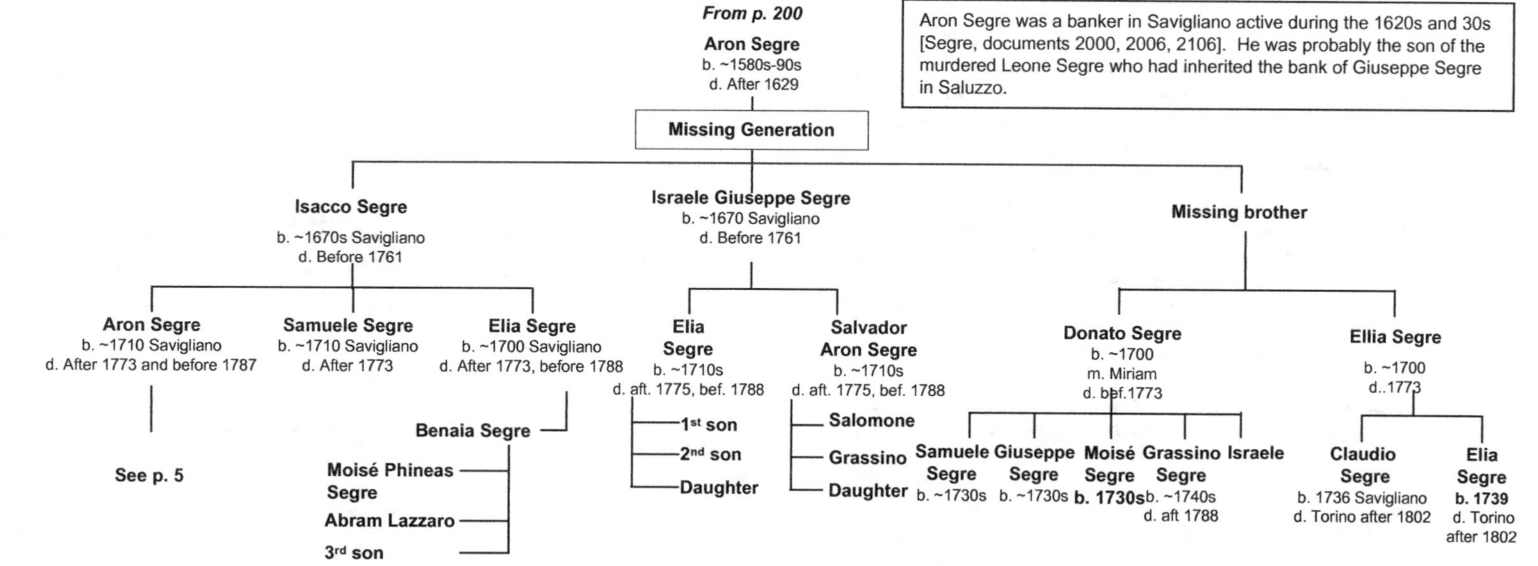

The Segre Ancestors of Elvira Montalcini

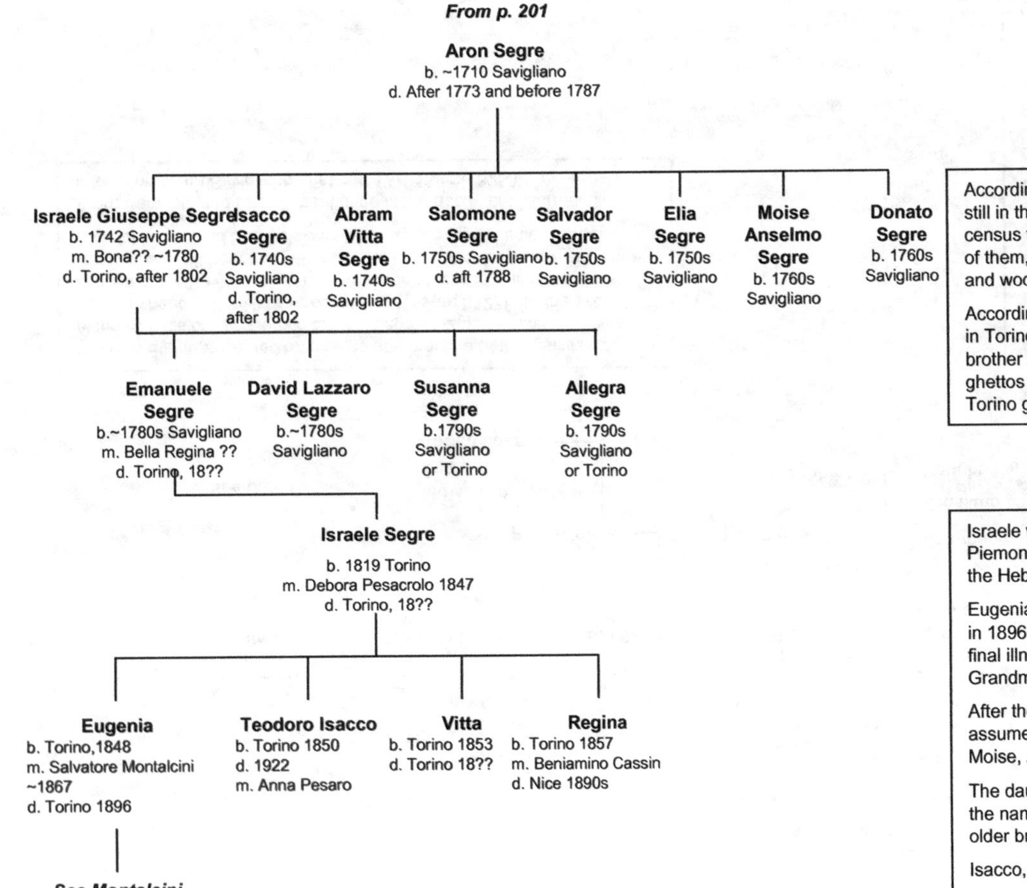

According to the 1788 census of Savigliano, all of this generation were still in that town. Isacco is listed as having a household of 10 in that census that included all brothers except Abram, and the wives of three of them, living in a total of two rooms; they were merchants in cotton and woolen cloth and silverware. [Segre 3376, 3404].

According the 1802 census of Torino, Israele was a wholesale merchant in Torino living with his brother, wife, and four children . He and his brother Isacco moved to Torino in the late 1700s, probably when the ghettos were opened during the Napoleonic period [1802 census of Torino ghetto].

Israele was a wholesale dealer in woolen cloth. He and his family spoke Piemontese as their primary language [source: 1858 partial census of the Hebrew community of Torino].

Eugenia was of frail constitution. She became ill in the 1890s and died in 1896, leaving five children in their teens and early 20s. During her final illness, her sister-in-law, Anna Segre nee Pesaro [Magna Anna, Grandmother Anna in Piemontese dialect] assumed the maternal role.

After the death of Salvatore Montalcini in 1901, Teodoro and Anna assumed guardianship for his as yet unmarried children, Emanuele, Moise, Alessandro, and Aldelina and Elvira.

The daughters Adelina and Elvira married Adamo Levi [who then took the name Levi-Montalcini] and Alberto Sacerdote, respectively. Their older brothers never married.

Isacco, Vitta, and Regina all died without issue.

The Segre Ancestors of Elvira Montalcini

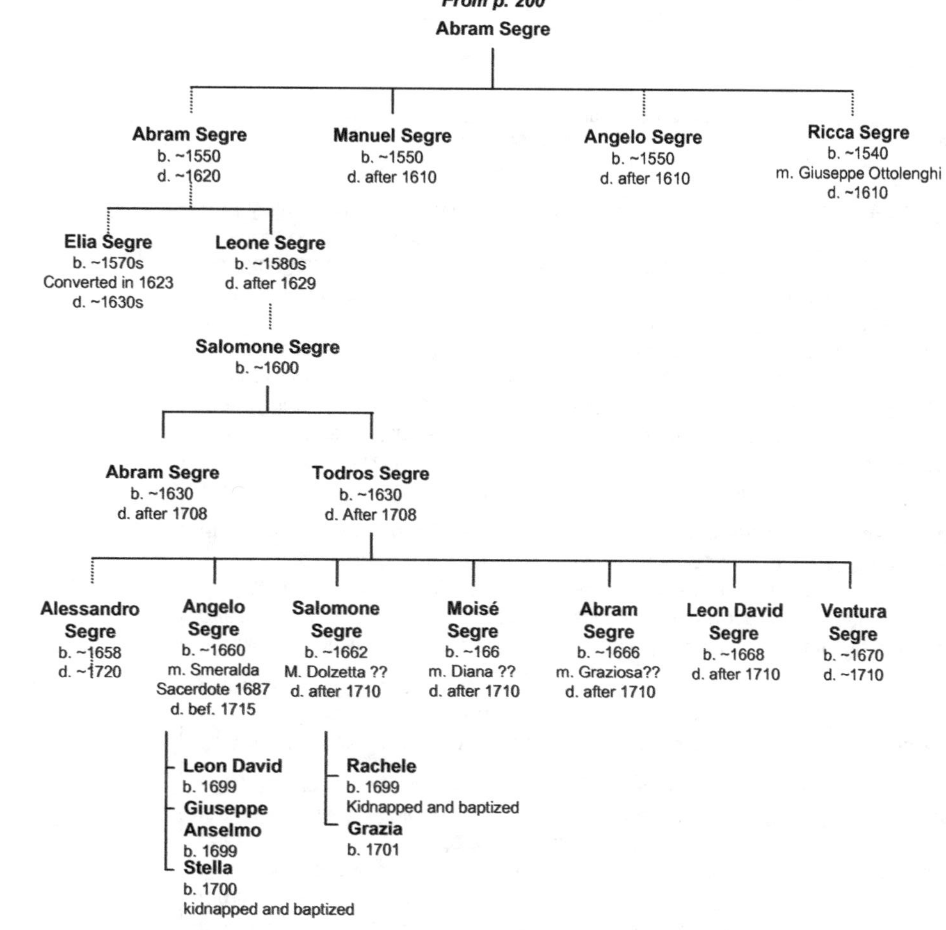

Abram, Manuel, and Angelo were bankers in Bene Vagienna and Dogliani active during the period from the mid 1570s to the mid 1630s [Segre 1167, 1361, 1472, 1484, 1639, 1645, 1676, 1860]. Abram was listed as resident in Chieri in 1596 along with his cousins Aron and Abram [Segre 1645]. Presumably Aron was the Aron, son of Abram and Ellea, and the cousin Abram was Aron's son.

Ricca figured in the lawsuit over the settlement of the estates of her late husband and his business partner Isacco Cavaglion in 1595 [Segre 1619].

Leone was a banker in Torino who also maintained a residence in Chieri; was most active during the period 1605-1630 [Segre 1839, 1912, 2037, 2040, 2046, 2049, 2106].

Elia's conversion is documented in [Segre 2022].

Abram moved from Chieri to Casale in 1662 [Segre 2310]. He and Todros bought the third Chieri bank from the heirs of Giuseppe Concio in 1672 [Segre 2487]. In 1708 he swore loyalty to the crown [Segre 2531].

Todros Segre became a silk manufacturer in the town of Racconigi. In 1678 he already had a large family [Segre 2370]. In 1702 four of his sons were married, and he had 5 grandchildren [Segre 2497]. In 1691 he produced 3500 florins worth of silk. On 1708, he was operating 4 silk factories employing 80 workers, producing 6000 pounds of silk [Segre 2526].

In 1687, Angelo Segre abducted Smeralda Sacerdote on her way to her wedding with Jona Todros [Segre 2425] and later married her. She subsequently became a property owner in Racconigi in 1715 [Segre 2594].

Their daughter and niece, Stella and Rachele, were kidnapped and baptized in 1708 despite the laws prohibiting the baptism of Hebrew children without the consent of their parents. Nonetheless, the Church would not return the children to their parents. The King subsequently demanded that the bishops issue a ruling that any such further incidents would lead to excommunications of the perpetrators [Segre 2516].

At the onset of the ghetto period the Hebrews of Racconigi were forced to move to a town with a ghetto. After much debate among the towns, all of which protested that their ghettos were already too crowded, Smeralda and her sons ended up in Carmagnola [Segre 2765, 2784, 2876, 2877, 2879, 2880].

Luciana's Levi Family from Nizza Monferrato

In tracing Luciana's ancestry back to their arrival in to Piemonte, we have had deal with the significant number of Levi families all of whom arrived in Piemonte in the 1500s. They all originated in a group of small towns in the Duchy of Milan: Pavia, Fiorenzuola, Lodi, and nearby towns and villages. We believe at least some of these families to have been closely related as they seemed to form business partnerships in the 1500s and 1600; such partnerships tended to form among families related by blood or marriage. At least some of these families were Ashkenazim, as a request by one of them in the early 1600s to establish a German-rite synagogue was turned down by the pope. [1]

A family tree assembled by Luciana's cousin, Giovanna Dompé begins with one Israele Levi from Nizza Monferrato, whom she describes as born around 1800, and of Ashkenazi Hungarian descent. His two surviving sons were named Leone and Samuele, and Leone's first two sons were named Israele and Abram.

Nizza Monferrato was and is a small, out of the way town. It its height the Hebrew ghetto could not have had a population over 100. In the 1700s, the ghetto was also quite poor, with only three or four families having material wealth. It seems unlikely that a wandering Hungarian would have found his way to a small, out-of-the-way, mostly poor community, married and settled down to raise a family. Instead it is much more likely that Israele's family had lived in Nizza M. for some time, and was descended from an Ashkenazi family, perhaps from Hungary, that had settled Piemonte much earlier.

We then began a process of working back from Levi families that lived in Nizza M. and the nearby, more important spa town of Acqui Terme [2] in the late 1700s and forward from Levi families that settled in Piemonte in the 1500s to reduce Luciana's possible ancestral lines to two. The first is a family is descended from an Aron Levi, born in Lodi, who settled in Asti in the late 1500s. We traced his descendents to Alessandria in the late 1600s, Nizza M. in the mid 1700s., and finally to a pair of brothers in Acqui, Abram Israele and Samuele Levi, one of whom may have been the father of the Israele Levi with whom Dompé begins her family tree. The second possible ancestral line leading to Dompé's Israele Levi begins with a banker Simon Levitis from Pavia. His son Giuseppe settled in Vercelli in the late 1500s. Giuseppe's cousins, sons and grandsons then built a network of banks serving the small towns in the foothills of the Alps between Vercelli and Biella. In the mid 1600s, Giuseppe's son Salomone and grandson Isacco decamped to the Monferrato, at the time foreign territory, probably to avoid onerous Piemontese taxes. From there we can easily trace the family to another pair of brothers, Abram Israele and Salvador Leone Levi in Nizza M. one of whom may be the father of Dompé's Israele Levi.

---

[1] In 1601, Giuseppe Levi's cousin Aron Levi sought to convert the Vercelli Synagogue to the German rite. Later that year the community asked to build a second synagogue to accommodate the German and Italian rites. The pope refused permission to build a second synagogue in the town [Segre, documents 1721, 1726].

[2] During the 1700s there seemed to be a lot of movement back and forth between the neighboring Hebrew communities in Nizza Monferrato and Acqui Terme

Luciana's Levi Family from Nizza Monferrato

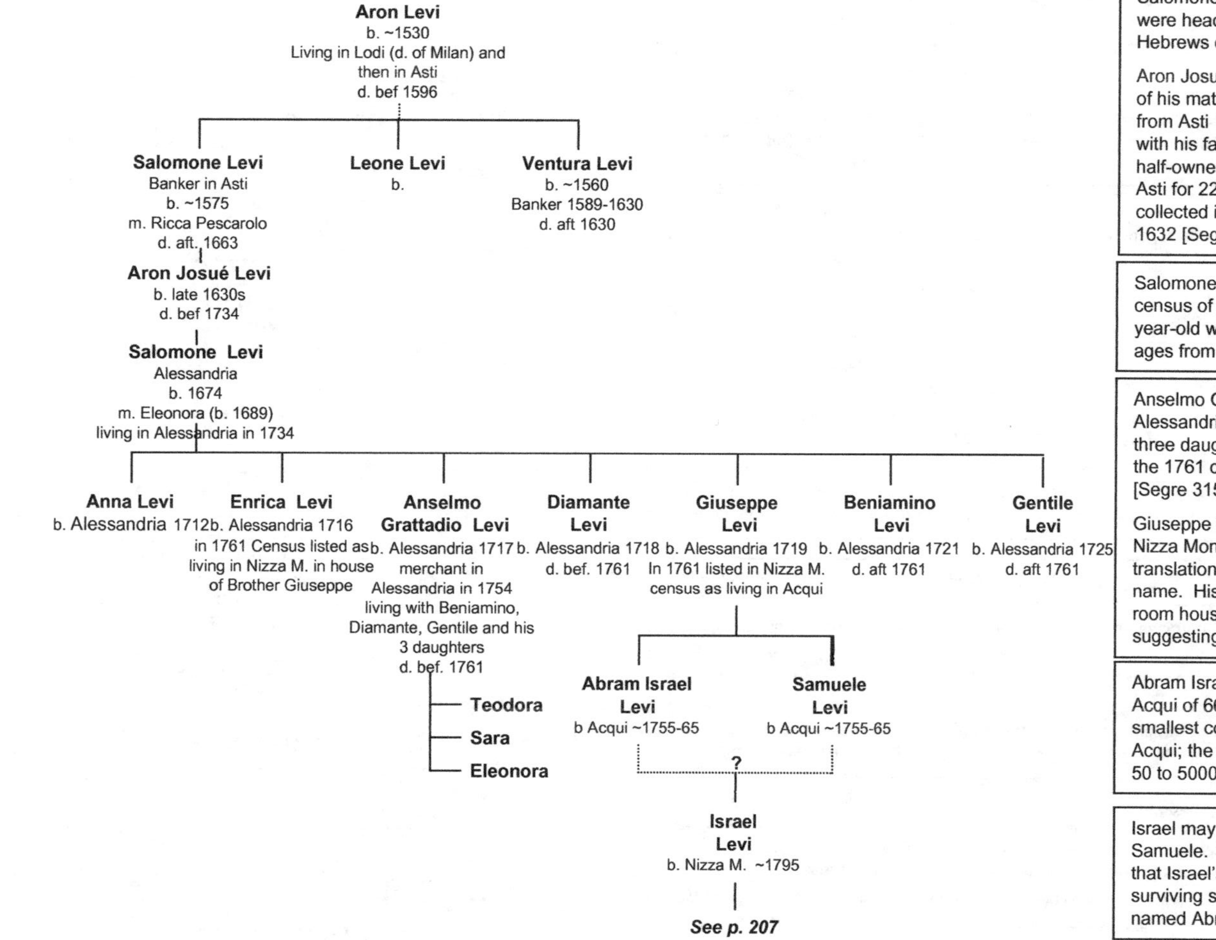

Salomone, Leone, and Ventura Levi, sons of Aron of Lodi, were heads of households in Asti the 1596 Census of the Hebrews of Piemonte [Segre 1645].

Aron Josué Levi, son of Salomone, was the heir in 1648 of his maternal grandfather, the banker Abram Pescarolo from Asti [Segre 2223]. In 1658, Aron Josué, still a minor with his father acting on his behalf, bought out the other half-owner of one of Pescarolo's credits from the town of Asti for 225 lire [Segre 2289]. These credits were finally collected in 1663 [Segre 2312], and they dated back before 1632 [Segre 2126].

Salomone Levi, son of Aron Josué was listed in the 1734 census of Alessandria as being 60 years old with his 45-year-old wife Eleanora and their seven children ranging in ages from 9 to 22 [Segre 2841].

Anselmo Grattiadio Levi listed in the 1754 census of Alessandria as a dealer in used clothing, living with his three daughters, brother and two sisters [Segre 3082]. By the 1761 census, Beniamino was head of this household [Segre 3155].

Giuseppe Salvador Levi was listed in the 1761 census of Nizza Monferrato as living in Acqui. Salvador is the translation into Italian of Josué, his grandfather's middle name. His maiden sister Ricca (Enrica) was living in his 5-room house in Nizza M. Both were listed as 40 years old, suggesting the ages were approximate [Segre 3147].

Abram Israel and Samuele, sons of Giuseppe, paid taxes in Acqui of 66 and 50 lire respectively in 1798, by far the smallest contributions of the Hebrew householders of Acqui; the average contribution was 895 lire in a range of 50 to 5000 lire [Segre 3466].

Israel may have been the son of either Abram Israel or Samuele. We know from the Dompé genealogy of the Levi that Israel's first son was named Leone and his second surviving son, Samuele. Leone's first two sons were named Abram and Israel.

Luciana's Levi Family from Nizza Monferrato

Simon Levitis of Pavia
b. ~1520s-30s?
had credits in Chivasso 1563

Giuseppe Levi
b. Pavia ~1560
Est. Bank in Vercelli in 1599

**Salomone Levi
[Gattinara]**
b. ~1600
At some point lived in Gattinara
d. aft. 1670

Moisé Levi
b. Vercelli ~1600

**Isacco Levi
[Gattinara]**
b. Vercelli ~1630
moved to Casale M w/ his father
1666, still active in 1690s,
ultimately lived in Acqui

**Giuseppe
Levi**
b. ~1655-1665
d. bef 1734

**Salom
Levi**
b. Nizza M. ~1690-1695
m. ? Ottolenghi (b. ~1730)
Living in Acqui in 1756
probably as a result of
marriage around 1750
d. aft. 1761, bef. 1775

**Abram Israel
Levi**
b. Nizza M. betw. 1750-54

**Salvador Leone
Levi**
b. Nizza M. betw. 1750-54

Daughter
b. betw. 1754-1759

?

**Israel
Levi**
b. Nizza M. ~1795

See p. 207

Simon Levitis, a Banker from Pavia, was extending loans to towns in Piemonte [Segre 1971].

Giuseppe Levi was a banker from Pavia in the Duchy of Milan. He established a bank in Vercelli in 1599, paying 45 ducatoni for the license and annual fee of 8 ducatoni [Segre 1697].

Salomone Levi became a prominent banker in Vercelli, and expanded the franchise to Gattinara, Biella and other towns of northern Piemonte. In 1648 he, along with his brother Moisé and his cousins Giuseppe Vita and Bonaiut Levi, negotiated an exemption from military service and guard duty for the Hebrew community of Vercelli in exchange for an annual payment of 6 scudi [Segre 2215]. In the same year he purchased a plot for a Hebrew cemetery for 25 scudi [Segre 2225].

In 1662 Salomone Levi along with two others negotiated a settlement with Abram Segre, formerly of Chieri, to get him to pay the taxes he had sought to avoid by moving to the foreign territory of the Monferrato [Segre 2310].

In 1666 Salomone and his son Isacco also left for the Monferrato, leaving behind annual taxes of 1100 lire apiece [Segre 2332].

In 1670 Isacco Levi, operating from Casale, supplied 1100 *sacchi* of wheat to Torino at 67.5 *soldi* per *sacco*.

In 1677 Salom Levi, now living in Acqui in Monferrese territory, purchased a bank in Torino, which was subsequently sold by heirs (Isacco and/or Giuseppe) in 1693 [Segre 2487].

Of Giuseppe Levi, we know nothing. He was presumably a son of Isacco Levi, named for his great-grandfather. His son Salomone was presumably named for his great-grandfather as well.

In 1734, Salom Levi, son of Giuseppe, claimed he was too poor to pay the salt tax in Nizza M. [Segre 2849].

In 1740, he owned a house that was deemed sufficiently large for use as a municipal charity hospice. Presumably this house was outside the ghetto [Segre, 2934].

In each of 1744, 1745, 1747, 1749 Salomone Levi of Nizza M. paid taxes varying from year to year in the range of 39-44 lire [Segre 2973, 2991, 3009, 3046].

Salomone Levi of Nizza M. paid taxes of 39 lire for 1749, and 23 lire for 1753 and 1755. These taxes were paid in Acqui along with those of his brother-in-law, Giuseppe Salvador Ottolenghi [Segre 3105.]

In 1756 Salom Levi testified in Acqui that he and others had been improperly denied licenses to raise silkworms [Segre 3108].

In 1761, Salom Levi, son of Giuseppe is listed in the census for Acqui along with his wife, two sons and daughter [Segre 3144].

Abram Israel and Salvador Leone Levi of Nizza M., sons of Salom and minors in 1775, brought suit against the Debenedetti brothers. The Levi brothers were represented by their guardian and uncle, Giuseppe Salvador Ottolenghi of Acqui. The Debenedetti had sought to remodel the building where both families lived, depriving the Levis of use of a common staircase. [Segre 3277]. Ottolenghi was the second largest taxpayer of the Acqui ghetto in 1798 at 3165 lire [Segre 3466].

Israel may have been the son of either Abram Israel or Salvador Leone. We know from the Dompé genealogy of the Levi that Israel's first son was named Leone, and Leone's first two sons were named Abram and Israel.

Luciana's Levi Family from Nizza Monferrato

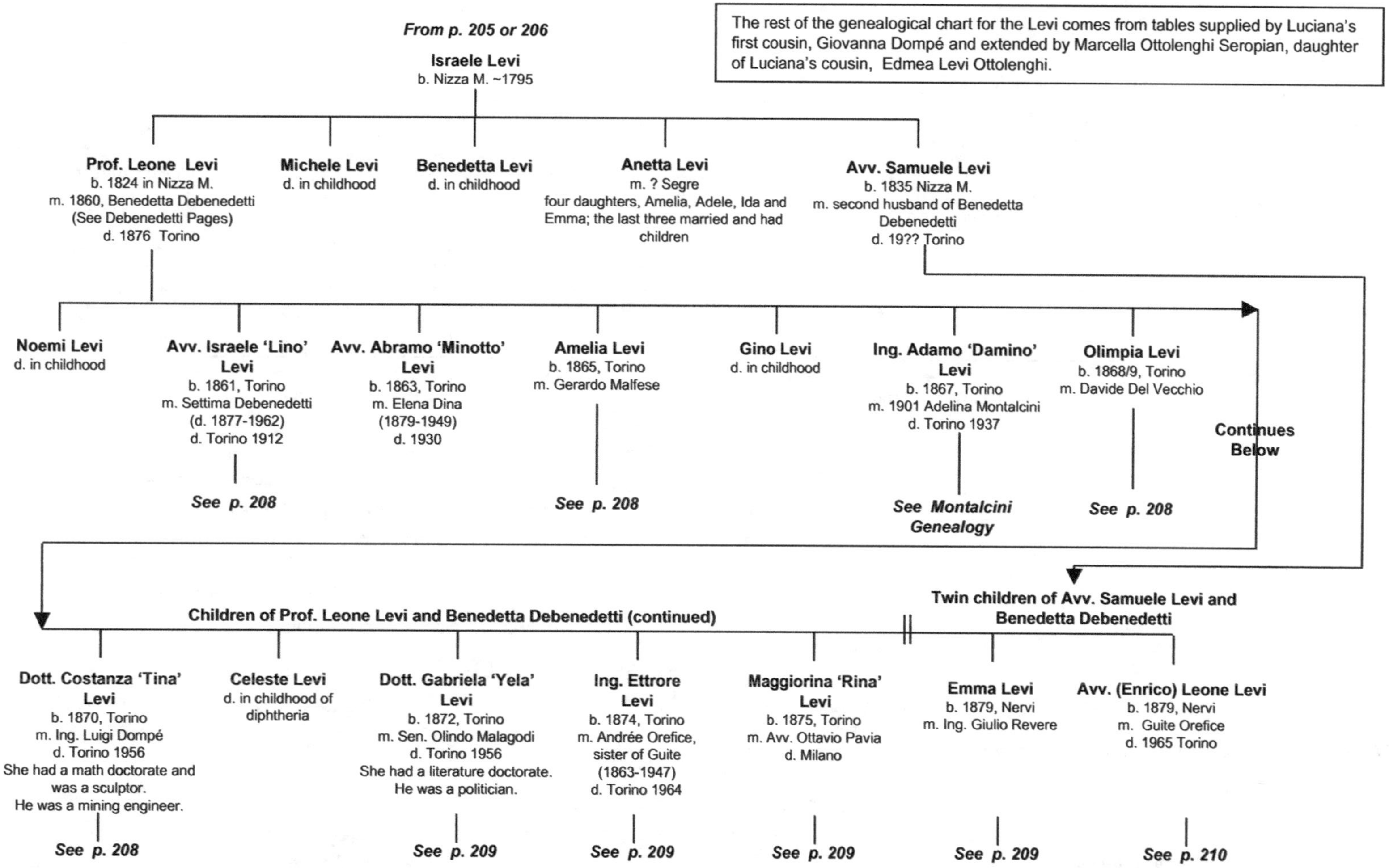

From p. 205 or 206

Israele Levi
b. Nizza M. ~1795

The rest of the genealogical chart for the Levi comes from tables supplied by Luciana's first cousin, Giovanna Dompé and extended by Marcella Ottolenghi Seropian, daughter of Luciana's cousin, Edmea Levi Ottolenghi.

Prof. Leone Levi
b. 1824 in Nizza M.
m. 1860, Benedetta Debenedetti
(See Debenedetti Pages)
d. 1876 Torino

Michele Levi
d. in childhood

Benedetta Levi
d. in childhood

Anetta Levi
m. ? Segre
four daughters, Amelia, Adele, Ida and Emma; the last three married and had children

Avv. Samuele Levi
b. 1835 Nizza M.
m. second husband of Benedetta Debenedetti
d. 19?? Torino

Noemi Levi
d. in childhood

Avv. Israele 'Lino' Levi
b. 1861, Torino
m. Settima Debenedetti
(d. 1877-1962)
d. Torino 1912

See p. 208

Avv. Abramo 'Minotto' Levi
b. 1863, Torino
m. Elena Dina
(1879-1949)
d. 1930

Amelia Levi
b. 1865, Torino
m. Gerardo Malfese

See p. 208

Gino Levi
d. in childhood

Ing. Adamo 'Damino' Levi
b. 1867, Torino
m. 1901 Adelina Montalcini
d. Torino 1937

See Montalcini Genealogy

Olimpia Levi
b. 1868/9, Torino
m. Davide Del Vecchio

See p. 208

Continues Below

Children of Prof. Leone Levi and Benedetta Debenedetti (continued)

Twin children of Avv. Samuele Levi and Benedetta Debenedetti

Dott. Costanza 'Tina' Levi
b. 1870, Torino
m. Ing. Luigi Dompé
d. Torino 1956
She had a math doctorate and was a sculptor.
He was a mining engineer.

See p. 208

Celeste Levi
d. in childhood of diphtheria

Dott. Gabriela 'Yela' Levi
b. 1872, Torino
m. Sen. Olindo Malagodi
d. Torino 1956
She had a literature doctorate.
He was a politician.

See p. 209

Ing. Ettrore Levi
b. 1874, Torino
m. Andrée Orefice, sister of Guite
(1863-1947)
d. Torino 1964

See p. 209

Maggiorina 'Rina' Levi
b. 1875, Torino
m. Avv. Ottavio Pavia
d. Milano

See p. 209

Emma Levi
b. 1879, Nervi
m. Ing. Giulio Revere

See p. 209

Avv. (Enrico) Leone Levi
b. 1879, Nervi
m. Guite Orefice
d. 1965 Torino

See p. 210

The Levi Family (Continued from Page 207)

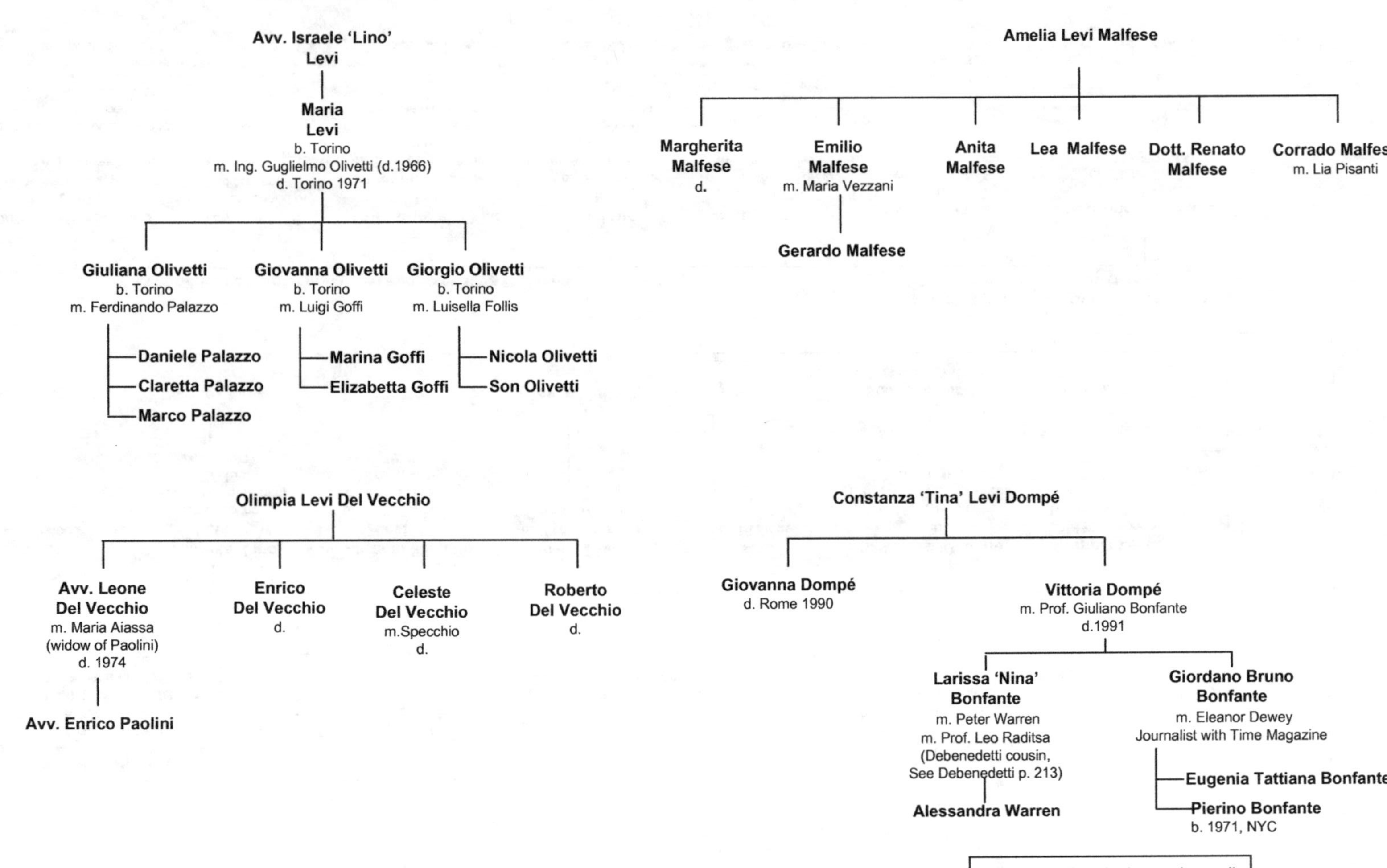

The Levi Family (Continued from Page 207)

(Continued from Page 207)

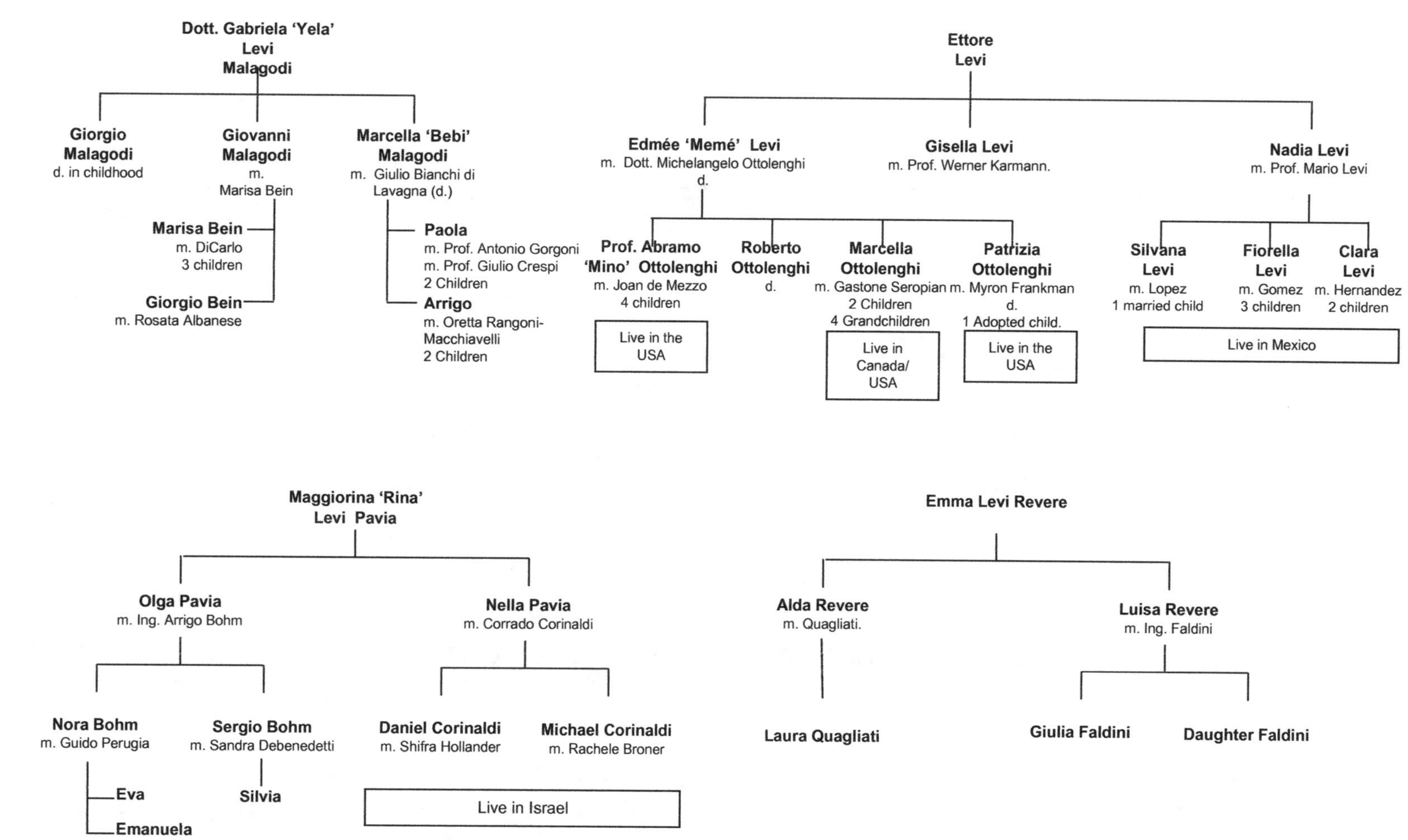

The Levi Family (Continued from Page 207)

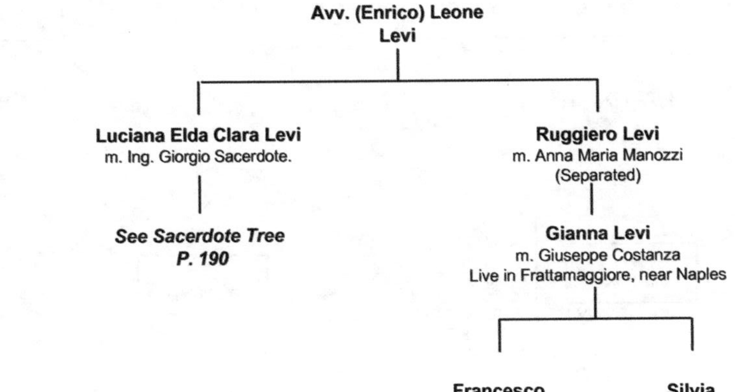

Luciana's Debenedetti Ancestry

The Piemontese Debenedetti all seem to have descended from a Spanish banker Benedictis de Benedictis who settled in Cherasco in the mid 1500s. His sons and grandsons built up their banking business until it spanned half a dozen or more towns by the mid-1600s, including Nizza Monferrato.

Dompé's genealogy of the Levi family's Debenedetti ancestors begins with a certain Sabato Debenedetti who was resident of Alessandria in the early 1800s. In a census of that town's Hebrew Ghetto in the late 1700s, there were only two families of that surname, headed by two brothers, Moisé and Giacobbe Salvador, who had moved there earlier in the eighteenth century from Nizza Monferrato. Since only Moisé had sons, we assume Sabato was the grandson of on of those sons, Tobia or Giuseppe Vita.

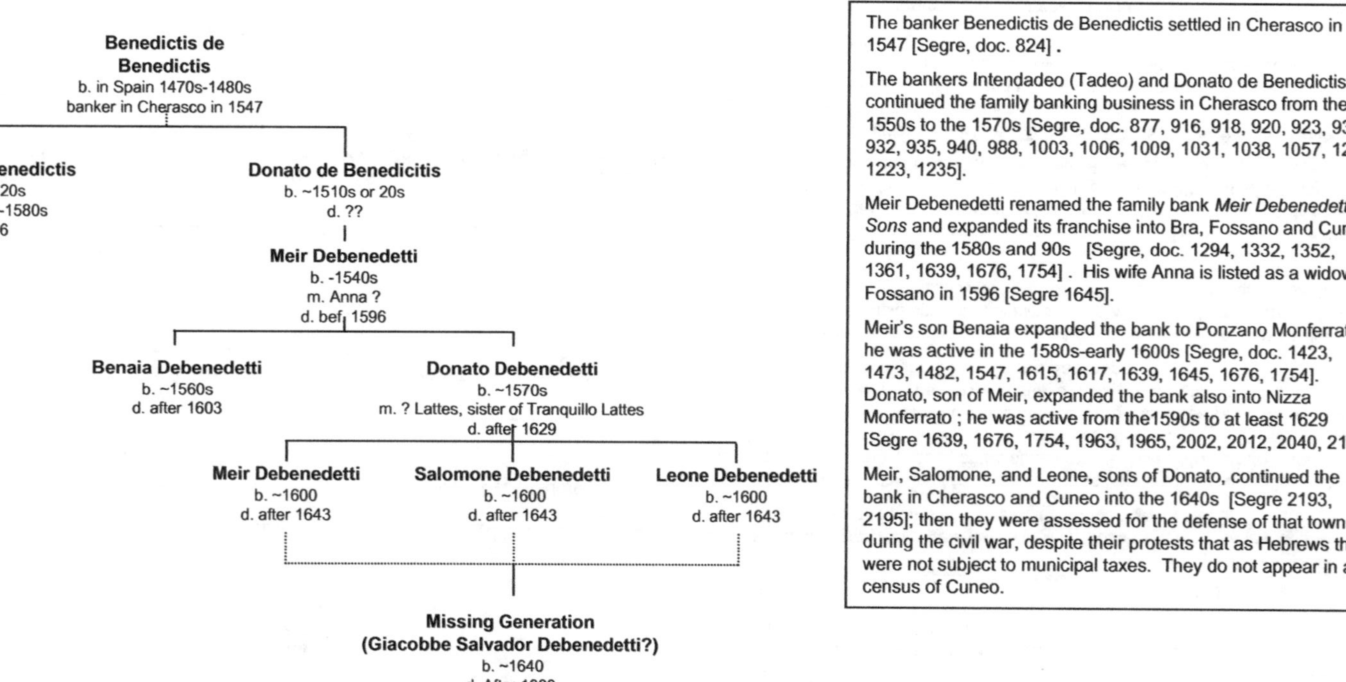

See p. 212

Luciana's Debenedetti Ancestry

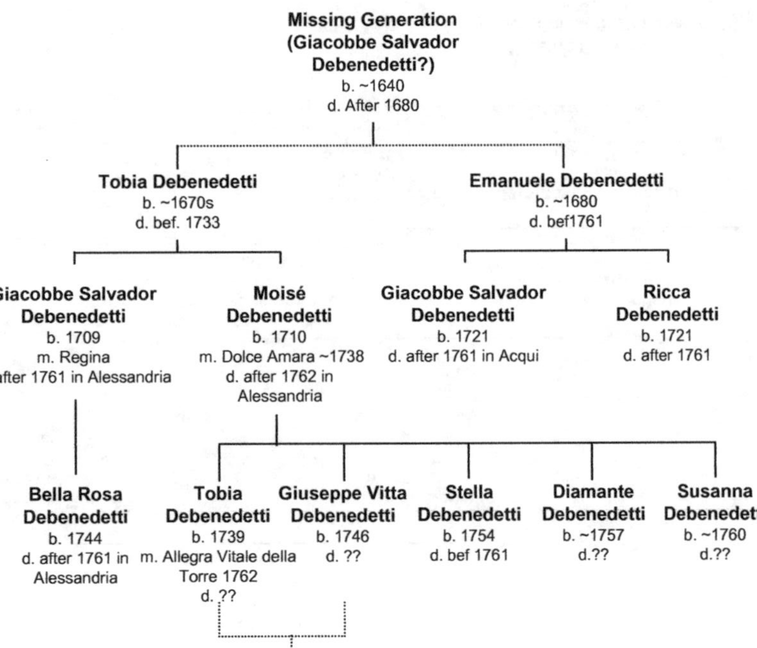

We inferred the name Giacobbe Salvador from the fact that two grandsons of that generation bore that name.

Emanuele was a banker in Nizza Monferrato in 1740s [Segre 2952]. His daughter Ricca was unmarried as of 1761.

About the elder Tobia we know virtually nil, other than that he loaned the town of Nizza Monferrato some 9500 lire in the 1690s [Segre, 2826].

Giacobbe Salvador and Moisé continued as bankers into the 1730s. Giacobbe was also the sublicensee of the state lottery in Nizza Monferrato in the 1740s [Segre 2826, 2964, 3147]. He obtained this sublicense from Moisé Davide Pavia, who had purchased the right to operate it for three years from the King for 114,200 lire. Giacobbe Salvador subsequently moved to Alessandria and was the personal assistant to Pavia's son Salomone.

Moise moved to Alessandria in 1735, where he was a prosperous banker. In 1754 his household consisted of himself, his wife, their four children, his wife's 70-year old uncle Sanson Amar, and two live-in servants [Segre 3082, 3155, 3162].

In 1754-61, Giacobbe Salvador Debenedetti, son of Tobia, was the personal secretary to the well-to-do merchant Salomone Pavia. He appeared in censuses of Nizza Monferrato and Alessandria in 1761 [Segre 3082, 3147, 3155]. He married Regina and had a daughter Bella Rosa [Segre, 3147].

Tobia married Allegra Vitale della Torre in 1762. She was the daughter of Israel Vitale della Torre and his wife Benedetta, the wealthiest Hebrew merchant in Alessandria. In 1761, Israel and Benedetta had a household of 26 including 4 daughters, 5 sons, 2 daughters-in law, 5 grandchildren, and 9 live-in servants [Segre, 2082, 3155].

In 1734, Allegra's grandfather, Raffaele Lazzaro Vitale della Torre paid 5000 lire, nearly 1/3 of the entire forced loan that the King levied on the city of Alessandria to help pay for the War of Polish Succession [Segre, 2842, 2844, 2856, 2957, 2985, 3025].

Shortly after Tobia and Allegra were married, they sued his father to gain control of her substantial dowry [Segre, 3162].

I believe that Sabato Debenedetti was descended from Tobia and Allegra, rather than Giuseppe Vita because he named his first daughter, Luciana's grandmother, Benedetta, the name of Tobia's mother-in-law.

Luciana's Debenedetti Ancestry

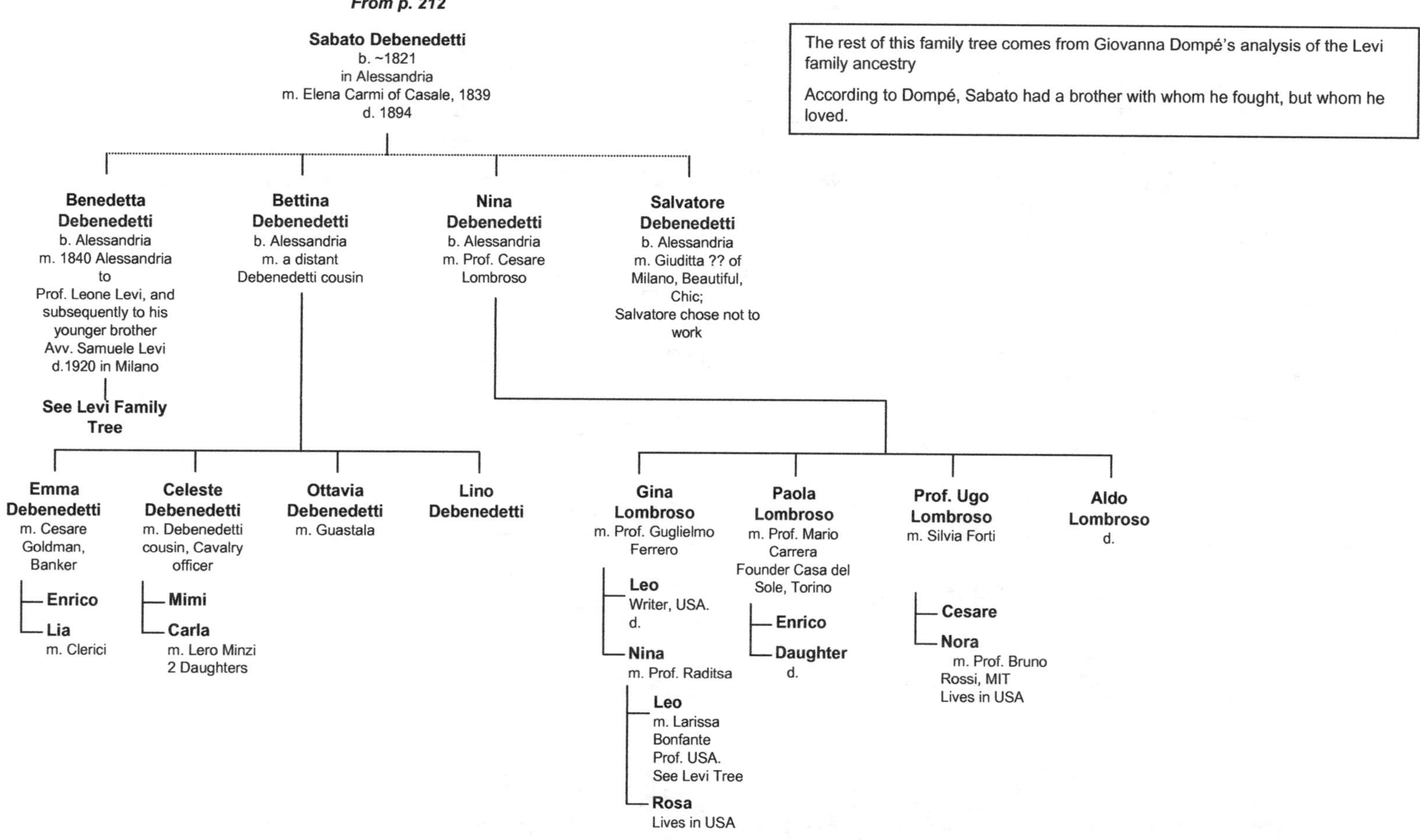

Appendix F
The Dukes of Savoy since 1343

	Born	Died	Reigned From	To	Notes
Amedeo VI, il Conte Verde	1334	1383	1343	1383	Count of Savoy
Amedeo VII, il Conte Rosso	1360	1391	1383	1391	Count of Savoy, probably assassinated
Amedeo VIII, il Pacifico	1383	1451	1391	1434	Dowager Duchess, widow of Amedeo VI as regent initially during a civil war from 1391–1395 with partisans of widow of Amedeo VII; first Duke of Savoy in 1416; Avignonese anti-Pope Felix V from 1434–1449
Ludovico	1415	1465	1434	1465	
Amedeo IX, il Beato	1435	1472	1465	1472	
Filiberto I, il Cacciatore	1465	1482	1472	1482	Dowager Duchess ruled as regent 1472–74
Carlo I, il Guerriero	1468	1490	1482	1490	French King Louis XI ruled as regent 1482–3
Carlo II	1489	1496	1490	1496	Minor, never actually ruled
Filippo II, Senza Terra	1443	1497	1496	1497	
Filiberto II, il Bello	1480	1504	1497	1504	
Carlo III, il Buono	1486	1553	1504	1553	French rule: 1536–59
Emanuele Filiberto, Testa di Ferro	1528	1580	1553	1580	
Carlo Emanule I	1562	1630	1580	1630	
Vittorio Amedeo I	1587	1637	1630	1637	
Francesco Giacinto	1632	1638	1637	1638	Minor; never actually ruled; dowager duchess as regent
Carlo Emanuele II	1634	1675	1638	1675	Dowager Duchess ruled as regent 1638–1648
Vittorio Amedeo II	1666	1732	1675	1730	Dowager Duchess ruled as regent 1675–1680; king of Sicily 1713–20; King of Sardina thereafter; abdicated 1630
Carlo Emanuele III	1701	1773	1730	1773	
Vittorio Amedeo III	1726	1796	1773	1796	
Carlo Emanuele IV	1751	1819	1796	1802	Abdicated 1802
Vittorio Emanuele I	1759	1824	1802	1821	Abdicated 1821
Carlo Felice	1765	1831	1821	1831	
Carlo Alberto	1798	1849	1831	1849	First King of the Savoia-Carignano Line; abdicated 1849
Vittorio Emanuel II	1820	1878	1849	1878	
Umberto I King of Italy	1844	1900	1878	1900	Assassinated
Vittorio Emanuel III	1869	1947	1900	1946	Abdicated 1946
Umberto II	1904	1983	1946	1946	Reigned one month; abdicated 1946

Appendix G
The Value of Piemontese and Italian Currency

In 1562, Emanuele Filiberto decreed a currency reform, setting the units of currency as the **lira**, divided into 20 **soldi**, with each soldo divided into 12 **denari**. In addition he created the **scudo d'oro** worth 3 lire. The value of the lira and scudo varied against the value of gold over time. This LSD monetary structure dated back at least to the days of Charlemagne, and survived in the UK until the 1970s when the pound was decimalized. In Italy the lira continued as a unit of currency until the advent of the euro. The soldo was still in use until after World War II, when the extreme depreciation of the lira made it pointless to continue to subdivide it.

In the 1500s and into the 1600s a Florentine currency, the **fiorino**, also circulated. The fiorino was divided into 12 grossi. Another common currency of the time was the Venetian **ducatone** or ducat. To further complicate matters, Spanish doubloons [doppie in Italian] also circulated at this time. The fiorino and the ducat had a fairly constant value in terms of gold over a long period of time: 1 fiorino = 3.5 gm of gold; 1 ducatone = 39 gm of gold. A Troy ounce, the unit in which gold is quoted today weighs 31.1 gm. Using this information, and exchange rates quoted in a number of Segre's documents, we can estimate the value of the Piemontese currency in terms of gold for the period 1570–1775. In short, while the currency fluctuated up and down, it remained in the range of LL1 = 9–17 gms of gold.

With the turbulent times of the French Revolution and the Napoleonic invasion, the lira fell to 1 lira = .36 gm of gold, a value that it more or less held until WW I, including the period from 1861–1915 when the lira, Swiss and French francs, and Spanish peseta were in a currency union with a common value of .26 gm of gold. After WW I, it went through periodic devaluations, until it was worth only .000050 gm of gold by 1995.

Year	Estimated Grams of Gold/Lira	Segre Document Reference	Year	Estimated Grams of Gold/Lira	Segre Document Reference
1570	9.12	1031	1626	14.82	2072
1575	10.26	1193	1629	10.26	2109
1575	10.83	1197	1770	9.05	3218
1575	9.12	1209	1776	9.69	3284
1576	11.40	1226	1793	0.36	3421
1576	11.60	1238	1816	0.32	
1579	12.57	1287	1824	0.32	
1580	9.12	1293	1834	0.32	
1586	12.89	1395	1861–1915	0.26	Currency Union
1586	11.39	1400	1927	0.079	
1590	13.68	1470	1931	0.088	
1591	10.26	1493	1936	0.056	41% devaluation
1591	11.40	1510	1945	0.0089	
1598	11.97	1675	1946	0.0089	
1598	10.26	1677	1947	0.0042	
1599	9.12	1699	1948	0.0025	
1600	11.97	1701	1949	0.0015	
1601	11.93	1711	1950	0.0015	
1603	15.39	1742	1955	0.0015	
1605	14.58	1788	1960	0.0015	
1608	17.68	1608	1965	0.0015	
1613	10.26	1900	1970	0.0013	
1613	9.12	1902	1975	0.00036	
1617	9.12	1958	1980	0.000063	
1620	9.12	2000	1985	0.000052	
1620	11.40	2004	1990	0.000065	
1622	11.40	2017	1995	0.000050	
1626	9.12	2052	2000	0.000056	

Appendix H
The Value of Pre-Metric Piemontese Measures

Before the metric system was created during the French Revolution, Piemonte had a system of metrics as quirky as the English system of miles, yards, feet and inches for length ; tons, pounds, and ounces for weight; bushels, pecks, quarts and pints for dry measures; gallons, quarts, and pints for liquids; and acres, square feet and square inches for areas.

The following table converts these archaic Italian measures into Metric and US units.

Italian Measures			*Metric*	*US*
Length				
trabucco	=	6 poedi	3.08 m	3.38 yd
piede	=	12 oncie	.513 m	1.68 ft
oncia	=	12 punti	4.28 cm	1.69 in
punto			3.56 mm	0.14 in
Area				
giornata	=	100 tavole	.38 ha	.939 ac
tavola	=	4 sq. trabucchi	38.01 sq m	405.8 sq ft
Dry Volume				
carro	=	6 sacchi	690 ltr	19.0 bu
sacco	=	5 emine	115 ltr	3.17 bu
emina	=	8 coppi	23 ltr	1.26 pk
coppo			5.575 ltr	5.22 qt
Weight				
rubbo	=	2.5 libbre	9.22 kg	20.3 lb
libbra	=	12 oncie	368 gm	12.95 oz
oncia	=	24 dinari	30.7 gm	1.08 oz
dinaro			1.28 gm	0.045 oz

Appendix I
1939 British Government Publication Concerning Concentration Camps and other Nazi Atrocities

While living in France in 1939–40, Giorgio and Luciana became well aware of the atrocities taking place in Germany and of what was happening in the death camps at Dachau and Buchenwald. A commission of the British government published a thirty-two page pamphlet in 1939 in multiple languages that included eleven detailed eye-witness accounts. I found a French language copy of this pamphlet in Giorgio's files, and have reproduced several pages of it in this appendix. This pamphlet disproves the common canard that the world was unaware that the Nazis were engaging in gross violations of the most basic human values, including horrific tortures and murder on a massive scale, until the end of World War II.

Note No. 8 is from R. T. Smallbones, the British Consul in Frankfurt. It describes events he witnessed or were experienced by a an educated Jewish businessman who was a personal acquaintance of Smallbones. The witness was one of 500 Jews rounded up in Frankfurt on November 11, 1938. The Jews were arrested, beaten at the local police station, and then transported to the Convention Center, where they were again brutally beaten. They were then trucked in garbage trucks to the railway depot and beaten again, resulting in many serious injuries including broken teeth and eye injuries, and subjected to mock executions. They were then transported by rail to Buchenwald, a camp near the city of Weimar. The camp was under construction, so there was no running water and it lacked latrines. It was surrounded by electrified barbed wire. Prisoners were selected at random for public whippings (fifty strokes of the lash, while tied to a hurdle), resulting in several prisoners going insane and/or dying during the whippings.

poser lui-même à de sévères représailles pour avoir agi selon sa conscience. Plus de 50 o/o des juges placés sous votre autorité sont obligés à faire violence à leur conscience, étant donné que les événements qui se sont produits sont de nature à nous faire honte d'être Allemands. De pareilles idées ne pouvaient jaillir que des cerveaux obtus et criminels d'un Hitler, d'un Hess, d'un Gœbbels, d'un Rosenberg, etc., et ils porteront à l'étranger la conviction qu'elles émanent des mêmes incendiaires, qui naguère ont mis le feu au Reichstag et qui sont responsables des crimes commis le 30 juin 1934. Il vaudrait mieux recommander à tous les juges allemands de prendre leur retraite. L'on ne peut s'attendre à ce que les juges allemands fassent œuvre de bourreaux.

Les événements du 10 courant ont prouvé au monde entier, clairement et sans erreur possible, qu'il n'y a plus de juges en Allemagne.

Vous, Monsieur le Ministre du Reich, Dr. Gurtner, êtes également responsable de ce qui est arrivé, et vous pouvez être certain que peut-être plus tôt que vous ne pensez, nous vous forcerons à venir à rescipicence. Assurez-vous votre propre retraite en donnant à tous les juges consciencieux l'occasion d'accomplir leur mission d'une façon humaine, et en exposant la vraie situation à votre ami Hitler, car le verdict qui sera prononcé par tous les juges honnêtes contre vous et vos bandits d'amis, sera la mort.

Signé : JUDEX.

No. 8

Sir G. Ogilvie-Forbes au Vicomte Halifax

Le Chargé d'Affaires de Sa Majesté à Berlin présente des compliments au Secrétaire d'Etat pour les Affaires Etrangères de Sa Majesté et a l'honneur de lui transmettre copie d'une dépêche du Consul général de Sa Majesté à Francfort-sur-le-Mein, datée du 14 décembre et se référant aux persécutions anti-juives.

Berlin, 15 décembre 1938.

Annexe au No. 8

Le Consul Général Smallbones à Sir G. Ogilvie-Forbes
Francfort-sur-le-Mein, 14 décembre 1938.

Monsieur,

Alors que le Gouvernement allemand a, sans beaucoup de conviction, fait répandre le bruit que l'action contre les juifs, l'incendie des synagogues, la destruction des magasins et des appartements privés, les attaques et le pillage, étaient l'œuvre de la populace rendue furieuse par la mort de Herr vom Rath, il lui sera difficile de nier sa responsabilité du traitement que les S. S. et la police régulière ont largement, et de façon systématique, fait subir aux personnes arrêtées. Je me permets donc de vous faire rapport sur le traitement de quelques-uns de ceux qui ont été arrêtés. J'ai peur que cette dépêche soit d'une lecture déplaisante, mais je considère de mon devoir d' « appeler un chat un chat ». Ceux qui ont été libérés des camps se sont vus menacés des pires conséquences s'ils divulguaient ce qui s'y est passé. Les faits que je rapporte m'ont été racontés, indépendamment les uns des autres, par un grand nombre de gens, et ils n'auraient pas pu inventer en même temps et au sujet d'événements identiques, les mêmes mensonges.

2. J'assure mon service en Allemagne depuis quelque huit ans. J'ai connu les Allemands quand j'étais en fonctions à Munich, à l'heure de

They were forced to sleep three men to a single, unpadded wooden bunk, cramming 500 people into a building designed for perhaps one fourth that number. Those few prisoners whose families could afford to buy them out of the camp [the witness was one of those] were freed only if they showed no scars or other visible signs from their ill treatment. They were forced to sign documents denying any ill treatment, requiring them not to divulge what was going on in the camps, and agreeing to leave Germany immediately upon their release. Upon leaving Germany, they were subject to forfeiture of all of their possessions and allowed to keep only ten marks to cover their future expenses. Smallbones concludes the document with comments about a rumored new roundup expected the following month, plans to build a new concentration camp near Darmstadt, and discussion of efforts led by British Quakers to buy the liberty of the camp prisoners.

leur humiliation après la guerre, et j'occupe mon poste actuel depuis 1932. Je m'étais flatté de comprendre le caractère allemand et j'ai travaillé au mieux de mes moyens pour une entente anglo-allemande. Les événements récents m'ont révélé un aspect du caractère allemand que je n'avais pas soupçonné. Il me semblait qu'il n'y avait point de cruauté dans leur nature. Habituellement, ils sont doux envers les animaux, les enfants, les vieillards et les infirmes. L'explication de cette éruption d'une cruauté sadique réside peut-être dans une perversion sexuelle et, plus particulièrement, l'homosexualité, chose très fréquente en Allemagne. Il me semble qu'une perversion sexuelle des masses pourrait offrir une explication à cette éruption autrement inexplicable. Je suis persuadé que si le Gouvernement de l'Allemagne dépendait du suffrage du peuple, ceux qui occupent le pouvoir et sont responsables de ces excès, seraient balayés par une tempête d'indignation, sinon alignés au mur et fusillés.

3. Ce qui suit est le récit de ce qui est arrivé à un juif, ancien combattant de première ligne, qui avait ici une entreprise prospère et qui est un homme de bonne éducation. Ces déclarations correspondent dans les détails à ce qui nous a été raconté par d'autres personnes qui ont subi la même épreuve. La police secrète l'a appelé au téléphone, le 11 du mois dernier, pour lui donner l'ordre de rester chez lui. On vint le chercher à 3 heures de l'après-midi. Il demanda l'autorisation de prendre du linge de rechange et quelques effets corporels chauds. On le lui refusa, mais on lui recommanda d'emporter quelque argent. Il fut emmené au poste de police le plus proche et y fut maintenu jusqu'à ce qu'un nombre suffisant de gens eussent été réunis pour remplir un camion automobile. Il fut alors emmené au Hall des Expositions, grand bâtiment utilisé pour les foires, et également pour des réunions politiques. A de telles occasions le hall contient bien plus de 20.000 personnes. Aux portes du bâtiment une grande foule s'était rassemblée et déversait injures et invectives au fur et à mesure de l'arrivée des convois. (M. Dowden y est passé deux fois au cours de la journée en question, et a observé que la foule se composait principalement de tout jeunes gens et de femmes. Il avait l'impression que les femmes n'étaient pas de cœur avec ces démonstrations, mais qu'on leur avait donné l'ordre d'y assister, tout comme leurs hommes avaient reçu celui de persécuter les juifs et de porter partout la destruction.) Une fois à l'intérieur du hall, mon informateur fut obligé de vider ses poches; leur contenu, y compris son mouchoir, fut enfermé dans une enveloppe et on lui dit qu'on lui rendrait son bien à sa mise en liberté. On le fit alors s'aligner avec les autres, dont quelques-uns se trouvaient là depuis la nuit précédente, privés de sommeil, de nourriture et d'eau.

4. Alors les S. S. et la police se mirent à s' « occuper » de ceux dont ils avaient la charge. Ils les firent s'agenouiller, croiser leurs mains derrière leur dos et se pencher en avant jusqu'à toucher du front la terre. Ceux qui étaient incapables de cet exploit furent « assistés » par leurs gardiens, qui leur donnaient des coups de pieds dans la nuque. A certains autres on fit faire au pas de gymnastique le tour de l'immeuble. Quelques-uns se mirent à rendre. Les gardiens firent disparaître les vomissures en saisissant les coupables par la peau du cou et en essuyant les déjections avec leur figure et leurs cheveux.

5. Vers 5 heures de l'après-midi, des camions chargés de S. S. arrivèrent et l'on y fit monter les prisonniers à coups de poings et de pieds. On leur fit traverser la ville jusqu'à une gare de banlieue. Après leur débarquement, on les fit descendre quelques marches qui conduisaient

à un couloir sombre, donnant accès au quai. Les gardiens faisaient pleuvoir des coups sur tous ceux qu'ils pouvaient atteindre. Une fois engagés dans le couloir, on les fit s'arrêter, face au mur. Ils pensaient qu'on allait les fusiller ; certains d'entre eux eurent des crises de nerfs. Les gardes passaient et repassaient dans leur dos en continuant à les battre et à leur donner des coups de pied. Quelques hommes en civil prirent part à ce sport. Puis, on les embarqua pour Buchenwald, près de Weimar. Pendant le voyage, qui prit plusieurs heures, les gardes passaient et repassaient, brisant les dents, frappant sur les têtes et meurtrissant les yeux. A Weimar, ils descendirent du train et se virent pousser à coups de pieds et coups de poings dans des camions chargés à refus. Pendant le trajet en camion on leur ordonna de mettre leur tête entre les genoux et, dans cette position, ils reçurent des volées de coups de bâtons.

6. A leur arrivée au camp, ils furent poussés, toujours à coups de poings et à coups de pieds, dans un enclos de fils barbelés. Le réseau était chargé de courant électrique et beaucoup de ceux qui tentèrent de s'échapper subirent de profondes brûlures. Ce détail me parvient d'autres sources. Ensuite, le Commandant du camp leur adressa un discours et leur dit ce qu'il pensait des juifs. Chaque homme eut la tête rasée et la moustache coupée. Le jeu paraissait plus particulièrement drôle avec les rabbins auxquels leurs prescriptions religieuses interdisent de se faire toucher la barbe avec des ciseaux.

Mon informateur qui faisait partie d'un groupe d'environ 500, fut parqué dans le hangar N° 1, celui qui se trouve le plus près de la porte. Les dimensions en étaient d'environ 200 pieds sur 80 et 2.500 personnes furent forcées de s'y entasser. A première vue cela paraît impossible. L'explication est qu'il y avait dans ce hangar, et jusqu'au plafond, des rangées superposées de couchettes, et trois hommes devaient s'étendre dans chacune de ces couchettes. (Un de mes amis a été obligé de dormir pendant seize nuits dans l'une de ces couchettes, entre deux conducteurs de bestiaux. Les trois hommes étaient forcés de demeurer couchés sur le côté, et quand ils désiraient se retourner pour se délasser un peu, le mouvement ne pouvait se faire que simultanément.)

7. Le camp de Buchenwald était à ce moment en cours de construction, ce qui ajoutait encore aux incommodités. Il n'existait pas de conduites d'eau, il n'y avait pas de latrines. Les prisonniers ne reçurent pas d'eau à boire le premier jour et n'eurent jamais d'eau pour se laver. (L'ami auquel j'ai fait allusion plus haut, passa seize jours sans se laver, sauf quand il pouvait recueillir un peu d'eau de pluie.) Le second jour, mon informateur reçut un peu d'eau chaude ayant une vague saveur de café, et un peu de pain. A ce moment, les prisonniers étaient à moitié fous de soif et de faim.

8. Au cours de la première nuit, des gardes entrèrent, choisirent quelques hommes au hasard et les firent sortir pour recevoir le fouet. Il y avait là, fixés au sol, des sortes de marche-pieds sur lesquels on ligotait les pieds de l'homme. Puis on le pliait en avant, par-dessus une perche, sa tête se trouvant fixée entre deux barres horizontales. On administrait jusqu'à 50 coups de fouet, sauf dans le cas des flagellations « hors série », infligées par pur plaisir. Chaque gardien ne devait porter que 10 coups, pour que sa force demeurât intacte. (On donnait le fouet pour les moindres motifs, tels que « lenteur à se mettre au garde à vous » ou « non obéissance à un ordre ». Un rabbin reçut le fouet parce qu'il refusait de signer son nom le jour du Sabbath. On le menaça d'une seconde flagella-

tion. Il n'eut pas assez de force de volonté et finit par signer.) Des hommes mouraient entre les perches. Ceux qui survivaient étaient ramenés à coups de pied dans le hangar. Le jour, les flagellations avaient lieu en public afin de donner un exemple aux autres. Quelques-uns devinrent fous. On les enchaina et leur enfonça la tête dans un sac pour étouffer leurs cris.

9. La première nuit, l'on n'autorisa personne à sortir du hangar, même pas pour satisfaire aux exigences de la nature. Ils se servaient de leurs chapeaux (1).

10. Mon informateur porte un ratelier et souffre de pyorrhée. Il demanda un verre d'eau supplémentaire pour nettoyer son dentier et se rincer la bouche. Le manque d'eau était tel, la soif si grande, qu'il buvait cette eau après s'en être servi.

11. Il faut rapporter un autre cas. Un officier prussien reçut l'ordre de s'agenouiller et de dire : « Je suis un sale juif et un traitre à mon pays. » Il refusa ; on le fouetta jusqu'à ce qu'il consentit à répéter ces mots.

12. Parmi les prisonniers, se trouvaient des chirurgiens et des médecins réputés. Ils ont accompli des miracles de science et de dévouement. Dans certains cas urgents, ils ont même procédé à des opérations. Les rabbins, eux aussi, se sont montrés dignes de leur mission. L'un d'eux à qui l'on offrait sa libération refusa de quitter le camp avant la dernière de ses ouailles. Je n'ai pas entendu citer un seul cas d'un gardien qui aurait montré quelque signe de charité chrétienne ou de simple humanité.

13. Quand on libérait les prisonniers, on les présentait au médecin du camp. Aucun de ceux qui portaient des blessures ouvertes n'était autorisé à partir. On rasait les autres, et on les conduisait devant des agents politiques qui les avertissaient que toute divulgation sur ce qu'ils avaient vu au camp, se ferait, de leur part, à leurs propres risques et périls. Ils ajoutaient que le parti était à même de les abattre après leur départ d'Allemagne et en quelque endroit qu'ils se trouveraient. On leur restituait ensuite ce qui restait des objets leur appartenant. Cependant, la plupart des objets de valeur avaient disparu, et l'argent qu'ils pouvaient avoir eu sur eux, avait singulièrement diminué en quantité. On leur disait que toute plainte équivaudrait à une accusation de vol portée contre les S. S. et que toute imputation de ce genre serait punie du fouet. On les forçait, suprême insulte, à contribuer de leurs deniers au Winter Hilfswerk (collecte pour le secours d'hiver) du parti. Presque tous ceux qui furent relâchés durent signer un engagement de quitter l'Allemagne dans un laps de temps déterminé, habituellement quatre ou six semaines, et cela sous peine d'être internés à nouveau. Dans la plupart des cas, ils ont signé un engagement inexécutable.

14. Au moment où se déclencha le récent mouvement, peu d'entre eux savaient ce que l'emprisonnement pouvait être. Un certain nombre cependant se suicidèrent ; d'autres se cachèrent dans les bois ; d'autres encore allèrent trouver un médecin ami et se firent ouvrir le ventre pour être admis à l'hôpital. Un homme que je connais à Stuttgart, considère qu'il a eu une chance toute particulière. Le jour fatal, on le réveilla à 4 h. 30 du matin ; sa femme répondit à la sonnette ; en apercevant les gardes S. S.

---

(1) *Suivent ici six lignes qui ont été supprimées. Impossible d'imprimer les détails qu'elles donnent.*

elle eut une crise de nerfs. Il s'élança à son secours, mais fut renversé à terre et reçut un coup de pied à la bouche. Le coup lui fit sauter environ dix dents et lui brisa la mâchoire. Courageusement, il demanda qu'on lui montrât un ordre d'arrestation. Les gardes s'éloignèrent pour aller s'en munir et, entre temps, il put se faire admettre à l'hôpital avec sa mâchoire fracturée.

15. L'on me dit, de bien des côtés, qu'un autre mouvement anti-juif est imminent et le 16 janvier est indiqué comme date de la nouvelle persécution. On affirme que cette fois les juives allemandes, elles aussi, iraient dans les camps de concentration. Des juifs ont été avertis par des amis qui prétendent avoir des informations confidentielles, d'avoir à quitter l'Allemagne avant cette date. A Obenrode, près de Dieburg, dans le district de Darmstadt, l'Arbeitsdienst, me dit-on, est occupé à la construction d'un camp de concentration pour loger les victimes de la répression prévue.

16. Pour autant qu'il soit possible d'alléger les malheurs des juifs en Allemagne, je pense que la politique à suivre en ce moment consiste non point à vouloir sauver « femmes et enfants d'abord », mais bien à s'occuper « des hommes d'abord ». Ce sont eux qui sont dans les camps de concentration et en danger de mort imminente, ce sont eux aussi qui peuvent gagner le pain des leurs. S'ils meurent, le problème soulevé par le sort des familles n'en apparaîtra que plus effrayant.

17. J'apprends que certains Quakers auraient l'intention de créer en Allemagne une organisation destinée à nourrir et à vêtir les non-aryens, et feraient également des projets pour une évacuation graduelle s'étendant sur un certain nombre d'années. Si le Gouvernement Allemand ne donne pas son assentiment à un projet de ce genre, il est impossible de calculer combien de ces malheureux survivront à leur séjour forcé en Allemagne. Lord Forrester qui est venu ici, envoyé lui-même en mission par les Quakers, semble envisager la création hors de l'Allemagne de camps où l'on pourrait rééduquer les émigrants avant de les transplanter dans leurs foyers futurs. Ce projet est probablement de nature à réduire le gaspillage en vies humaines.

18. Je regrette d'avoir à proposer que les informations contenues dans cette dépêche soient considérées comme confidentielles. Si l'on publiait ces faits, pour autant qu'ils ne soient pas déjà connus, l'opinion publique du monde atteindrait probablement un plus haut degré d'indignation. Mais ceux qui gouvernent l'Allemagne paraissent en ce moment mépriser l'opinion du monde. La seule réaction probable de leur part serait de se mettre en chasse pour découvrir mes informateurs et leur appliquer leur châtiment, ou alors de recourir à un châtiment collectif, s'il leur est impossible de les découvrir. La mention même de mon nom pourrait soulever un incident. Cependant il serait peut-être utile de porter confidentiellement les faits relatés à la connaissance des Gouvernements qui ont l'intention de faire quelque chose en vue de la solution de ce problème.

J'ai l'honneur, etc.

R. T. SMALLBONES.

No. 9

Le Consul Général Carvell au Vicomte Halifax.

Milord,   *Munich, 5 janvier* 1939.

J'ai l'honneur de vous faire connaître qu'en dépit des menaces des

Note No. 11 is the testimony of a Jew from Berlin; he was one of 4000 arrested in that city in June, 1938; he was released from Buchenwald in February, 1939. He gives graphic details of conditions in that camp, including lack of food, sanitation and medical care; the epidemics among the prisoners; the brutal hard labor to which the inmates were set; the selection of violent criminals as the chiefs of each vastly overcrowded bunkhouse and work detail; the singling out of the Jews among the prisoners [Jews were about one third of the inmates at the time; there were also Aryan Socialists, Gypsies, gays, Evangelical Christians, and common criminals in the camp] to receive half of the already grossly inadequate rations and double the brutalities; the random public whippings, hangings and shootings; and the disposal of the bodies of dead prisoners at the Weimar crematorium. Of the 2000 Berlin Jews who

No. 11

*Déclarations d'un ancien prisonnier au camp de concentration
de Buchenwald,*
communiquées au Ministère des Affaires Étrangères le 18 février 1939.

Dans l'Allemagne d'à présent, nul mot plus que le nom de Buchenwald, n'inspire de terreur au cœur des gens.

Située à quelques kilom. à peine du Weimar de Gœthe, au milieu d'une charmante forêt de hêtres, entourée d'un réseau de fils de fer barbelés, gardée par des détachements de S.S. et des mitrailleuses, s'élève la nouvelle « Cité des Lamentations », le camp de concentration de Buchenwald.

J'ai été arrêté à mon domicile, à Berlin, à 5 heures du matin, le 13 juin 1938, et l'on m'a emmené aux services centraux de la Police où l'on m'informa qu'en ma qualité de juif ayant un « casier judiciaire de criminel », j'étais dès maintenant en état de détention préventive et serais, en temps opportun, envoyé dans un camp de concentration. Dans les locaux surpeuplés de la police, où l'on me conduisit tout d'abord, j'ai rencontré beaucoup de connaissances parmi les prisonniers qui, pour la plupart, étaient des gens de bonne réputation, hommes d'affaires et professeurs d'Université. Les condamnations antérieures, qui servaient de prétexte à toutes ces arrestations, dataient souvent de plus de dix ans et se rapportaient à des « crimes » tels qu'infractions aux règles de la circulation et toutes sortes d'escapades puériles et sans importance.

De nouveaux prisonniers y étaient amenés, jusqu'au point de créer aux fonctionnaires de la Police eux-mêmes les pires difficultés à trouver de la place pour l'afflux des nouveaux arrivants. Au cours de ces deux journées, le 13 et le 14 juin, tout juif de sexe masculin sur lequel existait n'importe quel dossier de police fut arrêté. Certains des prisonniers avaient dépassé 70 ans et avaient été emmenés en prison des asiles de vieillards où ils vivaient.

A Berlin, le nombre des arrestations atteignit environ 4.000 ; pour le pays tout entier, le chiffre oscilla probablement entre 10 et 15.000. Ces prisonniers furent tous envoyés aux camps de concentration de Dachau, Sachsenhausen et Buchenwald. A la Police on informa chaque prisonnier qu'il ne pourrait s'attendre à être relâché qu'à la seule condition qu'il se fût procuré, d'une façon ou d'une autre, les papiers nécessaires pour quitter le pays. Il est clair, par conséquent, que les arrestations n'étaient qu'une mesure purement politique et que l'on avait adopté ce stratagème typiquement nazi, dans le seul but de hâter l'émigration juive qui, aux yeux des nazis, s'écoulait trop lentement. Néanmoins, les arrestations furent confiées à la police criminelle ordinaire et non point, comme on aurait dû s'y attendre, à la Gestapo. De cette façon, les journaux de Berlin purent annoncer simplement « qu'un certain nombre de criminels juifs avaient été arrêtés préventivement ».

Au cours de la nuit du 14 juin, 2.000 d'entre nous furent transférés de la prison au camp de concentration. Avant de quitter la prison, nous fûmes examinés par un médecin extrêmement jeune, qui déclara chacun de nous physiquement à même de supporter les rigueurs de la vie au camp de concentration, y compris les septuagénaires et un prisonnier tuberculeux qui crachait sans cesse le sang.

La gare d'Anhalt, par laquelle nous avons quitté Berlin, fut fermée au public à 2 heures du matin, heure de notre départ, et un fort détachement de police, armes chargées, montait la garde. Vers 6 heures du matin, le 15 juin, nous arrivâmes à Weimar, pour y trouver un détachement de

arrived at this camp on the 15th of June, 1938, 110 had been killed within the first five weeks and the witness estimated that 720 had perished by the time of his release eight months later. New SS guards were generally young men in their late teens; they were given two days "training" before being unleashed on the prisoners; they showed particular zeal in their brutalities. This prisoner was required to sign the same documents as the witness in the previous document and leave Germany immediately upon his release. He asked for time to sell his business and was re-arrested; the police told him that if he did not leave Germany immediately he would be returned to Buchenwald.

S.S. à la « Tête de Mort », qui nous attendait à la gare. Nous avions à peine mis le pied sur le quai qu'une grêle de coups de poing, de coups de pied et de coups de crosse nous poussa dans le souterrain qui menait à la route. Là, nous fûmes salués par le surintendant du camp, Rödl, dans les termes suivants :

« Certains d'entre vous ont déjà été en prison. Ce que vous avez goûté là-bas n'est rien en comparaison avec ce que vous allez connaître ici. Vous allez pénétrer dans un camp de concentration, et cela signifie que vous entrez en enfer. La moindre tentative de résister à l'autorité des gardes S.S., et vous serez fusillés sans autre forme de procès. Nous ne connaissons que deux sortes de châtiment dans ce camp, le fouet et la mort. »

L'entrée du camp était gardée par des mitrailleuses et au-dessus de la porte se trouvait inscrite la maxime : « Qu'il ait raison ou qu'il ait tort, c'est mon pays ! » Tout prisonnier entrant dans le camp était obligé de passer en courant entre deux rangs de gardiens ; les coups de poing et les coups de pied recommençaient à pleuvoir.

Immédiatement après cette réception, qui est plus ou moins usuelle dans tous les camps de concentration, on nous a rasé la tête comme on le fait à tous les criminels dangereux. Puis on nous donna l'ordre d'échanger nos vêtements civils contre l'uniforme des forçats. Le vêtement de chaque prisonnier est marqué d'un symbole spécial. Les prisonniers politiques portent des rayures rouges, les « Zélateurs » des rayures violettes et ceux qu'on appelle les « réfractaires au travail » sont distingués par des rayures noires.

Nos tuniques de forçats étaient décorées de « l'Etoile de David » (Sceau de Salomon) en noir sur fond jaune. Cela voulait dire « Juifs paresseux ». Il est utile d'indiquer ici que la plupart d'entre nous étaient des hommes d'affaires établis pour leur compte, le reste étant des travailleurs qui avaient été chassés de leur emploi ordinaire. Notre groupe comprenait également un dentiste et plusieurs avocats. Un numéro fut attribué à chacun de nous, cousu à nos vêtements de prisonniers, et à partir de cet instant, ce numéro anonyme fut substitué à notre nom.

Après les préliminaires que je viens de décrire, l'on nous emmena à nos nouveaux quartiers. Alors que six mille prisonniers aryens étaient logés dans des baraques en bois, dont chacune en contenait environ 140, nous avons été littéralement empilés dans un certain nombre d'écuries en groupes de 500 par bâtiment. Ces hangars ne contenaient ni tables, ni chaises. Il n'y avait même pas de lits. La nuit, nous nous couchions sur la terre nue, incapables de nous étendre ou de nous reposer, étant donné le manque de place. Chaque prisonnier toucha deux minces couvertures, souvent déchirées. Il n'y avait aucune installation pour se laver. Aucun de nous ne fut à même de se laver pendant la première semaine. Plus tard, huit cuvettes furent fournies pour chaque groupe de 500 ; il fallait aller chercher de l'eau à une pompe située à dix minutes de distance. Le plus difficilement supportable fut le fait qu'en exécution d'ordres donnés par les S.S., un groupe de criminels professionnels fut introduit dans chaque abri pour y « maintenir l'ordre ». On fit de ces criminels, eux-mêmes prisonniers dans le camp, des espèces de sous-officiers ayant pleine autorité pour punir les autres prisonniers. Le criminel à qui était confié la direction de notre abri, était un individu particulièrement brutal qui nous maltraitait honteusement et constamment au gré de sa fantaisie.

Nous étions tous bien trop épouvantés pour essayer de nous protéger nous-mêmes contre ces brutes inhumaines, car toute résistance, toute réplique même, considérée comme mutinerie, aurait été punie de mort. Un incident particulièrement horrible s'est fixé dans ma mémoire. Au cours d'une journée et pendant que nous étions au travail, un des prisonniers les plus âgés avait été à ce point maltraité par les gardiens S.S. que pendant la nuit, dans le hangar, il gémissait de façon continuelle. La brute qui surveillait le hangar frappa cet homme plusieurs fois à la figure en lui ordonnant de cesser ce bruit. Au matin, le vieillard était mort.

Pendant les deux premiers jours que nous passâmes au camp, l'on nous donna aucune nourriture. Et cependant l'on nous mit durement au travail. Une semaine tout entière se passa à remplir les différentes formalités exigées par notre entrée au camp; ce n'est qu'après que l'on nous assigna un travail régulier. Parmi ces formalités, il y avait la signature d'une déclaration aux termes de laquelle nous avions été arrêtés préventivement parce que nous étions « des juifs paresseux », réfractaires au travail. Le formulaire portait la mention imprimée que le signataire avait spontanément admis ce fait. Un des prisonniers, avocat à Breslau, refusa de signer le formulaire. Ce malheureux vit s'abattre sur lui tous les châtiments qui se trouvaient dans le répertoire de nos tortionnaires. Il maintint fermement son refus de signer le document. Après quatre jours de torture, mourant, le corps meurtri et brisé, à moitié évanoui, il y apposa son nom. Il me faut maintenant décrire certains des châtiments que nous infligeaient les S.S. La faute la plus légère — par exemple, boire de l'eau pendant les heures de travail — était punie de la suppression du repas de midi et de l'obligation de se tenir au garde à vous, pendant quatre heures, au cours des brefs « loisirs » normalement accordés le dimanche. Mais le châtiment principal était le fouet. La flagellation était donnée en public, pour punir des fautes bénignes; par exemple, si un prisonnier était surpris à fumer pendant le travail. A la fin de l'appel de l'après-midi, les prisonniers condamnés à être fouettés étaient appelés par leur nom — il y en avait plusieurs par jour — et les hommes étaient conduits vers le poteau d'exécution où on les attachait. Le châtiment habituel, vingt-cinq coups d'une cravache en cuir, appliqués sur les fesses, était confié à deux gardiens S.S. vigoureux qui maniaient la cravache à tour de rôle. Un troisième S.S. serrait les mâchoires de la victime pour étouffer ses cris. Quelques-uns des prisonniers, plus âgés et incapables de travailler plus rapidement, ont été fouettés de cette façon inhumaine pour les punir de leur « paresse ». Après la flagellation, l'on obligeait la victime à baisser son pantalon et à exhiber les marques sanglantes à un S.S. dont c'était l'affaire de juger si le fouet avait été appliqué avec assez de vigueur. Vingt-cinq coups constituaient le châtiment favori à Buchenwald, mais il y en avait d'autres. La « caisse à suer », par exemple. Il arrivait souvent que le prisonnier fût déjà mort avant que la « caisse à suer » ne fût ouverte pour l'en retirer.

Un autre châtiment était connu sous le nom de « ligotage à l'arbre », et les gardiens montraient beaucoup d'esprit d'invention à varier les modalités de cette torture. Si la faute commise était légère, les prisonniers étaient ligotés à l'arbre de façon à ce que, face tournée vers le tronc, leurs mains fussent liées comme pour l'embrasser. Les liens qui les attachaient étaient serrés si durement qu'ils avaient de la peine à faire le moindre mouvement. Alors les gardiens se mettaient à « jouer au carrousel » avec eux. C'est-à-dire qu'ils les forçaient à tourner tout autour de l'arbre. S'ils ne pouvaient se mouvoir assez rapidement, il était normal qu'on leur allongeât des coups de pied dans les chevilles.

Cela cependant n'était que la variante la moins sévère du « ligotage à l'arbre ». Une autre variété du même châtiment se terminait souvent par une issue fatale. La victime était attachée à l'arbre, dos au tronc, les bras tirés en arrière de façon à entourer ce dernier, puis ligotés. Les jambes et les pieds, ces derniers touchant à peine le sol, étaient ligotés à leur tour, d'une façon suffisamment serrée pour interrompre la circulation du sang. On laissait le prisonnier suspendu dans cette position pendant des heures consécutives. Il ne faut pas penser que ces tortures barbares étaient exceptionnelles. A Buchenwald, ces choses étaient des événements quotidiens. Une semaine après notre arrivée, l'on nous mit au travail régulier. La journée de travail au camp de Buchenwald était réglée comme suit. L'on nous réveillait à 3 h. 30 du matin, puis suivait l'appel qui durait de 4 h. 30 à 5 h. 30, ensuite on nous conduisait sous escorte au travail, qui commençait un peu avant 6 heures. Nous travaillions sans arrêt jusqu'à midi. A ce moment, une demi-heure de repos, pour boire le café de glands que l'on nous distribuait. Le travail recommençait à midi trente et continuait jusqu'à 3 h. 45. De 4 heures à 5 h. 30, second appel, suivi des flagellations publiques décrétées pour ce jour. De 5 h. 30 à 6 heures, nous prenions le repas principal de la journée pour recommencer le travail jusqu'à 8 heures ; suivait le « diner ». La journée se terminait ; à 9 heures. Dimanche, l'on nous faisait travailler de 6 heures du matin à 4 heures de l'après-midi. Aucune fête n'était observée au camp, pas même (des prisonniers qui s'y trouvaient depuis longtemps me l'on raconté) celle de Noël. Nous étions sur pied pendant 17 heures 1/2 par jour, qu'il plût ou qu'il fit beau. Cet emploi du temps s'appliquait aux prisonniers âgés aussi bien qu'aux plus jeunes. Les malades, pour autant qu'ils fussent capables de se tenir sur leurs jambes, étaient traités exactement comme les bien portants. Revêtus de nos habits de condamnés en tissus ersatz, nous étions obligés de sortir par n'importe quel temps, sous l'orage et la pluie battante, ou à la chaleur brûlante de l'été.

Et maintenant, venons-en à mon premier jour de travaux forcés, jour que je n'oublierai pas jusqu'à la fin de ma vie. Plusieurs des prisonniers, les plus âgés de notre équipe de travail, moururent dans la carrière, au cours de cette journée brûlante de juin. Après l'appel du matin, nous avions été répartis en groupes de travail, composé chacun de 100 hommes. Chaque groupe fut pourvu d'un contremaitre choisi, presque invariablement, parmi les criminels habituels, et qui avait le droit de nous frapper à sa guise. Nous étions accompagnés d'un détachement de S.S. dont aucun ne pouvait avoir dépassé ses dix-huit ans. Ils étaient cependant parfaitement habiles à nous maltraiter et à nous battre. Notre colonne, comprenant plusieurs prisonniers de soixante-cinq ans, se mit en marche, ou plus exactement fut poussée le long du chemin par la meute des S.S. dont chacun était armé d'une matraque, jusqu'à ce que nous eussions atteint la carrière de pierres, où nous devions travailler. Quatre-vingts sur cent n'avaient jamais fait de travail manuel auparavant et néanmoins l'on nous demandait de porter des blocs de pierre à ce point lourds, que le seul effort pour les lever de terre eût semblé considérable à un terrassier bien entrainé. Beaucoup de ces pierres étaient d'un tel poids qu'il fallait plusieurs hommes pour soulever le bloc et le placer sur l'épaule de l'homme qui devait le porter. Ces pierres devaient être transportées sur le chantier d'une nouvelle route distante d'un peu plus de quinze cents mètres et qui se construisait grâce à la main-d'œuvre des « forçats ». Le chemin qui allait à la nouvelle route était assez raide, et pendant le dernier tiers du voyage, les S.S. qui étaient stationnés le long du trajet nous aidaient à le franchir à coups de pied et à coups de crosse de fusil. Les prisonniers d'un certain âge qui se trouvaient dans l'incapacité physique de remplir leur tâche étaient les plus malheureux. Nous retournions de la route vers la carrière pour prendre un nouveau chargement et le même processus se répétait. Le soleil montait plus haut dans le ciel, la journée devenait de plus en plus chaude. Les voitures rapides des S.S. soulevaient des nuages de poussière blanche sur la route (elle n'était ouverte qu'au trafic officiel). Près de la carrière, il y avait une source d'où jaillissait une eau fraîche et limpide. Les prisonniers qui essayaient de se rapprocher de la source pour y boire étaient chassés par les gardiens S.S. L'après-midi, trente d'entre les cent que nous étions au départ s'étaient écroulés, certains frappés de coups de soleil ; les brutalités des gardes, essayant de les remettre sur pied, et de leur faire reprendre le travail, restaient elles-mêmes sans résultat. Il nous fallut, à la fin, les emporter à l'hôpital du camp — tous sauf deux, qui étaient morts.

En dehors de notre travail à la carrière, nous avions aussi à transporter des troncs d'arbres d'un lieu en un autre. L'on ne mettait pas plus de huit hommes au transport de la charge la plus lourde. Le long du chemin, des S.S. se tenaient à intervalles. Nous étions constamment sous observation. Les gardiens nous assenaient sans cesse des coups de matraque sur la tête et sur les épaules, ou nous frappaient de leurs lourdes bottes ; leurs cris résonnent encore à mes oreilles. « En avant, n... d... D... voulez-vous marcher ! » Il arrivait de temps en temps qu'un S.S. particulièrement « énergique » nous ordonnât de nous livrer à certain exercice qui consistait à plier les genoux pendant que nous portions notre charge. Cela n'était pas sans danger, car si l'un de nous était tombé, le tronc pesant aurait pu écraser les autres. Un jour, avant de nous envoyer au travail, l'on nous dit « que des juifs avaient jeté leur ration de pain » et l'on prit une décision qui n'a pas sa pareille, même dans les annales du camp de concentration de Dachau. A partir de ce jour, nous n'allions plus recevoir qu'un demi-litre de soupe (tous les autres en recevaient un litre) et 250 grammes de pain (la ration normale étant de 625 grammes) ! On exigeait de nous un travail écrasant et sans trêve, et en même temps on fixait nos rations aux quantités suivantes : 1/4 de litre de café de glands le matin, 1/2 litre de soupe à midi et 250 grammes de pain avec un soupçon de margarine et un peu de viande, le soir. Pendant trois dimanches successifs, et bien que nous fussions naturellement forcés de travailler comme à l'habitude, nous n'avons touché aucune espèce de nourriture.

Nos familles étaient autorisées à nous envoyer de l'argent de chez nous. Les colis de victuailles, par contre, étaient interdits, « *tout pouvant s'acheter au camp* ». Nous verrons dans un instant comment ce système fonctionnait en réalité. Pour les familles des prisonniers plus pauvres, chaque pfenning envoyé au camp représentait un sacrifice réel. En raison des arrestations en masse, il était arrivé que bien des foyers fussent privés de leur gagne-pain principal. Dans un certain nombre de cas, que je connais personnellement, les autorités de l'Assistance Publique refusèrent d'allouer ou de continuer à verser un secours aux familles dont le chef était en prison. Ceux qui, cependant, recevaient vraiment de l'argent, étaient loin de pouvoir augmenter de façon adéquate leur maigre ration. On retenait par exemple une partie de la somme pour régler les tickets de chemin de fer, pour le cas où le prisonnier serait relâché. Cette règle était particulièrement dure pour les prisonniers plus pauvres, étant donné qu'alors l'intégralité de la petite somme était « mise de côté » à cet effet. Les sommes plus importantes étaient distribuées par versements hebdomadaires de cinq marks. Cette somme, il est vrai, pouvait être dépensée à la cantine de la prison où des prix très élevés étaient pratiqués. La cantine était extrêmement mal pourvue. Il n'était jamais possible d'y acheter du pain et il arrivait souvent que la seule chose en vente fut de la « poudre de limonade ». En outre, il faut rappeler que nous avions à acheter de nos propres deniers le savon, la pâte dentifrice et autres objets de ce genre.

A Buchenwald, le nombre des décès, tant chez les juifs que chez les aryens, dépassait de beaucoup celui de n'importe lequel des autres camps. La liste des décès aryens comportait au moins un nom par jour. Des 2.000 prisonniers juifs qui y étaient arrivés le 15 juin, 80 sont morts au cours des quatre premières semaines, 30 autres au cours de la cinquième. Les autorités firent tout ce qui était en leur pouvoir pour cacher ces chiffres : le Comité de la Communauté Juive de Berlin ne fut officiellement informé que de 39 décès sur les 110 qui se produisirent. Comment ces décès se sont-ils produits? Une phrase bien connue, « tué au cours d'une tentative d'évasion », doit nécessairement fournir l'explication. Je dois témoigner ici du fait que, tout au moins pendant la période de ma propre détention, il n'y eut pas un seul cas d'un prisonnier tué au cours d'une véritable tentative d'évasion.

Le camp est entouré d'un réseau de fils de fer chargés électriquement. De place en place, il y a des postes de surveillance, avec des mitrailleuses servies par des détachements de S.S. Il est interdit aux prisonniers de s'approcher du réseau. S'ils le font, les S.S. ont des ordres pour tirer sur eux. Les prisonniers nouvellement arrivés ignoraient souvent ces règles et les S.S., s'ennuyant de l'immobilité que leur imposait leur mission de surveillance, s'amusaient parfois à faire signe à un prisonnier de s'approcher du réseau. Ces prisonniers nouveaux étaient portés à obéir à l'ordre, mais aussitôt qu'ils s'approchaient, la mitrailleuse des S.S. ouvrait le feu. Cette forme de « blague » était fréquemment employée. De temps en temps, quelques prisonniers, devenus à moitié fous, et incapables de supporter plus longtemps les conditions infernales du camp de concentration, s'élançaient vers le réseau, comme frappés de démence. Invariablement les S.S. ouvraient le feu, et tout de suite, bien qu'ils comprissent évidemment que ces malheureux étaient fous, et n'essayaient pas vraiment de s'évader du camp.

Mais la plupart des prisonniers qui décèdent à Buchenwald meurent à la carrière. Autour de cette carrière, était placée une chaîne de postes S.S.; s'approcher d'elle signifiait la mort. Il arrivait souvent que l'un des prisonniers, plus âgé ou plus faible, reçût l'ordre de porter un bloc de pierre, ce qui lui était physiquement impossible, même s'il avait employé la dernière parcelle d'une force déjà limitée. Le gardien S.S., alors, essayait à plusieurs reprises de forcer le prisonnier de porter sa charge. Naturellement, le malheureux traînait à l'arrière de ses compagnons. Quelques instants après, ceux qui avaient passé devant lui entendaient un coup de feu. C'est que le prisonnier, contraint par le gardien à quitter la file, avait été poussé du côté du poste des S.S., qui avaient ainsi abattu à coups de fusil une autre victime « pendant une tentative d'évasion ». Une histoire particulièrement tragique mérite d'être racontée. Parmi les prisonniers juifs se trouvait un tout jeune homme de vingt-deux ans, appelé Erich Löwenberg. Il avait été chantre dans une synagogue, s'était marié jeune, et sa femme attendait un bébé pour dans deux mois. Löwenberg — cela se passa aux environs du 15 juillet 1938 — fut emmené par un gardien S.S. sur la grande route, à proximité de la carrière, et poussé

devant un lourd camion conduit par un autre S.S. Une heure et demie
plus tard, le jeune homme était mort.

Les mauvais traitements physiques auxquels les prisonniers étaient
normalement soumis conduisaient parfois à l'apoplexie et à la mort. Les
causes du décès étaient alors indiquées par le docteur comme étant « fai-
blesse du cœur ». Les cercueils étaient fabriqués par les prisonniers eux-
mêmes, dans l'atelier de menuiserie. Les corps étaient habituellement trans-
portés au crématoire de Weimar et incinérés. La famille était informée
officiellement de la mort du prisonnier par une carte postale ouverte et
non affranchie, expédiée par le bureau du commandant du camp.

Beaucoup sont morts également à cause du manque de soins médi-
caux au camp. Dans les premières semaines, les infirmiers de l'ambulance
avaient des ordres formels de ne pas donner de médicaments aux juifs,
et l'on peut imputer à ce règlement la responsabilité d'un certain nombre
de décès. Plus tard, il arrivait assez souvent que le médecin-chef de l'hôpital refusât d'admettre des malades juifs. Je connais personnellement un
cas où le docteur a mis à la porte un homme malade, en déclarant qu'il
était un simulateur. Deux heures plus tard, l'homme était mort.

De nuit, dans nos hangars, nous n'avions aucun moyen de venir en
aide à un compagnon mourant. Nous ne pouvions pas même mettre la
main sur un verre d'eau, et bien moins encore obtenir des médicaments.
Il nous était également impossible de quitter le hangar pour aller chercher
une aide médicale, car les gardiens S.S. avaient des ordres pour tirer à
la mitrailleuse sur quiconque quittait le bâtiment pendant la nuit.

Quatre semaines après notre arrivée, une baraque-hôpital fut ouverte
pour les juifs. Les juifs eux-mêmes eurent à subvenir aux frais de son
installation. Les objets les plus essentiels y manquaient. Il n'y avait pas
de thermomètre. Même pas un pot de chambre.

Et cependant, même dans cet enfer, on rencontrait par hasard des
créatures humaines. Il y avait des S.S., en très petite minorité, qui ne nous
maltraitaient pas. Certains d'entre eux nous expliquaient qu'ils ne pouvaient rien faire pour améliorer des conditions régnant dans le camp. Ils
recevaient leurs ordres de « plus haut ». Cette autorité supérieure était
Herr Strandàrtenfülirer Kock, marqué d'infamie pour avoir perpétré des
brutalités sans nom aux Kolumbiahaus à Berlin, dans les camps Ester-
wege et de Sachsenhausen, et maintenant Directeur du camp de Buchenwald. Combien de morts de prisonniers sans défense cet homme a-t-il sur
sa conscience ?

Il y avait également, parmi les « contremaîtres », certains, qui au risque
de leur propre vie, essayaient de nous venir en aide. Certains d'entre eux
furent dénoncés par d'autres prisonniers comme « amis des juifs » et
fouettés en public. Le pire moment pour nous arriva après qu'un détachement de jeunes S.S. autrichien eût été envoyé de Wöllersdorf à Buchenwald. Les tortures que ces hommes nous infligèrent sont littéralement
indescriptibles.

Comment se compose, dans l'Allemagne d'aujourd'hui, la population
d'un camp de concentration ? De quels éléments le camp est-il formé ? A
Buchenwald, nous étions 8.000 : 2.000 juifs et 6.000 non-juifs. L'on a
maintenant l'intention d'agrandir le camp et d'en faire, avec une population de 25.000, le plus important d'Allemagne.

Nos 8.000 prisonniers comprenaient avant tout les « politiques », tels
par exemple les membres communistes du Reichstag (Neubauer, Sæfkow,
Woitinski et d'autres). Beaucoup d'entre eux avaient été dans différents
camps de concentration depuis 1933. Un autre prisonnier était l'avocat

d'Assises berlinois bien connu, Hans Litter. Il s'est cassé la jambe récemment dans la carrière de Buchenwald. Il n'était pas complètement guéri d'une blessure reçue auparavant. En plus des vrais prisonniers politiques, il y avait à Buchenwald plus d'un pauvre diable accusé d'avoir parlé d'une façon insultante de la personnalité sacrée du Führer. La plupart d'entre eux étaient envoyés au camp de concentration (c'est-à-dire mis en prison) après l'expiration de leur peine. Dans ce cas, la durée de leur séjour demeure indéterminée.

L'une des caractéristiques les plus infernales de l'emprisonnement dans un camp de concentration est précisément cette incertitude qui brise les nerfs. Une « arrestation de protection » peut signifier une détention pour une durée de trois mois, elle peut facilement signifier un emprisonnement pour trois ans. Ni règle, ni loi ne détermine la longueur de la sentence.

Après la catégorie « politique », celle des « réfractaires au travail » était la plus nombreuse. Quiconque s'imaginerait que ce groupe a quelque rapport avec les clochards et les vagabonds se tromperait lourdement. Voici un exemple : un employé de commerce avait perdu sa situation et avait demandé un secours de chômage. Un beau jour, il fut informé par la Bourse du Travail qu'il pouvait trouver de l'embauche comme terrassier sur les nouvelles autostrades. L'homme, qui recherchait un emploi commercial, déclina l'offre. La Bourse du Travail le signala à la Gestapo comme étant « réfractaire », il fut arrêté et envoyé dans un camp de concentration. Les techniciens, qui abandonnent un travail peu rémunéré pour rechercher un salaire plus élevé, sont souvent victimes du même sort.

Le groupe suivant était composé des Bibelforscher (Zélateurs de la Bible), une secte religieuse qui tire ses doctrines de la Bible et possède un grand nombre d'adhérents dans toutes les parties du pays, mais se trouve proscrite par la Gestapo, parce que ses membres refusent de faire du service militaire. Ces malheureux étaient presque aussi mal traités que les juifs.

La quatrième catégorie se composait d'homosexuels ou tout au moins de ceux contre lesquels la Gestapo jugeait utile de proférer l'accusation d'homosexualité. Accuser ceux qu'elle n'aime pas, de ce délit, est une tactique favorite de la police secrète. Au moment où j'y étais moi-même, Buchenwald ne comptait aucun représentant de cette catégorie.

La dernière classe de prisonniers était fournie par des criminels professionnels. C'est dans leurs rangs, je l'ai dit, que l'on choisissait nos « surveillants ». Ceux d'entre eux que l'on investissait d'une autorité sur nous avaient l'autorisation de nous maltraiter autant qu'ils le désiraient. Beaucoup d'entre eux essayaient de se concilier la faveur des S.S. en nous torturant, en nous faisant faire de l' « exercice » le dimanche, pendant la période de repos, ou en obligeant les prisonniers âgés à se rouler sur le sol humide et boueux.

Quand il arrivait qu'un prisonnier fût vraiment sur le point d'être libéré, il devait d'abord se soumettre à un examen médical pour montrer si son corps portait encore les marques du fouet ou paraissait contusionné d'une façon quelconque. Un prisonnier qui portait encore les traces des coups qu'il avait reçus n'était pas autorisé à partir, jusqu'à ce que toutes les cicatrices fussent guéries. De cette façon les autorités essayaient d'empêcher que le monde eût quelque connaissance des mauvais traitements physiques infligés aux prisonniers. Il est douteux que ces mesures de précaution préliminaires aient été le moins du monde couronnées de succès. Lentement, la vérité passe au travers des barrières.

Au moment de mon élargissement — j'étais un des très rares qui purent quitter le camp de concentration sans avoir obtenu un visa pour l'étranger — je fus averti par un haut fonctionnaire S.S. que la moindre indiscrétion concernant ma vie au camp de concentration serait punie de mort.

Les paroles exactes prononcées par ce chef des S.S. valent la peine d'être rapportées : « Le National-Socialisme, dit-il, n'a aucune raison de craindre la vérité, mais il ne tolérera pas que soient répandues de fantastiques histoires d'atrocités. »

Après la mise en liberté je fus averti que je devais quitter le pays en l'espace de cinq semaines, et que l'on me refuserait l'autorisation d'y rentrer.

Pendant ces cinq semaines, il était entendu que je resterais sous la surveillance de la Police, et que je devrais me présenter quotidiennement, tout d'abord au bureau central de la Police de Berlin, plus tard dans mon propre district. La première fois que je me présentai au bureau central de Police, quelque chose arriva qui m'apparut typique des conditions actuelles en Allemagne. A mon arrivée, je me suis trouvé entouré par un groupe de fonctionnaires de la Police régulière qui, avec beaucoup de curiosité, m'interrogèrent à propos de Buchenwald. Me rappelant les menaces qui avaient accompagné mon départ du camp de concentration, je refusai tout d'abord de répondre. Ils me montrèrent leurs pièces d'identité pour écarter tous mes soupçons et à nouveau ils insistèrent pour que je leur racontasse quelles étaient les conditions réelles à Buchenwald. Ils se chargeaient, disaient-ils, de faire en sorte que rien de mal ne m'arrivât. Alors je leur parlai des choses que j'avais vues. Ils s'en montrèrent émus au point qu'ils ne pouvaient s'empêcher de m'interrompre sans cesse. De telles conditions, disaient-ils, constituaient un scandale révoltant. Frick et Himmler étaient responsables. Personne d'autre. Ils s'efforcèrent à me bien faire comprendre qu'ils n'avaient aucune espèce de contrôle sur les camps de concentration, où l'autorité suprême et exclusive appartenait en fait aux S.S. J'ai moi-même vécu les choses et passé par les épreuves qui sont rapportées ici au sujet de Buchenwald. Je ne suis resté que six semaines dans le camp, et ma narration ne peut donc pas prétendre à être complète. Je sais de source digne de foi que la majorité de ceux qui furent arrêtés au mois de juin en même temps que moi, sont toujours prisonniers, et que la liste des décès parmi eux augmente sans cesse.

Index of Names and Places

Note: I have standardized given names with many variant spellings, for example, Mosé, Moise, and Moisé are all rendered as Moisé and Giuseppe, Joseffe, and Joseph are all rendered as Giuseppe.